D0099825

UNDERNEATH A HARLEM MOON

UNDERNEATH
A HARLEM MOON

THE HARLEM TO PARIS
YEARS OF
ADELAIDE HALL

IAIN CAMERON WILLIAMS

continuum
LONDON • NEW YORK

Continuum

The Tower Building, 11 York Road, London, SE1 7NX
370 Lexington Avenue, New York, NY 10017–6503

First published 2002 by Continuum by arrangement with Bayou Press Ltd

The author and publishers thank the following for permission to reprint copyright lyrics:

"I Can't Give You Anything But Love," words by Dorothy Fields and music by Jimmy McHugh. © 1928, EMI Mills Music Inc/Ireneadale Publishing Co., USA. Reproduced by permission of Lawrence Wright Music Co. Ltd/EMI Music Publishing Ltd, London, WC2H 0QY.

"Diga Diga Do," words by Dorothy Fields and music by Jimmy McHugh. © 1928, EMI Mills Music Inc/Ireneadele Publishing Co., USA. Reproduced by permission of Lawrence Wright Music Co. Ltd/EMI Music Publishing Ltd, London, WC2H 0QY.

"I Must Have That Man," words by Dorothy Fields and music by Jimmy McHugh. © 1928, EMI Mills Music Inc/Ireneadele Publishing Co., USA. Reproduced by permission of Lawrence Wright Music Co. Ltd/EMI Music Publishing Ltd, London, WC2H 0QY.

British Library Cataloguing-in-Publication Data

A catalogue record for this book is available from the British Library.

ISBN 0-8264-5893-9 (hardback)

Library of Congress Cataloging-in-Publication Data

Williams, Iain Cameron, 1953–
    Underneath a Harlem moon : the Harlem to Paris years of Adelaide Hall / Iain Cameron Williams.
       p. cm.
    Includes bibliographical references (p.   ) and index.
    ISBN 0-8264-5893-9
      1. Hall, Adelaide. 2. Women jazz singers—Biography. I. Series.

    ML420.H1166 W55 2002
    782.42165´092—dc21
    [B]   2001047749

Typeset by Kenneth Burnley, Wirral, Cheshire
Printed and bound in Great Britain by MPG Books Ltd, Bodmin, Cornwall

CONTENTS

PART I

SING TO THE MOON AND THE STARS WILL SHINE

1901–27

FOREWORD

I first met Adelaide in the 1950s when she was appearing in a West End musical.

I did not know about her legendary musical history at that time—only that she was an American singer now living in London. We became friends, and gradually I discovered I was a friend of someone who was a somebody . . . a somebody with a jazz history.

Although Adelaide's career started in 1921 in a Broadway musical, it was her 1927 recording with the great Duke Ellington of his "Creole Love Call" that catapulted her into the minds of the jazz public's world. It was her improvisation at the beginning of the instrumental that made it stand out, so making it into a smash hit classic. Every jazz singer who sings it does so in tribute to her. Whenever I sing this song I always tell the story of how, in 1927, Duke Ellington heard her improvising on his instrumental line and invited her to record it with his orchestra. The rest is history.

She loved to sing and, indeed, well into her late eighties would often get up to sing if she was in a club and liked the musicians playing, as she often did with John Dankworth.

I admired and loved her, and am so pleased that her story is at last being read, heard and seen.

DAME CLEO LAINE

TRIBUTES

Adelaide was a remarkable artist and an inspiration to work with. Not only was she a huge star; she was one of the major figures in the Harlem Renaissance and as such her biography is long overdue.

FAYARD NICHOLAS (of the Nicholas Brothers)

In recent years, jazz experts have invented for us the world of the "real" jazz singer. To be such a singer, you had of course to be black, preferably from a deprived family, to have had a man who mistreated you, to have learnt your trade in the world of smoke-filled basements and to have spent at least a part of your life enslaved to drink and/or drugs . . . only in this way could you really understand how to sing the blues and thus learn to be a true jazz singer.

This is all, of course, poppycock! The real way of becoming a great jazz singer was very simply to be endowed with talent and to work at it. Adelaide Hall had talent in abundance. She was discovered at school by a white impresario who heard her wonderful voice and knew immediately that she was destined for stardom and, as this meticulously researched book demonstrates, what a star she became.

Not for her a voice ruined by drug abuse but a high-quality vocal instrument of power and quality that could probably have made her a classical singer should she have chosen that route. For Adelaide, jazz meant an entry into a world of glamour (never a life of degradation) and she lived all her days with that attitude.

Most important of all, however, Adelaide, born in the same year as Louis Armstrong, was a pioneer of jazz. There was no previous generation to influence her. She was one of the exclusive band of musicians who created the whole genre of jazz and defined jazz-phrasing for all who followed her. There are those who think of jazz singing as what Billie Holiday did, but, great as she was, she came a generation later into a world of jazz already fully formed. Adelaide Hall was of the generation that built the foundations of jazz and it is to her that we should look to find out what it was all about.

Hers was the voice that first graced bands like Duke Ellington's and was backed by Art Tatum and other greats who produced the music for those glamorous Broadway and Cotton Club shows. And let us not forget her dancing ability. To have partnered Bojangles as regularly as she did is at least equivalent to being Ginger Rogers to Fred Astaire.

I only knew Addie after she was 70, but the voice was still powerful enough to fill London's Albert Hall without a microphone and when she sang songs like the one she introduced to the world, "I Can't Give You Anything But Love, Baby," nobody could out-swing her.

I'll always miss Adelaide Hall for the twinkle in her eyes and her warmth of personality but I'm delighted that at last a book has been written reminding all of us who sometimes took her for granted of her supreme importance both historically and as a great creative artist in her own right. I can just imagine her now, reading through the manuscript . . . and, as she turns the pages, giggling as she always did, like a naughty schoolgirl.

EARL OKIN

PREFACE

I consider myself very lucky to have started my career in show business during the Harlem Renaissance. In those early days, Harlem was a multiracial community. I grew up with Jewish, Italian and Irish kids playing around me and never encountered prejudice of any kind. It was much later, after I'd established my career, that I confronted prejudice full on in social situations, but never in my work. There is no color barrier in music; there are no boundaries you cannot cross with a song. To think back of all the wonderful musicians and songwriters I've worked with makes me realize how truly lucky I've been.

> Adelaide Hall in conversation with the author, 1990

THE FIRST LADY OF JAZZ

For a woman whose musical career spanned eight decades, luck could hardly have been responsible for the phenomenal success Adelaide achieved throughout her long life. Acknowledging a force other than that of her own talent was, characteristically, indicative of her humble nature. Hers was a voice that was destined to be heard. In later years, the jazz world would resoundingly refer to Adelaide as a "living legend," an expression that both amused and irritated her.

"It makes me sound like a dinosaur," she would mutter to herself whenever the phrase was mentioned, and we all knew how touchy she was about her age.

Adelaide was born in Brooklyn, New York, at the turn of the twentieth century, into an unequivocally poor family of mixed race. Her father was of African descent and worked from home as a piano teacher. Her mother, of combined Dutch and North American Indian lineage, took in washing to help relieve the continual burden of the debt collector. Despite Adelaide's later denials of racial prejudice during her childhood, she grew up believing that the color of her skin determined her destiny. After her father's unexpected death in 1916, she spent the rest of her adolescence taking care of her sickly younger sister, Evelyn. In the years that followed, relaxation became the one luxury Adelaide was never fortunate enough to enjoy.

During her formative years Adelaide learnt how to communicate through her natural ability to sing. Her girlish charm became her forte and beguiled all who came in contact with it. Throughout her long life she remained loyal to her heartfelt belief that she was born to entertain. In a quote taken from the biographical text included in her 1992 Carnegie Hall concert program, she sums up her philosophical approach to life with a very simple statement: "I have a feeling that I'm here to help people forget their worries and troubles. Thank God, I've been able to do it for so long."

In writing this book, I have tried to recreate an accurate account of what happened during the incredibly successful and influential "early" period of Adelaide's career. This period covers her conquests in America and subsequent visits to Europe that eventually led to her exile in Britain.

The story uses the Harlem Renaissance and all its colorful characters as a backdrop around which I have intertwined actual events, dates, incidents and biographical data relating to Adelaide's career, as well as reminiscences told by herself. Although her memory was still pretty sharp right up into her nineties, for personal reasons she conveniently chose not to disclose certain family recollections, which made my job as a biographer even more difficult.

In my quest for information, I visited New York, Toronto and Paris. I also spent over six months at the British Library newspaper archives at Colindale scanning microfiche tapes of every newspaper and periodical I could find, dating from 1910 through to 1940. My search revealed a wealth of information that had, hitherto, been either forgotten or neglected by historians and biographers of this period.

Adelaide epitomized the "Jazz Age" and all it represented, and in assessing her career one must remember that the history of jazz is not the same as the history of jazz recordings. Considering she was one of the most significant figures in twentieth-century black culture, recognition of this fact and the tremendous contribution she gave to her art has sadly been overlooked.

Underneath a Harlem Moon is my testament to the Harlem Renaissance, probably the most important period in black social history, through which Adelaide bravely fought adversity, rejection and racial segregation to become the greatest female star of her race.

I sincerely hope that within these pages I've faithfully captured a little of the spirit that drove Adelaide to reach the pinnacle of her career as an entertainer.

IAIN CAMERON WILLIAMS
November 2001

INTRODUCTION

I was first introduced to Adelaide Hall in 1971, soon after I moved to London from Sheffield. It was to be the beginning of a close friendship that ended only with her death in 1993.

As a penniless teenage singer/songwriter seeking lodgings, destiny steered me to a large theatrical household in Bloomsbury owned by Peter Barrett—an eccentric and well-acquainted philanthropist. This was to be my home for the next six years.

Through Peter, I met Jack Hockett, a theater ticket-agent who owned Premier Box Office on Shaftesbury Avenue. Peter and Jack played host to many visiting celebrities from the entertainment world. Like Laurel and Hardy, they were a formidable team. During my residency in the household I met many fascinating people, Josephine Baker and Adelaide included.

When Josephine Baker arrived in town everyone who knew her went on high alert. She had an uncanny habit of monopolizing one's time and thought nothing of arriving unannounced at our apartment with the youngest members of her Rainbow Tribe in tow—looking very much like fluffy chicks following a stern mother hen. Although Josephine was always genuinely pleased to see you, one couldn't help but sense the relief she felt at being able to offload her children on someone else for a few hours. Peter and I were expected to entertain and amuse them, which usually meant a visit to Madame Tussaud's, Regent's Park Zoo or some other tourist attraction.

It was during the evening, back at her hotel suite, after Josephine had completed her busy schedule for the day that she would relax. On a couple of occasions we invited her over to our apartment for dinner and I cooked her favorite spaghetti dish. If she felt a little more sociable, we might be summoned to escort her out to dinner, usually a simple meal at the French restaurant Chez Solange, just off Leicester Square. Only after she had unwound did the less demanding, more affectionate East St. Louis Josephine re-enter our lives.

Adelaide entered my life with less of a fanfare. At first, I didn't grasp how famous she had once been. In my ignorance I presumed that she was just another old-time jazz singer. Little did I realize that she was in fact a major historical figure of the American musical stage. Even though she had just witnessed her seventieth birthday, Adelaide looked considerably younger than her age and was still an attractive woman. I found her far more approachable than Josephine and much easier to befriend.

In 1990, I suggested to Adelaide that I write her biography, an idea she welcomed with great enthusiasm. The thought of her autographing copies of the book at its launch amused her. Little did I know what I was letting myself in for. Sadly, due to the extent of her career and the small amount of written documentation that exists relating to her personal life, the autographing session was never to take place. The book's compilation was to far outlast her.

When Adelaide returned to America in 1992, to perform her second series of solo concerts at Carnegie Hall, she remarked to the first-night audience, "It feels as if New York has, at long last, finally forgiven me for leaving." Even though she had spent over fifty years' exile in Britain, I sincerely believe that in her heart she never left America.

In writing this book, not only did I ascertain who Adelaide Hall really was; I unearthed a remarkable story—the missing link in Harlem's widely documented Renaissance. Hers truly was a gilded life, just waiting to be rediscovered.

ACKNOWLEDGMENTS

My gratitude and heartfelt thanks go out to all the people who gave assistance throughout the writing of this book. It is a pleasure for me to be able to say that *Underneath a Harlem Moon* is richer for your contributions. May I also confirm my sincere love and appreciation to Adelaide Hall for sharing over twenty years of friendship and secrets with me.

I should like to acknowledge the following people for kindly allowing me to invade their privacy: Kate and Thomas Greer for their understanding, dedication and belief in the project, Malcolm Crowthers for his diligence with editing, Roma King—a close friend of Adelaide's since 1952—for her patience, knowledge and time spent reading the text, Jack Hockett for introducing me to the rich and glorious past, Derek Wright for ably assisting me during my various trips, Neil and Maria Davey for their continual encouragement and faith, Adam Francon Lannon for his computer skills, Brian Moffat for his photographic expertise, Bob Larkin for his sound advice, Margaret Reutens for her uplifting enthusiasm, and Alan Long for his wisdom, guidance and, most of all, patience. May I also thank Kim Baker for her warm support and clear direction and a very special thank you to Sue Adams for giving me a chance when no one else was prepared to. I am indebted to you all.

I should also like to express my sincere gratitude to Dame Cleo Laine for contributing a foreword to the book.

Enormous thanks to the staff at Continuum International Publishing

Group, especially Janet Joyce, Sandra Margolies, and Valerie Hall in London and Nick Weir-Williams in New York. I should also like to thank Alyn Shipton at Bayou Press and my copy-editor, Sue Cope.

Thanks go to: June Hesler at the Larchmont Library in Westchester, Gladys A. Clark for searching the archives at St. Philip's Episcopal Church in Harlem, the Hotel St. Regis in Paris and the Algonquin Hotel in New York for looking after me so well, George Gibson for recounting his memories so vividly, the Wittich family in Westchester for kindly welcoming me into their home at Larchmont, Fayard Nicholas of the Nicholas Brothers and Fayard's fiancée Katherine Hopkins for granting me an interview at such short notice and allowing me to interrupt their marriage plans, Christopher Frith at the New York Public Library, archivist Billy Mitchell of the Apollo Theater Foundation in Harlem, Mary F. Yearwood and Diane Lachatanere—curators at the Schomburg Center for Research in Black Culture, Elisabeth Welch for narrating her stories to me, Josephine Baker and her Rainbow Tribe for their whirlwind visits to my apartment during my late teens and to Peter Barrett for making them possible, Jean-Luc Bonnin for his prompt French translations, Neil and Diji Richardson for their help early on in the project, Gary Holmes for his useful research in America, Rosemary Davis—a close friend of Adelaide's since 1941—for her lucid recollections, Patricia K. Reed for searching the archives in New Orleans, Carmela Piazza—assistant to New York's Mayor Giuliani, Michael Romei (head concierge at New York's Waldorf Astoria) for helping me locate where the Ritz–Carlton was originally sited in the Twenties, Earl Okin for his passionate tribute and help in tracking down certain musicians, Bill Egan (Florence Mills' biographer) for his generous gift of the original sheet music to "Diga Diga Do," the pianist Mike Renzi for his help in putting me in contact with Lena Horne, Helga Rothschild for her clarity with words, Petrine Archer-Straw (writer) for her knowledgeable directions and leads, Chris Hayes (writer for *Melody Maker*), Michael Nelligan (Dress Circle, Monmouth Street, London), Hugh Palmer, Pat Durham (Bert Hicks' niece), Lenora Rosamond Chapman (Adelaide's second cousin), Margaret Douglin (Bert Hicks' great-niece), Caroline Rostant (researcher in Trinidad), Eion Todd (Adelaide's clothing designer), Jon and Revie Jourrou, H. D. Rothschild, Stephen Bourne, Barry Sullivan and Laurie Wright (*Storyville* magazine).

I must also mention the help I received from various persons in fields and institutes of knowledge including: Father Alex Hill of All Saints' Church in Notting Hill Gate, Dominic Fisher at Keystone Photography Archives in Paris, Hulton-Getty Photography Archive in London, especially the Director of Collections, Matthew Butson, Mary Rakinson at the U.S. Department of Justice, Carla Coleman at the Passport Services Research Division in Washington, D.C., the Courtauld Institute of Art, the British Film Institute's Photography Stills Archive, La Galcante Archives in Paris, Bibliothèque Nationale de France, especially the performing arts and photography divisions, the British Library Newspaper Archives in Colindale, the staff at Notting Hill Library in Kensington for tracking down many out-of-stock books for me, Françoise Combes at the Observatoire de Paris, Bernie Corbett at the Writers' Guild of Great Britain and Gareth Shannon at Roger Palmer Ltd.

Photographic credits are due to Keystone–F. S. Pictures—courtesy of Michael Soulsby—for the two pictures of Adelaide arriving at Paris Gare St. Lazare in Chapter 10, to Stephen Bourne for the *Chocolate Kiddies* picture in Chapter 6 and *Desires of 1927* portrait in Chapter 7, to Rainer E. Lotz for the two *Chocolate Kiddies* pictures in Chapter 6 and the British Film Institute for the two pictures in Chapter 9 and the portrait in Chapter 13. Paul Colin's image in Chapter 11 is reproduced courtesy of DACS. All other photographs and illustrations appearing in this book that are not otherwise credited are from the private collection of Iain Cameron Williams and Kate Greer. Permission to use the song lyrics to "I Can't Give You Anything But Love," "I Must Have That Man" and "Diga Diga Do" has been issued by EMI Publishing. Authorization to use the poem "Black Black Black" has been granted by its writer, Malcolm Crowthers. Although every care has been taken, if, through inadvertence or failure to trace the present owners, I have included any copyright material without acknowledgment or permission, I offer my apologies to all concerned.

Finally, special thanks must also go to Alexe Knowles-Johnson, Barbara Austin, Barry Mishon, Catherine O'Connor, John W. Davey, Dora Haywood, Paul Brady, Anthony Crowthers, Granville King, Caroline Keene, Ann Man and all my former colleagues at Hogg Robinson Business Travel plc including George Buchanan, John Barker, Sally Shervington, Terry Lambert, Steve Garbutt, Jayne Flatman, Mita Khara,

Nikki Treweek, Jacque Cranston, Sophie Lazari, Victoria Gunn, Hayley Housden, Leanne Graham, Tina Clark, Noel Rabbetts, Thea Walker, Sarah Thompson, Ovril Laidlaw, Michelle O'Toole, Annemarie Hughes, Nicola Stapleton, Alan Punter, Jacqui Quy, Shaun Holroyd, Jackie Duck, Ron Clark, Rosie Wooding, Ami Shaidi, Helen Hudson, Brian Deehan, Charmaine Moseley, Hayley Walters, Nina Kaneira, Cara Driver, Sarah Hudson, Wendy Horn, Julie Bradley, Tracey Sweeney, Sergio Gomez, Mimie Moges, Jenny Oliver, Julie Burke, Suzie Hutson, Bradley Tong, Natasha Tong, Simon Blackie, Martin Drennan, Sue Cash, Lea Coots, Danny Akhtar, Brian McKay, Richard McLoughlin, Joanne King, Amanda Whittet, Maria Caton, Ann Till, Laura Wiggs, Annemarie Robinson, Georgina Cox, Rakhi Shah, Michelle Ward, Jo Vullo, Mario Tondina, Hannah Green, Martina Loftus, Stephen Ng, Emilio Eleftheriou, Nick Kotlarevsky, Mei-Ling Chung, Marion Fox, Thalia Wynard, Anna Skoczylas, Claudette Williams, Leigh Jarvis, Lisa Ljubojev, Jason Coutts and Sam Plested.

Last, but not least, nobody has done more to help bring this book to print than the characters contained within the story. I will always be indebted to their art. It's not what you take with you that matters; it's what you leave behind.

Iain Cameron Williams

*This book is dedicated to the memory of
my grandfather, Æneas Francon Williams
and
my father, Alfred Francon Williams*

As I stood before the theater, my attention was drawn to a photo of Miss Hall, posed as the Madonna. A halo encircles her brow, her eyes are raised aloft portraying within their depths a look of sincerity and holiness. One glance and the memory lingers forever. Some day this girl . . . will . . . step out into a world of keen competition to emerge with laurels, never before allotted a race actress.

Theophilus Lewis, *Baltimore Afro-American*, October 30, 1926

Black Madonna

Adelaide, posed as the Black Madonna in *Desires of 1927*. (Picture taken from the theater program)

PART I

SING TO THE MOON
AND THE STARS WILL SHINE

1901–27

TAXI FOR MISS HALL

LONDON, OCTOBER 1988

Written on a large scrap of cardboard and propped up against a cornflake packet on the small, cluttered kitchen table stood Kate's indispensable "Do not forget" checklist.

Adelaide read the list carefully and crossed off each item as she came to it. Publicity photos, address book, contract, musical arrangement scores, stage costumes, theatrical make-up, wigs, two fur coats—two fur coats?—air-tickets, itinerary, and so the list went on.

Written in bold capital letters at the bottom of the card was a gentle reminder, "AND DON'T FORGET YOUR PASSPORT!"

By the time she had finished reading it, Adelaide felt confident that she had, at last, managed to pack everything in her two suitcases. Kate had planned the trip down to the minutest detail and it had taken Adelaide the whole week to organize herself. Just the thought of all the upheaval and the amount of time it would take to prepare for the trip had exhausted her. Now, at the last moment, she felt a niggling sense of apprehension about the whole affair and couldn't help wondering, "would all the effort be worth it?"

At the beginning of the week, the list seemed endless. With the two large suitcases, locked, labeled and stacked in the hallway awaiting their removal, the effort did, somehow, now seem worthwhile. Anticipation, relief and the odd flutter of a butterfly in her stomach replaced the previous day's symptoms of fatigue but, no matter how Adelaide viewed the situation, she couldn't stop thinking that at her time of life she was far too old for all of this.

"Really . . . at my age, who would have thought it?" she kept chuckling.

There seemed little reason to have another cup of tea. She had already had three and it was still only 9 a.m. Happily she just sat and waited, fully dressed in her long mink coat, watching television with the sound turned down so she could listen out for the taxi's arrival.

Then it came, the long incessant ring on the front doorbell, just as Kate had arranged. Glancing at her wristwatch she noted the time, dot on 9:30.

"All right, all right . . . I'm coming," yelled Adelaide, fully expecting her voice to carry the distance and be heard outside in the street.

"Hello," she calmly spoke into the hall intercom.

"Taxi for Miss Hall," came back the reply.

"Well, I never, that'll be for me. I'll be with you in just a second."

Fifteen minutes later, with Adelaide's two large suitcases loaded, the taxi finally pulled away from Fairholme Road and headed off in the direction of Hammersmith and the M4 motorway. Kate sat next to Adelaide on the back seat. The relief of realizing that they had actually managed to get this far in the schedule produced a slight sense of disorientation in Kate's manner. Excitement had provoked her previous night's lack of sleep and, in an attempt to remain alert, she chatted continuously, oblivious of the early morning traffic chaos that accompanied their entire journey to Heathrow airport.

The weather that morning was uncharacteristically bright and mild for early October. Even the sun managed to make a brief appearance as it emerged from behind a large island of cloud.

"Great weather for flying," interrupted the taxi driver, as if he were an authority on such matters.

The thought hadn't really entered Adelaide's mind, but his comment seemed valid enough to warrant a reply.

"Oh, that's good . . . I've got a plane to catch."

"Yes, I thought you might have . . . that's why I said it," quipped the driver rather cheekily. "Where are you flying to?"

"New York, that's where I'm originally from," enthused Adelaide. "I'm giving a concert at Carnegie Hall."

Before replying, the taxi driver took a glance in his front mirror to see if he could recognize the old lady that he was talking to. He clearly had no idea who she was. After a brief pause he picked up the conversation where he had left it.

"I thought I recognized you. You've picked great weather for flying."

As the sun's glorious rays spun across the horizon even the clouds seemed a little hesitant to follow their gloomy course for the day.

Adelaide Hall at Carnegie Hall had a nice ring to it. The phrase sat happily on the tongue. It made one's eyebrows lift when one heard it spoken. It also dropped neatly into conversations, straight off the cuff without any need of an explanation. In plain English, it just sounded right. Even though she had mixed feelings about the trip, deep down Adelaide still couldn't stop thinking to herself, "Really . . . at my age, who would have thought it?"

Kate Greer had worked in television production for most of her career. It was in 1981, during her employment with the BBC on Michael Parkinson's Saturday night chat show, that Kate was first introduced to Adelaide. The program was a tribute to the pianist Harry Stoneham and Adelaide had been invited to participate as a special guest. Kate and Adelaide hit it off immediately and by the end of the recording Adelaide had invited herself over to Kate's house for dinner. They had been close friends ever since.

After a lengthy absence, Adelaide's return to America brought an ocean of fond memories flooding back. On her way to the hotel, the journey across Manhattan became an excursion down memory lane: Bojangles, Lew Leslie, Duke Ellington, the Cotton Club, Ethel Waters, George Gershwin, her beautiful home in Larchmont, "Creole Love Call," Harlem, her RKO concert tour across America, the Palace, the Lafayette, Fields and McHugh, Harold Arlen, Art Tatum and funnyman Fats Waller . . . all came back to greet her. Like fragmented stills from a silent movie, her former life flashed vividly before her and for a brief moment, as tears welled up in her eyes, the melody of "I Can't Give You Anything But Love, Baby" began to play inside her mind.

After gently wiping the tears away, Adelaide turned and gazed reflectively across at Kate, "All distant memories now but, boy, what memories."

Adelaide's immediate impression of New York was that it had changed little from how she remembered the city all those years ago, only now there appeared to be a lot more of everything. More people crowding the sidewalks, more shops and restaurants lining the streets and much more traffic. However, no matter how much cosmetic surgery had taken place over the years, Adelaide still found the ethos of the old place remained very much intact.

New York always has dominated its inhabitants. From the moment you catch sight of Manhattan's skyline, the panorama overwhelms your vision in every sense of the word. No matter how long you may have lived there or how well you might think you know it, the city has an amazing habit of throwing something unexpected at you, each time you look. Even the skyscrapers appear constantly to gaze down in amazement at the tangled web of activity beneath them.

The following day's rehearsal was arranged for 12:30. The streets were manic with midday traffic and the chances of arriving on time seemed slim. The trip across Manhattan, from the hotel to Carnegie Hall, should normally have taken ten minutes at most. For the past twenty minutes the cab had been stationary. As the fare ticked over Adelaide grew increasingly more anxious by the dollar.

When they eventually reached Carnegie Hall a great surprise awaited them. Displayed on the outside walls of the building were several large billboards advertising, "*Cabaret Comes to Carnegie* with the legendary Adelaide Hall in concert." Slashed across them in thick black lettering were the words, "SOLD RIGHT OUT."

"Well, would you take a look at that," Adelaide motioned to Kate.

Without so much as a raised eyebrow, as if it were the most natural thing in the world, Kate casually retorted, "There, I told you they hadn't forgotten you," then let out a squeal of delight that could clearly be heard on the opposite side of the street.

In the foyer, anxiously awaiting their arrival, stood the show's producer, Donald Smith. His flamboyant greeting also came as an unexpected surprise: "Welcome home, Miss Hall! It truly is an honor and a privilege to meet you at last."

The stage was much larger than Adelaide had imagined it. Only a few folding chairs stacked along the backstage wall and a discarded microphone stand remained from the previous night's concert. Perhaps it seemed so vast because it was deserted; she couldn't quite work it out. The house lights were turned on full and gave a clear perspective of every corner of the recital hall. Standing on the dais, peering out across row upon row of empty red velvet seats gave Adelaide's nerves a sudden jolt. Having traveled this far, she now realized that there was no turning back. Only then did the harsh reality of her situation kick in.

Turning to face Kate, Adelaide sighed deeply, then through half a smile remarked rather pensively, "To think I've had to travel halfway around the world to get here, when I only used to live up the road." Kate smiled back reassuringly whilst nodding her head slowly in agreement. "Yes, but just think . . . they've had to wait all these years for the privilege of seeing you."

In a sense, the long lapse in time since her heady days of fame back in the Twenties and Thirties made her act seem incongruous with today's concert-hall performers. Hers would be a performance of matured artistry and talent without the aid of flashy gimmickry, lavish production or record company hype. Those days were well and truly over, if indeed they ever did exist.

It had always been Adelaide's dream to appear in concert at Carnegie Hall. The long wait had been worth it. That evening, as she stepped out onto the stage, the standing ovation she received, before she had even sung a note, gave her a clear indication that the Big Apple had not forgotten who Adelaide Hall was.

Her reviews in the following day's papers were a testament to her legendary status in the jazz world. Back at their hotel suite, Kate excitedly read each one out aloud. Having someone else recite her reviews was a practice Adelaide's late husband, Bert, initiated and one she had grown accustomed to over the years.

" . . . and in the *New York Times*, no less, their music correspondent John Wilson heads his review with lavish compliments."

As Kate continued her narrative, Adelaide reclined deeper into the comfortable, oversized sofa, wallowing in all the praise.

She sang Duke Ellington's "Solitude" in the brisk, lightly swinging tempo in which he first recorded it rather than in the slow, mournful manner it has since taken. . . . With the ballad "Tenderly," her use of gentle, husky vocalizing enabled her to personalize what can easily be an overly familiar song. At an age that she describes as "somewhere over 75," Miss Hall placed her emphasis on skillful phrasing and secure rhythmic sense and combines bubbling vitality and enthusiasm with the skill of a veteran performer.[1]

Each time Adelaide heard something she liked, as if to make sure she had heard it correctly the first time, she would ask Kate to repeat it, after which she would shake her head and quietly mutter to herself under her breath, "Really . . . at my age, who would have thought it?"

However painful the process may be,
sometimes it's necessary to travel back in time,
in order to lay the ghosts that haunt . . .
to rest.

SING TO THE MOON

By the end of the nineteenth century, Harlem had grown into a desirable residential district for wealthy, white, middle-class New Yorkers, who brought with them their newly acquired status and prosperity. Real estate in the area boomed and developers were quick to cash in. Located uptown between Fifth Avenue and Broadway just north of Central Park, Harlem became one of the most fashionable addresses in town. With its wide, well-lit avenues, brand-new subway system, and attractive modern brownstone houses and apartment blocks, Harlem gave off an air of refined respectability. In the wake of the looming recession the area would soon find itself transformed beyond recognition.

At the turn of the century, economic depression and overdevelopment brought an unexpected reversal in Harlem's good fortune. Overnight, house prices plummeted and bankruptcy followed for many of its affluent residents. As prices hit rock bottom, property in the area suddenly became affordable for the working classes. This time the black and immigrant population struck lucky and capitalized on Harlem's misfortune. Although it was no longer one of the most fashionable addresses in town, Harlem's new inhabitants brought an alternative wealth and confidence to the area.

Harlem rapidly became a thriving self-sufficient neighborhood once more, catering solely for the black and immigrant population. Its new residents found department stores, theaters, schools, restaurants and a fully equipped hospital all within a stone's throw, eliminating any necessity to travel downtown. Harlem even published its own daily newspapers. For its citizens, this flourishing community symbolically represented hope and opportunity for the future. As if to acknowledge this startling regeneration, many white New Yorkers now referred to the district as "America's Black Capital."

This new air of optimism encouraged Arthur William Hall and his wife, Elizabeth, to uproot their family from Brooklyn and move across the East River to enjoy the benefits that Harlem had to offer. Their decision brought a dramatic change in their lifestyle. With property costing considerably less to rent, they could afford a larger, more comfortable, two-bedroom apartment. Situated on the first floor of a tenement block on 194 West 134th Street, their new home even boasted its own bathroom with hot and cold running water.

The family quickly settled into the neighborhood. Their first impressions of the area were more than favorable. Elizabeth couldn't help but notice how clean and well-maintained the sidewalks were and wondered naïvely if the street cleaners polished them each night. It hadn't occurred to her that the district's refuse department might be one of the finest in Manhattan.

As a classically trained musician, Arthur's qualifications helped establish him locally as a private piano teacher. He offered lessons in both light classical and popular music and taught from home, six days a week.[1] On Sundays, as director of music at their local Protestant church, St. Philip's Episcopal, he proudly played the organ whilst simultaneously conducting the church choir.

Arthur and Elizabeth's first home at 10 Steuben Street, in the Clinton Hill district of Brooklyn, had been a cramped one-room apartment, on the upper floor of a four-story, red-brick tenement block. Its residents mockingly referred to the area as the slums of Brooklyn's Navy Yard. The apartment had neither heating nor running hot water. The bathroom was out on the landing and shared by other tenants on the same floor. Water was heated on a potbellied coal stove which in winter helped heat the room, although far from adequately. In the summer you sweltered and the foul stench of excrement from the blocked drains hung around in the air like a poisonous gas. The streets were noisy, congested and dirty. There seemed no escape from the garbage that piled high in any available doorway or alley. Only the rats showed any interest in its disposal. Although accommodation in the area was cheap, Brooklyn's mean streets were hardly the right surroundings for a child's upbringing.

Known locally as the borough of many churches, a spire could be seen from almost every street corner and each vicinity had its own patron saint to whom you prayed constantly for salvation. Living within such a crowded, multiracial community created many problems. To the west of the neighborhood lived the Jews, to the east lived the Italians and in the south lived the transient Irish population. Blacks were viewed with suspicion by all factions. This fiery mixture proved volatile. Brooklyn was like a tinderbox; rivalry between the various ethnic groups was a daily hazard and gave the borough its well-earned reputation for violence. If your neighbors were of the wrong creed, it automatically created tension. Given the slightest provocation, hostilities and street fights erupted. Not only was the environment unsettling to live in, the chances of escaping from it unscathed were minimal.

By coincidence, on Navy Street, twelve blocks from the Hall home, lived the Capone family, recent *émigrés* from Sicily. As a grocer, Mr. Capone found his pitiful earnings impossible to live on so he established a barber's shop just off Steuben Street at 69 Park Avenue. In 1899, five years after the family's arrival in America, Alphonse Capone was born and registered as a U.S. citizen. As one of nine children, Al quickly learnt how to look after himself. By the time he had reached his teens, trial and error had taught him that being an honest citizen in a tough neighborhood was not the cleverest way of earning the respect of his rivals.

Early on in his career Arthur had worked part-time as a pianist in a small lounge orchestra, resident at an exclusive supper-club on Riverside Drive, along Manhattan's West Side. Many of his friends were fellow musicians. They would often call round to his apartment during the afternoon on their way to work. As most musicians worked seven nights a week, such visits were probably their only chance to socialize.

When Arthur was offered regular employment, playing the piano in a small traveling black orchestra, his decision to accept left Elizabeth heartbroken. The job kept him away from home, touring for long spells at a time. When his initial contract was extended for a further six months, Elizabeth, then aged 23, panicked. Unbeknownst to Arthur she was pregnant. To add to her distress, she now found herself alone, forced into a position where she had to fend for herself. Elizabeth gave birth to Adelaide Louise Hall in Brooklyn on October 20, 1901.

Although Arthur sent home to Elizabeth as much money as he could afford, his wage was not sufficient to cover the bills or indeed allow her to join him on tour. His prolonged absence and her uncertain predicament at home led Elizabeth to decide not to register the child at birth.

With no personal income to rely upon and now finding herself unable to work away from home, Elizabeth took in washing to help relieve her financial difficulties. Writing to her mother for guidance, she found little sympathy, "You've made your own bed. Now you must lie on it."

With help from friends who remained loyal, Elizabeth soldiered on. At the end of his contract, Arthur, unaware that he had fathered a child, returned to Brooklyn to find his situation at home changed dramatically. When he asked Elizabeth why she hadn't written to tell him that she was pregnant her reply confused him. "If you truly loved me, I felt sure you would come back, but if I'd told you that I was pregnant, I was afraid you might dodge the responsibility and never return."

Contrary to Elizabeth's worst fears, Arthur did come back and shouldered his responsibilities. With an addition to the family, their one-roomed apartment in Steuben Street became increasingly cramped and uncomfortable. Fourteen months later, Elizabeth became pregnant again. The time had finally come for Arthur to move his growing family into larger premises.

They moved across town to the East New York district of Brooklyn. It was here, at 985 Blake Avenue, on August 6, 1903, that Elizabeth gave birth to Evelyn Augusta. Throughout the pregnancy Elizabeth had remained unwell and during the latter stages her ill health created minor complications, which prompted her doctor to induce the birth prematurely. As a result, Evelyn was born with a weakened constitution and was to suffer greatly from poor health in later years.

Born in 1875, in Mifflintown, Pennsylvania, of African ancestry, Arthur Hall was the grandson of a freed slave from Port Jefferson on Long Island.

As one of thirteen children—his father had been married twice—Arthur's unhappy childhood memories of poverty, persecution and general hopelessness were often recounted to Adelaide and Evelyn, in the hope of teaching them to appreciate what little good fortune they had. Though money was scarce, the time and love Arthur and Elizabeth invested in the upbringing of their children was priceless, a commodity neither parent had been fortunate enough to experience during their own troubled childhood.

Tall, with a handsome smile and a sharp sense of humor, Arthur believed resolutely in the old biblical proverb, "For whatsoever a man soweth, that shall he also reap,"[2] and accordingly worked hard and long hours to support his growing family.

Fastidious and a habitual worrier, he suffered regular bouts of insomnia. On numerous occasions Elizabeth was roused from her sleep in the middle of the night to the sound of her husband playing through a whole piano concerto. This was his way of trying to relieve his pent-up anxiety.

Elizabeth's family was also large. She had seven brothers. Though none of them lived close by, Robert, Frank and Oscar regularly kept in touch. Born on November 4, 1877 in Port Jefferson, Long Island, Elizabeth Gerard grew up surrounded by the age-old traditions and superstitions that belonged to an Indian tribal settlement. Her family's ancestry boasted Pennsylvania Dutch and North American Shinnecock Indian blood of which her family were deeply proud.

Elizabeth adored her new home in Harlem. Each morning she rose early, long before the rest of the family. The warm, fragrant smell of freshly brewed coffee would rise from the percolator, as it often did throughout the day, and filter through the apartment. She ran her home efficiently and with ease and woe betide anyone who messed it up. If the parlor was considered Arthur's study, then the kitchen was strictly Elizabeth's domain and became the hub of the household. Here she regularly welcomed and entertained her many friends and visitors. Her closest friend, Gertrude Curtis, visited daily.[3] The girls adored her and adopted her as their aunt. Born of mixed descent, she had a soul as black as any Negro, yet her skin was as white as a Caucasian's. After qualifying as a dentist in 1911, Gertrude opened her own practice. It was the first dental practice ever to be owned by a black woman in New York. Gertrude's elevated position in society afforded her the unique privilege of mixing socially with all classes.

Sometimes, Gertrude would pop in on her way home from a smart supper party downtown to see Elizabeth for a chat. She was always full of exciting gossip and tremendous fun to have around but, more importantly for her adopted nieces, always remembered to bring a little treat with her.

The Hall household revolved dutifully around religion. St. Philip's Episcopal Church was the focal point of their worship and when they were old enough both Adelaide and Evelyn joined the church choir. On Sundays they learnt how heaven could exist here on earth, a philosophy that, at times, seemed difficult to comprehend, considering that the separation of blacks within society was still legal in certain states of America. The further south one traveled, the more evident such prejudice became.

Both Adelaide and Evelyn attended Public School 89, conveniently located in the street where they lived. The school had a well-structured educational system and was run strictly and efficiently by its headmaster. Music was taught by a young lady called Miss Corlias. Her energy and enthusiasm for the subject rubbed off on her pupils. She ran the school orchestra—which performed each morning during assembly—with great keenness. In future years several of her ex-pupils, including Thomas "Fats" Waller, would praise her diligence and assistance in helping to develop their musical skills. Most of the pupils were encouraged to learn an instrument even if it was only the triangle. Adelaide chose the ukulele and became quite a proficient player. When Miss Corlias picked her to play in the orchestra, Adelaide's interest in music suddenly took a giant leap forward.

The girls soon settled into the school's routine and quickly attracted a new circle of friends. One such girlfriend, Maude Mills, had a particularly good singing voice.[4] She and her two elder sisters, Florence and Olivia, had formed a vocal trio called the Mills Sisters. To earn pocket money, they performed at local functions and on special festive occasions. This inspired Adelaide to form her own act. With Evelyn playing the piano, they sang at similar events and billed themselves as the Hall Sisters.

Elizabeth would often invite friends and neighbors round in the evening for a glass of beer and a singsong. Before the mass invasion of the radio and phonograph, the upright piano was the main source of in-house entertainment. With the guests gathered around the keyboard listening to Arthur playing the latest popular songs, the party soon got swinging. Adelaide and Evelyn would eagerly join in with the singing. Sometimes, if they were really lucky, the girls might be rewarded for their efforts with a small tip from the guests. The fact that Elizabeth was tone-deaf did little to discourage her from joining in too, much to the amusement of her two daughters.

Elizabeth's favorite song, to which she knew all the words, was "Georgia Rose." Adelaide would pester her mother continually to sing it and then hide her head with embarrassment when she did. Crouched behind the piano, Arthur would call out mockingly, "And who said you can't sing, darling. It sounds beautiful," and the girls would fall about the room laughing their heads off. It was on occasions such as these that life could not have got much better for the Hall family.

As sisters, Adelaide and Evelyn were devoted to each other and treated one another as best friends. Very little jealousy or rivalry came between them. Though similar in appearance—they both inherited their mother's good looks, light copper-brown skin coloring and ginger hair—Adelaide looked slightly more like her mother than Evelyn. In Harlem, such children of mixed-race families, who were neither black nor white, were referred to as either brown or doeskin.

Due to the fine quality and coloring of their hair, early photographs of the sisters showed them looking very odd. They appeared to have little hair at all and looked almost bald. Adelaide was very upset by this trick of the camera but soon discovered a trick of her own to overcome it. If she was to be photographed she wore a black woolly bonnet. This gave the viewer the impression that she had a head full of thick, black hair. It seems that even at an early age, Adelaide was aware of how important her image was. The Hall Sisters became well known in the neighborhood, if not for their singing then certainly for their appearance, for which they acquired the colorful nickname "the carrot-top twins."

Each afternoon, when the girls returned home from school, Elizabeth made sure that the first thing they did was to change out of their school uniform and into their navy-blue, sleeved tunics. Only then would she permit the girls to play outside in the street until supper time.

On her thirteenth birthday, Adelaide received a surprise gift from her mother's brother, Uncle Frank. A brand-new pair of roller-skates. Before long these became her second feet, as she wore them almost constantly. Bruises and cuts on her elbows and knees regularly appeared, as did the tears that followed. However, Adelaide soon became a first-class skater and could outskate any of the boys in the neighborhood. She taught herself to glide as gracefully as a swan sails across the still waters on a pond. By watching other skaters perform in the street she developed her own interpretation of dance steps, adapting their movements and expressing them with a rhythm and style all of her own. Interestingly, this was how she initially learnt the first movements of dance. Gradually her confidence grew and with it came a determination to be the best skater in the borough.

Much to the fury of her mother, Adelaide would leap through the air and land perfectly still as if on a pinhead, then effortlessly jump over four garbage cans, just to compete with the boys. A crowd, forming a large circle, always gathered in the street to watch her perform. Spurred on by their cheers, Adelaide would pull out all the stops and skate like a seasoned professional. Her daredevil antics greatly distressed her mother, who kept a constant vigil from the kitchen window. Each time she leapt over the garbage cans her mother would wince and throw up her arms in dismay, convinced that Adelaide would hurt herself. Things finally came to a head when her mother became so anxious about her daughter's leaps that Arthur, fearing for his wife's health, forbade Adelaide from ever performing them again. Although she liked to watch her sister, Evelyn had no desire to skate. Her shyness kept her firmly on the sidelines, where she would proudly bask in Adelaide's glory.

Sometimes, for a dare, Evelyn would coax Adelaide to climb out through one of the apartment's large sash windows to walk along the narrow stone ledge that extended the length of the block. The danger and consequences of her actions never once entered Adelaide's head. It was only after a neighbor complained about Adelaide creeping past her first-floor window that Elizabeth became aware of her daughter's crazy antics. Both girls promptly received a severe scolding from their father, who then secured numerous locks to the apartment windows and banned them both from playing in the street for a week. Although his actions prevented

Adelaide from attempting any similar excursions in the future, her tom-foolery continued unabated.

After supper, on hot humid summer evenings, Elizabeth allowed the girls to sit outside on the front stoop of the house to cool down. They would happily have sat there all night long, if their mother had let them, just watching the world pass by . . . underneath a Harlem moon.

During the muggy summer months, New York became unbearable. By the time the school break arrived, those who could afford to take a vacation deserted the city. Being poor, Elizabeth could only manage to take the girls to Coney Island for day trips. For the price of a train ride the beach-front amusement resort gave working-class families a holiday they couldn't have otherwise afforded. Here they could escape the polluted claustrophobia that engulfed the city and breathe clear, fresh sea air. The resort had a charm that was hard to resist. On its wide, sandy beach, which seemed to stretch for miles in both directions, the girls had ample space and freedom to play contentedly all day.

Far off in the distance, along the penciled edge of the coastline, the thunderous sound of Atlantic breakers could be heard crashing down in a continuous flurry of motion. The water was always far too cold to swim in, but that never deterred the girls from taking the occasional dip. As Elizabeth kept herself occupied, crocheting under the shade of a large canvas parasol, she would watch in utter amazement at the pranks of her two hyperactive daughters. Sometimes, if the sun disappeared behind the clouds, the girls forgot about the sand and the sea and the squawking gulls overhead and, instead, fantasized about visiting foreign countries far across the ocean. Adelaide would tease Evelyn by pretending she could see Europe way off on the horizon. Not wanting to feel left out of the daydream Evelyn would squint her eyes together and agree that she too could just see the French coastline.

On Coney Island the sun's intensity was very deceiving and scorched everything in sight. Even the landscape's neutral color scheme seemed to contradict its tanning power. Having suffered from severe sunburn in her youth, Elizabeth was fully aware how harmful the sun's rays could be and was always worried that her daughters' delicate skin would burn. When the girls were playing on the beach she insisted they protect their arms and legs at all times with a thick layer of greasy coconut lotion. Much to their horror, the lotion smelled foul and stuck to everything it touched, causing them much embarrassment in front of other bathers.

If the weather wasn't up to much, there was always the famous amusement park to explore. Here the razzle-dazzle of its arcades, stomach-churning roller-coaster rides, musical carousels and scary freak shows kept the daytripper amused for hours. Where else could one see a headless woman, an illustrated man, a two-headed baby and the smallest pony in the world all on the same day? Elizabeth had learnt from earlier visits that it was pointless trying to steer Adelaide and Evelyn away from the amusements. It was far easier to let them get it out of their system.

When the sea became too rough for bathing, further along the promenade on Surf Avenue was the world's largest swimming pool. "The Palace of Joy" was advertised as having sterilized and heated water directly channeled from the ocean. Its waters certainly gained a healthy reputation with bathers, who claimed its special elixir benefited the body and mind. How much of this reputation was hearsay is anyone's guess but it certainly made good reading on the advertisements.

During the afternoon, synchronized swimming events were held, given by a squadron of diving girls. These were aimed primarily at the youngsters and were highly entertaining. Adelaide loved them and would concentrate hard trying to memorize the swimmers' movements. At the end of the display she would be the first one to dive into the pool to emulate what she had just seen. She never could get the routines right but had a good shot at trying. The exhibitions were accompanied by Victor's Famous Venetian Band. Quite what the band was famous for the posters never said. However, Adelaide grumbled that without their accompaniment she would never be able to keep her routine synchronized.

By sunset, the girls were thoroughly exhausted. On the train journey home, with their heads snuggled restfully upon their mother's lap, Adelaide and Evelyn would fall fast asleep, totally content. Elizabeth never could work out why the journey home seemed so much quicker than the journey out to Coney Island.

As a duo, the Hall Sisters performed regularly at their local church, St. Philip's Episcopal. Rather than sing, Evelyn accompanied Adelaide on the piano, although occasionally they did sing a cappella together. Performing did not come naturally to Evelyn. She always had been the quieter, more studious of the two. It was under her father's tutelage that Evelyn studied music. As a pianist she showed great aptitude and went on to pass her piano grades successfully, much to her father's delight. She loved ragtime music and would often play a rag tune to help speed up her mother's housework. Evelyn's bashfulness and lack of enthusiasm for the spotlight provoked Adelaide on many occasions to use bullying tactics in order to get her sister up on stage.

"Why do I always have to force her to sing with me?" Adelaide would deviously moan in her mother's presence, each time they were invited to perform.

Usually, with a little intervention from Elizabeth, Adelaide got her way and the Hall Sisters would appear at the end-of-term school concert. It was here that Adelaide would shine and show off in front of her friends. She would try to imitate the singers she had seen on stage in the local theaters. Her naive idea of performing was to throw herself all over the stage without any thought of co-ordination, allowing her legs to fly in one direction while her arms lashed out in the other. Whatever illusion the overall effect gave, her performance was always memorable and enthusiastically received by her school chums. From this early age Elizabeth could already see her daughter was going to be a difficult act to follow.

Even as a small child, singing came naturally to Adelaide. It was as if she had been born singing and had not stopped since. In the evenings, after her father finished tutoring, he would often call her into his study to sing for him.

"Sing to the moon, Addie, and the stars will shine," he used to bellow loudly across the room. Pointing to the window, he would then ask her, "Can you see the moon?"

Adelaide would rush to the window to take a look but always responded with the same answer,

"No!"

"Well, listen to the music and you will."

He then played the piano like a madman with his fingers falling all over the ivories from one end of the keyboard to the other. Adelaide would hoot with laughter as she tried hopelessly to sing along with his manic accompaniment.

Then he would call out, "Now look outside the window, Addie."

On one occasion, as if by magic, the largest full moon you could ever have imagined suddenly appeared from nowhere, suspended high up in the evening sky.

"There . . . I told you the moon would raise its head."

Adelaide peered through the window in amazement. "It looks more like a big apple to me."

She never could work out why it was but always insisted adamantly that it didn't look like the moon at all.

⋙

Though the Hall household could hardly have bragged that the theater was in their blood, on Elizabeth's side of the family, a much-talked-about cousin, Ada Overton Walker, had found modest acclaim as an actress on the black theater circuit across America.[5] Born in 1880, in New York City, she entered show business at an early age. It was during a vaudeville tour that she met and courted her future husband, George Walker. He appeared on stage as one half of the colored comedy duo Williams and Walker. As most minstrels in vaudeville were white they were billed as the "Two Real Coons."

In 1903, Williams and Walker's first starring role propelled them into the limelight. The show, *In Dahomey*, was the first all-black production to play on Broadway. In it they popularized the Cakewalk, a dance which originated in minstrel shows where white performers imitated slaves mimicking the dances of their masters. After a highly praised, profitable run the show traveled to Europe and was booked into the Shaftesbury Theatre in London. A command performance at Buckingham Palace, in front of Edward VII, guaranteed the show duplicated its American success in Britain.

For convenience, Ada always appeared in the same shows as her husband. Their next production, *In Abyssinia*, fared equally well in the eyes of the press and public alike. Even though much of their marriage was spent on the road touring, Ada and George did manage to set up home in New York. It was at their home that Elizabeth had, on several occasions, visited her famous relative. Unfortunately, the fruits of stardom were to be short-lived for both Ada and George. In 1908, during the lengthy run of their next and most accomplished musical to date, *Bandanna Land*, George contracted paresis. The weakening of his muscles brought on gradual dementia. During the final weeks of the show's run, George became too ill to perform. So advanced were the symptoms that he could no longer talk without stuttering. By way of a tribute to her husband, Ada blackened her face with burnt cork, donned his costume and, at each performance he missed, substituted for him He died in 1911. Ada found little solace in the theater after George's death and three years later succumbed to what her relatives termed "a mysterious illness." Those close to her thought differently and felt she had died of a broken heart.

The happy carefree years that colored Adelaide's adolescence with love and security changed forever, with the sudden death, in 1916, of her beloved father. Elizabeth turned to Adelaide as the elder of her two daughters, for comfort and support. Overnight, Adelaide suddenly found she was expected to mature from a carefree teenager into a responsible adult. She was now called upon to take charge of family responsibilities that her mother could neither manage nor comprehend.

Adelaide's middle name, Louise, was inherited from her grandmother, Louise Gerard. For many years Louise had lived and worked abroad, in France. Employed as a housekeeper by a wealthy French Canadian family, she had traveled to Europe as a member of their staff. When her employment with the family terminated, having grown accustomed to the French lifestyle, she remained in the country and continued to work in domestic service. In her spare time she studied nursing and became a fully qualified midwife. During the First World War she volunteered her nursing skills at a local Catholic hospital and helped attend to the steady stream of sick and wounded soldiers who were admitted.

In 1916 she suffered a mild stroke, which left her convalescing for several months. Being unfit to work, her exile in France came to an abrupt end and she returned to America. Arriving in New York homeless, without any means or an income to support herself, she turned to her daughter Elizabeth for temporary accommodation. Elizabeth now found that her mother, having lived in France for so long, spoke only broken English with a heavy French accent.

To Adelaide and Evelyn, who had never met their grandmother before, having a foreigner in the family came as quite a shock. They thought her manners peculiar and embarrassing and felt uneasy in her presence. Louise found Harlem difficult to adjust to. In her opinion nothing seemed good enough. She continually complained, not only about her own predicament but also about that of her daughter. She tried hard to convince Elizabeth that Adelaide should further her education in France where she could train to become a *modiste* in a proper fashion house. Although the idea greatly appealed to Adelaide, without proper finance the chance of it ever happening seemed like another one of her grandmother's pompous whims.

However, at Louise's insistence, Adelaide did attend evening classes to learn needlework and dressmaking. As most poor families were unable to afford new clothes, they would either make their own or adapt hand-me-downs that were given to them from the Salvation Halls. Knowing how to sew was deemed to be a very useful skill.

It was at an end-of-term school concert that the budding impresario Lew Leslie first saw Adelaide perform.[6] Leslie had been invited by Elizabeth's friend, the singer Lottie Gee (whom he later managed), under the pretext that she wanted him to accompany her to the show. Leslie arrived with no conception of what he was about to witness. During the concert Adelaide sang two songs, a gospel hymn that began with the line, "There is a green hill far away," followed by a more uptempo ragtime number.

He later likened Adelaide's performance to that of a whirling dervish, all movement without actually arriving anywhere. It was her voice that struck a chord with him. He instantly recognized her natural ability to pitch every note she sang perfectly. She could hit top C effortlessly. He knew then that, with the right training, Adelaide could have a tremendous career ahead of her as a professional singer. After talking the matter through with Lottie, it soon became apparent that the only obstacle he would have in putting his thoughts into practice would be convincing Elizabeth.

Lottie knew the family's financial situation was precarious, having little money to survive on since Arthur's death. She was also aware that it had already been arranged for Adelaide to enter the fashion industry to train as a seamstress when she left school. It was her grandmother's wish that she should enter the trade. Adelaide would have much preferred to remain at college and further her education, although the prospect of entering the rag trade did appeal to her growing interest in fashion.

After the concert Leslie introduced himself to Elizabeth and impressed upon her how much he had enjoyed Adelaide's singing. Respecting the family's lack of finance, he politely offered to pay for Adelaide to have voice training.

Elizabeth was flattered by his interest but saw little reason to alter the plans she had already made for Adelaide's future. It took a few days of continual nagging from Lottie before Elizabeth relented and finally accepted Leslie's offer to help. As it turned out, Adelaide only ever had one singing lesson, after which the voice coach announced in astonishment, "Tell Mr. Leslie that you have perfect pitch and the loveliest voice I've ever heard and there's little I can teach you that you don't already naturally know."

With Leslie's theatrical connections and persuasive personality and Lottie's constant encouragement, the only foreseeable obstacle keeping Adelaide from entering show business now . . . was timing.

The trauma of returning to New York caused Louise's fragile health to slowly deteriorate. At the age of 72, her tired heart and weary soul were no longer strong enough to cope with the sudden upheaval in her life. Each day Elizabeth found her mother's presence in the apartment increasingly more demanding. It reached a point where Sundays became the only day her mother ventured out, to attend church. At home the atmosphere became claustrophobic and highly charged. Clearly the situation was not going to alter overnight but somehow Elizabeth had to find a tactful solution to the problem.

With little funds to support her growing family, Elizabeth contacted her brothers for financial assistance. Between them they were unable to give more than a token gesture of support. However, her favorite brother, Oscar, who was in need of accommodation, suggested it might be helpful if he were to rent a room in their apartment. To keep the wolf from the door and help relieve some of the anxiety about and burden of her ailing mother, Elizabeth agreed. As the apartment only had two bedrooms Oscar moved into the parlor. This unsatisfactory arrangement now meant that Elizabeth had to share her mother's bedroom.

At the plush Riverside restaurant, where Arthur had worked, his colleagues clubbed together to raise a donation to help Elizabeth with her debts. The money brought a temporary respite. When the offer of an evening job came along, as a cloakroom attendant at the same Riverside restaurant, it seemed like a good omen and too good an opportunity to turn down.

Each evening before setting off, Elizabeth made the same announcement to her daughters, "Be sure to keep the front door securely locked while I'm away at work." Although the girls were quite capable of looking after their grandmother and Uncle Oscar, Elizabeth never felt easy about leaving them on their own.

On her way to work, Elizabeth met up with some of the musicians who played in the restaurant's orchestra. Together they would walk through St. Nicholas Park, over the hill, down the other side and along towards Riverside Drive. At the end of the evening the same musicians escorted her back home. During the bitterly cold winter months, to keep themselves warm, they walked briskly, singing gospel songs in rhythm to their own footsteps. In summer, when the sweltering heat became unbearable, they would saunter home slowly, marveling at the city's bright lights far off in the distance.

The restaurant catered exclusively for rich white folk. It was the sort of establishment where the clientele went purely to be seen, dressed up to the nines, in all their jewels and finery. Here, the famous and the celebrated rubbed shoulders with the upper echelons of American society who, in return, viewed this new breed of vulgar, ill-bred *nouveaux riches* with little more than suspicious contempt. As long as the overpriced check was settled at the end of the meal both fraternities were guaranteed to have their every whim catered for and served up without so much as a raised eyebrow from the waiters.

Confined below stairs, in the bowels of the ladies' cloakroom, Elizabeth soon learnt how to spend an entire evening attending to the needs of overpampered women. Each visitor to her rest room received fresh towels, scented soap, and an array of expensive perfumes to choose from. With practice and a little discretion, Elizabeth became familiar with each lady's preference of scent. She boasted that with one sniff she could instantly name any perfume that entered her cloakroom.

Some regulars made the effort to befriend her and, in doing so, found a willing soul in whom they could easily confide their personal problems. For Elizabeth, this privileged world, that revolved a million miles away from hers, became a welcome break from her own troubled existence. The hours may have been long and the pay low but the tips were generous, as much as three or four dollars a night.

With Uncle Oscar now resident under the same roof, Adelaide and Evelyn found themselves with a new father figure in their lives. As Oscar had the security of a regular job (he had held it for over twenty years), his presence brought an element of stability back into the household.

Then, without warning, the owners of the factory where Oscar worked announced the imminent closure of the company. This disturbing news sent Oscar into an immediate depression. At the age of 50, his chances of finding another job were slim. The longer he remained unemployed, the more depressed he became. He lost his appetite and started to lose weight. Elizabeth became concerned over her brother's health and called the doctor for a prognosis. Oscar's state of mind had deteriorated so rapidly, the doctor thought it highly unlikely that he would ever return to work. It was as if he had lost the will to live. Within six weeks of his redundancy Oscar died in his sleep. The suddenness of his death dealt another blow to the Hall household.

Gradually, Elizabeth's self-confidence returned. Once again, she found herself in the position of being the sole breadwinner. Her daily routine of managing a home on a pittance had become a necessity, and one, given past experience, at which she now excelled.

Through the church she discovered an inner strength and peace of mind that enabled her to stand up and fight for what she believed in. From then on, anyone who dared to cross her path, no matter how important they might be, soon got the sharp edge of her tongue.

With the Great War overshadowing world events, America braced itself as the eye of the storm drew ever closer in its direction. When the inevitable happened and American troops were drafted to join the Allied Forces, the United States become another casualty of man's aggressive and unreasonable behavior. Detailed descriptions of the war's horrific progress were reported in newspapers, newsreels and in the classroom.

At school, Adelaide and Evelyn were now taught how to act as responsible grown-up human beings even though at times it appeared their elders didn't. As the good Americans they were, they learnt how to help minimize the country's expenditure and were shown cost-cutting ways to save and economize at home in an attempt to support the war effort.

Elizabeth's eldest brother Frank had recently separated from his wife and was looking for temporary accommodation. It was agreed that he should move temporarily into their apartment and rent Uncle Oscar's old room. With two boisterous teenage daughters, her ailing mother and now her brother in residence, once again the sleeping arrangements in the apartment became totally inadequate. In order to retain some peace of mind, Elizabeth resolved to sleep in the kitchen. Frank's deep affection for his sister and her two young daughters helped bring back an element of much-needed fun into the household. He found that having the patience of a saint was an extremely useful trait when confronted with the tomfoolery of his nieces. A cruel twist of fate was yet to deal its hardest blow.

Towards the fall of 1918 the war appeared to be reaching an end. In the newspapers, daily reports were filtering through of a severe outbreak of influenza in the East. It was reported that over the past three months the virus had swept alarmingly quickly across India killing an estimated five million people in its path. As the virus spread from country to country, doctors discovered that they had no medicine to cure this particularly virulent strain of flu.

By the time the outbreak hit the American mainland in 1919, it had reached pandemic proportions and almost twenty million people had died from the disease. Concern that the young, elderly and infirm would spread the virus unchecked prompted New York's local health authorities to issue guidelines on prevention. Unfortunately, no matter how well prepared an individual was, the virus, which was carried invisibly through the air, spread uncontrollably without discrimination.

Having recently completed her schooling, Evelyn had started a job working as a machine operator in a small, local factory that made cotton hairnets. During her childhood Evelyn always had been more prone to illness than her sister. It was at work, in the cold and drafty surroundings of the inadequately heated factory that Evelyn went down with a slight fever. As a health precaution, her boss immediately sent her home. Overnight her condition rapidly deteriorated. Fearing the worst, Elizabeth sent for the doctor. His prognosis was, as Elizabeth had feared, flu. In order to contain the virus, the doctor insisted she be admitted to Harlem Hospital at once. Realizing the seriousness of her daughter's illness sent Elizabeth into shock. Her mistrust of hospital regime saw Elizabeth stand her ground. She adamantly refused to allow Evelyn's removal, arguing that she would be better cared for at home. Already severely weakened by her critical condition, within a week Evelyn contracted pneumonia. Her frail body was now incapable of building any resistance. On March 25, 1920, fourteen days after contracting the virus, Evelyn, aged only sixteen, passed away.

For Elizabeth and Adelaide, March 25 was the day their worst fears became reality. Not only did they now have to confront inconsolable grief, they found their whole world had irretrievably fallen apart.

Throughout the sleepless nights and restless days that followed, the only words of comfort that helped Adelaide make any sense of the desperate sorrow and sadness she experienced belonged with the memory of her father:

> "Sing to the moon . . . Addie,

> . . . and the stars will shine."

"Can you see the moon?"

"No!"

"Well, listen to the music and you will."

SHUFFLE ALONG NICELY

For over 60 years America's traditional white minstrel shows had portrayed blacks as uneducated, down-at-heel, banjo-strumming loafers. This portrayal, painted across the stage footlights, suited the perception that most white Americans held. It is, after all, an accepted practice to mimic and laugh at those less fortunate than oneself. However, in the 1920s this perception was spectacularly confronted. With the gradual influx of more and more black performers into vaudeville, the bright lights of Broadway grew darker by the day.

In 1921, the all-black musical *Shuffle Along* exploded onto Broadway. The glorification of black culture that followed subconsciously acted as a catalyst for questioning old racist taboos. In a remarkable turnaround, theaters where black patrons had normally been segregated and seated out of sight in the gods suddenly permitted them to sit anywhere. This acknowledgment of black culture that *Shuffle Along* instigated brought about the beginning of what would later be termed the Harlem Renaissance.

Like a breath of fresh air, jazz appeared from nowhere and in its wake blew a gale force wind. On street corners young black musicians gathered in small groups to improvise on whatever instruments they could lay their hands on. From this new age of expression, a catalog of strange sounds and dance steps were created of a kind that no Caucasian had ever witnessed before.

New York's ultra-conservative world of high society was thrown into disarray. How could the white man just sit and watch when his whole body, soaked in restless jungle rhythms, released wild sexual emotions he never knew existed. This was jazz . . . and, this time, the white man had to take notice.

Over the years, Harlem had nurtured a wealth of highly talented and individual artists who had yet to be discovered by a white audience. The Alhambra, Lincoln and Lafayette theaters, which catered exclusively for the black community, staged new productions regularly and it was here that many of vaudeville's future stars learnt their craft.

America had two major vaudeville chains, Keith's and the Orpheum Theater group. They later merged and became known as the RKO circuit. Theaters on the RKO circuit catered mainly for white audiences and presented most of America's top-notch variety acts.

Black acts worked mainly on the TOBA circuit, which catered solely for black audiences. The initials stood for Theater Owners' Booking Association but were jokingly referred to, by those in the profession, as "Tough on Black Asses." The crossover from the black circuit to the RKO circuit occurred only after a black artist had established a successful career on the TOBA circuit.

In their attempt to carve a notable career all black performers worked for the TOBA at some stage of their training. It was a well-known fact that the wages were very low. It was suggested that the reason for this was that the experience was more beneficial than the salary.

When touring, artists traveled from town to town by train on a third-class ticket. Their journey was booked in advance and paid for by the tour company's stage manager. It was his job to ensure the performers arrived at the contracted engagement on time. During the long grueling schedules many lifelong friendships developed between the artists, quality friendships bonded by the hardship and miserable conditions they encountered *en route*.

Even traveling third-class in a "Jim Crow" carriage seemed to hold a special magic about it. In its checkered history the railroad had employed thousands of blacks in a variety of menial jobs, from tracklayers and gravel trampers to baggage handlers and Pullman porters. It played a significant part in helping blacks to freedom after the Civil War, providing a means of escape from the misery and economic imprisonment of the cotton plantations. If you were black and were seen to be traveling as a passenger it meant you had either money or a good job.

The derogatory term "Jim Crow" referred to the impoverished Negroes who lived and toiled on the Southern cotton plantations. In 1832 a blackface minstrel called Daddy Rice wrote a song entitled "Jim Crow" about the plight of a Negro cotton picker. On stage he dressed in the customary shabby rags with burnt cork rubbed on his face. His novelty act catapulted him to overnight riches and stardom, and thereafter the name "Jim Crow" was used to refer to the black race.

While on tour, accommodation was provided in cheap "coloreds only" rooming houses usually located in the seediest area of the town they were visiting. The rooms were always sparsely furnished and decorated: a wooden floor, a bed and a cupboard in which to hang their stage outfit. One meal a day would be included in the rent and served early in the evening at six. It was customary for a guest to eat half of the meal at the dinner table and save the remainder in a bag to eat later, for fear of not knowing where the next meal would come from. The doggybag habit became a practice many black stars continued to exercise throughout the rest of their careers. Some of the towns on the TOBA circuit were located in the bible-bashing Southwestern States where it was an accepted practice to refuse blacks entry into restaurants. In such States, lynch law was still considered constitutional.

One of the most challenging aspects of touring was trying to get enough rest between engagements. If you arrived at your destination tired, there was little time to recover. As many as four shows were performed a day and you were contracted to appear in all of them. After the first few weeks, the thrill of traveling away from home soon wore thin.

Vaudeville theaters were the best venues for black performers to showcase their talents. Hopefully, somewhere along the line, the chief booker from one of the major circuits would catch your act and offer you a big-time coast-to-coast tour.

Shuffle Along arrived at the forefront of a daring new decade, arousing both curiosity and suspicion. Its impact permeated every aspect of American culture. The economy was still very much in recession, an after-effect of the First World War. For most of society the confines of poverty brought about dramatic changes in lifestyle. In a relentless quest for cheap pleasure the public hungered for more diverse and *risqué* distractions. Their search steered the Roaring Twenties through a heady initiation ceremony of artistic discovery.

Vaudeville's golden years were at their peak. Its stars were given celebrity status, the kind usually reserved for royalty, and paid handsome salaries that most people could only dream of. Blackface comedians had long since been an accepted part of vaudeville culture, white performers, shabbily dressed with over-exaggerated make-up, who would imitate and satirize the black population. It was a cheap gimmick that held the audience's attention every time.

Two such blackface comedians were the duo Miller and Lyles. They were still at the supple stage of their careers, forever dodging the rent collector. However, they had perfected a skillful comedy act based on an original sketch, "The Mayor of Dixie." The clever part of the act was the fact that they were black guys imitating white guys imitating blacks. Dressed in ragged suits with broken hats, white gloves and the customary clown's panstick, they fooled most of the audience, most of the time.

Although their act took them across the length and breadth of America, fame and fortune eluded them. They hit upon the novel idea of developing their "Mayor of Dixie" routine into a full-length show. In doing so they hoped to realize a yearning ambition: to star in their own Broadway revue. It was agreed a musical ingredient would be necessary. This arrived fortuitously after a chance meeting in the street with the black musical duo Sissle and Blake.

At the outset, the notion of presenting an all-black musical comedy on Broadway seemed ludicrous. Without a white producer behind it and with no finance to back it, the project seemed doomed. Relying solely on black talent and the will to succeed was a sure way of filing for bankruptcy. This was the reaction Miller and Lyles were anticipating. However, to their astonishment, Sissle and Blake took them seriously and listened closely to what they had to say. Strangely enough, they too had been toying with the idea of presenting a full-length revue. The four of them struck a deal and, to get the show up and running, pooled both their professional skills and whatever finances they could lay their hands on.

Working long hours in a borrowed Harlem apartment, Miller and Lyles set to work rewriting the script. Drawing mainly from their past slapstick vaudeville routine, they developed the "Mayor of Dixie" into a continuous story line. The plot revolved loosely around an election campaign and its conniving candidates. The two rival contenders, Steve Jenkins and Sam Peck, who hope to be elected as Mayor of Jimtown, just happen to be joint owners of the local grocery store. Each suspects the other of stealing from the till in order to finance his campaign. Suspicions are aroused and each hires a detective to investigate—unbeknown to either of them, the same detective. After both crooks are presented with the evidence, an argument ensues and a fight follows, with "Fisticuffs," a slick comedy routine the duo had perfected early on in their careers.

Through crooked deals, Jenkins becomes Mayor. As a form of consolation he appoints Peck as his Chief of Police. In the finale, the reform candidate Harry Walton, whom everyone is wild about, arrives in the nick of time and intervenes. Jenkins and Peck's double-dealings are revealed and both are promptly ousted from office. The pair are jailed, leaving the way clear for Harry to be elected as the new Mayor of Jimtown.

After two weeks, the show, with the working title of *Dixie*, was completed and ready for rehearsal. The next task, and possibly the most difficult, was securing the finance to produce it.

With America firmly held in the grasp of a financial recession, most people claimed they were broke. The few who did confess to having spare cash considered *Dixie* an unwise investment. Through theatrical contacts, Miller and Lyles secured help from John Cort, owner of Cort's Theater chain. Although he too claimed to have no spare capital, he did offer to provide costumes, scenery and a Broadway theater on one condition: that his son Harry was given a financial interest in the show.

The house on offer turned out to be the 63rd Street Theater, a dilapidated lecture hall at the wrong end of Broadway. With no proper stage facilities, the hall was far from adequate. For a start, the first four rows of seating had to be removed to house the orchestra. There were no curtains and the overhead lighting threw stark shadows upon the walls. The costumes Mr. Cort had promised were discovered in large trunks beneath the stage and were ragged, moth-eaten and in serious need of repair.

The cast-offs came from two previous Cort productions, *Roly Boly Eyes* and *Jim Jam Jems*.[1] Both musicals had starred blackface comedian Eddie Leonard. Even though Eddie's hits "Ida" and "Roll Dem Roly Boly Eyes" became hugely popular tunes of the day, the shows did not fare so well. Ironically, after amassing a fortune at the expense of the black race, it was Leonard's failed Broadway musicals that indirectly helped put *Dixie* on stage.

The costumes brought a new and unexpected dimension to the show. An oriental number would now have to be included to use the Japanese geisha kimonos. By adapting a song they had previously written Sissle and Blake inserted "Oriental Blues" into the score. However, the cotton-pickers' outfits defeated them. They finally came up with "Bandanna Days," an uptempo dance number set on a cotton planta- tion. Casting notices were placed in the local press and news of the auditions spread quickly throughout Harlem. The response was over- whelming. Queues formed around the block as all manner of entertainers arrived for the audition. Although their talents were varied, all the prospective hopefuls had one thing in common: a genuine desire to perform on Broadway.

Her grandmother's insistence that Adelaide attend night school to learn needlework had, to some extent, already paid off. Although she had not quite made it over to a Paris fashion house, Adelaide had secured a seam- stress's job in a local high-class fashion store on Lenox Avenue. The job paid fifteen dollars a week and at last allowed Adelaide a little independ- ence. Although she could now afford to buy the latest fashionable clothes, she realized that by making her own copies she could actually save herself money.

For a teenager, Harlem was an exciting vibrant community to live in. Adelaide and her friends made full use of its amenities. Her mother's dis- approval of the local bars and clubs did little to dissuade Adelaide from visiting them. She found the lure of the music too difficult to resist.

One bar that Adelaide visited frequently was Edmond's Cellar Bar.[2] Here she regularly sang during its amateur hour. The resident singer at the bar was Ethel Waters, a slightly older, rather plain-looking girl. Ethel instantly recognized Adelaide's talent and encouraged her to seriously consider a career in show business. Although the bar only had a small dance floor for its artists to perform on, for the first time in her life Adelaide began to experience the addictive buzz a performer gets on stage in front of an audience. At last she had found her calling.

The *Dixie* auditions that were being held in the old lecture hall hadn't escaped Adelaide's attention.

Elizabeth's friend Lottie Gee called round to their apartment one evening with some exciting news. She had auditioned for a part in the show and was thrilled at being chosen for a leading role. Adelaide listened intensely to what Lottie had to say, an unusual event for such a talkative young girl.

"The fat cat got your tongue, Addie?" remarked her mother suspiciously, wondering what had caused her daughter's sudden change in temperament.

"No . . . just wondering," came Adelaide's vague reply.

"Well, just you wander off and leave me and Lottie to talk in peace . . . do you hear?"

Adelaide laughed cheekily and shook her head whilst mimicking her mother's stern expression. She then headed out and left them in peace to carry on talking. Outside, Adelaide sat down on the front stoop of the house and began to think a little more seriously about the auditions.

In the kitchen, seated around the large wooden breakfast table, Elizabeth and Lottie continued to talk about the *Dixie* auditions. Lottie felt sure that Adelaide's dancing abilities might secure her a part in the chorus line, if only Elizabeth would allow her to audition. Although the thought had crossed her mind, Elizabeth was not convinced. Chorus girls have training. Adelaide had none, and surely she was far too young to be treading the boards on Broadway. During their chat, Lottie did her utmost to persuade Elizabeth to change her mind. Nevertheless, by the end of the conversation Elizabeth was still harboring doubts.

A few days later, Lew Leslie called unannounced at the Hall household. His visit was for one specific purpose. He, too, felt Adelaide should audition for the *Dixie* show and during his brief visit tried his hardest to convince Elizabeth that she should allow him to arrange it.

Elizabeth liked Lew. He always talked sensibly, to the point but with an air of assertiveness, which she liked. He reminded her of Arthur in many ways. He too had had a habit of being abrupt but only when he wanted you to listen.

"When making important decisions, Mrs. Hall, one should always feel a hundred percent sure of one's actions."

Elizabeth thought silently for a moment and then spoke to Lew in a calm whisper as if she were about to tell him an important secret. "Having given the matter much thought, if you believe Adelaide has a real chance, then I as her mother would never forgive myself if I did not allow her to take that chance."

Without further ado, Leslie arranged the audition. Luckily for Adelaide she already had one advantage in her favor—the producers were specifically looking for light-skinned girls. Her honeyed complexion would clearly enhance her chances.

Dressed casually in slacks and a top, Adelaide arrived at the old lecture hall feeling not the slightest bit nervous. Excited, yes, but not in the least bit apprehensive about her fate.

She began her audition by singing a spiritual. Her unaccompanied voice carried distinctly to the back of the hall. Its power lay in her clarity of diction.

"Sing to the moon and the stars will shine" was the saying her father used to encourage her to sing with more conviction. To all those present that afternoon, it appeared her father's advice had worked.

After her second song, a lively rag number, Adelaide leapt straight into an impromptu dance. As if in a state of frenzy, without showing any signs of restraint, she flung her arms and legs aimlessly in all directions. Her body gyrated with such ferocity that even the choreographer felt compelled to watch in amazement at her dexterity. What failings her lack of training showed, her enthusiasm certainly made up for.

"Thank you, Miss Hall," bellowed a stern voice from the back of the auditorium, announcing the audition over.

Her dance came to an abrupt halt. Breathless and feeling unsure what she should do next, Adelaide stood to one side of the stage and waited self-consciously whilst the panel of producers talked amongst themselves.

"How old are you, Miss Hall?" inquired the same booming voice.

A sudden attack of nerves made her temporarily forget how old she was and for a brief moment she became confused and fumbled her reply. An uneasy silence followed. Under local state law the employment of chorus girls below the age of sixteen was strictly forbidden in New York.

"Well, your mother will have to sign a document confirming your age to be sixteen or over. Is that understood?" barked back the same impatient voice.

"Er . . . yes, sir," Adelaide quickly replied, unsure of what it was she was agreeing to.

"Thank you Miss Hall, that'll be all for the time being."

Adelaide smiled courteously, shook her head, then walked off stage, relieved the ordeal was over. On their way back home Leslie explained everything. For a salary of thirty dollars a week she had been offered a part as a chorine. Surprisingly, it was her dancing skills that had clinched the job for her. Rehearsals commenced the following Monday and, should she have any worries, Lottie Gee would be there to take care of them. Adelaide's increase in salary meant she could now afford to use some of her earnings to help support her mother.

Leslie's involvement in the show was minimal, although his enthusiasm was a vital ingredient in furthering many of the artists' future careers. What was important for Adelaide was the fact that she had established a link with the one person who, as an impresario, would in future years glorify the Negro on the Great White Way.

Broadway was heading for a period of transition, as if taking a well-earned rest to catch its breath from the many spectaculars it had witnessed during the past decade. Jazz had yet to be discovered by the discerning critic. With ragtime dying a natural death, the public were hungry for a change. The producer Florenz Ziegfeld's latest revue, his lavish *Follies of 1921*, costing a mammoth quarter of a million dollars, appeared on Broadway like the last explosion at a firework display. Even its hugely popular stars, W. C. Fields and Fanny Brice, could only watch the show clock up an unimpressive 119 performances before the public saw fit to desert it.

Further along Broadway at the Shubert brothers' Jolson Theater, the torch singer Al Jolson was starring in the new musical *Bombo*. The theater had recently been built in Jolson's honor. Broadway audiences were becoming so blasé that the premiere looked doomed from the opening number. It took Jolson right up until the finale before he could steal any acclaim from the hardened first-nighters. The show may not have been to their taste, but Jolson's performance was still praiseworthy. Only when he returned for the encore—with his trademark blackened face—and bent down on one knee to sing his classic hit "My Mammy" did the audience show any signs of recognition.

Silent movies were already making a dent in the paying public's pocket. New movie stars were gracing the theaters, and the biggest star, Sicilian-born Rudolph Valentino, was attracting huge audiences. Women flocked to see his latest movie *The Sheikh of Araby* and gazed in rapture at his sultry image on the screen before them.

Some cynics thought the popularity of the cinema would bring gradual closure to many live theaters but most people thought the effect would be short-lived and brushed the craze off as a passing fad.

In the dingy old lecture hall up in Harlem, the producers of *Dixie* put the cast through their final paces. To cut costs, the performers were told to repair and customize their own costumes. Adelaide suddenly found her dressmaking skills extremely useful. After two weeks' rehearsal the show was considered ready for an out-of-town tryout tour which commenced at Trenton, New Jersey. To reflect the show's vitality, the writers renamed it *Shuffle Along* after the shuffle dance.[3] With no spare cash for wages, the cast agreed to tour without pay on the understanding that they would be reimbursed once the show hit Broadway. In order to cover traveling expenses the company performed one-night stands anywhere it could find an audience willing to pay. From New Jersey to Pennsylvania and then on to Washington, D.C., *Shuffle Along* gathered praise wherever it played. After its final stop in Burlington, New Jersey, the show limped back to New York, triumphant but with an $18,000 overdraft tied to its legs. Undeterred by their hefty burden of debt, the producers began hectic preparations for the show's Broadway premiere.

Although it had been a long arduous struggle for Sissle and Blake, Miller and Lyles, and the rest of the *Shuffle Along* cast, on May 23, 1921, it seemed that the effort had all been worth it when the show opened to ecstatic acclaim.

Critics saw *Shuffle Along* as a swift, bright, rollicking show, jam-packed with talent. *Billboard* described its power as "A rainbow of hope and encouragement to every artist of the race."[4] The term "speed dancing" was coined to describe the velocity of its dance routines. One reviewer wrote that he believed the cast executed such rapidity of motion in order to prevent heckling from the audience. How wrong could he be! In truth, the dancers were just dancing the way that black people normally danced, unselfconsciously, rhythmically and full of explosive energy.

The discipline and training Adelaide learnt from being in such a show taught her to dance correctly using proper jazz steps. Her skills saw her featured in a duet with Arthur Porter. The song "Bandanna Days" was supposedly set in the Deep South on a cotton plantation. Adelaide appeared on stage wearing a loose-fitting gingham dress and a spotted bandanna, looking very much like an overworked mammy. For some reason she danced with the aid of Arthur Porter's wooden cane around which she twirled and kicked. The song was catchy enough to become one of the most notable hits of the year. Even though its success pushed Adelaide to the forefront of the show's 28 female chorus dancers, for the remainder of the revue she appeared dutifully in line as a Jazz Jasmine.

The show's biggest hit songs were the annoyingly catchy "I'm Just Wild

Adelaide, dressed in an oriental outfit, poses with Noble Sissle and other chorus girls from the Jazz Jasmines.

About Harry" and the sentimental ballad "Love Will Find A Way." Both songs became huge money-spinners and helped propel the show into orbit.

Remarkably, it was the production's underfunding and raw simplicity that worked to its advantage. Many critics found its unpretentious look added to its appeal. Over the next few years the *Shuffle Along* effect acted as a benchmark for every black musical. The show's importance was paramount in helping set the trend for the Twenties and its success made jazz a bankable asset and created exciting new opportunities for black artists to explore.

Shuffle Along broke new ground in almost every sphere. Not only was it the first all-black production to hit Broadway, it was also the show that introduced white audiences to an all-black chorus line of scantily clad girls, as in the style of Ziegfeld's *Follies*. Their good looks and precision dancing made them an instant eye-catching hit with the public. The show also gave Broadway its first glimpse of a black love affair through the romantic duet "Love Will Find A Way," sung by Lottie Gee to her handsome co-star Roger Matthews.

The show certainly had an immediate effect on white revues. Doors that were normally locked were now politely swung open. Its success saw every musical in town clamoring for a black performer. Lucrative spin-offs and merchandising earned extra cash for the cast. Girls from the chorus line coached dance classes so that white showgirls from productions such as Ziegfeld's *Follies* and George White's *Scandals* could learn the new jazz dance steps. Ironically, in future years many of the star performers from *Shuffle Along* would further their careers under the guidance of a white producer.

WARM HANDS

After fourteen record-breaking months on Broadway, *Shuffle Along* finally danced to the end of its New York run. Following a short break the cast packed their bags and headed off on a national tour. Billed rather pretentiously as "The All Around the World Company," in late July 1922 the entire production moved into Boston's Selwyn Theater for a two-week engagement. The show's reputation preceded it and attracted record ticket sales at the box office.

Queues for tickets stretched around the block on a daily basis. So great was demand that the owner of the theater, Arch Selwyn, who knew when he was on to a good thing, extended the engagement for a further thirteen weeks. To publicize the event, Mr. Selwyn hastily arranged a photo shoot for the city press corps. All 53 members of the cast lined up outside the theater's main entrance and posed enthusiastically for the gathered media. Standing at the rear of the group, perched upon a chair so she could be seen, Adelaide leant forward and gave a big smile for the cameras. Somehow the prospect of living away from home seemed not to be as unpleasant as her mother had predicted.

During the show's long run in Boston, Adelaide became acquainted with Josephine Baker, a darkly tanned youngster from East St. Louis. Slim, to the point of appearing undernourished, with a highly-strung disposition, Josephine joined the cast as a chorus girl in August. Joining at such a late stage immediately put her at a disadvantage with the other girls. With no friends in the troupe to confide in, Josephine found that she had to rely on her wild sense of humor to help win admirers, a trick she had learnt and used to her advantage during her childhood. To protect herself from the violence of her mother's temper, Josephine discovered that by acting the clown, not only did people laugh, it also made them feel more amiable towards her. At the tender age of fifteen, Josephine was already seeking empathy and support from the older male members of the company.

As the tour steadily progressed, Adelaide's relationship with Josephine developed on a professional level rather than on a personal one. This was due mainly to Josephine's aloofness and inability to accept her colleagues on an equal footing. Josephine didn't make herself likable. She chose to be the odd one out. It was as if she found it easier to reject people straightaway before they had any chance of rejecting her.

Running away from school at the age of thirteen to pursue her dream of entering show business, Josephine had already gained first-hand experience of the hardships encountered on the TOBA circuit. She had previously been employed as a dresser and part-time chorus dancer in a troupe called The Dixie Steppers. Unhappy with her job and measly salary of nine dollars a week, she lied her way into the chorus line of *Shuffle Along*'s provincial touring company. It was here that her extraordinary talent shone through and came to the attention of Sissle and Blake.

After watching her performance at a matinée show in Brooklyn, Sissle and Blake went backstage to introduce themselves. Fearing the worst, Josephine fully expected to be fired on the spot. She was, after all, still only fifteen and the minimum legal age for theatrical performers, clearly specified in her contract, was sixteen and over. She need not have worried. The ruling was only a state law and not enforceable upon a touring company. It therefore came as quite a surprise when, instead of disapproval, Sissle and Blake expressed their encouragement and offered to promote her to the main touring company after the show's Broadway closure.

In Boston, Josephine made a conscious decision to gain recognition for herself. Aware of the limitations her role—at one end of the chorus line—imposed on her, she set about embellishing her performance. Emerging from the wings, cross-eyed and purposely out of step with the other girls, Josephine tried to ambush the audience's attention with her crazy antics. The public instantly became attracted to the skinny, dancing buffoon. Her unscripted tomfoolery produced the immediate response she desired and brought the focus of attention full beam upon her.

One afternoon during the show's run in Josephine's home town of St. Louis, her poverty-stricken mother, Carrie McDonald, arrived backstage to confront her estranged daughter. Josephine must have had a premonition that such a confrontation might take place and had, without explanation, gone absent from the cast before the show arrived in town. When the matinée performance was over, Carrie stood nervously outside the backstage door waiting for her daughter to emerge. As the chorus girls began to leave, Josephine was not to be seen. Carrie became more and more worried. She kept asking if Josephine was in the building but none of the chorus girls had the courtesy to reply. Instead they bluntly snubbed her. By the time she approached Adelaide, Carrie was visibly upset.[5] Adelaide was fully aware that Josephine had absconded from the show but didn't have the heart to tell Carrie the reason why. Although she had quickly put two and two together, Adelaide's sense of compassion got the better of her. Taking Carrie to one side, she tactfully told her of Josephine's absence. "Josephine's doing fine, there's no need for you to worry about her, she just didn't come with us to St. Louis. I'm sure she'll be in touch with you as soon as she has sorted herself out. Look . . . give me your address and if I hear anything, I'll let you know immediately."

Adelaide took a small leather address book from her handbag, opened it at the initial B, and handed it to Carrie with a pencil. Carrie looked hesitant and fumbled around for a moment as if she were unsure of what she was meant to do. Adelaide looked puzzled for a moment before it suddenly dawned upon her that Carrie might be illiterate.

"Here, let me help you, I'll write it in," she said sympathetically.

Carrie thanked Adelaide for all her help and concern. She then turned around and slowly began to walk away, back down the alleyway towards the main street. The pitiful sight of a disheartened mother's anguish brought a lump to Adelaide's throat. In the hope of comforting her further she ran and caught up with her in the street.

"I just thought . . . what I meant to say was . . . I'm sure Josephine would want me to give you this. It's just a little something to help you get home safely."

Opening her purse Adelaide took out a five-dollar bill and placed it firmly in Carrie's hand.

"In fact . . . I know she'd want you to have it."

Without letting go of Adelaide's hand, Carrie looked straight into her big brown eyes. For a moment she just stared without saying a word, then, as if to break her embarrassed silence, gave a pained half-smile of gratitude.

"Warm hands lead to a kind heart. May God thank you . . . you'll never know how grateful I am."

"It's all right," replied Adelaide reassuringly. "I already know."

As if by chance, Josephine's return to the chorus line coincided with the show's departure from St. Louis.

Josephine's antics began to pay dividends. By the time the show reached Philadelphia, the producers had singled her out and billed her in the program as the "comedy chorus girl" and increased her salary to $125. Sissle and Blake had also recruited her for a leading role in their next Broadway production, *Chocolate Dandies*. However, her attention-seeking and sudden promotion had an adverse effect backstage, alienating her even further from the rest of the chorus girls. Through petty jealousy her colleagues now took it upon themselves to ostracize her completely. However, their churlish behavior had the reverse effect from the one they desired and only made Josephine even more determined to succeed.

When *Shuffle Along* revisited St. Louis a few months later, Josephine's elevated position in the cast gave her the confidence she had both lacked and needed to finally break her silence with her mother and initiate a reconciliation.

For over a year the tour zigzagged across America, playing in fourteen towns in almost as many states.[6] For all its record-breaking acclaim, *Shuffle Along* would primarily be remembered for laying the groundwork that helped change the public's attitude towards the Negro. Inadvertently the stage of the black musical comedy had become a platform for changing white man's opinion. Viewed now as a skilled, polished performer, the Negro could finally relinquish the typecast image of the downtrodden ragamuffin. In future, black artists could concentrate on developing their talent.

Returning home to New York with the valuable experience of fifteen months' traveling on the road had given Adelaide an air of assurance that noticeably projected itself in her appearance. When she arrived home, the first thing Elizabeth noticed was how grown-up her daughter had become. Her unruly, teenage prodigy had blossomed into an attractive, mature young lady. She now wore make-up, styled her hair with pomade, wore tailored frocks and box-heeled shoes, and carried her confidence like a clutch bag.

Fortunately for Adelaide, her apprenticeship had paid handsome dividends. Not only could she now associate her name with the most successful black show to have played on Broadway and bask in all the connotations and accolades that were attached to it, but she had also acquired a taste for the big time. She was now hungry for more.

Unfortunately for Elizabeth, who had hoped her daughter's return to New York was for good and would much rather have seen her back working in an "honest" profession, Adelaide still had the reckless passion of youth and an uncompromising determination to follow her dream of stardom.

For the show's writers, Sissle and Blake and Miller and Lyles, not only did *Shuffle Along* clear the path for future black Broadway productions, but it also earned them undreamed-of wealth in royalties. Their hard work and tenacity paid handsome rewards. The show grossed over eight million dollars and the temptation to spend was too great to resist. Their extravagance and flamboyance became the talk of Harlem. To celebrate his good fortune, Aubrey Lyles purchased the most expensive Packard limousine on the market. In the days when all cars were painted in somber black he had his sprayed burgundy red. Its interior was fitted with solid gold and ivory trimmings. What made the car even more special was its facility to be transformed into an imitation Pullman sleeper by sliding the back pigskin-covered seats out to create a bed. Lyles could regularly be seen slowly driving his pride and joy up and down the streets of Harlem for all the residents to swoon over. Their free-spending attitude made good mileage in the gossip columns. It was reported in one Chicago newspaper that between them the quartet had eleven limousines with chauffeurs, and that they all owned genuine raccoon coats and only wore hand-made union suits (all-in-one underwear) costing forty dollars each.

Noble Sissle was rumored to have purchased two solid platinum watches trimmed with diamonds at a thousand dollars a throw, one for his wife, the other for his mistress Lottie Gee. However, not all their money was spent on luxury goods. Sissle opened his own songwriter's shop in Harlem to help encourage new black talent into the business.

The fact that Sissle and Blake, as the show's songwriters, were reaping far greater financial rewards than Miller and Lyles was obviously going to create a rift in their partnership at some point. That crisis occurred after the company returned to New York from touring. Miller and Lyles' growing discontent prompted the pair to deviously sign a contract with the producer George White to present their own show on Broadway in the fall of 1923. Having done so, they persuaded almost half of the original cast of *Shuffle Along* to join them in the venture. The show's title *Runnin' Wild* could almost have been purposely chosen to air the bitter resentment that Miller and Lyles now felt towards their former partners.

❧

Born in 1886 of Jewish parentage in Orangeburg, New York, Lewis Lessinsky acquired his ambition to enter show business at an early age. As a youngster, he was well known in his local neighborhood for his comic impressions of famous personalities. This, he felt, was an encouraging sign indicating that he too should enter show business professionally. After leaving school he tried his hand at numerous jobs without much enthusiasm. Meanwhile his interest in the theater grew stronger. Inspired by his many evenings spent observing variety acts from the audience, his theatrical career commenced via talent shows. He changed his stage name to Lew Leslie. As an impressionist, success came quickly but was to be short-lived. He tried expanding his repertoire by including songs in his routine and for a short period even formed a double act with the singer Belle Baker, whom he later married.

Small in stature, his looks were typically continental with slicked back, receding hair that showed quite an expanse of forehead. Artistic and well read but with limited talents, he soon grew bored with performing and acknowledged his involvement with the theater would have to be redirected, perhaps in production or on a management level. He set himself up as an agent and was constantly seen scouting for talent at variety shows. Having little money, he moved his lodgings to a cheaper district and housed himself in Harlem. It was here his fascination with black culture evolved. His swiftness in recognizing the potential of so much untapped talent, just waiting to be exploited, would reward his shrewdness handsomely. His ambitious plans had led him to the *Dixie* auditions. What he saw at those auditions fascinated him and immediately inspired him to start formulating ideas for his own future all-black musical productions.

As his stable of artists grew, so his business acumen increased. He cleverly coupled two of his best performers in a successful engagement at Broadway's Café de Paris. It was here that Leslie conceived the idea of expanding the cabaret into a full revue. With the management's consent he featured an all-black cast and renamed the show *Plantation Revue*. This too proved popular with the clientele. Realizing the dividends from such a venture, Leslie acquired his own, larger premises and opened the first late-night supper club in Manhattan to offer a full-scale all-black revue. He named it the Plantation Café and opened with the second edition of *Plantation Revue*. His ability to recognize talent finally paid off in 1922 when he signed the unique songstress Florence Mills to an exclusive management contract.

He discovered Miss Mills in the cast of *Shuffle Along* where she had taken over one of the leading roles previously played by Gertrude Saunders, after the star's impromptu departure for a burlesque tour. Florence auditioned so many times for the producers that even she was surprised when they offered her a contract. Apparently it was Noble Sissle's reluctance to hire an inexperienced showgirl that caused their indecision. On her opening night Florence more than proved her worth. She received seventeen encores at the end of her performance. After her contract with *Shuffle Along* expired, Leslie transferred her directly into the starring role at the Plantation Café. It was here, under Leslie's guidance, that Florence was launched on the road to international stardom.

Leslie's total commitment to his projects involved him in every aspect, from the management of the cast through to production. On certain occasions he was even known to conduct the orchestra. His revues were known for their fast tempo and would, at times, leave an audience breathless. He had already acquired a reputation for irrational behavior at rehearsals, where he would work the cast like a dedicated slave driver. He thought nothing of keeping them overtime until they produced the effect he desired. The quickness of pace and meager content of his revues became his trademarks. Unlike the great Broadway producer Florenz Ziegfeld, who relied heavily on lavish costumes and extravagant stage presentations, Leslie focused the audience's attention on the performer and used only crudely painted backdrops as scenery. Sometimes he would delete whole numbers from the program only to replace them overnight with additional ones. This, he felt, kept briskness in the show and alertness in the performer. He would fire and hire at whim and often without explanation. His vision became blinkered only by his own stubbornness.

Leslie managed his artists with an iron fist in a white glove. To some he appeared fair and honest; to others uncompromising and calculating. Whatever opinions his fold might have held, they all agreed on one point, he was a damn good manager. Over the next few years, slowly and methodically, Leslie began to build an empire that would soon rival the biggest theatrical agencies in town.

4

I'VE BEEN WAITING FOR SOMEONE LIKE YOU

On December 30, 1912, Bertram Errol Hicks, a restless teenager fresh out of school, enrolled in the merchant navy to free himself and discover the world. At Cardiff docks he joined the crew of the SS *Snowflake*, bound for Antwerp. He soon discovered that his rash decision to work at sea was not as congenial as he had hoped. In his mind the sea represented an escape route from the constraints and injustice he found prevalent on shore. On board the freighter he found a new, more stringent set of rules and restrictions were forced upon him. As a junior steward he was expected to labor hard and for long hours. His pay was miserable and the living conditions below deck were even worse. Being made to act as a responsible human being brought a new perspective to Bertram's life. It is said that travel broadens the mind. True, but it also makes you aware of your own shortcomings.

Bertram was born on July 4, 1894, to Aurora and Edward Hicks in Port of Spain on the British West Indies island of Trinidad.[1] At the age of thirteen his parents packed him off to Britain where he stayed with relatives in the Welsh capital, Cardiff. As Bert was one of nine children, his father, who worked as a cabinetmaker, believed his son would receive a far better education in Britain than in Trinidad. Unfortunately, Bertram's academic skills were limited to his imagination. He missed Trinidad and his parents, and found it difficult to forgive them for sending him to such a cold and unfriendly country. A proud and self-willed teenager, he rebelled at school by flunking his exams. He informed his teacher that his dream was to go to sea and discover the four corners of the world. As soon as the opportunity arose, Bertram grabbed it and waved goodbye to his academic career and a life he found oppressive and stifling.

As the most junior of stewards Bertram was made to feel uncomfortable about his ethnic origins by his seniors. To remind him of his lowly position in life they constantly taunted him with racist remarks. Gradually, with time and initiative, Bertram won the respect of his elders, the term "Nigger" was dropped and his name was abbreviated to Bert. This turnaround marked the crew's acceptance of him on their terms.

Although Bert's home port was Cardiff, many of the ships he worked on docked in the bustling port of London. During shore leave it was far more convenient for him to rent lodgings in the capital than to travel to and from Cardiff. Close to London's docks were many small boarding houses that were favored by visiting seamen. The Sandringham Hotel in Upper Sydenham was one such dwelling. Its landlady, the widow of a merchant seaman, regarded her establishment as being slightly more upmarket than other such boarding houses. She had a soft spot for visiting sailors and it was here that Bert stayed regularly during shore leave.

Throughout the next eight years, including the duration of the First World War, Bert's career in the merchant navy took him to many exciting and culturally diverse countries and continents. After numerous trips to northern Europe and a visit to Murmansk in the Arctic Circle, which he later described as being "the coldest place on earth," he sailed to the warmer climate of the Mediterranean, before heading down the narrow straits of the Suez Canal for South Africa. From the Cape of Good Hope he sailed halfway round the globe to South America before his final discharge papers were issued in Philadelphia on May 24, 1920. He was admitted to the United States on a temporary visa for the purpose of reshipping foreign freight.

During his shore leave Bert didn't waste his time sampling the delights of the local hospitality. To help further his employment prospects and relieve the continual boredom he suffered during the long months spent at sea, Bert taught himself various foreign languages. He liked to flatter his ego by claiming he could speak fluent Spanish, Italian, German and French. This was not altogether true, as his visits to foreign ports proved.

To impress his shipmates he would often converse with the locals in their native tongue. Bert soon discovered to his embarrassment and expense that by trading in this manner he frequently bought more than he had bargained for.

On board ship Bert worked his way up through the various ranks and was promoted to chief steward for his last three voyages. His certificate of discharge, signed by the ship's master, gave him a glowing character report. His "ability" and "general conduct" ratings were stamped "very good" on all his trips and were indicative of his attitude towards work and colleagues.

After disembarking in Philadelphia, Bert traveled north to the port of New York where he fully expected to find work awaiting him. Instead, when he arrived he was handed an envelope that contained his dismissal papers. Due to a fall in exports the shipping company had been forced to make cutbacks and subsequent redundancies. As a form of conciliation they offered him repatriation to Britain with the promise of a free passage.

For the first time in his life Bert felt rich. His leather wallet was stuffed with $1,400 of redundancy pay. On the night before he was due to sail, he celebrated his sudden good fortune by making his last evening in New York City a memorable one. Looking handsome, dressed in his best English suit, Bert set off from the docks in a jovial mood and headed straight for Harlem.

The fact that he had "sucker" written across his forehead never occurred to him. He never did reach Harlem nor did he ever see his wallet with its 1,400 green bucks again. His naïve lack of judgment failed to recognize his first American con man. His stupidity taught him a costly lesson.

By nightfall Bert was broke. He couldn't even afford to catch the bus back to the docks. Needless to say, he missed his free passage to Britain. In utter panic, he found his way to a nearby hotel where his friend Elmer worked as an elevator porter. As fate would have it, Elmer was on night duty. There's an unspoken freemasonry amongst colored folk and after hearing Bert's hard-luck story, Elmer immediately offered help. He smuggled Bert into the hotel through an underground trade entrance and gave him the use of an attic room used purely for storage. Located at the rear of the building, it was the perfect hideout. Although only a short-term arrangement, it gave Bert the time to wire his relatives in Cardiff for assistance. With no money in his pocket and only the clothes he stood up in, Bert took a temporary job to tide him over, as a kitchen porter in a local restaurant.

In later years, blessed with good fortune, Bert would often recount an amusing incident that occurred during this impoverished period of his life. Finding himself without even a cent in his pocket, and in desperate need to travel uptown for a job interview, he made his way to the subway wondering how on earth he could find the money to buy a train ticket. At the top of the stairs leading down to the subway entrance sat a blind beggar. Holding out his cap the beggar called to passers-by, "Money for the blind!"

Bert stopped in his tracks. Peering down at the huddled body that appeared oblivious to the comings and goings of the rushing world around him made Bert feel even sadder.

"Poor sod," he muttered under his breath. "At least I can see."

No sooner had the words left his mouth than Bert noticed the beggar's cap. It was full of cents, nickels and dimes. In a strange way the beggar seemed to be holding the cap out to him as an offering.

"I need this more than you'll ever know," said Bert, matter of factly. Without giving it a second thought he bent down and took a handful of change.

"If you lend me this now . . . I'll pay you back double at the end of the week." Bert never waited to hear the beggar's reply. He disappeared as fast as he could down into the maze of subway tunnels to catch his train.

Bert got the job. On pay-day at the end of the week he returned to find the blind beggar. As usual he was sat at the top of the subway stairs. Bert bent down to thank him and repay the loan.

"Hi, I'm the guy you gave a loan to at the beginning of the week."

"Not you again," replied the disgruntled beggar. "This is the third time this week." Before Bert got the chance to explain his irrational behavior a punch landed straight between his eyes and knocked him backwards onto the sidewalk.

"I'm not that blind that I can't see," cursed the beggar, as he fled down the street, leaving his white stick behind propped against the wall.

The following evening Bert and Elmer headed straight back to Harlem.

Bertram Errol Hicks

Before they went anywhere Elmer insisted that he deliver a message to his sister, Fleck. She happened to live at 194 West 134th Street, in the same tenement block as the Hall family. They arrived at Fleck's apartment to discover she was out. As it was quite important that she got the message, Elmer decided to leave it with one of her neighbors. He rapped the knocker on Mrs. Hall's front door. After a lengthy pause it finally opened just enough for the person inside to see who was there, while veiling her identity.

"Sorry to bother you . . . is Mrs. Hall in?"

"Oh! Right . . . I'll just go and get her. Who shall I say is calling?" inquired the mysterious voice.

"Tell her it's Elmer, Fleck's brother."

"OK, I'll just go and get her." The door slammed shut once more. A few moments later it re-opened, only this time wide open so Elmer and Bert could see exactly who they were talking to. It was Mrs. Hall herself with a look of surprise on her face.

"Hello, young Elmer, and what brings you knocking at my front door?" she inquired in a jocular manner.

"Hello, Mrs. Hall, I'm sorry to bother you. I've come to give Fleck an important message."

"Well, in that case you'd better come in. Fleck is sitting in my kitchen." Elmer and Bert entered the apartment to find Fleck and Adelaide and Adelaide's grandmother all sat around a large wooden table in the kitchen. Surprised by the sudden appearance of her brother, Fleck totally ignored Bert who stood conspicuously aloof to one side. However, Bert wasn't too bothered about having Fleck's attention; it was Adelaide who had caught his eye, a fact both her mother and grandmother immediately noticed.

After Elmer and Fleck had finished their conversation, Adelaide's mother—Elizabeth—asked the name of Elmer's friend.

"Oh! I'm sorry, I forgot to introduce everybody." Turning to face Bert, one by one Elmer introduced all the four ladies that were seated round the kitchen table.

". . . And this is Bert Hicks," concluded Elmer. "He's a steward in the merchant navy."

Elizabeth, more than anybody else in the room, seemed very interested in the handsome, smartly dressed visitor from Brooklyn dockyards. She began to question him about his life. During their conversation, Adelaide grew visibly restless and kept asking Fleck the time.

When Fleck announced it was seven-thirty, Adelaide abruptly got up from the table and interrupted her mother's conversation.

"Mum, it's time for me to leave." She had arranged an evening out with some of her girlfriends.

After saying goodbye to everybody in the room, Adelaide's polite farewell to Bert was returned with an extraordinary reply, "If we were meant to meet, our paths will cross again."

Although their meeting had been brief, Adelaide's presence left an indelible impression upon Bert's mind, so much so that he spent the rest of the evening thinking about her.

After making their farewells, Elmer and Bert visited a local hop called Edmond's Cellar Bar. Situated at the corner of 132nd Street and Fifth Avenue, Edmond's had acquired a reputation for hard living and even harder liquor.

To accommodate its flighty clientele the bar stayed open until the early hours of the morning. Housed in a basement, the place was dingy, hot and heavy with the sweet smell of stale tobacco smoke. On a busy night the place could squeeze in around 200 people at a push. That night the bar was crowded.

Named after its Irish owner Edmond Johnson, a boxing fanatic, the bar was a haven for hookers, sportsmen and other assorted underworld figures. Although he had a heart of gold, Edmond was known for his meanness. He'd begrudge anybody smelling his cigarette smoke. He paid his staff the lowest wages possible and his mean habits earned him the nickname "Mule," a name he detested. His entertainers, including the three members of the band, were each paid a measly two dollars a night and, in return, were expected to perform up to four sets an evening. If it hadn't been for the customers' tips the artists could have earned more money begging on the streets.

To cheer the joint up, Edmond decorated the bar's precariously low ceiling with paper chrysanthemums and hanging streamers. Along the walls hung numerous nicotine-stained photographs of famous prize-winning fighters and black entertainers. As most of these pictures were autographed personally to him, they were his pride and joy. At the far end of the bar a battered upright piano and a small set of drums were squashed alongside the tiny dance floor, which was just large enough for the cabaret to perform on. During the course of the evening, if business was slack, Edmond would hold an amateur hour. The audience loved it and, better still for Edmond, it was free entertainment.

On the circuit, Edmond's was known as either the last or the first rung on the show business ladder, depending on which way you were going. Over the past few months, blues singer Ethel Waters had been the resident artist at the bar. Her repertoire varied from night to night depending on the mood and state of the audience she was entertaining. The later it got, the louder she sang. Not only did this keep the audience awake but, more importantly for Edmond, it kept them drinking at the bar. She could pull your heartstrings tighter than a belt with a soul-wrenching ballad. Her rendition of "He Done Me Wrong" had men cowering in corners from shame. If the need arose, her vocabulary could also blacken the teeth of any honest-living Christian who might mistakenly wander into the joint. Down on her luck and finding regular work difficult to come by, Edmond had persuaded Ethel to work temporarily at the bar while she was "resting." It was during her residency that Ethel gradually began to build a reputation for herself as an entertainer, not only among the local punters who flocked nightly to hear her risqué repertoire but also among downtown white theatrical circles. Over the next ten years, Ethel's career would travel tempestuously along the rickety rails of a roller coaster, before she would finally see herself financially solvent and recognized as the truly talented singer and actress that she was.

One of the customers who stepped out of the audience that evening to give an impromptu performance during amateur hour was a young slip of a girl who could barely have been out of her teens. Small in stature, with pretty features and a perfectly formed smile, she sang a couple of sentimental ballads followed by an energetic flatfoot-time buck dance.[2] Her girlish charm instantly won over the audience. For most of the evening Bert had stood towards the back of the crowded bar where his view of the entertainment was obstructed and unclear. As the room was so dimly lit he hadn't been able to see who the vocalist was. Later that evening, as fate would have it, Bert was introduced to the girl with the velvet voice. It was Adelaide . . . Adelaide Hall.[3]

As an illegal immigrant, Bert's situation was becoming more desperate by the day. Fortunately, money finally arrived from his relatives in Britain and at last he could afford to buy new clothes and find legitimate accommodation. For eight dollars a month he rented a small room in a Brooklyn lodging house close to the naval dockyard.

By dint of perseverance Bert secured regular employment at the local docks as chief steward on board an inland freighter. His new job allowed him plenty of shore leave, time he spent frequenting Harlem, especially Edmond's Cellar Bar, in the hope of meeting up with Adelaide again.

Many youngsters tried their luck during Edmond's nightly amateur hour but not many were talented. Some were out-of-work professionals hoping to be spotted by a visiting producer; others were just out for a good time. Living in the heart of Harlem, close to the bar, gave Adelaide the perfect excuse to hang out there regularly, even though it was one of the places her mother had forbidden her to go to. Each night, she cleverly managed to sneak in past the bouncer to watch Ethel's performance. Adelaide wasn't difficult to spot. She was about the only fresh-faced teenager in the crowd. Her visits became so frequent that at one point Edmond was under the impression he had hired her as a waitress.

Ethel became accustomed to seeing Adelaide around the place and offered to help her develop her act. Adelaide's talent and genuine enthusiasm made her an easy pupil to coach. She paid careful attention as Ethel worked the room. Her technique and delivery seemed effortless and her clever use of sexual innuendoes had the audience eating out of the palm of her hand. Adelaide soon realized that if she could project herself confidently in front of a half-baked audience, she could easily win the admiration of a sober crowd. Ethel taught her the art of voice control so she could pitch her vocals over the heads of an audience and ensure the sound carried clearly to the opposite end of the room. Within a short space of time Adelaide had shaped her performance into a more cohesive routine. Not only was she quick to learn, but she was now attracting fans.

Bert had little trouble finding the girl he couldn't stop thinking about. On his very next visit to Edmond's bar, there she stood, singing her heart out on the dance floor. During the following weeks, Adelaide and Bert's relationship steadily began to grow beyond the boundaries of friendship. For the first time in his life, Bert had fallen in love.

Although Adelaide adored all the attention and gifts Bert showered upon her, she was still young and inexperienced in matters of love. At first she found Bert's persuasive personality and flamboyant dress sense off-putting. One friend, whom Adelaide often confided in, was the singer Alberta Hunter. Alberta was a keen judge of character and could size a person up in a minute. Her only concern was that Bert might try to dissuade Adelaide from pursuing a career in show business. At that point in time Adelaide was in no rush to settle down. Besides, she already had a boyfriend.

Dudley St. John had been Adelaide's intended suitor since her early teens. Although he was slightly older than Adelaide, they had attended the same public school in Harlem, and it was there that their relationship developed. As teenage sweethearts, both sets of parents believed their courtship would advance into marriage.

Adelaide had grown accustomed to Dudley and thought little about other young men in the neighborhood. Having secured a steady job in the retail business, Dudley's future prospects looked very promising. He had a clever brain without appearing to be a know-it-all and had a good head for figures. His calm and easy manner made him instantly likable. Dudley's philosophical approach to life never allowed problems to get blown out of proportion. However, his lackadaisical manner, no matter how well intended and endearing it might have seemed, would often annoy both Adelaide and his elders.

Bert and Dudley were complete opposites. If Bert's character was best described as being hot and fiery, then Dudley's had the cooling effect of a mountain spring. Both men were handsome in their own way and each had attributes Adelaide found attractive. There was one big problem, though. Dudley had already asked Adelaide to marry him and Adelaide had, more or less, accepted. Dudley's proposal hadn't just been a spur of the moment whim; it was a serious proposition and Adelaide and her mother had given it a great deal of thought and consideration. They had decided that Dudley was a sensible young man with good prospects and would make an ideal and loving husband. Although she didn't say anything to either her mother or Dudley, Adelaide now began to feel differently about the whole affair.

With a mounting sense of guilt Adelaide found herself unable to handle the situation any longer. She finally plucked up the courage to tell Bert of her intended marriage. The news came as a bitter blow. At first Bert felt as though he had been duped, but he soon collected himself. If there was to be any rival contender for Adelaide's affections then he was not the kind of guy to give up without a fight. With the belligerent spirit of a boxer, Bert proudly announced his intentions. Perhaps that was what Adelaide had needed to hear—their secret love affair continued.

Meanwhile, Adelaide's career in show business had taken off with her employment in the chorus line of *Shuffle Along*. Each shore leave Bert arrived back in Harlem and continued wooing Adelaide's affections. The real test of their love came when *Shuffle Along* went on tour for fifteen months. Bert vowed to remain faithful and await her return.

When Adelaide returned to New York their courtship resumed. As their love grew richer so did Bert's gifts, until one day he arrived with a special gift, a small leather box containing an engagement ring.

In a sense Adelaide had always found Dudley's predictability dull. She much preferred Bert's get up and go and joy for life. Even though she hadn't realized it at the time, she had been waiting for someone to sweep her off her feet and Bert knew exactly how to raise the air from under her soles. Their secret courtship progressed at its own pace and on its own terms, and their commitment to each other grew stronger by the day. The time finally arrived for Adelaide to break her silence and tell both her mother and Dudley about Bert. Their response was not what she had expected.

Elizabeth was no fool and confessed to having known for some time that Adelaide didn't love Dudley. Her only concerns were for her daughter's welfare, which Dudley would have amply provided for.

Elizabeth fully understood the situation and accepted Adelaide's decision, but saw no reason to encourage her to reconsider. She could still vividly remember her own strength of will whilst courting her late husband.

"There's no point in me trying to change your mind, I can see that. So who is this fellow and when am I going to meet him?" Little did she know she already had.

Dudley did not take the matter so calmly. He truly was heartbroken to hear the news, especially as he felt betrayed by the one person he felt he could trust.

Bert knew full well how important initial impressions were. It was one of the first things he had learnt when he joined the merchant navy. At her mother's request, Adelaide arranged for Bert to have dinner at their apartment. Bert felt sure that if he could impress Elizabeth on this meeting, his foot would be halfway in the door. From then on, he reckoned he would be on a home run. He also believed that his acceptance into the family would depend on his manners and dress sense, so he went to town and dressed as smartly as if he were going to a wedding reception. With grey spats over his highly polished shoes and a white handkerchief neatly folded in his topcoat pocket, Bert arrived at the Halls' apartment looking very much the dandy.

From the moment Elizabeth saw Adelaide and Bert together, she thought they made a dashing couple. She found him personable, decent, trustworthy and, most importantly, humane. Looking remarkably like a slimmer version of Fats Waller, Bert's cheeky grin and weathered sense of humor held him in good stead for Elizabeth's grilling. Elizabeth had no doubts as to their compatibility. Her only concern centered on Bert's career prospects.

Knowing little about the machinations of the entertainment industry, Bert's intense feelings for Adelaide prompted him to take a genuine interest in her fledgling career. Already his mind had begun to work overtime. He could clearly see, just from Adelaide's small role in *Shuffle Along*, that the possibilities for developing and exploiting her talent were endless. To him, her future prospects in show business seemed obvious. He honestly believed that with the right management push she could reach the top.

Adelaide had never heard anyone talk so enthusiastically about her career before but at the back of her mind she felt a little uneasy about what she heard. She liked Bert's ambitious plans but couldn't stop thinking to herself that maybe he was sweet-talking his way into her affections. On the other hand she could clearly see that he would be the ideal candidate to act as her manager. Bert's efficient and analytical mind was moving faster than Adelaide could dance. Although strong-willed, she needed time to think things over. She got that time when she was picked by Miller and Lyles for a featured role in their next musical, *Runnin' Wild*. Rehearsals were to commence immediately before leaving New York for a tryout tour.[4]

At this point in her life only one thing was certain: her role in *Shuffle Along* had taught Adelaide how to dance for her supper. Now she had to decide exactly how hungry she was to make it to the top.

RUNNIN' WILD AND FREE

In 1923 *Runnin' Wild* introduced the greatest dance craze the world had ever seen, the Charleston.[1] It was the dawning of F. Scott Fitzgerald's "Jazz Age," an age of discovery, where sleeping was deemed to befit only the faint-hearted. What better way to discover oneself than in a darkened club dancing the night away? After all, jazz music called for new dances and who better to invent them than the hardened clubbers themselves? In fact so many dances were concocted that it became an occupation just keeping track of them. In an era where nothing remained constant, it was commonly joked that a new dance would arrive in the morning with the milkman.

Not only did *Runnin' Wild* introduce its audience to the Charleston; it was also the first Broadway musical to present the "flapper" to the public. Perhaps the term came from the fashion for women to wear skirts that flapped above their knees, revealing legs enmeshed in flesh-colored silk stockings. Epitomized by Scott Fitzgerald's wife, Zelda, a "flapper" was regarded as courageous, reckless and, above all, a spendthrift. Her unconventional, gay, light-hearted approach to life was the perfect accompaniment for jazz.

Once again Miller and Lyles dipped into their fictitious characters, Sam Peck and Steve Jenkins, and based the plot of *Runnin' Wild* around their comical antics. Elida Webb, also a veteran of *Shuffle Along*, was drafted in to choreograph the dance routines and various songwriters were commissioned to write the score. The respected Broadway producer George White, of *George White's Scandals* fame, produced the show and, this time, the venture had substantial financial backing.

Plucked from the chorus of *Shuffle Along* Adelaide now had three numbers to perform: a duet, "Old Fashioned Love," in which she teamed up with Arthur Porter again; "Love Bug," an up-tempo love yearner; and "Ginger Brown," which incorporated a strutting dance backed with a full chorus of flappers.

Intensive rehearsals soon had the show up and running. To inject speed into its stride, the company jogged off on a tryout tour that opened on August 23, in Washington, D.C. From there the troupe raced on to Boston.

Whilst on tour the show ran into financial difficulties. Much of the money that was invested in the venture had reportedly been raised from a gambler called Arnold Rothstein. By the end of the second week the money dried up. As well as paying Miller and Lyles a weekly salary of $2,000 the show carried 82 people and a fifteen-piece band. In order to keep the production afloat, George White asked the cast to take part pay. He promised that any outstanding balance would be reimbursed when they got back to New York. Healthy reviews in Washington, D.C., and Boston had convinced him the production would hit Broadway with a bang.

The show had originally been called *Shuffle Along Two*. However, concern for their own livelihood caused Sissle and Blake to issue a court injunction prohibiting Miller and Lyles from using the name. In court, when the judge asked exactly who owned the new revue, Miller and Lyles' representative seemed somewhat confused. It finally transpired that the writers had no rights to it whatsoever. Having run up incredible debts in staging the production, the duo had been forced to sell their option to three backers: Clarence Gray, a New York agent called Harry Bestry, and the movie star Rudolph Valentino.

After an extended eight-week workout the show was deemed fit and ready for its Broadway premiere and opened at the Colonial Theater on October 23.

"A tour de force of excellence" was how one critic tried explaining the show's stamina. Good reviews meant demand for tickets was higher than for any other colored show on Broadway. The Charleston took full credit

for helping steer the show's course and the song James P. Johnson composed to accompany the dance attained national recognition.

The *New York Times* critic heralded the show as "vastly entertaining, and a good deal smarter than *Shuffle Along*" and praised George White highly for his sympathetic production skills.[2] *Variety* singled out Adelaide and called her "a real find. She jazzes a number as Paul Whiteman would have it done. Her singing in 'Old Fashioned Love' is a knock-out."[3] The title may have been old-fashioned but the song went on to become a huge best-seller.

Runnin' Wild ran at a furious pace and hardly gave the audience time to catch their breath in between numbers. One has to say that the high point of the evening had to be claimed by the Charleston. Billed originally in the program as the "Charston," once the dance gained popularity its spelling was altered to read as it was pronounced. Surprisingly, the song that accompanied it was presented without any musical instrumentation. A team of male dancers, billed as the Dancing Redcaps, performed to the lone accompaniment of loud hand clapping and foot stamping such as is found in gospel chapels. To one side of the stage stood the diminutive figure of schoolgirl Elisabeth Welch who, with her honeyed alto voice, sang a cappella in time with the complex foot and hand rhythms.[4] She was picked to lead the song purely because of her vocal prowess. In his book *Black Manhattan*, the writer James Weldon Johnson captured the song's power with four words: "the effect was electric." Certainly the sound that resonated throughout the auditorium was so loud that when the audience left the theater the song was still ringing in their ears. To impair their hearing further, the number took several encores nightly without fail.

Rudolph Valentino's staggering ascent in popularity came after his role in the 1921 movie *The Four Horsemen of the Apocalypse*, in which he danced the sensual Argentinian tango. His sultry Italian good looks and overpowering sexuality instantly set the screen alight. The press dubbed him the screen's greatest lover and confirmed his role as every woman's sweetheart. Valentino's joy for dancing stemmed from his teenage years spent studying at the Collegio della Sapienza, a military academy in the medieval Umbrian town of Perugia. He first learnt to dance whilst he was resident at this college. On the large, red-tiled floor of the recreation room, the cadets would spend free evenings dancing to the lush accompaniment of guitars, mandolins and violins. As no females were allowed on the premises, the boys, dressed in full uniform with heavy hob-nailed army boots, were forced to dance with each other. These jolly evenings fostered Valentino's love for dancing and ultimately led to his desire to become an actor. Although to date he had only starred in a handful of movies, by 1923 Valentino was easily the most famous movie star in the world.

On October 21, 1923, Valentino arrived back in New York from his European honeymoon looking radiantly happy. Not only did he have a new wife, he also had a new male lover, the exceptionally handsome André Daven, whom he had met in Paris.[5] Valentino immediately started work on his next movie, *Monsieur Beaucaire*. Contractual difficulties had prevented Valentino from working for the past two years and he was now banking on his new movie to reconfirm his status as the number-one box-office heart-throb. As the film was to be shot at Paramount's studio on Long Island, rather than occupy his own house in Manhattan, which was undergoing refurbishment, Valentino rented a luxury suite at New York's

Ritz-Carlton Hotel, located on the corner of East 46th Street and Madison Avenue.

Valentino had recently appointed S. George Ullman as his personal manager, primarily to help reorganize his financial affairs, which were in a sorry state. His lavish lifestyle and inability to work for two years had left him heavily in debt. Ullman advised Valentino to consider certain short-term investments. One such idea was to become an angel in a Broadway production, where the dividends were handsome if the show was a hit. It was a suggestion Valentino liked. With Broadway's sudden fixation for black revues, when the offer came to invest in *Runnin' Wild* it looked like a sure-fire money-spinner.

After the show's Broadway opening it was only a matter of days before Valentino visited the Colonial Theater to view his investment. The musical more than lived up to his expectations, especially the Charleston dance, which fascinated him. As a professional dancer and ex-dance teacher, Valentino felt compelled to learn this exciting new dance that everybody was raving about. Post-haste he sent a message to Miller and Lyles requesting that a dancer from the show be sent to his Ritz-Carlton hotel suite to teach him the Charleston.

It was with trepidation and trembling knees that Adelaide arrived at the Ritz-Carlton to teach Rudolph Valentino the Charleston. Outside the hotel's imposing main entrance a permanent crowd of fans besieged the building in all weathers, eager to get a glimpse of their hero. Adelaide pushed uneasily through the throng and entered the hotel lobby where she informed reception of her arrival. "Ah, yes! Mr. Valentino is expecting you, Miss Hall," replied the receptionist reassuringly. "The porter will show you the way."

When Adelaide walked into Valentino's suite, she discovered to her surprise that all the furniture in the main room had been placed against the walls to create a makeshift dance floor.

The lesson ran for just over an hour. Valentino turned out to be an excellent pupil. He danced with the agility of a gazelle and the vigor of a leopard. His intense concentration made Adelaide's job far easier than she had anticipated. By the end of the lesson Valentino had not only mastered the Charleston, but he had also acquired another besotted fan.

To show his appreciation, Valentino kissed Adelaide on both cheeks before she departed. The following day a beautifully packaged gift, wrapped in gold tissue paper, was delivered to her dressing room at the Colonial Theater. Inside she found a large bottle of French perfume. Attached to it was a parchment card upon which were written a few words of gratitude:

To my teacher
I will say my thank you's with perfume . . . it lasts longer.
Love Rudolph Valentino

The Charleston had a history and the history had controversy attached to it. As the dance became more and more popular, more and more people wanted to connect their name to it. It was said to have originated in the South on the cotton plantations and arrived in the city with freed black slaves. That was how the story read in *Runnin' Wild*'s program. In fact, in 1922 a version of the dance had appeared in a Broadway show called *Liza* but for some reason it never caught the public's imagination.

In a letter to *Variety* the show's choreographer, Elida Webb, laid her claim to inventing the dance.[6] Her version went as follows. After watching kids dancing in a Harlem street, she had noticed a new step they were using. Asking them where they got the step from, she was told that a family had just moved into the area from Charleston, South Carolina, and the kids from the family had brought it with them. Miss Webb claimed that she took the step and joined others of the same character to it, thereby inventing the Charleston, which she duly incorporated into *Runnin' Wild*. The story certainly seemed feasible. However, in following issues of the magazine various dance tutors wrote in to lay their claim to its invention, thereby creating even more confusion about the Charleston's true origins.

Whoever invented it, the dance took America by storm and went on to symbolize the wild youth of the Twenties. It was the first true black dance to gain mass popularity and *Runnin' Wild* had the good fortune to spearhead its vogue. Charleston contests, some running for days, were held all over the country, prompting many religious groups to condemn the dance as wicked and sinful. Their outrage only helped push ticket sales even higher. The show galloped ahead, clocking up a respectable

213 performances on Broadway. After taking a deep breath, *Runnin' Wild* then raced off on tour and at the tail end of spring in 1924 opened in Philadelphia.

⚭

1924 would have been a memorable year in anyone's diary. It was the year George Gershwin gave jazz to the orchestra when he introduced his magnificent piano concerto "Rhapsody in Blue" to rapturous acclaim at New York's Aeolian Hall.

The year was also to be an especially important one for Adelaide. Everybody likes punctuation in their life. Both Adelaide and Bert's frequent absences had kept their relationship permanently on hold. Marriage seemed the perfect way of sealing their attachment with a full stop. Bert already spent most of his shore leave attending to Adelaide's fledgling career. With her popularity increasing by leaps and bounds, it now seemed only a matter of time before managing her affairs would require his full-time attention.

When *Runnin' Wild* closed in Philadelphia, Adelaide returned to New York to prepare for her wedding. With help from her friend Elida Webb, who organized the reception, the ceremony took place on June 18, 1924.

In the old-fashioned Protestant church of St. Philip's Episcopal, Adelaide Louise Hall and Bertram Errol Hicks were wed in front of a packed house, including the majority of the cast from *Runnin' Wild*. Bert arrived for the service in poor shape suffering from the effects of a severe hangover. Throughout the service he felt and looked extremely sick. His best man, Wilfred Rodriguez, suggested Bert chew spearmint gum to help prevent him from vomiting. When the time came for Bert to pledge his vows he had such a large ball of the stuff protruding from the inside of his cheek that he could barely speak. Although the trick delayed his sickness, nobody in the congregation, including the vicar, could understand a word he said.

After their marriage Bert no longer sought employment at the dockyard. At the beginning of the year his close friend Elmer propositioned him with the idea of opening a bar in Harlem, nothing grand, just a local joint aimed at a young, fashionable crowd. Although Bert thought the venture viable, finance and the lack of suitable premises delayed their planned opening. Meanwhile, Bert took a temporary job as a salesman in the men's department of a clothing store. When an interested third party offered financial backing and an unused basement beneath a shop on one of the four corners of 135th Street and Seventh Avenue the bar soon began to take shape. The deal was for Bert to manage the establishment whilst Elmer hosted the entertainment. To reduce running costs Bert suggested they hire only amateur performers. By inviting Adelaide and several of her theatrical friends along to christen the place he hoped to guarantee a full house on opening night.

With only one week to go Bert and Elmer still had not agreed upon a name for the establishment. As time was rapidly running out, they were both working all hours to try and finish the renovations. One afternoon Bert invited Adelaide over to view their progress. Although much work had still to be done, Adelaide was suitably impressed with what she saw. Painted in silver on the far wall, behind what was to be the stage, shone a gigantic full moon surrounded by small glittering stars. Whilst she was there the second-hand piano that Bert had ordered was delivered. By coincidence it turned out to be an identical make to her father's old piano at home. Bert asked the deliverymen to position the piano on the stage by the far wall, directly beneath the silver moon.

When the driver inquired if the bar had a name, Bert explained that they hadn't yet made a decision but were open to suggestions. During the conversation Adelaide's attention was drawn towards the small stage, and in particular to the large full moon which now had the piano sitting beneath it. The set with the piano sitting under the silver moon immediately made her recall the words her father would bellow out whilst he was playing the piano: "Sing to the moon, Addie . . . and the stars will shine," and her mischievous reply, "It looks more like a big apple to me."

After the deliverymen had departed, Adelaide kissed Bert goodbye and left him to carry on decorating. As she made her exit up the tall stone steps towards street level she hesitated for a moment. Turning around, she called out to Bert rather smugly,

"Honey . . . I know what name to call the bar."

". . . And what's that, babe?"

"The Big Apple."

THE CHOCOLATE KIDDIES
COME TO TOWN

Blackest girl in blackest night
Invisible till I strike a light
When your smile puts a moon up in the sky
And stars, the glint of fire in your eye[1]

Malcolm Crowthers

THE CHOCOLATE KIDDIES REVUE, 1925

Although the occasional spark from Broadway's explosion of black talent had reached the Continent, Europe had yet to witness a full firework display. Paris had yet to succumb to the beguiling spell of Josephine Baker's exotic dancing and Bricktop was still a relatively unknown hostess struggling to front a back-street nightclub in Montmartre. Berlin was busy chaperoning the avant-garde Bauhaus Movement and Scandinavia's climate seemed far too cold for hot syncopated dance music. Europeans were complaining that they had been starved of authentic American jazz for too long. In one spectacular flourish, *Chocolate Kiddies* was to introduce the Continent to Harlem, the Charleston and real, live black jazz.

Like the stirring melodies and powerful rhythms in Gershwin's "Rhapsody in Blue" which conjure up zany, frantic images of America in the Twenties, *Chocolate Kiddies* grouped together in one choreographed swoop all that was jazz and blew it right out front into the public's lap. The show couldn't fail to impress. It was innovative, exciting and came with a bold sign attached to it: "This is America, this is jazz and it don't get much better than this."

The show was conceived by a stubborn impresario from Berlin called Dr. Leonidow. He believed the German palate was craving for a spicier taste of jazz than the bland symphonic sound that Paul Whiteman dished up. After briefly visiting Europe with his orchestra at the beginning of 1925, Whiteman's concerts had merely acted as an *hors d'œuvre* without actually satisfying the hunger. By creating his own revue, hand-picked from the best available black performers in New York, Leonidow was convinced he could cash in on Europe's growing appetite for real American jazz.

Armed with an open checkbook and strong determination, Leonidow set sail for the U.S.A. He arrived in New York in early March and promptly arranged a meeting with agent and sometime producer Arthur Lyons. Lyons was no stranger to organizing tours to Europe. He had already promoted Lew Leslie's *From Dover to Dixie* revue, which visited Britain in 1924. Leonidow put his proposal across with great Germanic gusto. By the end of the meeting, Lyons was hooked. Leonidow's enthusiasm so impressed Lyons that he immediately volunteered to guide Leonidow around the city's most colorful nightclubs to sample the menu of talent on offer.

Lyons knew exactly what Leonidow was looking for and cunningly offered his own services as agent, writer and producer. He thought he knew the perfect band to accompany the revue—the Sam Wooding Orchestra, which, in his opinion, was waiting to be discovered. As luck would have it, he was their agent. During the next few days, Lyons and Leonidow could be seen tirelessly traipsing across Manhattan, scouring countless clubs and theaters in search of gifted artists.

At Club Alabam on West 44th Street they heard a dazzling set from Sam Wooding's orchestra that almost blew the pair of them back out into the street. Leonidow also singled out various performers in the revue that he felt stood out from the rest. The duo Bobby and Babe Goins floored him with their acrobatic comedy and a pretty young vocalist called Adelaide Hall caught his eye. At the Plantation Café he marveled at the zany Three Eddies' clever dance routines and watched Arthur Payne's dextrous footwork in amazement as he strutted his stuff across the dance floor.

The following afternoon they caught the matinée performance of Sissle and Blake's latest Broadway offering, the *Chocolate Dandies*. Here they propositioned numerous performers including the star of the show, the highly acclaimed singer and actress Lottie Gee.

By the end of the week the pair had visited most of the clubs and theaters in town. Their tenacity paid off. Not only had they managed to enlist a striking array of talent, but it seemed like the whole of Harlem was now clamoring to jump on the bandwagon. Charlie Davis, who shot to fame with his superb show-stopping dance routines in *Shuffle Along*, agreed to choreograph the show and several composers, including a talented new bandleader from Washington called Duke Ellington, were commissioned to write songs for the score.

For the tour, Sam Wooding rearranged his orchestra and recruited some of the finest musicians in Harlem. The band's impressive line-up included Willie Lewis, Garvin Bushell, Maceo Edwards and the outstanding tenor saxophonist Eugene Sedric. Enlisted for the rhythm section were George Howe on drums and Johnny Mitchell on banjo. Wooding even tried to persuade Louis Armstrong to sign up, only to discover that Fletcher Henderson had beaten him to it.

During Wooding's final days at his Club Alabam residency, the new outfit had the whole of Manhattan jumping and most of the celebrated musicians who weren't lucky enough to be enlisted made a beeline to the venue, to check the band out.

Back at his hotel, an elated Leonidow congratulated Lyons upon their good fortune and, to celebrate, cracked open a bottle of German Apfelsaft.

"Not bad going for a week'z work, ya," Leonidow growled in his heavy German accent and proceeded to toast his partner's good health and continuous wealth, "and here'z to zee show'z continuoz zuccezz."

The hardest part for Lyons was yet to come. Contracts had to be negotiated, the script had to be written and a musical score composed, all at breathtaking speed. As Leonidow bid farewell and departed for home, he gave Lyons one last order—that the revue be rehearsed and ready to open in Berlin by the end of May.

That an unassuming, short and stockily built German, who, from a distance, took on the unflattering shape of a penguin, should not only have the foresight to see what the public wanted but also the courage of his convictions to see it through was a fortuitous stroke of luck for all those who became involved in the project.

In Berlin, Leonidow was known as a man of spirit and already had a reputation for his entrepreneurial skills, although they usually involved more dignified opera singers. He was well liked in the business and known to be fair. His austere Germanic features hid his sense of humor, which at times could be quite wicked. At least he had a humorous side. He suffered from myopic vision and found it difficult to focus without wearing his circular, gold-rimmed spectacles resting upon the tip of his nose. He hid his receding hairline beneath a black trilby hat, which he never removed, even indoors. Sweet-tasting Apfelsaft, the German equivalent to cider, was his favorite drink and he was extremely persnickety about the food he ate. This, he explained, was due to a temperamental stomach ulcer that became inflamed if his diet was too rich. Although he wasn't a misogynist he much preferred the company of men. For some unfathomable reason he found female company irritating.

Arthur Lyons grew very fond of his new, odd-looking business partner and over the next few months the pair struck up a great kinship.

By late March the cast had been chosen and rehearsals were already under way at Bryant Hall up in Harlem. After her recent Broadway success, Lottie Gee had secured the leading role and Adelaide was hired as a featured vocalist.

For many of the cast just the idea of traveling abroad was in itself an exciting prospect. Budapest, Vienna, Zurich and Berlin all sounded such romantic cities to visit. The tour would be the first of its kind to visit Europe and for the majority of the performers it would be their inaugural trip to a foreign land. Although their thoughts were occupied with the more aesthetically pleasing aspects of the trip, the main priority for the cast was a little more mundane—the acquisition of a passport. For Adelaide this turned out to be a tricky task. Theoretically, as she hadn't been registered at birth, she didn't exist.

Preparation for the tour took weeks to organize. It was customary for a performer traveling on such a lengthy trip to purchase a whole new wardrobe of clothing. In Harlem there were certain fashion stores that catered exclusively for such events. As most performers had little or no spare cash to pay upfront for their purchases, it was common practice for shopowners to allow credit. This was granted on the understanding that weekly payments were wired back as soon as their work started, until the loan was paid off. This arrangement enabled most of the female performers to have at least one mink coat in their closet.

From an early age Adelaide's mother had instilled the belief in her that as long as she wore good-quality, strong, sensible shoes they would stand her in good stead. It was with this notion placed firmly at the back of her mind that Adelaide went shopping and bought two pairs of the most outrageously expensive snakeskin shoes that she could find. She too had every intention of showing a good footing in life.

"It's a long way from home," remarked Elizabeth, who was more concerned about her daughter's welfare than her hopeless lack of direction.

"And it's a long way from Broadway," interrupted Bert, as if to remind her of the geographical implications of the tour.

Adelaide took little notice of either her mother or Bert's concerns. She jumped without hesitation at the opportunity to travel to Europe and had happily signed along the dotted line. It was, after all, her childhood dream to visit the Continent, especially after listening to all the fascinating tales her grandmother had told. Whereas her mother's anxiety was focused on her daughter's well-being, Bert's apprehensions revolved around the professional aspects of the tour. To him the tour seemed a bit of a hit-and-miss affair. He was anxious to know what would happen if the troupe were stranded. Bert need not have worried. All the members of the cast were issued with return tickets to guarantee their safe passage home.

On May 6, 1925, 43 musicians and performers descended upon New York's harbor to board the SS *Arabic*, bound for the German port of Hamburg.[2] Excited and high spirited, the cast lined up along the quayside to pose for the waiting press photographers. Conspicuous by her absence from all the revelry was the principal member of the cast . . . Miss Lottie Gee. Desperately unhappy at the thought of spending time away from her lover, Noble Sissle, Lottie decided at the last minute to cancel her passage and quit the tour.

Her rash decision was frowned upon by Sissle. He refused to listen to her feeble excuse and continued to lecture her on the legality of the contract she had signed. He explained how her unprofessional conduct could very easily jeopardize her future career in show business. His stern words were not what she had hoped to hear. She tried to explain her behavior as being more of a cry for help than an act of sabotage. Sissle was not convinced. Perhaps his strong disapproval was influenced by his own precarious situation at home. Nevertheless, he stuck to his guns.

Sissle's wife, Harriet, suffered from high blood pressure and low self-esteem. Over the years her fondness for alcohol had produced a well-known temper but beneath her flaws lay a remarkably kind spirit.[3] It was Harriet who discovered Florence Mills singing in a cheap bar. Their meeting led directly to Florence being chosen by Sissle to star in *Shuffle Along*.

To help pacify the situation Sissle informed Lottie that his own European tour with Eubie Blake had been rescheduled.[4] It would now commence in a few weeks' time, so realistically they could very easily liaise in France.

In her heart Lottie knew all along that she must honor her contract. Her protest had merely been her way of making Sissle face up to his selfish philandering ways. She truly loved him and to prove it was prepared to lay her career on the line.

After digesting Sissle's advice, Lottie's anger began to surface. Not only had she missed the sailing, she had also miscalculated Sissle's response. In a fit of fury she telephoned the shipping line and rebooked her passage on the next boat bound for Hamburg.

The excitement of the tour traveled with the troupe well into the first few days of the voyage. By the time they reached mid-Atlantic though a different picture emerged. Most of the cast had never set foot onboard a ship before, let alone sailed across a vast ocean. The particularly rough seas that they encountered began to take their toll.

Those who could no longer stomach the boat's pitching and rolling took solace below deck, where they remained for the duration of the trip, convalescing in the discomfort of their own cabins. For the rest of the cast, the eleven-day voyage provided ample free time to rehearse their dance routines along the promenade deck, adding much to the amusement of fellow passengers.

Like the welcome effects of a sedative, the last night on board was spent anchored in the calm waters of Hamburg's port. After a hearty farewell dinner, a surprise announcement was relayed to the passengers. Following a request from the captain and by way of saying *danke schön* to the crew for the attentive care they had received during the voyage, the much depleted cast had agreed to perform a shortened version of the show for that evening's entertainment.

After disembarkation the troupe spent the entire day restlessly hanging around Hamburg's bitterly cold Hauptbahnhof railroad station. For some reason the train to Berlin had been delayed. All the tannoy announcements were in a foreign tongue and difficult to decipher. Taking out his small German phrase book, Arthur Lyons went in search of assistance. However, the stationmaster was just as much in the dark as to the cause of the delay as the waiting passengers. It transpired that the train had developed mechanical problems and was still coupled in the railroad shed, awaiting repair. Frustratingly for the cast, the next available train to Berlin would not be in service until later that evening.

Situated in the center of Berlin on Friedrichstrasse, the Admirals Palast Theater was housed in a magnificent, cavernous, ornately decorated building, which was more used to staging grand opera than black musical revues. Opposite the theater lay a beautifully maintained garden where rows of metallic tables and chairs were neatly arranged. It was here that theatergoers would congregate on warm summer evenings after a performance to enjoy a social drink whilst keenly scouting for their latest beau.

On opening night the show was still without a title. Advertisements simply billed it as a "Negro Production." Its name arrived by fluke.

Ever since Lyons stepped off the train in Berlin, he had kept noticing large billboards promoting a candy bar called Schokolade. The word stuck in his memory. As publicity for the show grew, Lyons decided it was time to christen it with a proper title. To reflect the number of youngsters in the cast, the candy bar inspired him to choose the name *Chocolate Kiddies*.

Even before the curtain rose on the first half, the prevailing hype surrounding the show's arrival in the city created quite a rush for tickets. From the response of the audience on opening night, it was obvious the show lived up to the public's expectations. They went berserk. As is the German manner, after each number they stood up and cheered wildly. At first, the cast were confused by the raucous conduct and mistakenly took the loud calls of "Bis!" to mean "Beasts!" Thinking they were about to cause a riot, the performers hastily retreated into the wings only to be confronted by an angry-looking Leonidow. Realizing their confusion, Leonidow quickly reassured the cast that "Bis!" translated, in fact, meant "Encore!" then promptly pushed them back on stage to perform one.

By American standards the show depicted a fanciful spectrum of Negro life. The comedy duo, Greenlee and Drayton, acted as narrators and guided the audience through four acts. The first scene reflected the hardships on a Southern cotton plantation where the cast sang heartfelt spirituals recounting their repressed heritage. This was offset by a visit to the salacious temptations of Harlem's nightlife. During one number, "Jungle Nights In Dixie," in which the public were expected to believe the cast had just stepped off a banana boat, Adelaide performed in a short white wig, a matching grass skirt and brassiere, and very little else. The next routine saw the Three Eddies in a clever comedy skit based upon the way white folks perceive blacks and had the audience rolling in the aisles laughing at themselves.

The second act presented a musical *mélange*. It saw the hoydenish chorus parading in ridiculous tin soldier outfits, had Arthur Payne chanting more Negro spirituals, heard Adelaide singing "Rabbit Hop" and witnessed Lottie Gee pouring her heart out in "With You," which she dedicated each night to an absent friend. The high point of the act was definitely Duke Ellington's "Jig Walk," during which Adelaide introduced the public to the Charleston.

After an interval, the third act introduced a little refinement into the program. Wooding's orchestra performed a 30-minute symphonic jazz concert, which gave the rest of the cast a breather before their final energetic onslaught.

Act four took place inside a Harlem cabaret club where the audience was invited on a wild dancing spree. It opened with Ellington's "Deacon Jazz" performed by Adelaide in a sophisticated mode. It set the mood beautifully. Any preconceived impressions that the public might have arrived with, expecting to see a jungle-bunny revue, were soon eliminated. For the cast, the production's content was nothing new but for the German public it was to be a revelation.

The finale, a reprise of "Jig Walk," had the whole cast dancing the Charleston. "Jig Walk" turned out to be the big hit of the show, taking several encores nightly. Even after several encores, the audience still yelled for more, leaving the theater manager with the dilemma of not knowing how or when to empty the building. He soon overcame the problem and devised a simple but effective method of evacuation, by bringing down the curtain unannounced on the cast.

The program's content changed regularly depending on which city the troupe were appearing in. This allowed for improvisation, an integral part of jazz make-up, and kept the spontaneity flowing.

If any one artist got singled out for more attention than the rest it was Lottie Gee.[5] In a country known for its chill factor, both the media and public alike found her sincerity and warmth endearing. It has to be said though that Wooding's orchestra came out tops. Praise rained upon them like confetti at a wedding.[6]

The cast attracted great interest wherever they went, especially from women, who were fascinated by their fashionable dress sense. In the street, people just stood around and stared at them. It was as if they had never seen a well-turned-out black person before. One can only assume that such inquisitive behavior stemmed from a sense of intrigue rather than suspicion. However, in time the constant scrutiny of the cast became a hindrance, for not only did it restrict their movements socially, it also created problems with certain minority groups who would single them out to initiate trouble. Although such incidents were isolated they did become a worry.

Following two equally unpleasant incidents, the band's clarinetist,

Garvin Bushell, decided to take matters into his own hands and seek protection. He visited the local dog pound and adopted the largest stray dog he could find. He chose a Great Dane—and named it Ajax. Never was there a dopier dog but somehow its size detracted from its stupidness and its mere presence did the trick.

Post-war Berlin had blossomed into a multicultural city, attracting artisans and musicians from all across Europe. The restrained effects of the depression that followed the war had gradually worn off, revealing a carefree society whose etiquette was hell-bent on reckless living.

Nicknamed the "Cabaret City," Berlin was known for partying furiously all night, every night. Although the city appeared to have a permanent hangover, in reality it was just a city that never slept. Many of its cafés and cabaret bars were notorious for their lack of morals. Here, homosexuals and lesbians were accepted and, if you knew where to look, any sexual deviation could be found. Such self-gratification, where there was no

The *Chocolate Kiddies* troupe in Berlin, 1925.
Front line from left, Lottie Gee (5th), Adelaide (7th). (Photograph courtesy of Stephen Bourne)

distinction between right and wrong, encouraged many visitors on a journey of inner exploration.

Berlin was an education in itself. The city's racing pulse and relaxed moral attitude formed an ideal background against which experimentalism and raw talent could develop and grow without interference from prejudice. To the open-minded German, American jazz brought the equivalent apotheosis to music that the Bauhaus Movement had brought to the art world. That these two diverse forms of expression should at some point collide seemed a foregone conclusion to Berlin's artistic circles.

For all its excesses and seedy attractions, Adelaide couldn't help but find Berlin incredibly exciting. It wasn't just the expanse of culture on offer that she found so interesting, it was the liberated feel of its people. She discovered a side to herself she never knew existed and a reason to question her own beliefs and sexuality. Only the answers would not be that simple. Her journey of self-discovery through the wild temptations of Berlin's nightlife was an exercise in restraint for a newly married woman. She could hardly have known how right Leonidow had been when he proclaimed that the city was "full of contradiction" and the ideal location for launching such a revue. Noble yet feeble, frivolous yet staid, cautious yet wild, awkward yet challenging, patriotic yet abandoned—there seemed to be no two adjectives that best described its character. In a sense Adelaide had now reached that same point of discovery. There were also two sides to her make-up.

During their Berlin engagement the Victor Company invited the cast to record the principal songs from the production. Wooding and his orchestra arrived early at Vox Studios to prepare for the first day's recording session. The musicians were promptly told to set up their instruments in a studio that turned out to be no larger than a one-automobile garage.

For the musicians, the cramped conditions made playing their instruments with any feeling almost impossible. Whilst running through various numbers to set a sound level, the studio engineers complained that the orchestra was too loud for their monitoring equipment. The musicians were politely asked to play a little quieter. The art of dubbing had not yet been perfected, so it was vitally important that each take was played perfectly. For Wooding, this created a problem. How could the orchestra be expected to recreate faithfully what they did on stage, in the confines of a shoebox?

After much knob twiddling, blank stares and overheated arguments inside the engineering booth, it was suggested they all take a short break. As the temperature inside the studio had risen to an unbearable degree, the doors that led out on to a yard were opened to let in fresh air. Suddenly someone came up with an idea. As it was far too hot and uncomfortable to perform inside the studio, why not have the brass section play their instruments outside in the yard, where it was a lot cooler? Miraculously, not only did this resolve the frayed tempers, it also gave the engineers an accurate sound level to record.

Thankfully for those involved, all the tracks were laid down in one day. Lottie Gee sang lead vocals on "With You" in German, Thaddeus Drayton sang "Love Is Just A Wish," also in German, and the whole cast grouped together to sing Ellington's lively "Jig Walk." Although the recordings were only ever released in Europe, they did help promote the tour.[7]

Tickets for *Chocolate Kiddies* became the most coveted in Berlin. Demand was so great that Leonidow hastily extended the itinerary, taking in several new countries *en route*. Sadly for Lottie Gee, whose restless heart was in a tangle, the prospect of an early return to the States grew less likely by the day.

At the end of its Berlin run the show traveled to Hamburg and performed at the Thalia Theater. On opening night a surprise awaited the audience. Lottie Gee's name had been mysteriously omitted from the program. Although it was a printing error, it turned out to be an omen. At the end of the first week, Lottie defected from the tour. Her numbers were swiftly delegated to Adelaide and Evelyn Dove to perform.

Although Lottie's decision to leave the show had not been unexpected, her departure caused much speculation and gossip amongst the ranks. No official explanation was given but certain rumors suggested that Sissle and Blake's imminent arrival in Europe might have been the catalyst that prompted her to quit.

News travels fast but scandal travels even quicker. Back home, the *New York Amsterdam News* theater correspondent, whilst reporting on the phenomenal success of the tour, was quick to mention Miss Gee's unexpected departure in his column: "Lottie Gee's hasty departure from the show would see her arriving back in the States on 19 August."[8] Although the news was misinformed, perhaps this was intentional. Lottie's return would not take place until the end of April the following year.

Whatever the circumstances surrounding Lottie's defection, it clearly was not for health reasons. On August 6, in the early hours of the morning she was sighted in Paris, celebrating at the Grand Duc, the nightclub American entertainer Bricktop hosted in Montmartre.[9] That night the club was particularly crowded, playing host to a large party of visiting black Americans. Some were personally acquainted with Lottie and carried confirmation of Sissle's impending departure from the States.

Visibly happy to be amongst friends again, yet rather the worse for wear from the effects of drinking too much champagne, Lottie climbed on top of the bar and gave an impromptu rendition of "I'm Just Wild About Harry," the Sissle and Blake song she had made famous in *Shuffle Along*.[10]

From country to country the *Chocolate Kiddies* tour accelerated on full throttle and with each new city extraordinary new adventures unfolded.[11]

In Sweden, as the cast stepped off the boat at Malmö, an army of police and soldiers was waiting to greet them. A diplomatic emergency had arisen. Someone on board had stolen a diplomatic bag that contained important papers from Berlin destined for King Gustaf V of Sweden. After searching everyone's cabin and personal luggage, nothing was found. It transpired that the diplomat had left the bag behind in Stettin and to cover his carelessness falsely reported it stolen. His ineptitude resulted in the cast being left stranded and having to spend the entire night huddled together in a cold uncoupled railroad carriage that was parked right on the water's edge.

One evening, during their engagement in Stockholm, Sweden's Crown

Prince, Adolf, attended. After the performance, the cast were introduced to him backstage. He was genuinely dismayed to hear of the incident at Malmö and the discomfort the cast had consequently endured. As a gesture of goodwill, he invited them all to attend an informal party at the palace. Although some of the cast did accept, the prospect of attending any sort of party at the palace was far too daunting for most of them. To those that declined, the invitation was in itself enough of a memory to cherish.

In Vienna, the cast were given a civic reception and invited to tour the city's famous fourteenth-century catacombs beneath St. Stephen's Cathedral. Underground lay a labyrinth of narrow, dimly lit passageways leading to row upon row of crypts and sarcophagi belonging to former Austrian emperors and princes. Their guide was an elderly war veteran, who was less than steady on his legs. As the tour delved deeper and deeper underground, Adelaide clung tighter and tighter to Garvin Bushell's arm for support. With each step, the air grew thinner and the lighting grew dimmer. Adelaide began to feel scared. At the next corner, a sudden surge in the electricity power caused Adelaide to screech out in panic, at which point the elderly tour guide tripped and fell crashing to the floor.

"Oh, my God!" yelled Adelaide hysterically. "He's dead. . . . Now we'll never get out of here!"

At the end of their Vienna engagement Adelaide quit the tour and returned to America. Christmas was looming and the idea of spending the festive season away from her family made her feel homesick. Numerous unheeded requests from both her husband and mother to reconsider any extension of her contract had finally taken effect. For Adelaide, the tour had taught her many things. Not only was she now returning to New York as a leading lady but also, more importantly, she had discovered her inner self.

After its phenomenally successful trek across the Continent and all the praise that was heaped upon it, it seemed ironic that a show conceived, rehearsed and arranged in Harlem should never perform to a paying audience in America. Arthur Lyons felt the show's content was too naïve for sophisticated Broadway tastes. In later years, Ellington would brag how he had written the entire score for the show in one night and was

Adelaide (center) on stage in *Chocolate Kiddies*. (Photograph courtesy of Rainer E. Lotz)

paid an advance of $500 for his effort. In truth, his evening's work produced only four songs that were actually used in the revue: "Jig Walk," "Deacon Jazz," "Jim Dandy" and the ballad "Love Is Just A Wish." However, the show did continue to run for a remarkable length of time. It was presented in most of the European capitals and even visited Russia before crossing the globe to perform in South America. Its profits made Leonidow and Arthur Lyons millionaires and paid Duke Ellington hefty royalty checks.

By the time the tour invaded Russia in the spring of 1926, little of the original revue which opened in Berlin the previous year remained.[12] After six months on the road, many of the cast, like Adelaide, felt it was time to return home. New recruits quickly replaced those performers that abandoned it. Only Sam Wooding and his eponymous orchestra stayed loyal, seeing the tour through to the end.

The impact *Chocolate Kiddies* had on Europe opened the floodgates for American black performers. European producers, impresarios and nightclub owners were all keen to jump on the bandwagon and capitalize on the sudden vogue for all things African. A steady stream of black entertainers poured across the Atlantic to fulfill lucrative engagements. Many were so impressed with what they found that they stayed far longer than their contracts stipulated.

THE SEEDS ARE PLANTED

Just as Adelaide had been slowly building and developing her career in show business since her audition for *Shuffle Along*, so too had her friend and mentor Lew Leslie.

In February 1922, Leslie's *Plantation Revue* starring Florence Mills opened at the Plantation Café. The nightclub was the first in New York to offer supper, dancing and a fully staged black revue.[13] Situated over Ziegfeld's Winter Garden Theater, at the junction of 50th Street and Broadway, the café attracted the wealthy, after-theater dinner crowd. Leslie's revue was hugely popular and imitations soon sprang up at similar clubs around town.

Not only was Leslie a damned good producer, but he was also his own best publicist. However, his inspired idea of presenting a Harlem floorshow in a midtown location did not succeed without its teething hiccups. Initially his gamble looked like floundering. To put it bluntly, no customers turned up. Believing his concept to be viable, Leslie held on and devised his own way of packing the place out. Each night during the first week, he paid Florence Mills and the Plantation Orchestra to perform in front of an empty club. Outside in the street, when the after-theater crowds walked by the club's entrance, all they could hear were wild exotic jungle rhythms exploding from within the premises. Those that asked for entrance were politely denied and told to queue, as the place was already full to capacity. Leslie had the doorman follow the same procedure nightly until word gradually got around that the Planta-tion Café was so hot you just couldn't get in. The trick worked and at the end of the week Leslie began to admit paying customers. From then on the club was continually packed.

When Harlem's Mafia-owned Cotton Club opened in 1923, its manager, Walter Brooks, realized that if he were to compete with the Plantation Café he would need a producer to equal Leslie's standing. Without further ado, Brooks had Leslie marched uptown and ordered him to duplicate his success at the Cotton Club. Whether he liked it or not, Leslie was hired. Leslie contracted the Boston songwriter Jimmy McHugh to write the score, thus establishing an acquaintance that would be of great value to him in later years. The club became an overnight

Lew Leslie

success and gave Leslie the confidence to push his production talents even further.

Unlike the Cotton Club, the Plantation Café had no mob connections, thus allowing Leslie the freedom to exercise total control over the artists that appeared in its revues. Part of the attraction of dining at the Plantation was witnessing the charismatic performance of Florence Mills. Petite and delicate in frame, with light skin the color of *café au lait,* her large brown eyes and wayward smile charmed the dollars out of the customers' wallets. She was good for business and Leslie instantly clocked her pulling power. He built each revue around her and within a short space of time had molded her into a star attraction who could draw a sell-out audience solely on her own merit.

As Florence's exclusive manager, Leslie cleverly developed her image to suit the white public she was now attracting thereby pushing her career to new heights. His winning formula at the Plantation prompted him to plan a full Broadway revue.

It seemed the obvious step to transpose the whole show across the street into a legitimate theater. With *Plantation Revue* Leslie tasted his first success as a Broadway producer. His relentless hard work finally began to pay dividends, for both himself and those involved in the show. In theatrical circles he became known as the patron of black musical revue and renowned for his autocratic behavior which kept his artists in check and his bank account in checks. After its short Broadway run,

Leslie renamed the show *From Dover to Dixie* and took it on tour to Britain, supervising the move like a general on an army maneuver.

On his return to New York, Leslie conceived his next production, *Dixie to Broadway*, which paved the way for every black revue that followed. For the next couple of years if Florence wasn't starring on Broadway she could be found heading the revue at the Plantation Café. In the summer of 1925, under strict doctor's orders, Florence pulled out of her starring role at the club in order to take a well-earned break. Four years of continual hard work had finally taken their toll upon her health. With no immediate replacement to hand, Leslie was left in a quandary.

When he contacted fellow club owners to recommend a stand-in, Edmond Johnson suggested he audition Ethel Waters.[14] Ethel had been resident at Edmond's Cellar Bar for a number of years and during her tenure become as neglected as the club's furnishings. Having already heard Ethel's bawdy repertoire, Leslie felt reluctant to audition her for the refined Plantation Café. However, purely as a favor to Edmond, he agreed. At the audition Leslie was pleasantly surprised to find that Ethel's expanded repertoire now incorporated sophisticated show standards. Her performance so impressed him that he hired her on the spot.

"Risqué, but never blue, and polish without brass" was how Leslie viewed his revue. Although Ethel was hardly going to step into Florence's shoes, she intended to make a good enough impression to get her out of the pit at Edmond's Cellar Bar for good.

In the summer of 1925, Ethel took the leading role at the Plantation Café, replacing Florence during her convalescence. Also featured in the chorus, having just left Sissle and Blake's production of the *Chocolate Dandies*, was Josephine Baker. One evening Caroline Dudley arrived at the Plantation, scouting talent for a proposed all-black revue she was organizing to ship over to Europe.

Married to Donald Regan—a commercial attaché at the American Embassy in Paris—Caroline's position as a society hostess kept her in regular touch with the city's artistic circles. Originally from Chicago, she felt a kindred spirit with American jazz and in her own small way wanted to impress the French with what she termed "the real flavor." Where better to start her hunt for talent than in the after-hours clubs of New York? She had already read about *Chocolate Kiddies'* extraordinary success in Germany. What she didn't know was that only a few months earlier the German impresario Dr. Leonidow had also arrived in New York pushing the same idea, treading the same path. The *Chocolate Kiddies* revue was now blowing a gale-force storm everywhere it played in Europe. If Caroline was to create any impression on the French she had to move quickly, before the *Kiddies* tour beat her to it.

Initially Caroline chose Ethel Waters to head the cast. Ethel was not keen on the idea, so she asked for the ridiculous salary of $1,000 a week, knowing full well Caroline's budget wouldn't stretch that far. Caroline's second choice was the vocalist Aida Ward who accepted the role, only to be fired before rehearsals commenced because of her alcohol dependency. The blues singer Maude de Forest finally took the lead and Josephine Baker accepted a featured role in the chorus. Josephine had also read press reports documenting the astounding progress of the *Chocolate Kiddies* tour and was eager to discover the rewards that Europe had to offer her. On September 15, the cast of Caroline's *Revue Nègre* sailed to France in search of untold fame and fortune.[15]

During Florence's convalescence, Leslie formulated ideas for his next presentation. *Blackbirds of 1926* was to be his biggest show to date and would once again center around Florence Mills. He also announced elaborate plans for future productions, including the creation of an annual edition of the *Blackbirds* revue, a formula that would be imitated widely by many gold-digging producers in the years to follow.

Detail from the *Chocolate Kiddies* poster (courtesy of Rainer E. Lotz).

THE CHOCOLATE KIDDIES EUROPEAN TOUR, 1925

GERMANY
May 25: Berlin, Admirals Palast Theater, ran for eight weeks and
played 65 performances
July 28: Hamburg, Thalia Theater, ran for four weeks and played
32 performances

SWEDEN
Aug. 25: Stockholm, Cirkus Theater, ran for three weeks and
played 21 performances

DENMARK
Sept. 15–21: Copenhagen, Scala Theater
Sept. 22–26: Copenhagen, Benneweis Cirkus

GERMANY
Sept. 27–Oct. 3: Hanover
Oct. 5: Magdeburg, Zentral Theater
Oct.: Dresden

CZECHOSLOVAKIA
Nov.: Prague

HUNGARY
Nov.: Budapest

AUSTRIA
Dec. 1–14: Vienna

Please note this is not a comprehensive listing of all the tour dates as certain newspapers containing relevant information to complete the itinerary could not be located.

7

NO PLACE MORE SO
THAN IN HARLEM

1926

Adelaide's return to America produced a sigh of relief all round. She was pleased to be home again, back amongst her family and friends, but the thought of remaining static was the last thing on her mind. Although *Chocolate Kiddies* had nourished her with a valuable source of education, she felt her absence from Harlem had produced a sense of inertia in her career. Eight months was a long time to be away from the action. Over the past few years, American black culture had evolved into a driving creative force. Many respected journalists, including Carl Van Vechten, had used their influence in the media to encourage and promote Negro writers, artists and musicians. Harlem was viewed as fertile ground for such talent and harvested regularly.

Adelaide's attention was clearly focused on reaching the top of her profession. It had taken five slow years to reach this point in her life—too long in her opinion. If nothing else, Europe had bolstered her confidence bringing forth a new impetus of motivation and drive. She knew exactly what she wanted: success, wealth and fame. From her perspective, the only obstacle preventing her from achieving this was timing. Somehow, Bert had to devise a plan to eliminate the time factor. The challenge had now become "how" not "if," "when" not "maybe." His role as a full-time manager was about to commence.

Bert's management of the Big Apple had turned the bar into a reasonably profitable concern. The place attracted a young fashionable crowd but was limited by its size. Unless it moved to larger premises, its profitability would never greatly increase. Bert's heart was set on bigger things. If he were to concentrate on promoting Adelaide's career, he would have to relinquish his job at the bar.

Curiously, the bar's popularity inspired many Negroes to use its name—the Big Apple—as slang when referring to the geographical region in Harlem where it was located.[1] Gradually, the nickname became known to visiting white New Yorkers who, thinking the term novel, adopted it and began referring to New York in general as the Big Apple. No one really knows who first referred to the metropolis in this manner, but most jazz historians agree the terminology came from Harlem in the early Twenties. As with all aspects of fashion, the original idea emanates from street level and is then expanded upon by others. Certainly, Adelaide's story and her lifetime claim that she popularized the name seems valid enough when put into context.

Since their marriage, Adelaide and Bert had resided at her mother's apartment at 194 West 134th Street. For obvious reasons, the arrangement was far from ideal. Bert would have much preferred their own place. Only Adelaide's insistence on remaining there prevented them from moving. However, Bert did negotiate a compromise. After Adelaide returned from Europe, he rented a roomier three-bedroom apartment on St. Nicholas Avenue. At first, Elizabeth, who was convinced she would be alienated from her friends, refused to budge. Considering the location of the new dwelling was but a few hundred yards away, the absurdity of her stance seemed laughable. However, only after reassurance from her best friend Gertrude Curtis did Elizabeth finally relent and reluctantly move the few blocks down the street into their new address.

Throughout the first half of 1926, Adelaide starred in a series of black revues that played exclusively on the TOBA circuit. These included *Lincoln Frolics*, *Tan Town Topics*, the *Bill Robinson Revue* and *Shake, Rattle and Roll*. With the ill-fated production *My Magnolia* she briefly appeared on Broadway again in front of a white audience, but it was to be her leading role at the later end of the year in *Desires of 1927* that finally set her on the right path.

On March 8, 1926, Adelaide co-starred with the blues singer Lucille Hegamin in *Lincoln Frolics* at Harlem's Lincoln Theater.[2] Miss Hegamin had achieved considerable success as a Columbia recording artist and, as such, was well known on the TOBA circuit. The show attracted much local publicity as the theater had recently been refurbished. As well as offering its customers a live revue, at the back of the stage the management had installed a wide cinema screen on which to project the latest film releases. After a successful week's run at the Lincoln, the show traveled to Washington, D.C., where it appeared at the Broadway Theater for a limited engagement. Although the revue was nothing spectacular, *Lincoln Frolics* did establish Adelaide in her first starring role in an American production and thus became a turning point in her career.

From Washington, D.C., Adelaide returned to Harlem and went straight into rehearsals at the Lafayette Theater for her next featured role.

TAN TOWN TOPICS

Tan Town Topics was Fats Waller's first attempt at writing a full-length stage revue. Commissioned by the Lafayette's owner, Frank Schiffman, Fats only agreed to write the score if a suitable lyricist could be found to assist him. Schiffman suggested he collaborate with Spencer Williams who turned out to be an ideal writing partner. Fats had been in-house organist at the Lafayette Theater since 1921 and during his tenure accompanied countless revues. He knew exactly what kind of show Schiffman was looking for. The assignment seemed a doddle.

On April 5, *Tan Town Topics* opened for a four-week run.[3] Produced by Leonard Harper on the lowest budget possible, the revue showcased many of Harlem's local black vaudeville acts. Included in the line-up were Eddie Rector, Ralph Cooper and Florence Mills' younger sister Maude. Many of the cast had previously worked in the floorshow at Connie's Inn (located adjacent to the Lafayette), which now felt lost without their presence. The most memorable scene in the production entitled "Valencia," a big Spanish spectacle that included a bullfight, featured Adelaide singing the sentimental ballad "Senorita Mine." The song gave Fats his first legitimate hit.

The Lafayette was famous for presenting the best black stage shows in the country but as most of its revues showcased local talent they commanded little attention in the weekly entertainment bible *Variety*. The theater held around 1,500 people and played continuous performances from 10:30 a.m. to midnight, six days a week. To recoup the expense of staging such a production, the revue would run for at least one week. If the show proved popular and sold out, it would be held over before hitting the TOBA circuit for a short tour. For the first time, Adelaide got the prestige of having her name emblazoned in bright lights across the entrance marquee. If you headlined at the Lafayette, you truly had made it to the top of the black show-biz ladder. The next rung up was the white vaudeville circuit and, ultimately, starring on Broadway.

To add status to her name, the producer billed Adelaide as having just arrived back from Europe. The show had to be good. It was running in direct competition with Florence Mills at the Alhambra Theater in Lew Leslie's *Blackbirds of 1926*. In a calculated move, the Lafayette's management reduced the cost of seat prices to 25, 35 and 50 cents, thereby guaranteeing themselves a full house nightly. Not wanting to be outwitted, Leslie announced Florence Mills' imminent departure to Europe and stressed it would be the last time the public would be able to see her for a whole year. He then reduced the Alhambra seat prices from $1 to 50 cents, prompting the Lafayette's owner, Frank Schiffman, to remark in the press, "Competition is the life of trade." Such rivalry added more loose change to the public's pocket, which consequently afforded them the opportunity of catching both shows.

Fats loved being in the limelight. He played the clown and people adored him for it. As well as being a heavy drinker, he also had a tremendous appetite and given the chance would eat anyone under the table. He had a great passion for grits and rice, especially the way his mother cooked it. Even though Prohibition was in force, when Fats was around, alcohol was readily available.

When *Tan Town Topics* played in Philadelphia the *Tribune* raved ecstatically, heaping praise upon it as if it were the greatest show on earth. "The world's greatest tap dancer arrives in town," referring to Eddie Rector, "and is coupled with one of the finest singers of her race, Adelaide Hall, who are complemented by the hottest rhythmic sounds to be found in the land, executed by Fats Waller's Tan Town Orchestra."[4]

Encouraged by *Topics'* initial success, Schiffman commissioned a second score from Fats, only this time Spencer Williams was unavailable to collaborate on the project. (Williams had previously written the lyrics for the *Revue Nègre*, the show that had recently propelled Josephine Baker into the limelight in Paris, and had been summoned by the producer to join the troupe in Paris.) Undeterred by his lyricist's departure, Fats' new-found confidence prompted him to write both the music and lyrics himself.

Outside the Lafayette Theater, on the edge of the sidewalk, stood the famous "Tree of Hope." This tree was said to hold magical powers. Unemployed performers, who touched its bark and made a wish for a job, believed emphatically that their request would come true. Before Fats commenced writing his new show, Schiffman ordered him to go outside and rub the tree's bark as hard as he could. This time he wanted a Broadway hit.

With the hope of cashing in on Broadway's hunger for black musicals and Florence Mills' departure, Schiffman modeled the new revue along the lines of Lew Leslie's latest hit, *Blackbirds of 1926*, and cheekily called it *Junior Blackbirds*. Without a star like Florence Mills or Adelaide at the helm, the show flopped and for a while left a sour aftertaste on Fats' palate for writing any further musicals.

After *Tan Town Topics'* run in Philadelphia, Adelaide returned to Harlem to guest at the Alhambra Theater for two weeks in the *Bill Robinson Revue*. The show was cheekily billed as an "all-new revue" when it did in fact have the majority of the cast from *Lincoln Frolics* in it.

To the American public Bill Robinson was known endearingly as Bojangles and rated as the world's leading tap dancer. He was revered in the black community as something of a hero, having made it to the big-time white vaudeville circuit where he commanded a fee in excess of $2,000 a week.

With Bojangles at the helm the show looked set to reap huge dividends, until disaster struck. After a promising opening night, business tailed off dramatically to the point where it was playing to half-empty houses. The management of the Alhambra couldn't understand why this should be and sent spies out to question the public at large. It transpired that the previous weeks' price war between the Lafayette and Alhambra had fueled such a demand for tickets that the public now felt short-changed when asked to pay full price for a ticket.

Rumor spread quickly amongst the cast that the revue couldn't survive and their pay check might not be forthcoming at the end of the week. After Saturday night's performance hearsay turned into fact. No moneys were paid. The cast stormed out, refusing to return. Needless to say, the revue folded.

MY MAGNOLIA

Broadway had had its fill of meager black productions. The public had become weary and wary of the same run-of-the-mill formula and showed their dissatisfaction by staying away in droves. *My Magnolia* was a belated attempt to cash in on the black revue formula.

The show originally started out on the TOBA circuit under the name *Struttin' Time* where it played for twenty weeks. A theater booker in Philadelphia became interested, took it over, revamped it and booked it into Broadway's Mansfield Theater in the heart of Times Square. Billed loosely as a musical comedy, *My Magnolia* starred the talented comedian Eddie Hunter. Adelaide had a small featured role playing a character called Jenny, the daughter of a wealthy industrialist. Her big production number was "Spend It," a flapper-inspired ditty that exalted the joys of having too much money and not enough imagination. It was hardly a demanding role. In fact, during rehearsals Adelaide had enough spare time to star in another revue at the Lafayette called *Shake, Rattle and Roll*.[5]

Production credits for *My Magnolia* went to Eddie Hunter and Alex Rogers but also included input from Lew Leslie. This was the first show Adelaide worked in under the direct guidance of Mr. Leslie.

The revamped show opened in Atlantic City for its tryout with high hopes of success but things rapidly went downhill from then on. Under-rehearsed, a badly written script and the lack of hit tunes were sour points on the reviewer's nib. It hoisted as much support from the audience as a broken crane and sent them home wishing they had never ventured out in the first place.

My Magnolia limped into New York's Mansfield Theater like a three-legged horse. With hindsight, it probably wasn't such a wise decision on the part of the show's owner to have leased the theater for three months. As the continuing summer heatwave gave great concern to everyone its premiere was postponed. The show eventually opened three days late on July 12. It couldn't have been more badly timed. Due to the soaring heat and a subway strike, it was Broadway's worst week ever for ticket sales. Even the cut-price ticket booths couldn't get rid of seats.

It's fair to say that the musical didn't entice the critics' attention.[6] Some were seen to walk out in dismay before the interval, and those that did stay until the finale were thought to represent the race papers. The fact that the show ran for three hours didn't help and was unanimously thought to be too long by two.

Variety dismissed the production kindly as "a quick flop," as opposed to a nail-scraping cliffhanger, and must have watched with amusement when it did just that.

"A long and sorry affair insufficiently rehearsed. It lacks the sustained speed and native abandon of previous Negro entertainments. Eddie Hunter is featured and he is not even moderately amusing." So spoke the harsh words of the *New York Times* critic.

To survive after such disastrous reviews the show now had the challenge of scaling a precipice that even a seasoned mountaineer would have shirked from climbing. It seemed much fairer for all concerned to call it a day. The hard-boiled critics' mauling saw the show axed after only five performances and left Eddie Hunter nursing a bruised ego.

Perhaps its failure could best have been described by one of Tallulah Bankhead's astringent one-liners: "Darling, there's less here than meets the eye."[7] *My Magnolia* didn't woo anyone, least of all the audience, who fled the theater disheartened. If a writer were to perform an autopsy upon its reviews he or she would be lucky to fill one paragraph with praise.

The sudden closure of *My Magnolia* came as no surprise to the cast. Most of them had already accepted its fate in Atlantic City. Strangely, the show's quick demise was in total contrast with the success of other black revues that week. It was reported in the *New York Amsterdam News* that business at Harlem's theaters was so brisk that customers trying to purchase tickets were forced to wait in long queues, with little hope of gaining admission.[8] Clearly the black musical, if handled correctly, could still attract punters.

Receiving one of the few commendable mentions in the press, "Miss Hall handled 'Spend It' well and displayed grace in her dancing," saw Adelaide come out of the fiasco unscathed, although her intention of bypassing the career ladder and taking the elevator was temporarily halted.[9] Serious consideration was now called for before agreeing to any future choice of production.

After digesting the reviews, a look of disappointment settled upon Adelaide's face. There seemed little point in arguing with destiny. Fate has a peculiar way of profiting from adversity.

THE SWEET SHOP AT THE TOP OF THE AVENUE

> Love would turn your head around
> Make you wild and hit the town
> And make you stay out gambling all night long

Harlem was famous for its nightlife and catered for all tastes no matter how simple or bizarre. Situated within a concentrated zone of around fifteen streets, the area boasted over 125 entertainment venues ranging from theaters, supper clubs, ballrooms, lounges, speakeasies, cellar-bars and nightclubs. Since the introduction of Prohibition in 1920 most of the local off-street drinking bars had shut down. Those that remained were mob-owned and operated illegally, usually hidden in dark dingy basements. More often than not locals rather than downtown visitors would frequent these establishments.

Lenox Avenue cut directly through the center of Harlem and operated like the main artery in a heart, continuously feeding life in and out of the area. It was the glitzy expensive extravaganzas that the plusher venues offered their clientele, available at such venues as Smalls' Paradise, the Cotton Club and Connie's Inn, that attracted a new breed of clubber to Harlem—the white socialites of New York. After eating their main course at dinner downtown, it was common practice within such circles to visit the sweet shop at the top of Lenox Avenue for dessert.

At nightfall, Harlem transformed itself into a glittering playground. After Broadway's theaters had closed their doors for the evening, Harlem swung into action and flung its doors wide open. New Yorkers, with an insatiable fixation to party, gravitated towards the hospitable welcome that awaited uptown. With its reputation for being the only place in New York where the exotic and the erotic could be found at any hour of the night, the thought of returning home held little appeal for the discerning reveler.

Into the early hours of the morning, Harlem's main thoroughfare bustled with crowded activity. Along its broad avenues stretched a continual line of taxicabs and gleaming limousines all touting for business. Clubbers were well known for hopping in and out of cabs even if it was just to visit the club around the corner.

Outside on the sidewalk, beneath smart canopies that hung over a club's entrance, stood impeccably dressed doormen. This was their territory and they ruled the sidewalk with iron fists. Their job was to meet, greet and choose the customers who either could or could not enter the premises. Needless to say, many a golden handshake took place during the course of an evening in the hope of swaying their opinion.

Most of Harlem's establishments encouraged their patrons to drink bootleg alcohol, eat authentic Creole food or simply learn the latest dance craze. As America's black capital willingly played host to this lucrative nightly invasion, the intoxicating rhythms of jazz inadvertently became the canvas on which the town was painted red. Those that delved a little deeper inside this seemingly risqué world could even find new and more potently expensive addictions to satisfy their curiosity.

Harlem's prosperity came hand in hand with the seedier elements of affluence. Racketeers, vice barons and sordid drug peddlers all mixed openly with the very punters they exploited. Their illegal investments and subsequent evasion of taxes saw vast sums of undeclared profits channeled out of the country and deposited into offshore accounts.

Jazz became inextricably associated with the underworld and, for the talented black performer, Harlem became an oilfield. Fortunes were readily made overnight by those who were quick to tap its source. Ironically, the very people who had kept black performers in poverty for so long were now content to throw bundles of cash at them. During what would later be dubbed "the Harlem Renaissance," the currency was talent and the nightclub barons dealt bountifully in its fertile trade.

Black stars were in vogue. With their newly acquired prosperity, they could now afford to drive expensive cars, own luxury apartments and wear fancy jewelry and furs. Those that were really well off even hired a servant or two.

Harlem's Renaissance brought Broadway's bigwig impresarios sniffing. Hauling themselves uptown in hot pursuit came Ziegfeld, Earl Carroll and RKO's vaudeville booking agents. Waving open checkbooks like flags, they signed up anyone with an inkling of talent and promptly transported them downtown to feature in their latest Broadway revue. Unfortunately, this created the reverse effect on the public's imagination from the one desired. Producing watered-down versions of Harlem's so-called "jungle music" and "sexually explicit" dance routines only served to whet the public's appetite for the real thing. Their craving and curiosity for a more authentic setting consequently sent the customers flocking back uptown to discover the real McCoy for themselves.

Harlem holds a unique position in the history of American black culture. For the white man, Harlem's appeal lay in its geography. Tucked away uptown, it was far enough away to have a debauched night of sin without the fear of being recognized yet close enough to get a cab home in the morning.

Not only did Harlem supply a wealth of musical talent, but soon black literature, poetry, art and fashion began to infiltrate the mainstream. As with any new trend, its novelty factor ranked high in its sudden popularity but, nevertheless, its influence would gradually be seen in all walks of society. Some people felt the vogue for all things black would only last a season, like the latest shade of color in a fashion designer's new collection. Others, rather naïvely, felt stronger and declared that Negro art had at last helped solve the race problem. Whatever the outcome, the attention black culture received made Harlemites think the Millennium had arrived early.

Speakeasies opened and closed with such frequency in the neighborhood that it was impossible for newspapers to make a comprehensive listing of the area's nightlife without it becoming dated before it was published. The uncertainty of a venue's existence made the excitement of discovering it was open for business even more compelling for its clientele. To the outsider, the whole community appeared to be money grabbing and cashing in on the Negro boom, even if it did involve staying awake all night in order to line one's pocket.

Perhaps the black poet Langston Hughes best describes Harlem's rich tapestry of flavors and attractions, in his narrative poem "Harlem Sweeties." With his elaborate use of adjectives, he likens it to a candy store brimming full with every conceivable kind of confectionery imaginable, just waiting to be sampled by the paying customer.

If, by nightfall, Harlem took on the dynamic personality of a hostess who warmly welcomed you into her extended bosom, then by day only the scent of her sweet perfume lingered.

For Harlem's residents, the nightly influx of downtown New Yorkers brought noisy congestion to the neighborhood, and also inhibited their choice of evening's entertainment. Harlem's smart supper clubs with their astringent "Whites Only" door policy admitted blacks only as performers or waiters, never as paying customers. As most of Harlem's best clubs were playing host to whites, this meant the locals were limited to frequenting the seedier joints in the area. Many residents complained, claiming they were being short-changed: "If we can't go downtown and dance in a white man's club where can we go?"

This predicament led to the invention of "Bottle", "Food" and "Rent" parties. These took place in private apartments at weekends and were attended by invitation only. As the term "Bottle" implied, guests were expected to bring their own liquor. "Rent" parties were thrown when the tenant of an apartment had fallen into arrears with the landlord—throwing a party was deemed to be a quick solution to paying the rent—and strapped-for-cash landladies renowned for their culinary skills organized "Food" parties.

Various methods were used to announce these parties—word of mouth, small advertisements in the local press or elaborately designed visiting cards placed on the grilles of apartment elevators. At the howl of the midnight owl the parties would begin and last until dawn. Such was the demand for new places to go that the events were always over-attended. "Bottle" parties became so popular with the locals that visiting whites, who thought that they were missing out, would try anything to gatecrash.

Celebrity parties were also held regularly around town and were heavily attended by the show-biz glitterati. Anyone who could beg, steal or borrow an invitation suddenly became your best friend for the evening. George

Gershwin, the writer and philanthropist Carl Van Vechten and the black heiress A'lelia Walker threw some of the most memorable and lavish functions in the calendar. A'lelia's inheritance—she was America's wealthiest black woman—came from her mother whose invention, patented as the "Madame Walker hair straightening process," worked wonders at taming unruly Negro hair. Sadly her spendthrift habits would see her penniless within years.

So grand were these affairs that many had accounts of them written up in the society pages of the following day's papers. Every class, color and creed, from royalty down to mere chorus girls, would attend. A more eclectic mix of personalities could not have been found in a telephone directory. Many of these parties created first-rate scandal that set society tongues wagging for weeks.

One occasion that caused much excitement in the gossip columns occurred at one of Carl Van Vechten's parties. As a highly controversial writer, he wrote what he thought and suffered the consequences later. He was known to favor the more exotic personalities around town and at one of his soirées, to charge the atmosphere he invited an array of rival show business celebrities just for the hell of it. As was usual at such events, various cabaret acts had been lined up to entertain the guests. One of the performers, Chief Long Lance, who attained modest success in silent movies playing the role of a Cherokee, had been invited to perform an Indian war dance dressed in full costume. As there was no musical accompaniment to enliven his routine, after much cajoling from the guests, Adelaide courageously stepped in to help spice up his performance by offering to play the drums.

Having never played the drums before, Adelaide's attempt to add rhythm to his seriously dull war dance turned the party into a riot. The audience laughed uncontrollably at her comical interpretation of how she thought war drums should sound. Needless to say, Chief Long Lance, who was far too serious for his own good, was fearsomely unhappy with the reception he received. After brandishing his bow and arrow in the air to halt the charade, which made the guests roar even louder, he then threatened to shoot them if they continued to laugh at his performance. His threats went unheeded. Like cupid on a busy night the arrows began to fly. It took five waiters to restrain him. Before being forcibly evicted from the party, the Chief threatened Vechten with a lawsuit for embarrassing his honorable name in front of so many famous and important people. The poor fellow never did see the funny side to it all.

DESIRES OF 1927

In August, Rudolph Valentino's sudden death from a perforated ulcer caused the most sensational scenes of grief ever witnessed for an entertainer.[10] His funeral attracted mass hysteria and rioting, causing scores of people to be injured. Thousands of grieving females took to New York's streets in a maudlin display of hero worship. The press fueled their disbelief by publishing every snippet of information about the actor that they could lay their grubby hands on. It transpired later that Valentino's manager, S. George Ullman, had staged the whole event with uncanny skill to generate as much publicity as possible from the event. In the lovesick eyes of the public, Valentino's death proved, without any shadow of doubt, that stars of the silver screen had the capability of becoming modern-day gods.

It had been five years since Adelaide first stepped out in front of a Broadway audience in the chorus line of *Shuffle Along*. Now, with a great sense of elation, Elizabeth could proudly stroll along Lenox Avenue and see her daughter's name displayed in bold lettering on enormous billboards, advertising the latest show in which she starred.

> Irvin C. Miller's smash hit
> **DESIRES OF 1927**
> starring
> ADELAIDE HALL

Fate's peculiar way of profiteering from adversity became evident with *Desires of 1927*. Even though the revue's title suggested otherwise, its premiere at the Orpheum Theater in Newark, New Jersey, took place on October 18, 1926. At a cost of $50,000 to stage, the production was everything a black revue should be. It had direction, an abundance of talent, a hit producer behind it and it was slick and snappy. The show was so appealing that the audience wrapped it up and took it home with them in their pockets each night.

Irvin C. Miller was one of the few remaining black impresarios in the business. Having his name endorse a revue guaranteed quality and class. The show's underlying theme was the three desires of the mind: success, fame and wealth, coincidentally, the same three desires Adelaide had. However, in this script her come-uppance in the finale came in the form of disappointment.

Adelaide's role was tailor-made to incorporate her many talents— singing, acting, dancing and strumming the ukulele. Supporting her were J. Homer Tutt, a bevy of brownskin beauties and her old partner from *Shuffle Along*, Arthur Porter. The revue ran for 90 minutes, of which 30 were allotted to Adelaide. Her performance was credited with charm, wit and vitality and her rendition of "Sweet Virginia Blues" stopped the show nightly, producing a massive hit for the song's writers. The *Chicago Defender*, America's foremost black newspaper, described it as "exceptional" entertainment and proclaimed Adelaide to be "the only rival to Florence Mills," urging the public to "go see for yourself."[11]

With the Charleston appearing passé, the introduction of the Black Bottom shimmied in as the next dance craze. It had only just been introduced on Broadway in *George White's Scandals* but was already creating a sensation. The singer Alberta Hunter claimed she had invented the dance in 1925 by accident during her vaudeville act. When she heard Adelaide was to perform it in *Desires of 1927* she immediately offered to coach her. The dance steps were said to have been derived from the dragging of feet through the muddy black bed of the Suwannee River—a fanciful description if ever there was one. Fortunately for the public, it was far easier to learn than the Charleston. It consisted of forward and backward hops and the slapping of one's behind in between movements. Adelaide's interpretation in *Desires of 1927* certainly helped the dance achieve mass popularity across northeast America.

After a hugely successful engagement at Harlem's Lafayette, *Desires of 1927* went on a national tour of the TOBA circuit where it performed to "Sold Right Out" notices. The show catapulted Adelaide into the top ranks as one of America's leading black female artists. This was to be the first time that Bert accompanied Adelaide on tour.

Adelaide in *Desires of 1927*.
Success, wealth and fame—her three desires.
(Photograph courtesy of Stephen Bourne)

In Chicago she appeared at the Grand Theater in direct opposition to Bojangles who was starring at the newly opened Palace Theater. By co-incidence, Lew Leslie was in town scouting for talent and caught both their performances during the same evening.

As the show gathered momentum, recognition of Adelaide's talent snowballed. Theophilus Lewis, in the *Baltimore Afro-American*, pro-claimed her to be the premier star of the day: "I know that Josephine Baker, Florence Mills and Gertrude Saunders' fans are ready to rip me up the back, but how many of them are ready to deny it and upon what grounds? As I stood before the theater, my attention was drawn to a photo of Miss Hall, posed as the Madonna. A halo encircles her brow, her eyes are raised aloft portraying within their depths a look of sincerity and holiness. One glance and the memory lingers forever. Some day this girl . . . will . . . step out into a world of keen competition to emerge with laurels, never before allotted a race actress."[12]

Not only was she melting the audience's heart and receiving critical acclaim in the process, but her performance also confirmed without doubt that she could now carry an entire production. To her nearest and dearest it appeared that the three desires of Adelaide's heart—success, wealth and fame—were almost within her grasp.

YOU AIN'T HEARD NOTHIN' YET!

"Wait a minute! Wait a minute! You ain't heard nothin' yet," were the first words ever to be uttered in a talking movie. They were spoken by Al Jolson in his motion picture debut and created the kind of impact no film director could ever have dreamt of.

In anyone's diary 1927 was to be an extraordinary year.

On October 6, *The Jazz Singer* opened in a hail of publicity at the Strand Theater on Broadway. It was a date that would later be sanctioned in movie history as the birth of the "talkie" and one that would revolutionize the entertainment industry for ever. New Yorkers watched with emotional scenes of disbelief as Jolson knelt down on one knee and sang his way into the hearts of the public. Overnight, he alone rendered the silent movie obsolete. Fearing for their livelihood, those who worked in legitimate theater viewed this beautiful moment in the history of film with ugly suspicion. Even Jolson's single prophetic exclamation could never have predicted the breathtaking events that transformed man's perception of the world in 1927.

This was also an historic year for aviation. On May 20, 25-year-old Charles Lindbergh took off from New York in his specially designed monoplane, *Spirit of St. Louis,* in an attempt to fly across the Atlantic single-handed.

Tall, blond, with fearless blue eyes and strong Scandinavian features, his courage captured the public's imagination. Navigating his plane alone across the open sea, he touched down in Paris 33 hours later to a hero's welcome. His brave endeavor suddenly made the world that little bit smaller.

Newspapers proclaimed him the prophet of a new era and bestowed upon him the status of a celebrity. Parisians adopted him as their own son and treated him like royalty. They presented him with the freedom of the city and granted him privileges usually reserved for visiting heads of state. He soon discovered his sudden fame made the honor impossible to utilize.

Americans followed his every step with patriotic fervor. His boyish good looks and impeccable manners—he neither smoked nor drank alcohol—turned him into the media's dream personality. When he returned to the States, another hero's welcome awaited him. He was paraded through New York in an open-topped limousine. Thousands lined the streets along the motorcade route. It seemed like the whole of America had turned out to pay homage to him. From skyscraper windows, they waved the American flag and showered him with ticker tape and torn-up sheets from the newspapers in which he appeared constantly.

Fueled with determination and a dream, this dare-devil youngster entered aviation history as a comic-book hero, typifying the adventurous spirit of new-age American idealism. He became the most celebrated human being on the planet and spent the rest of his life desperately trying to escape the glare of publicity that surrounded his every move.

To celebrate this momentous and historic occasion, struggling song-writing partners Dorothy Fields and Jimmy McHugh penned a catchy ballad called "I Can't Give You Anything But Love, Lindy." Although the writers were genuinely inspired by Lindbergh's triumphant achievement, they hoped to cash in on the public's enthusiasm for America's unlikeliest idol. When the producers of *Delmar's Revels* heard it, they inserted the number, for its novelty value, into their latest Broadway revue. On opening night the song received a slating from the critics. They found it oversentimental and crass. Needless to say, the ballad was quickly dropped from the show.

Unruffled by its dismissal, Fields and McHugh's belief in the song's commercial appeal remained intact. Fortunately they would only have to wait a few months longer before their big break in show business arrived.

If *The Jazz Singer* caused a tidal wave of concern throughout the theatrical world, then the opening of the Jerome Kern–Oscar Hammerstein musical *Show Boat* momentarily calmed the waters. If anything, it proved the pulling power of a live musical still existed. Ziegfeld's lavish production had all the trappings of a money-spinner and saw the crowds queuing endlessly round the block for the voyage.

1927 was also the year Mae West took on the establishment. Her performance on Broadway in *Sex* saw her arrested and charged with indecent behavior. During her trial, Miss West's defense pointed out that on opening night, at which officers from the police department were in attendance, there had been no complaints about her performance. However, the prosecution argued that in later shows she had sneaked in more graphic and suggestive lewdness. Her seductive charms and quick-witted humor did little to impress the judge. On April 19, the jury found her guilty and the judge sentenced her to a ten-day prison sentence and a fine of $500. For a static moment in time, it seemed as if the Roaring Twenties had momentarily burped to a halt.

For the first quarter of the year Adelaide continued her tour on the TOBA circuit in *Desires of 1927*—Memphis, New Orleans, Birmingham, Atlanta, Louisville and Cincinnati with a return visit to Chicago followed by Detroit and Columbus where the show finally folded in April. Her reviews were nothing short of sensational. Some critics claimed her to be the new Florence Mills. Others simply compared the two as equals. However one viewed the praise, most critics agreed that with the right vehicle Adelaide was now ready to take Broadway by storm.

It was during the show's return engagement in Chicago that fate dealt Adelaide's next card. Her growing popularity had not gone unnoticed by the city's powerful underworld figures. A temperamental fit of rage from her buddy Ethel Waters gave Adelaide her first contact with the machinations of Mafia nightlife and, in particular, with one gangster, Al Capone.

∿

When the American Government introduced the Volstead Act, known generally as Prohibition, on January 17, 1920, bootleg liquor with all its implications emerged. Still readily available behind closed doors of Mafia-owned restaurants, nightclubs, casinos and whorehouses, the next thirteen years saw the sale of illicit alcohol amass fortunes for its sponsors. Chicago boasted a hive of such establishments. Most were situated in the north–south boundary divide along South Wabash Avenue. The area was referred to locally as the Levee. Not only were underworld bosses beneficiaries of this newly acquired wealth, but certain politicians and police officers, whose jobs primarily were to enforce the Prohibition laws, were also discreetly included on the gangsters' pay-roll. The pay-offs were seen as an insurance policy, thereby protecting the mob establishments from police raids and certain closure.

Big Jim Colosimo headed the Sicilian Mafia syndicate from his headquarters in Chicago's South Side. As owner of the hugely popular Colosimo's Café on South Wabash Avenue, he commanded an air of respectability, behind which he confidently conducted his criminal dealings. Content with his success and the enormous revenue it generated, Colosimo arranged for his nephew, John Torrio, to help run the more mundane operations he controlled. As a small-time New York racketeer, Torrio was known for double-dealing. Frustrated by his uncle's powerful grip, Torrio secretly branched out into the vice business, opening his own gambling rooms and a brothel.

Torrio wired back to New York to enlist fellow cohort Al Capone to front the business operation. His scheming ambition to supersede Colosimo as vice boss came to a head. Seeing the limitless potential Prohibition offered, Torrio had his uncle gunned down in cold blood inside Colosimo's Café. By eliminating the opposition, Torrio now had the freedom to reap the profits.

With the acquisition of breweries that had been forced to close down, Torrio instigated a bootleg industry of his own. This move instantly increased his stature in Chicago's underworld. His consistent earning power brought a battle for control by competitors. An attempt on his life left Torrio severely injured and forced him to retreat to the relative sobriety of New York. Relinquishing his stranglehold left his second in command, Al Capone, in charge. Capone was inexperienced but determined and fought back to take control of Torrio's badly bruised empire.

As the largest industrial city in America, Chicago's economy thrived upon stability. When the Mafia took control things rapidly changed.

Through violence, murder and intimidation their lawless administration spread fear and panic. Their closed regime operated the highest concentration of organized crime in the world. With such high rewards at stake, life in the Windy City took on a rich kaleidoscope of power struggles that finally led to Capone successfully becoming as Chicago's overlord of crime.

Under Capone's reign, nightlife in Chicago flourished and its benefits filtered throughout the entertainment world. To take advantage of Prohibition, society had to push aside the restrictive barriers that governed it. In doing so, show business became fortuitously linked with the dangers and excitement that the underworld prospered upon.

Although its revues were on a smaller scale than those in Harlem, Chicago's cabaret clubs were fiercely competitive. Situated at 459 East 31st Street, the Café de Paris was the latest Mafia-owned supper club to compete for business. Costing an extravagant $65,000 to refurbish, the café, advertised as a "Parisian Palace," swung open its French doors to the public in November 1926. After a shaky start, its winter revue *Black Cargo*, starring the tempestuous Ethel Waters, saw the place packed. With Ethel at its helm, the café's reputation as a first-class supper club was guaranteed.

The establishment was fronted and managed by Martin B. Paley but the true proprietors of the café were C. Fleming Lewis and Al Capone. Obtaining their license to operate through influence rather than legal avenues, especially when other clubs in the area had had their applications turned down, caused considerable grievance amongst local underworld figures.

The Mafia were known for paying their star performers handsome salaries. Unfortunately, certain unwritten conditions were expected in return, one being the necessity to mix and socialize with their employers. To be seen acquainted with show business celebrities made the Mafia feel and look more socially acceptable.

Ethel Waters' exhausting ten-week contract began to take its toll upon her health. Weary and frustrated by the constant hostility she received from the management over her generous weekly salary, her temper finally snapped. On Friday March 4, 1927, in a fit of rage, she stormed out, canceling that evening's performance. In a desperate bid to find a replacement the café's manager, Martin Paley, called his booking agent for help.

By coincidence Adelaide was playing a return engagement at Chicago's Grand Theater in *Desires of 1927*. On the strength of its previous reviews, the show had sold out for its duration. After numerous frantic phone calls, Paley's agent successfully secured Adelaide and several cast members from *Desires* to cover for Ethel's disappearance. Adelaide's assistance would not go unrewarded. Capone was so impressed with her performance that he immediately offered her a contract to star in the café's next production, *Parisian Follies*. Scheduled to open on April 12, the revue's budget was to be double that of its predecessor.

Unfortunately, Adelaide had already signed a month's contract at the end of her term with *Desires of 1927* to appear at the Swiss Gardens in Cincinnati, Ohio.[1] The show commenced on April 18, so realistically her options were restricted. After swift negotiations between Adelaide's agent, Ralph Cooper, and Paley, a compromise was reached. Capone's determination to secure Adelaide's services led Paley to accept a crazy contract that allowed her to star in his revue for the first five nights yet still honor her engagement at the Swiss Gardens. When Adelaide left for Ohio, the vocalist Ada Brown was booked to take over. Adelaide had her first brush with Capone during rehearsals for the new show. He made it a regular habit to keep an eye on his employees, especially if they were famous and attractive.

From outside, the Café de Paris cleverly resembled a provincial French bistro with rows of tables and bentwood chairs neatly set out along the sidewalk, encouraging passers-by to stop for a coffee. The café's freshly baked buttered brioche was the best in town. Inside, the décor was more elaborate and reminiscent of the classic Art Nouveau epoch. Here, the menu was expensive and offered authentic French cuisine.

At great expense the café employed its own ten-piece orchestra, the Symphonic Syncopators, under the baton of maestro Dave Peyton. In the evening, dancing commenced at 10 p.m. followed at midnight by the main floorshow.

Adelaide's appearance in the Easter presentation of *Parisian Follies* caused quite a sensation in the Levee. As its name suggested, the production adopted a French flavor for its theme. Steeped in patriotism, the opening number, "Marseillaise," a jazzed-up rendition of the French national anthem, lit the torch for what would follow. As Dave Peyton struck up his band, out marched a troupe of bronzed beauties dressed in matching red, white and blue military outfits. Step-kicking as high as their elastic bloomers would allow, the girls performed a rousing tribute to the can-can dancers of the Folies-Bergère. As master of ceremonies, Lew Lamar introduced the cast. One by one, each performer's entrance received louder and more enthusiastic applause. To deliver his final announcement, Lamar stepped to one side of the stage:

"Ladies and Gentlemen, the Café de Paris has enormous pleasure in welcoming Harlem's brightest new celebrity and star of tonight's show. Please put your hands together and give a warm Chicago welcome to the one and only . . . Miss Adelaide Hall."

To the sound of a thunderous cannon explosion and the unfurling of numerous banner-size tricolor flags, the stage took on the sudden appearance of a battlefield. In the midst of the revolution, from behind a large drum, stepped an apparition—Adelaide. Caught in the flickering rays of a bright light, with arms outstretched as on the cross, she stood motionless. Wearing a blonde wig and a long, sleeveless white gown, her silky skin shimmered like a polished jewel. The effect was dazzling. With the crack of a drum roll, she burst into song, giving what can only be described as an uptempo rendition of the "Marseillaise." Rising to their feet, the audience whistled and cheered like a wild pack of howling coyotes. Even the French would have been impressed with the reception.

Compared to the extravagant spectacles French music halls offered, the number was clumsy and passé but this was Chicago and most of the punters hadn't traveled further than the borders of Illinois so, for all the wrong reasons, as an opening number, the pastiche worked. As the orchestra reached the last few bars of the song, the stage lights went cold and the tableau vanished.

In its review, the *Chicago Defender* praised the spectacle as "The most lavish parade number yet seen in a South Side café," and stated "the offering was another innovation in floor show entertainment."[2]

The Café de Paris became a victim of its own success.[3] A few weeks later, in the early hours of the morning, a black limousine was seen speeding along East 31st Street before it screeched to an ear-piercing halt directly outside the empty café. One of the passengers jumped out of the vehicle carrying a small package. He calmly placed the parcel on the sidewalk directly in front of the café's entrance, then leapt back into the car before it sped off into the night. Three minutes later a bomb ripped through the restaurant with the force of a hurricane, destroying its interior beyond recognition. Although the show came to an abrupt end, Adelaide's performance in *Parisian Follies* would remain in Al Capone's memory for a long time.[4]

Chicago was home to a large black community, in fact the largest outside of Harlem. Many Negroes had migrated to the city from the Southern states at the turn of the century in search of regular paid work. The south of the city was occupied largely by the ethnic populations. Chicago's black belt, known as the Stroll, stretched from 31st to 35th Street.

The area was controlled by its own Negro vice bosses, the most notorious being Bobb Motts and Henry Teenan Jones, who between them owned most of the neighborhood's colored entertainment venues. These included the Elite, Grand and Vendôme Theaters and the Deluxe, Dreamland and Sunset Cafés.

With such a thriving trade the Stroll became a Mecca for musicians, actors, hookers and equally varied professionals. Unlike New York's clubs, Chicago's black nightspots had no discrimination policy, allowing Negroes and whites to mix freely. At nightfall, the wild hypnotic rhythms of jazz charged the air with energy and packed the Stroll with so many club hoppers, one could have easily been forgiven for thinking you were in Harlem.

No matter what its reputation, Chicago was a hip city to be in. Every street corner generated style and class. It was, after all, the home of Al Capone. If jazz created an aura of chic, then its performers were seen as purveyors of high fashion. Adelaide certainly developed a special love–hate relationship with the city. She loved its citizens but hated what the city represented. It was an affair that was reciprocal and long-standing and one that rewarded her with many friendships.

After her engagement in Cincinnati, the lure of Chicago drew Adelaide back for a residency at the Sunset Café.[5] Known to be mob-owned, it was a tough place to play and raided regularly by the police. This time her contract lasted three months, during which time she starred in two successive shows. The first, *Sunset Revue*, ended on July 10. That was succeeded by *Sunset Glories*, which opened on July 15.[6] Both revues were produced by Percy Venables and packed with talented black acts, including Edith Wilson, Jazz Lips Richardson, Cab Calloway and Louis Armstrong.

As one of the Stroll's premier supper clubs, the Sunset Café hosted some of the best jazz in town. Housed in a long, narrow, ornately decorated room, its limited size made the restaurant appear more intimate than it actually was. Along the full length of the furthest wall stood a slightly raised platform on which played the twelve-piece orchestra. Directly in front, beneath a pleated fabric canopy, stretched a wooden dance floor on which stood two grand pianos, one at either end. Without the luxury of a stage to appear on, the evening's cabaret was expected to perform directly in front of the seated clientele. It was during Adelaide's residency at the Sunset Café that one very important friendship developed.

The house orchestra, Armstrong's Sunset Café Stompers, had created quite a buzz about town. Among its ranks were many notable musicians, including the violinists Erskine Tate and Caroll Dickerson, the pianist Earl Hines and, of course, its leader, Louis Armstrong, on trumpet.[7]

At a certain point in the show, Armstrong would step down from the dais on to the dance floor and accompany the evening's featured artist. His happy-go-lucky character made him an instant favorite with the punters. At first, his forays into the spotlight caused him much anxiety but with time he learnt to relax and grew to enjoy the experience.

Armstrong had recently developed a style of vocalizing that used the voice as an instrument. Some called it meaningless sounds—Bop, De-Bop—put to music. The technique was later termed scat. He had just recorded "Heebie Jeebies," the first record to incorporate such a vocal. Scat singing is best described as the technique of translating percussive patterns into vocal lines by assigning certain syllables to characteristic rhythms. By coincidence, Adelaide had also experimented with wordless vocalizing. It was a common practice of hers to scat along to new songs she hadn't yet learnt the lyrics to, something she had regularly done at rehearsals for years.

The prospect of a scat duet between Adelaide and Armstrong during their Sunset Café residency seemed inevitable and too good an opportunity to miss. It seems more than probable that Adelaide expanded her technique under Armstrong's guidance. Although it's never been acknowledged in print before, Adelaide did confirm to me that Armstrong certainly influenced her greatly during this period by encouraging her to utilize the full potential of her voice. The rapport between them during their impromptu duets on stage, with their two vocals intertwined around a melody, must have been as intense as an illicit love affair. In later years, Armstrong referred to this period in Chicago as the happiest time of his life.

Adelaide returned to New York in October and the series of events that followed altered the course of her career dramatically. The star of a revue was suddenly taken ill and Adelaide was asked to cover temporarily. The revue could have been either *Messin' Around* at the Plantation Café or *Jazzmania* at Harlem's Lafayette Theater.[8] Annoyingly, as Adelaide was a last-minute replacement her name was not advertised in the press, so it's difficult to ascertain which revue it was. The offer to appear in a show, as a stand-in, for a short period was not very tempting. However, the fact that one of the hottest bands in New York, Duke Ellington's Washingtonians, was on the same bill, may well have swayed her decision. Adelaide accepted.

≈≈≈

"And now, 'Creole Love Call,' . . . I shall never forget 1927. I was three weeks old that year" was how Duke Ellington later referred to this extraordinary year. It was the year Adelaide and Ellington both savored their first real taste of success in the recording industry.

Adelaide's account of how "Creole Love Call" was originally conceived, which she vehemently stuck to over the years, is an interesting story to relate from an historical point of view. It also gives an insight into how Duke Ellington conducted his songwriting during this period.

Adelaide was singing in the first half of the show and Ellington's Washingtonians were performing in the second. After her set, Adelaide returned to her backstage dressing-room to change out of her stage outfit. During her performance, Ellington's band had accompanied her from the orchestra pit. For his own program, Duke had the band's instruments repositioned on stage. Just before the second act began, Adelaide made a dash from her dressing-room to catch Duke's set. Standing in the wings, obscured from the band by a wing drop, Adelaide got the best view in the house.

When the music hotted up, so did Adelaide and the sound of her improvised scat vocal began to carry effortlessly across the stage. Looking around in bewilderment, Duke became more and more intrigued as to where the mystery voice was coming from. When the band struck up "Creole Love Call" Adelaide's vocal knocked Duke off his piano stool. The counter-melody she improvised was the melody he had been searching for to complete the song. Unable to contain his curiosity any longer, he rushed off stage into the wings and to his astonishment found Adelaide singing her heart out. Duke grabbed hold of her arm and immediately led her back on stage.

"Whatever you're singing, Addie, keep doing it. We'll start again from the top."

After quietening the band, Duke turned to face the audience and made a brief announcement.

"Ladies and gentlemen there's going to be a slight change in the program. Please put your hands together and welcome back Miss Adelaide Hall. She'll be joining us for the next number, 'Creole Love Call.'"

Adelaide repeated what she had been singing backstage, in front of the audience. At the end of the number she received the loudest ovation of the night. Sensing he had got a sure-fire hit on his hands Duke then made her repeat the song as an encore. Before leaving the stage Duke whispered in her ear, "Addie, don't forget what you've just sung. We'll record it in the next couple of days."

26 OCTOBER 1927

Adelaide looked across at the telephone impatiently. It hadn't rung all morning. "How immediate is urgent?" she thought to herself. Having wasted most of the morning cooped up indoors waiting for Duke's call, her frustration finally took its toll.

"That's it," she snapped angrily, "I've waited long enough." Then, as if to rid herself of any negative thoughts, she decided she had far more pressing matters to attend to. After fastening the top button on her coat, she gathered up her belongings and headed out to the shops. No sooner had the front door slammed behind her than she stopped, dead in her tracks.

"Would you believe it?" she yelled in exasperation, as the dull trill from a phone rang in the distance.

"Hang on, I'll be there in a second," she hollered whilst fumbling through her handbag for the door keys. Once back inside the apartment she managed to get to the phone just in time to catch Duke on the end of the line issuing instructions.

"I've got a session booked this afternoon at Victor Recording Studios. I'll see you in half an hour at my manager's office at 150 West 46th Street, and don't be late, it's costing me money," then without so much as a "how are you?" he slammed the receiver down.

Victor Talking Machine Company was located on the outskirts of Philadelphia in Camden, New Jersey. Known principally for their phonograph machines, "Victrolas," the company had also built a record-pressing plant on site. A subsidiary of the company was the Victor record label, devoted solely to promoting race and hillbilly music. They also had two recording studios, one in New York and the other—a disused church, which they had converted—in Camden.

As director of the Artist and Repertoire Department, Ralph Peer was responsible for signing up new artists to the label. Peer had an ear for spotting fresh talent but, more importantly for the company, talent that sold bucket loads of records. He had already been responsible for signing Fletcher Henderson, Fats Waller and Jelly Roll Morton on to the label's roster and was now keen to sign up Duke Ellington.

With the steady increase worldwide in phonogram sales, record royalties often supplemented an entertainer's career, especially during "rest" periods. In the Twenties, radio rarely broadcast records—live music was the standard. Unlike the theater, though, radio didn't discriminate. Over the airwaves, an audience had very little chance of knowing if a particular vocalist was black or white. Singing live on the radio would, hopefully, generate high record sales for the artist.

"Creole Love Call" took only two takes to "can."[9] Upon its release, the record attracted both outrage and praise from the media and public alike. The controversy that ensued resulted in a flurry of attention for the artists and high demand for the record.

In his diary, New York columnist Edmund Wilson recounted an incident relating to the record's release.[10] It occurred during a leisurely afternoon walk along upper Broadway in the company of the wealthy socialite, Margaret Canby.

Whilst passing a phonograph store, they heard music emanating from a megaphone installed above the shop doorway. Inspired by its melody, Wilson spontaneously rushed in and purchased a copy, thinking it to be the latest composition by Gershwin in one of his more serious moods. When he got back to his apartment, Wilson played the recording only to discover to his horror that it wasn't what he had expected at all. Nothing short of a monstrosity that seemingly conjured up evil forces from the devil was how he described the recording.

"I'll never believe in God again, never believe in anything again," he exclaimed to his bemused friend Margaret and, as if an exorcism were in order to rid the vile recording of its immorality, she suggested they paste prayers of love, God and the resurrection upon it.

Why a wordless vocal should provoke such an outcry of hostility is unfathomable, but it did . . . and with far-reaching consequences. From that moment onwards, life for Adelaide and Ellington would never be the same. It wasn't as if the song was heralding the end of civilization, let alone the birth of an anti-Christ. In trying to understand Wilson's outrage, one can only assume his powerful imagination had played an illusory game upon his ear. However, over the coming weeks it transpired that Wilson was not the only person to hold such a viewpoint.

During the recording industry's brief history, such blatant sexual overtones had never been captured on a phonograph disc before. In the puritanical minds of certain factions of the American public, Adelaide, the seductress, had overstepped the mark of decency and public morality was deemed to be at risk. When a journalist asked her what she had been thinking about whilst recording the track, Adelaide declined to answer, thereby unwittingly adding more fuel to the fire.

Was this the prime reason why the recording attracted so much attention? I believe not. The timing of its release also played a crucial role in helping it achieve mass recognition.

Ever since *Shuffle Along* had popularized Negro talent, jazz had steadily progressed into the mainstream to become the vogue of a new generation. Charged on adrenaline, this spirited breed of hedonist felt no inhibitions about displaying their idiosyncratic behavior in public. They perfected and reveled in the art of shocking those who decried their every move. For them, "Creole Love Call" became a battle cry.

"Hey! . . . Look at me, I'm in control of my own destiny," purportedly yelled the novelist and guru of the movement, F. Scott Fitzgerald, whilst perched upon the roof of a taxi. As it drove down Fifth Avenue, he taunted bemused passers-by with a bottle of champagne toasting them one by one. Such reckless living typified the values of his doctrine.

From a rudimentary stance, little of the record's magic can be discovered from dissecting the musical arrangement. As it stands, it's fair to say Adelaide's effortless vocal steals the production from right under Ellington's baton to transcend even his expectations. From the moment her ululating vocal is first heard one could forgive the listener for thinking it was the sound of an instrument and not the human voice. Like smoke plumes drifting slowly towards a ventilation shaft, the melody lingers in your mind long after you've heard it. For me, the song evokes the impression of unrequited love. The captured effect is one of pure unadulterated passion. No wonder the bible bashers saw fit to denounce its release. Honest lust never did figure high in their vocabulary.

Perhaps, in essence, Adelaide's vocal captured the voice of an oppressed race, enslaved through decades of enforced persecution at the hands of its captors.[11] If so, by touching such a nerve, she would have automatically fired the public's imagination into controversy.

Ellington must have thought an angel had fallen out of the clouds when he first heard Adelaide singing in the wings. Her counter-melody was certainly a flash of inspiration. She claimed she merely responded to his simple eight-note piano melody. To her ears, the song sounded incomplete and lacked a hook. The dips and peaks of her vocal response not only produced that hook; they completed the song.

Ellington recognized this fact instantly and pounced. As with the song's main chord sequence, which he borrowed from King Oliver's classic "Camp Meeting Blues," Ellington had every intention of acquiring Adelaide's melody on permanent loan. In the days when the infringement of copyright laws were wide open to abuse, Ellington's manager, Irving Mills, knew exactly how to take full advantage of the loopholes. Rather stupidly and to his cost, King Oliver never registered himself as the composer of "Camp Meeting Blues." By coincidence, Ellington's clarinetist, Rudy Jackson, had previously played in King Oliver's band and it was he who introduced Ellington to the song.

To understand the copyright laws in the Twenties, one must remember that most black musicians had no manager and were usually refused copyright protection by any agent, publisher or record company that might show an interest in one of their compositions.

For some unknown reason, Ellington regularly changed the name of his band during this period in his career, adding more confusion to the issue. From the Washingtonians he changed the name to Duke Ellington's Band and for "Creole Love Call" amended it to Duke Ellington and his Orchestra. The disc credited Ellington, Bubber Miley and Rudy Jackson as the songwriters. When he came to copyright the song, Miley and Jackson's names were mysteriously omitted, leaving only Ellington's name listed as the composer. Jackson's dissatisfaction over the omission led him to quit the orchestra. The fact that Adelaide wrote the counter-melody has never been disputed. The fact that her name was not credited as such on either the record or the copyright has been a contentious issue ever since. To set the record straight historically once and for all, as Adelaide repeatedly explained in interviews throughout her career, she composed the counter-melody but was never credited as such on the copyright.

After the record's release, both Adelaide and Ellington's careers took a dynamic leap forward. Unbeknown to them at the time, their sudden juxtaposition gave jazz a temporary benchmark, from which future recordings could be viewed. They would have to wait for history to carve its granite niche before the full importance of the recording would rightfully be recognized.

LIKE A CANDLE BURNING AT BOTH ENDS . . .

Following her resounding success in London and Paris, Florence Mills was all set to repeat the process on Broadway. However, as soon as she returned to New York, she underwent an emergency appendectomy that went drastically wrong.

A second operation and blood transfusion left Florence in a coma. Her surgeon believed it would be a miracle if she recovered. On Tuesday November 1, in the early hours of the morning, she finally lost her battle to regain consciousness.[12] The death of Florence Mills caused a sudden turn in Adelaide's life and closed the first chapter in the history of black musical theater. A miracle is something that causes one to wonder. So too does tragedy.

Florence's death shocked America's black community, and sent ripples of grief throughout the world of entertainment. The people of Harlem, especially, felt her passing and wept openly in the streets, grieving the loss of their own little songbird.

Florence had just arrived back in New York after completing an exhaustive European tour starring in *Blackbirds of 1926*. The trip had been an enormous success. Her appeal lay in her quirky looks and innocent manner. With lightly tanned skin and wide eyes, she looked almost boyish. On stage she seemed vulnerable and slightly awkward, as if she were lost, but when she sang, her voice reached out and touched every heart in the house. "One couldn't help but love her," professed London's top producer, C. B. Cochran, who called her "The greatest performer that ever graced a stage." Sadly, she never released any recordings and no film footage of her act exists.

Lew Leslie had managed her career for five years during which his shrewdness and Florence's continual hard work had seen her attain the distinction of becoming the highest earning black female in show business.

Her determination to succeed ultimately weakened her fragile body to exhaustion. The light that shines twice as bright only burns half as long. That fate should deal such a cruel and callous blow in the hour of her finest glory made her untimely death seem even sadder and more poignant.

Leslie was determined to stage his protegée's funeral as an unforgettable tribute to a remarkable career. Harlem rose to the occasion. The funeral was bigger than that of Rudolph Valentino. Her body lay in state in a $10,000 bronze coffin at Howell's Chapel on 137th Street for five days. Ten thousand people filed past her coffin daily to pay their last respects.

The funeral took place on Sunday November 6. During the procession the whole of Harlem came to a standstill. Over 200,000 people lined the streets to watch. The motionless crowds stood in eerie silence as they waited for the cortege. Only the occasional sound of a bystander weeping broke the hush. As the coffin left the chapel, hidden beneath a blanket of roses, mayhem broke loose. Some spectators found their emotions too difficult to control and sobbed uncontrollably. Others called her name as if to try and awaken her. People pushed forward in desperation to touch the coffin; in the rush many fell to the ground. Those who were too overwhelmed simply fainted on the spot. The police tried valiantly to keep control but they too felt incapable of responding.

Lew Leslie led the procession. Forty flower girls carrying baskets of rose buds walked in front of the hearse. Eight honorary pallbearers, who were all close friends of Florence, filed behind the funeral car. Dressed in matching two-piece costumes made from gray crepe de Chine with close-fitting cloche hats, they included Ethel Waters, Lottie Gee, Gertrude Saunders, Aida Ward and Adelaide. Behind them drove a fleet of limousines conveying wreaths. Many of Florence's contemporaries from the entertainment world including Duke Ellington, Al Jolson, Miller and Lyles, Sissle and Blake, Paul Whiteman, Fred and Adele Astaire, and Bojangles joined the procession. Directly behind the hearse walked Florence's distraught husband, Ulysses "Kid" Thompson, who was comforted by close relatives. A program of solemn music played by a simple jazz band provided accompaniment along the route.

Though the funeral procession was very somber, there was a touch of humor. Leslie arranged for a group of well-known comedians to attend, dressed as minstrels, wearing ill-fitting costumes and crooked top hats. At one point along the route, the road surface became slightly uneven and created an unexpected dip. As the cortege moved over the uneven road surface several of the comedians lost their balance and stumbled, creating an amusing diversion for the onlookers.

The service took place at Harlem's Mother Zion Church. The flowers used to decorate its interior were estimated to have cost over $100,000. After the service the coffin was finally laid to rest at Woodlawn Cemetery. By Florence's graveside stood an enormous tower of roses, eight feet high, attached to which was a card that read simply "From a Friend." It was suggested the friend was the Prince of Wales, the future Edward VIII, who was said to have seen her perform over twenty times at London's Pavilion Theatre. Leslie arranged for a flock of blackbirds to be released overhead from an airplane at the exact moment her coffin was lowered into the ground. As they flew off, it is said, another flock of blackbirds, unordered, appeared from nowhere and flew over her grave.

If S. George Ullman had been accused of staging Rudolph Valentino's funeral to gain the maximum amount of publicity from it, then Lew Leslie co-ordinated Florence Mills' funeral like the finale in a Broadway musical.

DANCE MANIA

To the casual onlooker, Harlem appeared to dance non-stop. It had now become essential not only for a show's producer to commission a composer to write new songs but also to showcase a new dance to accompany them. Trying to keep track of all the complicated dance routines became a full-time headache for choreographers. If a new dance became fashionable with the public, it automatically helped boost record and manuscript sales for the song's composer.

Dance Mania opened at Harlem's Lafayette Theater on Monday November 14 to a wildly expectant audience. In spirit, the show captured the public's fascination with young girls wiggling their bodies around like contortionists. The choreography exhibited an array of current dance crazes and held the audience in a perpetual state of exhilaration.

It had been just over two weeks since Adelaide and Ellington recorded "Creole Love Call." Rumors were rife that Adelaide might be joining the Ellington band full time as its lead vocalist. Pairing the couple in his latest venture was a clever move on behalf of the show's producer, Clarence Robinson. It gave the public further grounds for speculating that the hottest gossip on the circuit could well be true. The publicity certainly attracted swift business at the box office.

The opening night was to be Adelaide's first publicized appearance at the theater for over a year since her acclaimed role in *Desires of 1927*. In a sense, the audience, many of whom in real life were her neighbors, came along to welcome her home.

With Ellington providing musical accompaniment from the pit, the fast pace of the show was assured. Not only would he get bums on seats but also off them, jiggling in the aisles. Lafayette audiences were well known for showing their appreciation by physically joining in with the musical numbers. At times, the auditorium would take on the lively atmosphere of a party. If the audience liked a song, they would holler for it to be repeated, adding considerably to the running time of the show.

Far from being a spectacular, *Dance Mania* was assembled to fit a tight budget. With little scenery, few props and costumes that would appear tame and uninteresting to a seasoned Broadway theatergoer, the show was standard fodder on the black theater circuit and easily rehearsed within a matter of days. In order to attract a wider audience, ticket prices were kept low, as little as 75 cents for a matinée performance. By all accounts, the show's producer, Clarence Robinson, was a master of many disguises. He dipped his hand into every aspect of the show, from its conception through to the finished product. He also danced in several numbers and, in-between, even found time to compere the evening. The cast found Robinson a nightmare to work for but his vision assured the theater management the top results they expected.

The revue consisted of the usual array of diverse variety acts that the public expected to see in such a production. The comedy duo Joyner and Foster took credit for gaining the most laughs during the evening and Lena Wilson, having just returned to the States after touring Europe with Florence Mills and the *Blackbirds* troupe, belted out a couple of knee-trembling blues numbers.

The show had two acts. Adelaide starred in the first and Ellington in the second. As a headliner, Adelaide had the luxury of a dance troupe—Twelve Dance Mania Maidens—to back her. Their job was to mirror Adelaide's movements and enhance her performance. On opening night, Robinson's wrath saw one of the Maidens fired on the spot, simply for stepping out of line during a routine. He need not have fretted: hidden in the orchestra pit, Ellington's band proved the best accompaniment a girl could ever ask for. In reviewing Adelaide's performance the *Age* confirmed what the audience already knew, "She can dance and sing and strum on a ukulele to one's unbounded delight."[13]

Dance Mania came at the height of heady Harlemism and the revue encompassed a whole variety of dance crazes. Many dances, including the Charleston, Black Bottom, Monkey Hunch and Shim Sham Shimmy had caught the public's imagination during the past few years. By cleverly placing them all together in one show, Robinson created a mass retrospective of black modern dance unsurpassed at that moment in time.

After the interval, Ellington took to the stage and for the next forty minutes proceeded to melt the hearts of every female in the theater. Tall, debonair and extremely handsome, women found his charismatic personality irresistible. At the end of his set, Adelaide reappeared on stage to add vocals to "Creole Love Call" and "The Blues I Love To Sing."

The show was hailed as one of the best the Lafayette had ever staged and received plaudits from the media and public alike. "Adelaide Hall delights Lafayette audience" announced the *Amsterdam News* and, in a prophetic statement, proclaimed "If Miss Hall can continue to enrapture audiences, as she did at the Lafayette on opening night, the world will soon hear a lot more of her."[14]

A strange quirk of fate steered Adelaide and Ellington's next career move along the same path. Harlem's Cotton Club was hunting for a new resident band to replace Andy Preer's Missourians after Andy Preer's death. Numerous bands had been auditioned but none were thought suitable. Dorothy Fields and Jimmy McHugh had been commissioned to write the next revue's score and it was McHugh's recommendation that prompted the Cotton Club's manager, Herman Stark, to go hear the Ellington band at the Lafayette. According to a band member, after the show, Ellington joined Stark for a drink in a tavern adjoining the theater. Although Ellington was under contract to tour with *Dance Mania*, it was here he secretly signed a contract for his orchestra to perform at the Cotton Club.

After its run at the Lafayette, *Dance Mania* hit the road for a short tour. First stop on the itinerary was a two-week engagement at Gibson's Standard Theater in Philadelphia.

Unbeknown to Adelaide and the rest of the cast, Ellington had no intention of seeing the tour through. News got back to Stark that Ellington had left New York and was performing in Philadelphia when he should have already commenced rehearsals at the Cotton Club. Before the week's end, Ellington and his band were summoned back to Harlem. It later transpired that Stark had contacted an underworld boss in Philadelphia to help persuade the Gibson's theater manager to release Ellington from his contract. "Be big or you'll be dead," he was warned. The trick worked and Ellington defected back to New York, leaving the cast of *Dance Mania* stranded.[15] With a temporary replacement band, the cast rallied round to fulfill the remaining week's contract. At the end of her Philadelphia engagement Adelaide also returned to New York where an unexpected proposition awaited her.

The aftermath of Florence Mills' death had left the black community starved of a female role model and Lew Leslie without a major star.[16] Adelaide fitted that role perfectly. Her good looks, charm and exceptional talent had already steered her career to the top of the black show-business ladder. Her next career move was to make the transition over to the white circuit. Leslie knew exactly how to help her make that transition. His proposal was simple: "I'll make you into the biggest black female star on Broadway." Adelaide's decision was not a difficult one to make.

Leslie immediately began preparations for his next revue. His swift announcement to the press that Adelaide would take the leading role in his next major production gave the Hall–Hicks household an almighty jolt and Adelaide's career a new dimension.

On December 4, Duke Ellington and his Orchestra opened uptown at Harlem's Cotton Club in *Rhythmania*, a specially written revue that included songs by Dorothy Fields and Jimmy McHugh. It was the first revue they had collaborated on. Four weeks later downtown, Adelaide would open at the plush Ambassadeurs Club in Lew Leslie's *Blackbird Revue*, the second show scored by Fields and McHugh.

In the meantime, no sooner had Ellington and his orchestra commenced their residency at the Cotton Club than record sales of "Creole Love Call" took off. Its sudden popularity put Ellington and the club's management in a dilemma . . . should the song be included in the show? The problem was Ellington found it difficult to perform the song live without Adelaide's vocal. In practical terms there seemed only one solution—to install Adelaide temporarily in the Cotton Club revue. Sensing such a collaboration would create real public interest, the management hastily contacted Bert. In an unprecedented move—inserting a hit song after the show had premiered—for the month of December Adelaide was added to the program of *Rhythmania* as featured vocalist on "Creole Love Call."[17] To complement the number, the producer Dan Healy choreographed an evocative dance duet featuring Paul Meeres and Lita Rose that left little to the imagination.

To celebrate Adelaide's newly signed contract with Lew Leslie, Bert threw a surprise dinner party at a smart restaurant on Seventh Avenue that served the best fried chicken and waffles in Harlem. The guest list included her mother and other family members as well as various black celebrities from the entertainment world.

Bert made the fatal mistake of announcing to the manager in advance who the guests would be. In response, the management decided they could use the occasion to create good publicity for the restaurant. The local press were tipped off and the manager went to town with decorations. Anticipating a large crowd of onlookers might turn up he hired a doorman for the evening and had roped barriers erected outside the entrance. As often happens in a tightly knit community, rumors of the party spread around the neighborhood like wildfire. The restaurant had large plate-glass windows on either side of its entrance that gave a clear view inside to passers-by. A table for twenty guests was booked for nine-thirty. By eight o'clock, the place was already full to capacity and crowds of curious onlookers had begun to gather outside on the sidewalk.

Neither Bert nor any of the other invited guests had any idea of what lay ahead. By nine o'clock, the sidewalk was blocked with eager pedestrians all waiting to catch a glimpse of Florence Mills' successor. The situation rapidly became chaotic and the local police were called in to take control. The first guests were met with unbelievable scenes of confusion. What was to have been a quiet private affair had developed into a public spectacle. With each celebrity's arrival, the cameras flashed brighter and the crowds pushed further forward to get a closer look. At nine-thirty, Elizabeth Hall and her brother Frank drew up in a taxi.

Although they were ushered inside the restaurant safely, Frank's concern for Adelaide prompted him to telephone Bert immediately to forewarn him of the situation.

Frank's call was too late. Bert's car had already departed.

By the time Bert drove into Seventh Avenue within close proximity of the restaurant, the sidewalk had become besieged. Confused by the disturbance, Bert's second mistake was to park close to the entrance. When the doorman recognized Adelaide, he rushed across to open her car door. The crowd surged forward to catch a glimpse. Fearing for Adelaide's safety, Bert leapt from the driver's seat and ran round to help protect her. In a moment of panic he began to push aside violently anyone who got in his way. Several bystanders, thinking he was a member of the public, grew aggravated by his behavior and fists began to fly. A fight flared up. In the following confusion Adelaide became trapped amidst the throng. Police efforts to release her only pinned the crowd tighter against the restaurant walls. The crush shattered a windowpane, scattering glass upon bystanders. Hysterical screams rang from inside the restaurant. In all, it took the full force of truncheon-wielding police officers before Adelaide was finally freed and returned to the car, shaken but luckily unscathed. Bert was not so lucky; he received a bruised eye and a battered self-esteem. They never did get to eat their celebratory dinner.

When the image becomes real, fantasy turns into reality. With the mass radio exposure "Creole Love Call" generated and her ascension to the throne as Florence Mills' successor, Adelaide's fame spread much further than Harlem. Overnight, her name became etched into the American public's consciousness.

. . . The madness of Queen Adelaide had commenced.

PART II

FOUR AND TWENTY BLACKBIRDS
BAKED IN A PIE

1928–29

Sing a song of sixpence, a pocket full of rye,
Four and twenty blackbirds baked in a pie.
When the pie was opened the birds began to sing.
Wasn't that a dainty dish to put before the King!

BLACKBIRDS

In 1928, musical theater on Broadway peaked. The quality of works was astoundingly high and audiences clambered for tickets to see such hit shows as *The Three Musketeers*, *Rosalie*, *Show Boat* and *Funny Face*.

Up against such stiff competition, no one could have predicted the impact Lew Leslie's next venture was to have on the Great White Way, least of all the man himself. The show captured the public's heart and imagination like no other black revue before or after, and clocked up an astonishing 518 performances, a Broadway record for an all-black production that it still holds to this day. Its catchy songs are as memorable as one's first love affair. The revue's remarkable success helped many of its cast establish a lifetime's career in show business. In retrospect, it therefore comes as no coincidence to note that Harlem's Renaissance reached its zenith when, on May 9, the curtain rose at 42nd Street's Liberty Theater to reveal Lew Leslie's latest and greatest production . . .

BLACKBIRDS OF 1928

January, New York, Les Ambassadeurs nightclub
Leslie had matured into a steam-rolling fireball entrepreneur. His stable of artists had grown into an impressive coterie and represented some of the finest talented black performers in the country. Aida Ward, Edith

Wilson, Johnny Hudgins, Tim Moore, Gertrude Saunders, Lottie Gee and the bandleader Will Vodery, to name but a few, were all discovered and managed by Leslie's organization. Being a clever businessman, Leslie featured most of his artists in his own presentations, thereby guaranteeing his 20 per cent management fee was always paid on time.

Announcing Adelaide as Miss Mills' successor was tricky and would obviously have provoked doubts and suspicion in the eyes of the public.[1] It wasn't Leslie's position to give her such a label. Her ascension would be determined by recognition, not hype. For Adelaide the role was the most coveted and challenging of her career. Stepping into the glare of another person's persona and hoping to further one's own career in the process is, invariably, a risky move. Somehow Leslie had to package Adelaide as an artist in her own right without any stigma of comparison. To develop her role away from media scrutiny, Leslie originally announced the show would first tour Europe before playing Broadway.[2] Dissatisfied with her salary, which she found unsatisfactory for the duration of time to be spent abroad, Adelaide stubbornly refused to sign the contract. As no compromise could be reached, the show opened in New York.

As with previous productions Leslie previewed his new show at a supper club. Sensing the public's interest would be considerable, following the enormous publicity generated by Florence Mills' death, he staged it at Les Ambassadeurs, one of the largest and swankiest restaurants in Manhattan. Known to be expensive—the cover charge was $3 a head—its exclusive reputation afforded Leslie the perfect platform from which to launch his latest venture.

For want of a better title he chose *The Blackbird Revue*. The name allowed the public familiarity without presumption and Leslie the freedom to maneuver, evolve and rework the content. Revues were easy for an audience to navigate around. With no restricting story line to adhere to, it was the ideal vehicle in which to introduce new talent.

Leslie's pick of supporting artists was chosen to enhance Adelaide's role yet still create individual interest. His ace in the pack was Miss Mills' husband—the dancer Ulysses "Kid" Thompson. The tenor Eddie Gray from the Three Eddies was hired as M.C., Brown and McGraw led the specialty dance routines and Will Vodery's Band provided musical accompaniment.

As an arranger, Vodery was in great demand. During the day he helped run the auditions for Ziegfeld's proposed London production of *Show Boat*, which some said made him the most popular guy in Harlem. Ziegfeld also offered to employ him in the musical full time. The offer was a difficult one to refuse, especially as Paul Robeson was cast in the leading role.

Blackbirds' premiere, advertised for December 29, 1927, came just in time for New Year's Eve celebrations.[3] Frustratingly for Leslie, an electrical fault delayed the opening until January 4. Such was the scramble for bookings that the management issued preferred table position passes for preferential guests, creating élitist segregation within an already upper-class establishment.

Situated on 57th Street in the heart of the theater district, Les Ambassadeurs had an air of Parisian gentility to it, acquired from its former incarnation as Le Perroquet de Paris. The maître d'hôtel and most of the waiters were of foreign stock and were encouraged to use French colloquialisms, which added to the club's ambiance. The orchestra performed from a raised balcony that overlooked a glass dance floor beneath which colored lights shimmered. Circular tables draped with crisp white linen seated over 500 diners who enjoyed the best French cuisine this side of the Seine.

Jimmy McHugh, who had composed the score for the revue, had only recently begun collaborating with the lyricist Dorothy Fields. Both writers were relatively new to Broadway and the project gave them the ideal vehicle to test each other's abilities. When the score was completed, Fields and McHugh hand delivered it to Leslie's office. It soon became apparent their partnership worked beautifully. Leslie had an old upright piano in his office on which Fields and McHugh ran through their numbers. Each song seemed catchier than the last. After listening attentively to them all, Leslie asked if they might have what he termed, "A crooning ballad that could also be used as a dance number."

"We have one we wrote last year that might just be what you're looking for," enthused Dorothy.

To begin with McHugh ran through the song unaccompanied on the piano. Leslie listened in silence. When the chorus hit, Dorothy joined in singing the lyrics:

I can't give you anything but love, baby.
That's the only thing I've plenty of, baby.
Dream awhile, scheme awhile, we're sure to find
Happiness and, I guess, all those things you've always pined for.
Gee, I'd like to see you looking swell, baby.
Diamond bracelets Woolworth doesn't sell, baby.
'Til that lucky day, you know darn well, baby,
I can't give you anything but love.

By the end of the song, Leslie knew he was on to a winner. After only one hearing, the melody had become embedded in his brain.

"That's the one," shouted Leslie, elated by what he had just heard. "If it can make the hairs on the back of my neck erect," he mused, "just think what it'll do to the public's follicles."

"I must warn you, though," interrupted McHugh, "this song's deceptive. It's already been in a show and was thrown out at the last minute."

"Listen," effused Leslie, "I don't give a damn what's happened to this song in the past. I'm gonna make it into the biggest hit in the country. Mark my words, today will go down as one of the most memorable in Broadway's history of popular music."

Leslie was a great believer in fate and intuition but never before had he experienced the two phenomena simultaneously. He was also convinced that any tune would become memorable, no matter how good or bad it was, if it was heard often enough. To pound it into the audience's subconscious, his theory demanded the reprise of "I Can't Give You Anything But Love, Baby" to be played three times throughout the show without raising suspicion from the critics. Of course, this didn't take into account any encores that might be requested. Leslie was determined that this little baby wasn't getting away without clocking up at least a million in sheet music sales.

Since the song's failure in *Delmar's Revels*, Dorothy had reworked the lyrics. Legend has it that in her quest for inspiration she went for a walk along Fifth Avenue and stopped outside Tiffany's store to gaze into the jewelry windows. Whilst peering at the splendid goods on display she overheard an impoverished courting couple admiring engagement rings. The man said to his girlfriend, "Gee, honey, I'd like to get you a sparkler like that right now, but I can't give you nothin' but love." The scenario became the vision Dorothy had been searching for.

Variety gave a lengthy, if somewhat mediocre, review of the show's opening at Les Ambassadeurs.[4] As Leslie had feared, comparisons were made between Adelaide and Florence Mills. "Miss Hall does not approach being a Florence Mills," bitched the critic, "nor even a Gertrude Saunders," he continued to hammer. Although praise was forthcoming for her "vocal callisthenics" and "torrid" rendition of semi-ballads, which he found becoming and more to his taste, his overall impression was not laudatory. He felt the production had been compromised and tailored to suit a white palate and lacked the abandonment of native Harlem. He also debased the all-black cast by claiming they tried to "out do the whites for class." However, he did compliment Leslie on his efforts in transforming the spacious club into a warm atmospheric environment and, taking all things into consideration, ended on a more favorable note by admitting the Broadway mob would probably find the club "a great bet."

Unruffled by the tepid media response, Leslie set to work formulating future plans for the production. If it were to transfer to a Broadway stage, he would need to enlarge the cast and feature more supporting artists. With this in mind he wired Josephine Baker in Paris.[5] Josephine swiftly wired back with news that she intended to go back to New York in March and was keen to discuss the matter further upon her return.[6] Surprisingly, Josephine never did make it back to the States in 1928. Her agenda took another course, an action she no doubt regretted for the rest of her life.

On February 15, vocalist Aida Ward was added to the bill. Aida was talented but headstrong and had a fearful temper.[7] Although she was recruited as a supporting vocalist, her potential as a lead was obvious. It was her bad attitude that let her down. She had recently starred at the Cotton Club for a short period on the same bill as Edith Wilson and Duke Ellington. Her disagreeable nature brought her into conflict with the orchestra which led to the show's producer, Dan Healy, issuing her with a final warning, "Any more bad behavior from you, Aida, and you're out." Needless to say the Cotton Club's second edition with Ellington opened without Miss Ward in the cast.

Leslie knew Aida better than she knew herself. Not only did he manage her career, he regularly counseled her mind. Her straight and narrow had permanent bends and cul-de-sacs where she would frequently drop anchor to hide from reality. Most of her secret stops were alcoholic watering holes although she had been known to spend the occasional night on a sobering park bench.

Before her role in *Blackbirds*, Aida's career had taken a somewhat uneven course. In 1925, Caroline Dudley hired her to star in *Revue Nègre* as a replacement for Ethel Waters whose demand of an unreasonably high fee could not be met. Not unexpectedly, Aida's volatile temper prompted Mrs. Dudley to have second thoughts about her role. Aida was dismissed before the cast departed for Paris. Her replacement was Maude de Forest. Lost chances, ill health and bitter regrets forced Aida to take stock of her life. By giving her the opportunity to appear on Broadway, Lew Leslie gave her back a career but only after first laying down the rules: "Any more boozing, Aida, and you're fired."

Included in the expanded line-up was a real find, the comedian Tim Moore. His act excelled in graveyard and poker-game humor and in the show he presented two hysterical skits—"Picking a Plot" and "Playing according to Hoyle." Remarkably, after playing vaudeville for the past fifteen years, *Blackbirds* was his Broadway debut.

At the end of the shake-up, Leslie had expanded the cast to feature 100 colored artists, a full orchestra, Cecil Mack's Choir and a chorus line featuring 24 female dancers. To capture the spirit of the moment, he renamed the revue *Blackbirds of 1928* and took it on a road tour to put wind into its feathers.

April, Atlantic City, Nixon's Apollo Theater
"You know what they say," Aida Ward flippantly remarked as she stormed off stage. "A bad dress rehearsal means we'll have a great opening night."

Leslie saw things differently. A bad dress rehearsal meant the show wasn't pulling together. That meant more work, more rehearsals and an overhaul of the content. As it stood, the weight of the show laid heavily upon Adelaide's shoulders. In Leslie's opinion the balance appeared uneven.

His decision to take an amplified version of the show on tour was purely to see if it adapted from an intimate club environment to a large theatrical setting. If the production worked on a traditional stage his intentions were to take it directly to Broadway. This process was not to be as straightforward as he had hoped. The tryout was the longest evaluation ever of any black musical before a Broadway opening.

As if to forewarn the cast what they were up against, at the first rehearsal in Atlantic City, Leslie assembled them all on stage and made a sharp announcement, "However tough you think it's gonna be, then double it and start from there."

Leslie was known to be impulsive and unpredictable. At rehearsals he lived up to his reputation. He governed them on the three Ts principle— in time, in tune and together. If an artist failed on any account he or she was out. Leslie's uncanny way of making failed performers feel they were only failing themselves made him appear harder than he really was. He never did play the role of the "White Father" as other impresarios were known to do, and much preferred to instill strength rather than molly-coddle an artist.

In practical terms, the transition did not go smoothly. At each perform-ance Leslie judged the show obsessively from various vantage points around the theater. His discerning eye missed nothing. The continuity felt wrong and at times the pace dragged. The use of stark white lighting threw too many shadows on the chorus girls coloring their flesh overtly black. More worryingly, the show lasted nearly three hours—an hour too long for Broadway—and the eleven o'clock slot needed a lift.

One of the first songs to be unceremoniously axed was Adelaide's "Baby." He felt it was too similar in sentiment to "I Can't Give You Anything But Love, Baby." Next went a comedy sketch that nobody found amusing and out went the big production number in memory of Florence Mills. In its place he dressed Aida Ward in an immaculate black evening suit and had her impersonate the songbird by singing one of her hits— "Mandy Make Up Your Mind." To warm the audience up, Adelaide's "Diga Diga Do" was moved from the second half to the first. Surprisingly, Ulysses "Kid" Thompson's contract was terminated. Although Ulysses was a spectacular dancer, Leslie felt he lacked star quality. Leslie's intentions of molding *Blackbirds* into a sure-fire hit were uncompromising. For the performer, at times it felt as if just singing and dancing brilliantly weren't enough. By the end of the week Leslie had completely restructured the production. By filleting the songs and acts into the running order according to their punch, the show now acquired the rapidity and slickness he sought.

Blackbirds made no pretense of being anything other than a revue. It had no thread of a story line and held no hidden messages for the public. Neither did the production rely on elaborate sets; simple drapes constituted the principal stage dressing. It was nothing other than first-class, upfront entertainment with irritatingly memorable songs, comedy sketches that made the punter laugh, dance routines that thrilled the eyes and buckled your feet and hugely lovable, talented performers. Even the amended tribute to Florence Mills, titled "Here Comes My Blackbird," was handled with finesse and brought a dry tear to the eye.

From Atlantic City the show journeyed to Philadelphia and appeared at Cort's Jamaica Theater for its final tryout before hitting Broadway. The press were already showing considerable interest in the venture, especially as Leslie was now openly promoting Adelaide as Florence Mills' successor.[8] In spite of all his alterations to the show, Leslie was still worried about the eleven o'clock slot in the running order. When they returned to New York, at the eleventh hour Bill "Bojangles" Robinson was brought in to do just that. His inclusion was too late to be announced in the press, which made his appearance on opening night even more surprising.

Leslie's aim of making "I Can't Give You Anything But Love, Baby," which Adelaide had originally sung solo, into the biggest hit in America gave him the inspired idea of presenting it on Broadway first as a duet, then reprised as a trio.[9] He passed the number to Aida Ward and Bojangles and in a clever move brought Adelaide on stage halfway through to sing a counter-melody over the chorus. As with her refrain in "Creole Love Call" the trick worked magic. The arrangement not only made the song twice as long, which pleased Leslie no end, but it turned the number into one of the high points of the revue.

◆◆◆

Born in Richmond, Virginia, on May 25, 1878, Luther was the youngest child of Maxwell and Maria Robinson.[10] Shortly after his birth, Luther's parents died tragically, leaving him and his brother Bill to be cared for by their grandmother. From an early age Luther disliked his name so much that he asked his brother to swap names. When Bill disagreed, Luther tried coercing him into changing his mind. The bullying succeeded. Luther and Bill exchanged names, leaving members of their family totally confused.

At the age of six, with his new name attached to his lapel, Bill began dancing as a hoofer in local beer gardens for pocket money. Because he always danced with a smile upon his face, he acquired the nickname Bojangles—Negro slang for happy-go-lucky. The name stuck, so Bill incorporated it into his stage name.

Over the next few years Bojangles gradually developed his routine into a slick act. He then turned professional and progressed onto the TOBA circuit. During an appearance in Chicago in 1908 Bojangles met Marty Forkins, an Irish immigrant and theatrical agent. After catching his performance and realizing Bojangles' earning potential, like dollar signs in front of his eyes, Forkins offered to manage him. Unusually, no contract was ever signed. Only a handshake marked their agreement. To vaudeville audiences Bojangles was known as "The Dark Cloud of Joy," a term he despised. Lest he should forget who he really was, Forkins inscribed "The greatest hoofer of all time" on his weekly pay packet, an expression Bojangles much preferred.

By 1928, aged 50, Bojangles had devoted almost his entire life to dance. Ironically, apart from his appearances at New York's Palace Theater, he had performed exclusively to black audiences. Only now, at this late stage in his career, under Leslie's command, would a white Broadway audience finally have the chance to see the gifted Bojangles perform. His prowess was not just limited to the stage. He was also a tremendously fit athlete. It was said he could outrun backwards any forward runner who cared to challenge him. He had already beaten ten competitors. During his visit to London in 1926 he challenged a former professional sprinter to a 100-yard race. Bojangles ran backwards and won by six yards. As well as being a perfectly trained athlete, he was known in show business as a living thesaurus of dance steps. Unbelievably, he claimed never to have had a dance class—"I dance as the spirit moves me"—and created many of his own steps.

Bojangles' famous stair dance was said to have been invented on the spur of the moment during an audience with King George V in London.

He had been invited to Buckingham Palace to receive an award for his dancing skills, which the King was to present. Bojangles found his visit to the royal residence daunting. The rooms were large and intimidating. When he stood at one end, he had no idea who stood at the other. As the palace guard ushered him into the Throne Room, Bojangles gave a gasp. Way down at the far end of the hall, at the top of a flight of marble stairs, stood a tiny figure who, he was duly informed, was the King. To walk the distance would have taken half an hour. To save time, Bojangles took to his heels and tapped down the entire length of the room and then proceeded to dance up the staircase until he came to a halt, directly in front of His Majesty. Not only was George V impressed by Bojangles' dexterity, but his audacity amused him no end.

For a man of few skills, Bojangles' meteoric rise in the entertainment industry was an inspiration to all budding youngsters. His lack of education was sorely apparent. His conversation was said to be largely anecdotal, his language mostly laconic and his singing uninspired. Partially illiterate, the only writing he attempted was autographs. He had the gift of the one-liner and would often quote, "If you think too long, you think wrong." His dancing feet were the tools of his trade and he never felt the necessity to acquire any other ability. As with all overnight success stories, what the public didn't see were the years of long hard slog that preceded it.

His act involved many tricks, most of which he invented. To increase the clarity of his taps, he attached wooden soles and heels to his shoes. This created a far brighter sound than that made by metal caps. The famous shoemaker Capezio made all his dance shoes. They were hand-crafted from hollow plaster casts of Bojangles' feet, which enabled him to order footwear no matter where he was, without having to visit the store. To stop imitators he patented his ideas, be it dance steps, routines or new movements, and thought nothing of suing anyone who plagiarized them.

Leslie's last-minute offer to feature him in *Blackbirds* couldn't have arrived at a better time.[11] His career in vaudeville had gone as far as it could go. Amazingly, Bojangles accepted on the spot, without any discussion of salary. "You can speak to my manager about the money. The only figures I worry about are those I'm dancing with."

⌁⌁

In preparation for her Broadway opening, Adelaide went on a strict diet—very difficult for someone with a sweet tooth. The lack of clothing in certain numbers necessitated a slimline figure. Her diet worked. During the tryout tour, each night, without fail, her entrance to "Diga Diga Do" drew gasps of astonishment. Emerging from the wings wearing what she later described as "a little bit here," pointing to her bosom, "a little bit there," pointing to her knicker line, "and a lot less round the back," the sight of so much black flesh left the audience panting. The spirited jungle number was sexy but fun. Set in Samoa by the sea—the sort of weird geographical displacement accepted in songs of that era—it had her extolling the love of her Zulu man. During a dress rehearsal in Atlanta, Adelaide discovered the large tail-feathered fan that hung at the back of her costume was top heavy and prevented her achieving certain movements. It eventually had to be strapped invisibly around her waist to balance the weight evenly upon the base of her spine. Trying to dance erotically whilst carrying such a cumbersome projection was no mean feat and took hours of practice to perfect.

No matter how seasoned a professional you are, any first night on Broadway brings with it an almanac of worries. Backstage, as Adelaide prepared to make her entrance, all she could remember were the last words Bert told her back in the dressing room. "Just remember, honey, people who try their hardest need not fear their critics. Nothing is impossible when you have a dream."

WHEN THE PIE WAS OPENED! . . .

. . . the blackbirds began to sing. (Photograph courtesy of the B.F.I.)

May 9, Blackbirds of 1928 *Premiere, Liberty Theater, Broadway*

Broadway was having a spectacularly good season.[12] The standard never slackened and competition was fierce. With each new production, the critics became more and more discerning in their judgment. An all-white creation for an all-black cast was hardly a novelty. Leslie was gambling heavily on Adelaide, Bojangles and Fields and McHugh's songwriting abilities.

Sadly, the first-night reviews were far from unanimous in their appraisal of the show. Several were blatantly unfavorable, others mediocre but a couple were encouraging.[13] "*Blackbirds of 1928* is the best of its kind on Broadway in recent seasons," claimed Burns Mantle in the *Daily News*. "Best colored revue since *Shuffle Along*," wrote Thomas Van Dyke in the *Morning Telegraph*.

Julius Cohen in the *Journal of Commerce* saw it as a "fast-stepping, melodious concoction of Negro tomfoolery at its best," whilst Leonard Hill in the *Telegram* noted rather mundanely that the show had "Speed, more speed and then a little speed." J. Brooks Atkinson in the *New York Times* thought *Blackbirds* "An amusing spectacle of rolling, mischievous eyes and gleaming teeth . . . it has the knack of finding the stuff of entertainment in simplicities." In the *Brooklyn Eagle* William Weer viewed the show as "Vivid, bright and rhythmical" and predicted it would easily run "well past the dull slow months of summer and into the fall."

But the praise was sparse. Renowned theater critic Alexander Woollcott reported in the *World*: "*Blackbirds of 1928* might be described as a kind of Harlem Follies, and would be better, I think, if it had some good songs or some good comedians or, to be extravagant in one's demands, both."[14] He then pushed in the dagger even further by suggesting the content would probably "seem more interesting after a few drinks." In its present format he regarded it as "a third-rate Broadway musical show, tinted brown." However, at the end of his critique he redeemed himself by encouraging the theatergoer not to leave the building before the finale otherwise they would miss "A sleek, pleased young man about Harlem named Bill Robinson" whose "dancing as an expert", lifts the show out of the doldrums, and then concludes "There is no sound in all the noisy, flagrant evening which approaches in gaiety and infectiousness the neat confiding whisper of his gifted shoon." Wilfred J.

"Nothing is impossible when you have a dream." Adelaide in *Blackbirds of 1928*. (Photograph courtesy of the B.F.I.)

Riley's account in *Billboard* was direct and straight to the point "a cheap imitation of lesser revues. The comedy is terrible, the music hackneyed and the lyrics fair to middlin'."[15] Gilbert Gabriel's vicious account went even further.[16] He panned the show and characterized "I Can't Give You Anything But Love, Baby" as "sickly" and "puerile." Even Leslie's financial backers were heard to mumble "Too bad, Lew. Sorry, it looks like a flop."

Critics can get it wrong and Leslie set out to prove them so. What his bankers hadn't taken into account was public reaction, the cast's tenacity and Leslie's unfloundering determination. If the critics' words were depressingly harsh, the audiences' were ecstatic.

Wit, glamour and style! Adelaide in *Blackbirds of 1928.*

The *Chicago Defender* did, as its name suggests, encouragingly defend Leslie's choice for the starring role by claiming Adelaide to be "the logical successor to the late Florence Mills."[17] It was this reassurance and the effect Adelaide's performance had upon an audience that convinced Leslie he had a winner. On opening night alone, she scored seven encores for "Diga Diga Do." The number was a guaranteed showstopper.

Though the reviews had been a mixed bag, Leslie felt they weren't significantly life threatening. After analyzing the show in detail he clearly saw where he had gone wrong. At the following day's rehearsal, in a bid to bolster cast morale, he made an announcement: "If *Blackbirds* is to survive, we must be united in our goal." To counteract the critics' hostility, he also issued a hastily arranged press statement, "The show will continue. Let the audience be its judge." Then, rather arrogantly, he had a bold declaration inserted inside *Blackbirds'* theater program: "Program subject to change owing to magnitude of the production."

However, more important than Leslie's confidence was the fact that *Blackbirds* captured the mood of the day. What Leslie had cleverly done was package the cream of Harlem's talent into a presentation unequaled by anything else Broadway had on offer and Leslie had every intention of proving this fact to his doggedly opinionated critics.

On opening night, Bojangles' rendition of "I Can't Give You Anything But Love, Baby," which he sang with Adelaide and Aida Ward, was a disaster. Halfway through the number he forgot the lyrics and had to improvise. In the process the song suffered. Leslie decided Bojangles' voice hadn't been strong enough to carry the melody in the first place and plucked Willard McLean from the choir to replace him. This gave Bojangles the freedom to concentrate on his one big number, "Doin' The New Low-Down," during which he performed his celebrated stair dance.

Although Bojangles was a familiar face in vaudeville, Leslie had taken a gamble by featuring him in *Blackbirds*. That gamble paid off. When Bojangles first appeared on stage, immaculately attired in a suit, carrying a bowler hat and cane, the audience could hardly have imagined he was capable of dancing with such extraordinary deftness and dexterity but his feet spoke with an eloquence peculiarly of his own making. Bojangles became an overnight Broadway success. What Leslie did next was even smarter. He paired Adelaide with Bojangles in a surprise dance sequence. Adelaide had glamour, charm and a superb singing voice. Bojangles was an undeniably skilled dancer. She flattered him with grace. In return he worshiped her with his feet. Their partnership was an inspired move that created the first direct black equivalent to Fred and Adele Astaire.

Initially, Leslie had followed friends' advice and placed his musical adaptation of "Porgy"—a capsule version of Dorothy and DuBose Heywood's play—at the beginning of the second act.[18] The number, which preceded Gershwin's opera by six years, "died" purely because it was in the wrong place. The scene, wherein the mourners try to raise the dead, was sung as a choral chant to "I've Got A Man Now," led by the lusty mezzo vocal of Aida Ward. After repositioning it at the end of the first act "Porgy" did eventually receive tremendous acclaim for its depth of emotion and went on to be considered as one of the outstanding features of the revue.

Two comedy skits, which were said to be weak and unfunny, were also cut and replaced with new ones. To keep the pace of the dancers up to tempo Leslie ordered daily rehearsals for the chorus girls. Even the musicians were given new orchestral arrangements. To stress their solidarity Fields and McHugh agreed to waive their initial royalties to help the production pay for itself. By the end of the week Leslie's strenuous reworking of the show saw *Blackbirds* become unquestionably tighter.

The Liberty Theater seated 1,500 people. Top price orchestra stalls were $3.30, first balcony was $2.75 and second balcony $1.10. In an attempt to attract custom, Leslie released 1,000 seats for every performance to the cut-price ticket agencies to sell for $1.[19] For the first few weeks a good percentage of the show's trade came from such agencies. To secure a full house nightly, Leslie also gave hundreds of free tickets away. A midnight performance was introduced on Thursdays to encourage stage folk to visit. This move swiftly promoted talk of the show amongst theatrical circles. Although the strategy was financially crippling for Leslie, his credit with the theater owner was good. As his debts mounted, for the time being, all he could do was nervously await the public's verdict.

AS ELEPHANTS MIGHT SAY . . .

It didn't take long for the public to discover *Blackbirds* had wit, glamour and style. Within days, Leslie's plan saw positive results and during the next five weeks the box office takings never dropped. Thereafter business steadily began to climb. The cast worked their butts off to make the show a success. Praise from the black press was soon forthcoming and helped attract punters by the score. "One of the best of its kind ever presented on Broadway," heralded the *New York Amsterdam News*.[20]

Like the domino effect, word quickly spread around town that Adelaide's performance in "Diga Diga Do" was nothing short of sensational and, as he had predicted and much to Leslie's delight, the song on everybody's lips was "I Can't Give You Anything But Love, Baby."

By the eighth week Leslie's persistence paid off. Weekly box office takings hit $17,000, shifting the gross over to the right side of the ledger.

Gradually the theater released fewer and fewer cut-price tickets until, by the tenth week the show was selling only full-price tickets. On its sixteenth week the weekly gross smashed the $20,000 mark. By September, *Blackbirds* was doing storming business in anybody's books. It now sold out with such regularity that one simply couldn't get a seat and in an unprecedented move the theater arranged to have 200 standing tickets released for each performance. So strong was demand that by the twentieth week its gross had reached $25,000. By October it was peaking at $34,000.[21]

Blackbirds' popularity left white Broadway producers in a state of confusion. The public had taken Adelaide and Bojangles to their heart. Each night the audience left the theater humming the hit songs all the way home. At last, Leslie had struck the jackpot. The show was more than memorable . . . it was addictive.

Leslie rapidly recouped his losses and in October organized a second company for a Western tour to capitalize on his investment.[22] This troupe he gave to his brother Sol to manage. They opened in Boston with Gertrude Saunders taking Adelaide's role.[23] He had no need to borrow money for this production. Banks were throwing the stuff at him. The fact that Leslie didn't quit, even when the signs pointed to nothing but failure, proved to everyone around him just how strong sublime confidence can be. "Only my faith in the show turned what looked like a failure into a huge success," he would proudly boast.[24] "I knew I had one of the greatest colored shows that ever came to New York." By the end of the year, *Blackbird* mania was sweeping the nation. To add to his nest egg, Leslie lined up a third troupe to tour the Pacific coast.[25] His philosophy always had been "manipulate to accumulate" and, as sole owner of one of the hottest shows on Broadway, he saw no reason to halt his exploitation now. As elephants might say if they could talk, "I'm living life in a gigantic colossal way."

For the first time in Broadway's history a colored performer was attracting more attention than any other entertainer on stage. Single-handedly Adelaide had redefined the role of the black female in show business. The rewards were to be considerable, both artistically and financially.

Her salary was known to be higher than that of her predecessor

Florence Mills, who was paid a weekly guarantee of $1,000 back in 1926.[26] Bojangles received $2,000 a week on the vaudeville circuit and his manager would probably have demanded a similar fee for *Blackbirds*, so one can confidently assume that Adelaide's earnings would have been comparable. On top of their fee, Leslie paid his stars a percentage of the profits from weekly box office takings. Needless to say as *Blackbirds'* popularity grew so did Adelaide's income.

Adelaide's new-found wealth suddenly gave her the confidence to cut the umbilical cord and move from her mother's residence. She acquired a spacious apartment on Seventh Avenue, which was the first home she could call her own. Although dismayed by her daughter's departure, Elizabeth remained happily in her abode at St. Nicholas Avenue in the neighborhood she knew best overlooking her beloved St. Nicholas Park.

Certain agitators in the press cruelly suggested Bojangles should have had top billing. In an open letter printed in several newspapers redressing the critics' defamation, Bojangles explained how pleased he was that Adelaide had top billing above his name.[27] He felt it only fair that black actresses should receive the same amount of exposure as their male counterparts and stated categorically that it was at his request Leslie had billed her as the leading star, to prevent his name overshadowing her importance in the production. He claimed that it was almost impossible for a colored actress to hit the "Big Time" and as long as he was working on stage he would give his full support to any black female performer who had the slightest chance of making it big.

Camaraderie amongst the cast was said to be genuine, with little back-stabbing or bitching reported. A revealing insight into the working relationship between the artists appeared in an article written in the *Chicago Defender* that dealt with the supportive spirit of the production.[28] It claimed that the stars of the show did not envy each other's success or feel threatened by it but instead rejoiced in it, often participating backstage in the applause. Emphasis was clearly put on teamwork. Jealousy and negative self-seeking were not tolerated and "mutual encouragement" was the watchword. The volume of fan mail and gifts delivered to both Adelaide and Aida Ward's dressing rooms was shown to be indicative of the individual artists' appeal. "Competition may be the life of the trade but cooperation is the life of *Blackbirds*," concluded the article.

After Vitaphone approached Bojangles to make a movie short of his famed stair dance, Leslie thought it prudent to insure both his and Adelaide's legs for a premium of $500,000 a pair. The stair dance had become Bojangles' trademark and attracted many imitators around the world. He could glide so effortlessly up and down the stairs that viewers often claimed he possessed an unnatural ability to levitate. Acts of piracy within the business were not uncommon but sometimes the culprits would go one step further and steal a whole act. Performers went to great lengths to copyright their routines, none more so than Bojangles. In an unusual move to control plagiarism, he placed a full-page advertisement in *Variety* condemning anybody who blatantly copied his act: "The many imitators of me at the present time are injuring the value of my perform-ance. I have suffered in silence as one after another have stolen my creation of tap dancing up and down a flight of stairs . . . I now declare that I am entitled to as much recognition, protection and consideration as anyone." His caution continued rather confusingly, "No imitation permitted, with or without my consent, credit or by mention of my name or otherwise."[29] Should any performer not take heed of his advice he ended his statement rather menacingly, "This is a fair warning. It goes for both sides of the ocean and I go everywhere sooner or later. You be nice and I'll be nice . . . or else!"

It's hard to judge if the advertisement discouraged any would-be imper-sonators. It certainly caused considerable alarm in the theatrical world as the idea of patenting a dance routine was unheard of and seemed totally absurd. If anything, Bojangles' concern over ownership probably encour-aged many resourceful performers to learn and insert the dance into their own act. If nothing else, the advertisement certainly informed the public exactly who had invented the stair dance.

Try to imagine the sound of 24 pairs of dancing feet, their metal taps slicing the beat in unison on a bare wooden stage, perfectly in time with the most addictive rhythm you've ever heard. Then, picture the audience reaction as the girls collectively raise their naked legs on every eighth beat. Unleash Adelaide's seductive charm generated by a battery of loco-motive energy. Position her out front, dressed only in flesh, sequins and a fantail of ostrich feathers, just close enough for the audience to smell the

DIGA DIGA DO

Adelaide was on stage singing like a honey
Bert was in her dressing room counting all the
money
Elizabeth was in the wings vetting Addie's clothes
When down flew Leslie and pecked off her nose

trail of her sweet perfume, then let her tease you with a voice that'll melt the wax in your ears. In a spectacular display of vocal agility she'll cast aside your inhibitions with a lyric that'll become permanently attached to your brain cells. Add the heat of a hot-blooded jazz orchestra to the equation, pounding their instruments in an attack of rage and what do you have? THE most impressive, resonant *mélange* ever to have hit you between the eyes. That was "Diga Diga Do" and DO, it surely did.

Nothing could have prepared the public for the riotous effect it had. By the time she hit the chorus, Adelaide had coaxed the whole audience into submission. There was no one to compare her to. Her delivery was unique and every performance a one-off. She created one of those unforgettable moments in theater that audiences continue to talk about for years. Even the backstage crew would stand in the wings to watch. In 1993, when I interviewed Elisabeth Welch (who sang in the production), she could still vividly recall the impact Adelaide had on an audience during the number: "She was fantastic beyond belief and brought the house down every night. Loud singing and wild dancing with the orchestra roaring from the pit . . . there wasn't a still foot in the house."

If Adelaide's performance was said to be calculated, a lot of Bojangles' was ad-libbed and reflected the audience's mood on that particular night.

On opening night,
Adelaide scored
seven encores for
"Diga Diga Do."

When he hit the stage his xylophonic feet filled the theater with musical cadences. He was so skilled at his craft that he could keep the drowsiest person wide awake or rock a lively baby asleep. Adelaide and Bojangles regularly rehearsed together and as the weeks progressed, added new, more complicated dance steps to their routine. They also composed songs together. Their first collaboration, "Lazy Moon," impressed Leslie enough for him immediately to include it in the show.[30]

Throughout its Broadway run, many amusing events took place involving the show and its performers that titillated the tabloids with endless stories, theories and gossip. Much hullabaloo was made over Adelaide's *risqué* rendition of "Diga Diga Do" and many column inches were written discussing her apparel, or lack of it.

Nudity on Broadway had always been represented in statue form, with the artist never moving more than an eyelash. In this role Ziegfeld glorified the white chorus girl who, frozen to the spot, revealed as much as State law would permit. In comparison, Adelaide's rendition of "Diga Diga Do" pushed those limits to the brink. Wearing as little as possible without dishonoring her name, the number had many conservative members of the public outraged. Some felt she forced the boundaries of decency too far. In their eyes the sight of so much black flesh threatened their morals and certain factions saw fit to complain. None more so than Adelaide's mother.

Elizabeth Hall had been out of town on an extended convalescence staying with relatives in Nashville, Tennessee. Having read about her daughter's accomplishment on Broadway in the newspapers, as soon as Elizabeth returned to New York she asked to see the show. Lew Leslie arranged for her and a friend to attend the evening performance on Tuesday July 31 and gave them the best seats in the house—on the front row in the center. As the show commenced, Elizabeth took little notice of the numbers until the announcement of "Diga Diga Do" when her companion nudged her and exclaimed excitedly, "Here she comes. This is Addie's first number." Elizabeth's face warmed with pride and anticipation as the orchestra's conductor, Allie Ross, banged out the introduction's syncopated rhythm. One by one, the chorus girls paraded on stage, 24 in all. From their midst burst Adelaide, her glorious butterfly smile striking the audience like a ray of blinding sunlight. Elizabeth sat bolt upright in her seat. As Adelaide's smile broadened, her mother's contracted. "There must be a mistake," she thought to herself. "Could Adelaide have been so late and in such a hurry to dress that she'd forgotten to put on her costume?" Mrs. Hall's startled eyes closed in shock, then looked again. It was Adelaide all right, and all her daughter had on was a smile. No skirt, no bodice, no stockings, just a simple pair of satin slippers. Upon closer inspection the rest of the audience were able to detect a tail fan of ostrich feathers and a rhinestone spangle or two, but these accessories only served to intensify and accentuate the superb, supple beauty of Adelaide's near-naked body.

Grim lines of disapproval etched deeply along the corners of Elizabeth's mouth. A moment of indecision followed, then, as Adelaide began shaking her hips in time to the beat, she could take no more. Elizabeth hurriedly vacated her seat and hurled herself backstage. Just what happened behind the scenes is obscured in a welter of conflicting reports.

The commotion that followed took Leslie, Bojangles, Bert and the rest of the cast totally by surprise. Pleading her disapproval with loud expletives, Mrs. Hall's voice rose clearly and decisively above the sound of the orchestra and singing on stage.

"Where is she? Let me at her. No daughter of mine's going to flaunt her nakedness in the face of the public. I'll show her who her mother is. I don't care if she's been married seven times with a backside as big as the side of a house. When I get her I'll spank the place her clothes should be hiding!" No matter who tried to pacify her, the ranting raged unabated. To add further injury to Elizabeth's pride, Leslie categorically denied her access to Adelaide's dressing room. At the end of the show, to escape the wrath of her mother's tongue, Adelaide fled from the theater and headed straight for home.

Back home, fearing for her physical appearance, Adelaide locked herself in her bedroom leaving Bert to mollify Elizabeth. His attempts at appeasement fell on willful ears, "This is show business. Adelaide's a big Broadway star. She's no longer a little schoolgirl in a blue-sleeved smock." The words stung. In Elizabeth's eyes, Adelaide would always be a little girl. As much as Elizabeth refused to listen, Adelaide stubbornly refused to budge from the bedroom. It took Lew Leslie's intervention, whose opinion Elizabeth always had respected, for a compromise to be reached. He promised to limit Adelaide's hip wiggles each performance to a specific number and agreed to add more material to her costume. How this was to be achieved he had no idea but he felt the peace offering would calm the situation for the time being. Clearly, he hadn't anticipated Elizabeth's next request. "Good. Then I shall sit in the wings at each performance and count the wiggles."

Leslie had no intention of limiting Adelaide's hip wiggles nor did he intend to add cloth to her outfit but somehow he had to soothe Elizabeth into believing he would. Clearly there was no alternative. He had to have another costume made, and quickly. The redesigned garment was tailored the following day and hand delivered to the Hall apartment for Elizabeth to vet. Neither Adelaide nor Leslie liked the costume. Needless to say,

Elizabeth did. Their argument resulted in Adelaide being forced to cancel her appearance that evening. The only person who found any reason to be cheerful about the day's events was her understudy, Ruth Johnston. On Thursday Adelaide returned to the theater for the matinée performance. Elizabeth sat in the wings, stony-faced, censoring her daughter's every move, meticulously counting each hip wiggle she included. At the end of the show, feeling satisfied with the outcome, Elizabeth departed under the impression that Adelaide would conduct all future performances in such a restrained manner.

With Mrs. Hall safely escorted from the building Leslie immediately issued a restraining order, prohibiting her from any future entrance backstage. News of the outburst reached the tabloids. To quell further speculation Leslie released a brief press statement: "The whole thing is ridiculous. Until Adelaide's mother came to see her daughter on stage there was no word of criticism from anybody regarding indecency in the 'Diga Diga Do' number. It's a simple dance, if erotic, done with grace and finesse. The reason Mrs. Hall forced Adelaide to stay out of the production is because she's a pious woman who very rarely goes to the theater. If she interferes again and forces her daughter to remain out of any more numbers in *Blackbirds* I will have her forcibly ejected from the building."[31] Elizabeth never was officially informed of the ban as nobody dared tell her. Fortunately, she returned to Nashville soon after to resume her convalescence giving Adelaide the freedom once more to parade on the Liberty stage in all her glory.

As can be imagined, the incident created quite a stir in the gossip columns. From Broadway to Harlem and back again, Adelaide's name was suddenly on everybody's lips. In aesthetic circles the dance was discussed as a matter of art. In the puritanical establishment it was judged upon its morals. Some claimed it to be a clever stunt, to lure the prurient minded to the box office. Others hailed it as highbrow entertainment beyond the realms of smut. "Did the dance cheapen Negro womanhood?" pondered Theophilus Lewis in the *Baltimore Afro-American*.[32] The *Amsterdam News* asked its readers, "Was 'Diga Diga Do' too hot?" then outlined the pros and cons, allowing them to decide.[33] The *Chicago Defender*'s editor was a little more direct.[34] Although he sympathized with Mrs. Hall's viewpoint, he found her judgment old-fashioned and felt nudity on stage meant little to the ultramoderns: "Girls and women wear their dresses so short that when they sit on a subway car they must keep their legs pressed closely together in order not to expose what they've eaten for lunch." He concluded his commentary by brazenly stating that these days even lesbianism was an accepted part of the profession.

If nothing else, the scandal compelled the public to sit up and take note and from their stampede for tickets it appeared everyone aired an opinion on the matter.

Looking back at the incident, what seems even more extraordinary in the light of all the fuss made over Adelaide's exposure was the fact that the main Negro comedian in the show, Tim Moore, in the age-old tradition of blackface, still saw fit to "black up" and wear white gloves in order to make fun of his origins.

If Leslie thought a momentary truce had been called regarding "Diga Diga Do," he was in for a big shock. On Tuesday September 11, a large party of Southern whites from Dixie attended the evening performance.[35] The delegation, numbering over 60 in total, were seated together in the orchestra stalls. Clearly boisterous from the offset—no doubt as a result of consuming too much illicit alcohol—as the show commenced they continued their disturbance by wolf whistling, hurling racist comments at the cast and generally acting disorderly. Members of the audience seated close by vacated their seats in disgust and complained to the management. Ushers were sent to politely calm their behavior, but all to no avail. No matter how loud the orchestra played, the barrage of derogatory innuendoes could still be heard. When the introduction to "Diga Diga Do" commenced and out danced Adelaide with her line of scantily clad chorus girls, the sight of so much nubile flesh brought the matter to a head. The worst tirade of insults imaginable rained upon them. "How'd you like to have that Nigger wench?" called out the ringleader. "I'd give you $5 to sleep with her," yelled another, and so the banter persisted. Fearing for their reputation, one by one the tearful chorus girls fled the stage. Finally, in a fit of desperation, Adelaide brought the number to a halt. Stepping out front she yelled to the perpetrators, "Call yourself men? I dare you to come up on stage and insult me to my face," to which a roar of approval filled the auditorium. In defiance the rednecks threw a further diatribe of indignities in Adelaide's direction along with programs, coins and anything else that came to hand. As members of the public became embroiled in the fracas, the situation rapidly deteriorated. In panic, Adelaide hitched up her feathers and flew off stage.

Backstage, Bojangles heard the commotion and rushed out to defend his colleagues. On stage he too was met with abusive threats. Unruffled, Bojangles stood his ground and declared he would personally return the admission fee to all who wished to leave. Several of the unruly crowd jumped over their seats and ran threateningly towards him, throwing firecrackers indiscriminately on the way. They fully intended to confront Bojangles face to face. In a brave attempt to stop them, other members of the audience intervened and punches flew.

Within minutes, news of the uproar spread to neighboring theaters. In a show of camaraderie, lighting technicians, stagehands and anybody else they could rally rushed to the Liberty to assist. At the start of the rumpus, the theater management had wisely called the local constabulary. The emergency riot squad burst through the exit doors, menacingly waving truncheons above their heads. The sight of so many police vehicles screeching to a halt on 42nd Street aroused much public curiosity. Huge crowds gathered outside the theater. The atmosphere became charged with excitement as onlookers clamored round the building in a bid to catch sight of the action.

Inside the officers soon took control of the situation. The culprits were herded up, handcuffed and marched off to cheers of approval from the audience. By now the entire cast of the show had re-emerged on stage to lend their support. The orchestra even struck up a marching tune. Once again Bojangles addressed the public, "Would anybody like their admission fee refunded?"

"No," hollered the audience unanimously.

"Then we shall continue the show."

The sergeant-in-charge retained a detachment of officers and positioned them on guard in front of the stage for the remainder of the performance in case any further trouble should flare up. During the interval, in an impromptu gesture to thank the public for their support, various cast members and musicians climbed out onto the theater's front balcony and gave a rousing rendition of "I Can't Give You Anything But Love, Baby," bringing 42nd Street to a standstill.

Lew Leslie had been absent from the theater at the time of the commotion, and did not return until the affair had subsided. After being briefed, he made no public statement. Presumably he felt the incident had incited enough newspaper coverage without his involvement. His presumption was correct. The story hit the front page of many editorials.

In contrast to Adelaide's native abandon in "Diga Diga Do," for her solo number in the second act she appeared on stage like a solitary rose. "I Must Have That Man" is a yearning torch song that pulls at the heart-strings. During the number her crystal-clear diction and emotional directness are used to dynamic effect as she cleverly communicates singularly with each person in the house. With every muscle in her body she pleads to the audience,

> I need that person much worse than just bad,
> I'm half-alive, he's driving me mad.
> He's only human, if he's to be had,
> I must have that man.

With sales of "Creole Love Call" exceeding everybody's expectations, record company interest in signing Adelaide as a solo artist had begun to grow. The music industry was booming.[36] Over 104 million record sales were logged in 1927 and agents were constantly scouting for fresh talent. Victor was the first major label to approach Adelaide with a contract proposal. The company's owner, Mr. King, invited her to his studio for a tone test. He suggested she record two songs from *Blackbirds* and chose her big showstopper "I Must Have That Man" and "Baby," the song Lew Leslie discarded at the last minute. On June 21, Adelaide, with her piano accompanist George Rickson, was driven to Victor Studios to record her vocals.

Leslie got wind of the proposed Victor deal and asked Mr. King if he could hear the demos. Much as he liked them Leslie was adamant that in order to get the best out of the songs they should be recorded with a full orchestra, as they were heard in the show. Leslie then had his lawyer write a polite but stern letter to Mr. King stipulating that unless he was satisfied with the finished recordings he would have no option but to issue an injunction to prevent their release. As a way of mediating the situation Leslie offered Mr. King the use of his own orchestra from *Blackbirds*. Leslie knew full well that if King accepted his proposition such a recording would require his signed approval. At this point King felt he was being held to ransom and put the negotiations on hold.

However, in the meantime, Leslie secretly negotiated with Jack Kapp (Brunswick's recording manager) to sell him the rights to release the cast recordings of the show. Brunswick was also very keen to sign Adelaide on to their growing roster of black artists. Kapp agreed to Leslie's suggestion that full orchestral versions of "I Must Have That Man" and "Baby" would achieve higher sales. The recordings were mastered on July 13 and took two days to complete.

The 78-rpm single was issued under the title of "Adelaide Hall accompanied by Lew Leslie's Blackbirds Orchestra." This time the record was made with the full co-operation of the Leslie Organization. Although Will Vodery's Plantation Orchestra performed on the recordings, for some reason Brunswick failed to credit them on the label. When the record was released music stores reported high demand for the record with supplies selling out as soon as they were delivered.[37] Encouraged by the disc's success, Kapp commissioned another recording from the show. This time Bojangles was the featured artist and once again Leslie's Blackbirds Orchestra accompanied the track.

Many of the songs from *Blackbirds* became international hits and were covered by most of the major record labels using an array of artists and instrumentalists including Louis Armstrong, Duke Ellington and Cab Calloway. Their release added further laurels to *Blackbirds'* fame.

During the notoriously slow hot summer months, when Broadway producers are known to tighten the money belt, *Blackbirds* surprised everyone by continuing to attract record attendance figures.[38] As there was no air conditioning inside the theater, if the heat became insufferable the management simply ordered all doors to be opened, allowing fresh air to flow throughout the building. Some said the show was hotter than the temperature. Certainly, for the performers it seemed that way. In between numbers, many of the chorus girls sat outside on the iron fire escape to cool down. Several theaters around Times Square backed on to each other and the colorful display of scantily clad females dangling their legs betwixt the metal rails gave passers-by a pleasing distraction. Only the warning notice beneath the stairs, "When klaxon sounds, keep clear," kept any resemblance of order.

Blackbirds cleverly brought together a cornucopia of colored artistry, unsurpassed on Broadway at that moment in time. The press referred to it as an institution and people began to visit it repeatedly, in the same way they might go to see the window displays at Gimbels or Wanamakers, always pre-assured they would see something worthwhile. By upgrading the cast periodically to include a wider spectrum of what black entertainment had to offer, Leslie kept the public's curiosity aroused. In a sense, *Blackbirds* became an exhibition for Negro talent and as such one of the most sought after shows for black performers to appear in. The artists who were chosen won an instant trip to stardom.

Peg Leg Bates was one such inclusion in the cast. He acquired his curious name as a youngster after being involved in a serious automobile accident in his home town of Greenville, South Carolina. His injuries resulted in the amputation of a leg. As a one-legged twelve-year-old hobbling around on ill-fitting crutches, he soon experienced cruel taunts from his school chums. Feeling thoroughly dejected and unable to take any more ridicule, his pride got the better of him. In defiance he recklessly threw down the sticks and attempted to hop around on one leg. Of course, he fell over. His bitter tears of woe prompted even more jeers from his classmates. Their taunts were to be double-sided. On the one hand they were discouraging but on the other they motivated him to think more positively about his predicament. His uncle took pity on him and promised to help by making him a wooden leg that would be stronger than any human leg in Greenville. From that day onwards Bates' life changed. For the next three years he walked the two-mile journey to and from school on his peg leg. This strengthened the muscles in his good leg, and thus enabled him to enjoy his passion for dancing. In the strictly two-legged world of dance, Peg Leg Bates became a phenomenon. *Blackbirds* was to be the first of many Broadway appearances that earned him recognition as one of America's top solo dancers.

In September, the comedian Johnny Hudgins was drafted into the cast.[39] Acclaimed as the successor to the late Bert Williams, Hudgins had carved a name for himself amongst Europe's capitals where he had performed in front of royalty and the social elite. Billed as a pantomime artist, his skill so impressed the Prince of Wales in London that he was invited to Buckingham Palace to teach his Highness the intricacies of mimicry.

On September 3, the night Hudgins gave his debut, an incident on stage brought the show to an abrupt halt. Bojangles came a cropper.[40] Whilst he was performing an intricate step during his famous stair dance he suddenly became dizzy. He missed his footing and fell headfirst onto the footlights knocking himself unconscious. Seated in the front row were two of Bojangles' great showbiz friends, Eddie Cantor and George Olsen, who both jumped from their seats to help break his fall. Fortunately, their assistance was not required. The orchestra leader, Allie Ross, leapt from his dais just in time to break Bojangles' descent mid-flight. His quick thinking prevented any serious ligament injury. Whilst the audience gasped in disbelief, Leslie rushed on stage to stop the show. "Is there a doctor in the house?" he yelled frantically. As luck would have it, Eddie Cantor had his personal physician with him. After a brief examination, the dancer was found to have severely bruised both legs and wrenched a shoulder. Bojangles finally managed to compose himself before hobbling off stage for further medical attention.

In the best theatrical spirit, Leslie proclaimed to the audience, "The show must go on," and so it did. However, fifteen minutes later he reappeared to make a surprise announcement, "Bojangles has requested that he be permitted to perform his scheduled number with Adelaide Hall and as such

I should like to welcome them back on stage." As the two artists stepped cautiously from the wings, warmly clutching each other's hand, the whole house instantaneously leapt from their seats to express their admiration.

After the show's initial mixed reviews, the Liberty Theater's manager, J. W. Mayer, allotted Leslie only a five-month lease and signed a new comedy—*Mr. Moneypenny*—to run from mid-October. Now, with the biggest success story of the year on his stage, Mayer was left with egg on his face. As luck would have it, the Eltinge Theater directly next door to the Liberty became available and overnight the entire production trans-ferred from one theater to another. Trade was so strong that bookings were being taken six months in advance.[41] The move encouraged Leslie to increase ticket prices and *Blackbirds'* weekly gross now became one of the highest on Broadway, overtaking Mae West's blockbuster *Diamond Lil*.[42] "*Blackbirds* is packing them in. Remarkable business for a colored revue, which is breaking all records," confirmed *Variety* in its financial rundown of Broadway's economy.

On October 8, at the end of its Liberty Theater run, Bojangles threw a lavish dinner party for the entire company to celebrate *Blackbirds'* triumph.[43] The meal was held at Small's Paradise (where even the waiters danced) and given in appreciation of the tireless work done by his fellow colleagues. The press noted it as the first time a black performer had paid for such an occasion out of his own pocket. Even the menu, which included filet mignon topped with a light mushroom sauce, was specially concocted for the affair. What made the event more noteworthy was Bojangles' insistence that the backstage crew and theater executives be invited. As is customary at such functions, the host made a speech during which he publicly expressed his thanks to Lew Leslie and claimed his own success in the show had increased his worth on the RKO circuit by an extra $2,000. In all, 168 persons were present including the husbands of Adelaide and Aida Ward. Bojangles' generosity only furthered his repu-tation for being the kindest man in the business.

His unsolicited role as Uncle Bill to all around regularly brought him a whole heap of mischief. His fondness for ice cream was well known and his dressing-room fridge was always well stocked with it. He bragged that over the past forty years he had regularly consumed a pint of the stuff for breakfast, claiming it awakened his mind and helped relieve headaches.

Whatever its remedial properties, his fridge full of ice cream certainly made him popular with the ladies, who constantly raided it.

Adelaide dressed in her ragamuffin outfit from *Blackbirds of 1928*.

THIS SIDE OF HEAVEN

Leslie cleverly tailored Adelaide's image to fit her role as a Broadway star and constantly bombarded journalists with reams of press releases to feed the public's interest in her. Some critics accused her of selling her credibility to gain mass acceptance in the white man's world. If she did, it was purely to reach the widest audience possible. By breaking the mold, she had become a viable product with commercial appeal. Irrespective of what her antagonists thought, her sudden high profile brought an array of interesting opportunities. She soon found her name embossed on some of the most sought after invitations in town. Though the recognition was pleasing, those precious moments at the end of a performance, when the curtain falls saturated with the rain of applause, were more valuable to her than anything else on offer. No one can ever evaluate their worth. This income was personal, the priceless reward of her art.

In the midst of all the brouhaha there clearly were times when Adelaide's feet did not touch the ground but, fortunately for her, Bert's soles were firmly placed this side of heaven. His intrepid business sense took full advantage of Adelaide's growing popularity and good looks. Her triumph in *Blackbirds* was not just a personal achievement; it reflected upon the whole of America's black community. She had become a role model, someone whom black people could identify with and emulate. Her name became a bankable asset and Bert seized every possibility to capitalize upon it, encouraging her to endorse a range of products from cosmetics to memorabilia. Her image promoted a new line of cosmetics named "Florence Mills Beauty Preparations," extolled the virtues of "Youth Eternal" facial creams for Joelet Cosmetics, and praised the versatility of "Pluko" hairdressing gel in their extensive advertising campaign.[44] She even opened her own dance classes in Harlem, which became so oversubscribed they had to be conducted on an open-air recreation ground to accommodate the hundreds of eager attendees.[45]

Cosmetics aimed exclusively at the black female had become increasingly popular in the Twenties and a huge array of merchandise appeared on beauty counters. Some made wild claims that would be banned in today's highly vetted marketplace. One product, "Nardinola" moisturizing cream, which Josephine Baker was said to use liberally, claimed to lighten

Advertisement in the *Chicago Defender*, June 16, 1928.

one's skin overnight. Sadly, young girls wishing to imitate their stage heroine's skin coloring genuinely believed such misguided claims.

"Pluko" gel was advertised to stimulate hair growth and straighten the most harsh, wiry, unruly Negro hair without using hot irons. It was disgustingly oily to handle and impossible to remove from clothing but it did just as the advertising claimed—straighten Negro hair. Adelaide posed for "Pluko" with a spit curl, sometimes referred to as a heart-hook or Marcel wave, pasted on the center of her forehead. Marcel waving was all the rage and the brittle quality of black hair made it impossible to set. The look was imported from Paris fashion houses where hair was slicked back with scented pomade. To set a fringe curl one had to hold it firmly in place with a grip until the gel dried, which could take up to an hour. The more adventurous arranged a whole row, up to a dozen, across the fringe line. Unbelievably, the art was even taught at college. Throughout *Blackbirds'* run, Adelaide's spit curl became known as her "hallmark" and was adopted by many fashion-conscious young ladies.

〜

Al Jolson's unimaginable success in *The Jazz Singer* transformed him from a Broadway star into the biggest box-office movie draw across the States. The more the film grossed the bolder the writing on Hollywood's contracts became. The changeover from silent to talkie created new opportunities for singers with deeper-toned voices. Early sound equipment rendered actors' voices slightly higher and thinner than in real life, thus destroying many a silent movie star's career. Suddenly, Broadway stars were in big demand. In a bid by the studios to find fresh talent, countless stage performers paraded before the microphone. George Jessell, Rudy Vallee, Eddie Cantor, Lillian Roth, Ethel Merman, Jack Benny, Ginger Rogers, Miriam Hopkins and Helen Morgan—almost every big name in vaudeville made a one-reel sound short in a bid to break into movies.[46] Today's wink in the camera could be tomorrow's brightest star. Some were lucky and struck it rich. It seemed only a matter of time before Adelaide's success in *Blackbirds* would bring her to the attention of the movie moguls. In true Hollywood fashion a limousine arrived to escort her to Paramount Studio on Long Island where she filmed a one-reel test for Sam Goldwyn. Bearing in mind there were few leading roles in movies for black females, not surprisingly nothing transpired from the taping.

In the entertainment world many black females were known amongst their colleagues to have lesbian tendencies.[47] Both Alberta Hunter and Ethel Waters openly displayed their gay lovers. Some of the strangest, yet most entertaining events to happen in New York's social calendar were the annual homosexual balls. These were always grand affairs. The two most spectacular were the Rochester Ball and the Hamilton Club Lodge Ball. Both attracted a real fruit salad of characters. They were drag balls where it was customary for men to dress as women and women to dress as men. Some looked so convincing that the confusion caused much debate during the course of the evening.

Many effeminate homosexuals arrived overdressed as their favorite Broadway or Hollywood actress. Not only did this cause much hilarity if the real celebrity happened to be a guest, it often caused acute paranoia for the stars, finding themselves confronted by their own distorted image. Situations of this kind were delicately handled by the organizers who diplomatically declined any knowledge of the real celebrity's presence. Towards the end of the evening a huge fashion parade took place at which the new Queen of the Ball was crowned. It was customary to have a famous star crown the Queen. In 1928, the organizers of one such ball invited Adelaide to perform that duty.[48]

The affair was staged in a huge casino that held over 2,000 people. For security reasons Adelaide and her entourage were assigned a private box. It conveniently looked directly down upon the crowded dance floor and afforded an uninterrupted view of the evening's proceedings. Queens aren't known for their modesty and at such balls they lived up to their sovereignty. Every historical female figure from Sheba to Cleopatra, to the more recent Goddesses of Hollywood made an appearance, in outfits elaborately tailored from sumptuous satins, yards of sequins and more plumage than could be found in an aviary. They looked gloriously camp and colorful.

For the crowning ceremony Adelaide was escorted on stage to present the prize. Unbeknown to her the organizers had arranged a special Adelaide Hall lookalike category that she was asked to judge. The prospect of having her own double parade up and down in front of her was not one she welcomed. She need not have worried. The ten contestants were all black males with the most enviable bodies in the house. It was a hard decision, in fact so hard that Adelaide chose two winners, much to the organizers' annoyance, as both expected an award. An outrageous Mae West imitator clinched top prize and was duly crowned new Queen of the Ball. For the rest of the evening she swanned around the casino drinking champagne from a gold high-heeled shoe, insulting all the old Queens in attendance. Just before dawn, when the magic of mascara and amphetamines had begun to fade and the cloakroom mirror showed little sympathy, the threat of daylight saw a mass exodus of Cinderellas scampering from the building. It certainly was a night to remember.

By November all performances of *Blackbirds* were playing to capacity houses and Leslie was heading for a nervous breakdown.[49] At the beginning of the production he had been full of fun and expectancy. At Les Ambassadeurs he would watch the show nightly with excitement. To cheer the cast, he would try and make out he was a dancer by imitating steps from the dance routines. At the time, they found it amusing. Only later, after the show opened on Broadway, did his temperament alter. As anxiety mounted so did his blood pressure. He became ruthless, dictatorial and scheming.

His histrionics and tiring workload took its toll upon his health. In December, much to the relief of the cast, his doctor ordered him to take an immediate vacation, as far away from Broadway as possible. The following week, accompanied by his actress wife, Belle Baker, he set sail for the Caribbean on a fishing holiday. Although his empire was built from relentless hard work, perseverance and the ability to recognize talent, behind his back many jealous competitors callously dubbed him a "Blackbirder"—someone who sells Negro slaves to whites. At times the nickname fitted him to a tee.

As 1928 bid adieu, Leslie's prediction that "I Can't Give You Anything But Love, Baby" would be the biggest hit of the year had come true. During the previous twelve months the song had become the most recorded and performed on the airwaves and was reckoned by *Billboard* to have been heard by every citizen in America. The ballad went on to achieve record sales of over 3 million copies. *Variety* hailed the show as the second most successful musical on Broadway for that year.[50] In a special live Yuletide radio broadcast across America the whole cast relayed a festive greeting of thanks.[51] Christmas had come at last.

Unhappily for Adelaide's friend and arch-rival Ethel Waters, her festivities were not so jolly. She was declared bankrupt, owing thousands in debts.[52] Her career still hadn't reached its full potential and Ethel was sick and tired of waiting for it to happen. In a rash decision, she quit show business and traveled to Europe for a break. The vacation rejuvenated her spirits and within a few months she returned to rebuild her career.

1929

Leslie arrived back from his West-Indian vacation fueled with inspiration and promptly announced to the media that his next venture, a musical version of Leon Gordon's stage play *White Cargo*, would open the following fall with Adelaide in the leading role as a libidinous African native girl.[53] The musical, titled *Tondelayo*, would be his most expensive production to date. Despite his enthusiasm, the show was destined to remain on the drawing board.

Hiding behind the small print, Leslie governed his empire like a judge. Working within an industry that encourages one's foibles makes it very difficult for an artist to decipher where the dividing line between reality and fantasy lies and Leslie played upon this. It's not easy saying "no" to a child. It's even harder denying sweeteners to a star. As with all relationships under intense pressure, at times Adelaide and Leslie's took a pounding. In the heat of their disagreements both parties were wise enough to recognize that for the time being each was reliant upon the other but for how long remained the question.

Hardly a week went by without news concerning *Blackbirds* hitting the press. On February 7, it was the comedian Johnny Hudgins' turn to make the front page.[54] His home in the Bronx was the scene of a fatal shooting in a crime of passion. At the time of the incident Hudgins was asleep upstairs with his wife, Mildred, and was only awoken by the sound of gun shots ringing from the lower floor of his home. When he went downstairs to investigate he discovered his lodger, Seymour Irick, lying in a pool of blood having been shot by his common-law wife, Mary, in a fierce fit of jealousy. When the police arrived the melodrama unfolded. It transpired that Mary had discovered Seymour was still married to his first wife. Mary, who felt no remorse for the consequences of her actions, was immediately placed under arrest and Hudgins' home was cordoned off for twenty-four hours so that an autopsy could be performed upon the body. The tragedy took on an even more bizarre twist when thorough police investigation yielded evidence that Mr. Irick had in fact got three wives.

As a Broadway star, Adelaide's presence was regularly requested at countless charity events, often alongside established stars such as Al Jolson, Ethel Merman, Helen Morgan, Sophie Tucker, and Fred and Adele Astaire.[55] Not only did such appearances benefit the cause, but they increased her profile as a media personality.

One charitable event that Adelaide and Bojangles headlined set quite a precedent historically. The concert was staged in Philadelphia at the Gibson Theater in aid of the Brotherhood of Sleeping Car Porters and was organized by Lew Leslie's brother Sol.[56] It was held on February 27, at the unsightly hour of midnight. However, there was a reason for its late commencement. It featured cast members from both the Broadway and touring company of *Blackbirds* (who just happened to be appearing in Philadelphia). What made the event sensational was the fact that New York's performers had to travel to Philadelphia after their evening show finished at 11 p.m. Realistically this gave the artists an hour to complete the journey. Adelaide, Bojangles, Peg Leg Bates, Snakehips and the conductor Allie Ross all offered their services. After careful consideration, it was decided that the only feasible way of transporting the artists to Philadelphia in time for the show would be to charter an airplane. Such a thing had never been done before and added greatly to the excitement of the occasion.

The final arrangements were finely honed to the last minute. Limousines with a police escort were placed at the cast's disposal at both ends of the flight. After Wednesday night's Broadway performance Adelaide and the rest of the gang piled into their respective vehicles and sped off towards Newark Airport amid a hail of cheers from well-wishers. Needless to say many bets were placed as to whether or not they would arrive in Philadelphia in time. For all the doubting Thomases, the trip was accomplished and the performers did appear at the concert, although not in time for the overture.

"Adelaide Hall, whose songs are important to *Blackbirds*, the Negro revue, which this week will round out a year on Broadway." (*New York Times*, May 5, 1929)

No matter how one viewed *Blackbirds*, the show had become an emblem of its time.[57] In April 1929, *Billboard* announced it to be "one of the most profitable attractions on Broadway."[58] Its popularity sent Adelaide's career rocketing sky-high. She may have been dancing to someone else's tune but in all fairness it was her powerful artistry that gave the show an identity. She had now become the most feted black female performer in America; she was up among Broadway's biggest stars, rivaling Mae West, Marilyn Miller and Helen Morgan.

In April, Leslie confirmed his plans to take the Broadway production of *Blackbirds* to Europe.[59] They would open in Paris, for a limited season at the famous Moulin Rouge.

On May 5, by way of celebrating a full year's run on Broadway and thanking the cast for their persistent hard work, Leslie threw a huge anniversary party at Lexington Hall on East 116th Street to which he invited over 500 guests.[60] The bash was the talk of the town and dubbed one of the season's outstanding social events. No expense was spared—no doubt it was tax deductible—and the dinner menu read like a gastronomic whim: Hors d'oeuvres à la Monsieur Bill Robinson, Celery and olives à la Chick Chick Chorus, Filet of sole à la Mlle. Adelaide Hall, Chicken noodle soup à la Mlle. Aida Ward, Roast spring chicken à la

Gigolo Tim Moore, etc., etc., culminating in richly roasted Demi-tasse café à la Blackbird Orchestra.

Guest of honor was New York's Mayor James J. Walker. In attendance, as well as the entire cast of *Blackbirds*, were numerous stars from other Broadway shows, celebrities, publishers, agents, journalists, backstage theater crew, aldermen, in fact everyone who had in some way contributed to the show's success. Even Elizabeth Hall received an invitation and arrived at the affair looking rather gleeful, on the arm of her son-in-law. Needless to say the function attracted much interest in the press and paid Leslie back handsomely with even more column inches of free newspaper coverage. Leslie truly was the happiest man in town.

In a gesture of gratitude to the people of Harlem for all the loyal support they had shown throughout *Blackbirds*' run, Leslie threw a massive free May Party in Central Park to which he invited a thousand children from Harlem's poorest families.[61] Thousands more turned up uninvited. An enormous marquee and stage was erected on the grass from which Adelaide, Bojangles, Aida Ward and the Blackbirds Orchestra entertained the youngsters. To the stars that attended, the occasion poignantly brought home exactly how fortunate they all were.

A decade elapsed before another white Broadway revue notched up as many performances as *Blackbirds of 1928*. However, to this day, no other all-black revue has ever beaten its record-breaking run.[62]

After such a precarious start, the reasoning behind *Blackbirds*' tremendous popularity was questioned by every white theater critic in New York and, after much deliberation, most unanimously agreed, "The reason it became such a resounding success was because it was turned into a brilliant show and the public found out." It would probably have been much fairer to say that the show triumphed because of its stellar black cast and superlative score.

When asked by one particularly inquisitive journalist about her views on the nobility of fame, Adelaide's enigmatic reply puzzled him, "I used to think one couldn't change the weather. It seems you can."

YOU'RE NOT THE ONLY OYSTER
IN THE STEW

APRIL 1929, PARIS

Josephine Baker's unannounced return to Paris for a short vacation in April 1929 came as a welcome respite during her lengthy and tiring European tour. After an absence of twelve months, the city seemed positively stimulating. She and her manager, Pepito, stayed as house guests at the home of Monsieur and Madame Dalliez and it was here that Josephine began reorganizing her life.[1] For the first time in her career, she began to question her future.

For reasons Josephine never could quite comprehend, her popularity in America had failed to grow with the same fervor she had encountered in Europe. Perhaps the principle "it's better to be a single fish in a small pond than one of a shoal in a vast ocean" held an element of truth in her particular situation.

She wondered if her fellow Americans still bore her a grudge for deserting them so early on in her career. It worried and puzzled her unduly, so much so that each week she had all the important American entertainment magazines shipped directly to her in Paris. In them she scrutinized each page for news of her competitors' progress, for that is how she viewed her fellow black artists—as competition.

Adelaide's phenomenal success on Broadway had not escaped her attention. Josephine's fixation with *Blackbirds* became paramount in her thoughts. If the show's success proved anything to her, it was that with the right vehicle a black performer can compete with any top white star on Broadway. It was a role for which she would have willingly traded her healthy fat bank balance. Having already missed out on the opportunity to be in the original production, she was now contemplating the prospect of eating humble pie.

Josephine insisted Pepito wire Lew Leslie with a proposal. If Leslie could produce a similar revue for Josephine to star in, she would return to New York immediately and by way of an enticement offered to take a reduction in her salary.

"How can Leslie not take my offer seriously?" she confidently informed Pepito.

Indeed Leslie did take her proposal seriously, very seriously, but not quite in the same light as Josephine had anticipated. Unprepared to alter a winning formula, Leslie had no intention of releasing Adelaide from her recently extended contract. She was, after all, the prime reason why *Blackbirds* had run so successfully on Broadway for the past year. Why compete with oneself on the Great White Way, especially when Europe had yet to experience *Blackbirds'* magic?

Leslie knew that if he were to try and keep *Blackbirds* running on Broadway after the original cast had sailed for Europe he would need a substantial replacement to fill Adelaide's shoes. In his swift reply, he offered Josephine the leading role in *Blackbirds* replacing Adelaide during the show's forthcoming visit to Paris—with a reduction in salary, of course.

Incensed by his offer, Josephine wired Leslie straight back.

"My dear Mr. Leslie, I have never in my life stepped into anyone else's shoes and I do not intend to start now!"

The following week Leslie announced to the press that *Blackbirds* would close on Broadway whilst the cast were in Paris to fulfill a three-month engagement at the famous Moulin Rouge.

Josephine was quick to react to this sobering news and had Pepito hastily arrange a press call at which she announced her own imminent departure from Paris. For a year she would undertake a mammoth world tour, the first of its kind ever to be undertaken by a black performer. In fact this was not strictly the truth. Over the past year Josephine had undertaken concerts in most of the major cities in Europe. As more dates were scheduled into her future itinerary, an offer to perform in various

South American countries prompted Josephine to elaborate on the size and length of her tour.

Pepito's reasons for persuading Josephine to leave Paris and travel were somewhat different. The sudden announcement of *Blackbirds'* impending arrival in the city brought with it the real fear that Adelaide could usurp Josephine's position. This created a headache Pepito could well have done without. The novelty factor which brought Josephine to prominence, enabling her to step out of the chorus and into the spotlight had, like a protecting veil, hidden her real talent within. In a sense, her public disguise could now be viewed as her downfall. Pepito knew that what the public had seen up until now was only the image that appeared through that flimsy veil. Dancing barefoot and practically naked with only a string of satin bananas hanging around her waist had, for a fleeting moment, captured the public's imagination. The time had arrived for Josephine to move on and reveal all her talents. Josephine, however, thought differently and still had her heart set on conquering Broadway.

For over twenty years, Mistinguett, a petite pretty songstress with near perfectly shaped legs, had triumphed unchallenged as "The Darling of Paris Music Halls." Since Josephine's ascent to stardom, Mistinguett had been on the warpath looking for ways to avenge her success. Fearing her position, as France's sweetheart, to be seriously under threat, Mistinguett's acrid tongue began spitting missiles. Competition can bring out the worst as well as the best in a person. With Mistinguett, her true colors were now beginning to come to light. The more bitterly she complained to the press, the more outrageously Josephine retaliated. After all, Josephine was young and American with nothing to lose and everything to gain.

Their feuding grew out of all proportion and was viewed by the press as an open slanging match. In public, Mistinguett brazenly referred to Josephine as "that vulgar woman" and nicknamed her "old banana tits" and "the black pearl." Josephine, whose sexual appetite needed feeding daily, got her revenge by stealing or luring away Mistinguett's lovers. The battle continued for many years, at great expense, with each star continually trying to outshine the other.

Adelaide's imminent arrival in Paris posed no threat to Mistinguett. In fact it was quite the reverse; she welcomed the competition, for clearly it would be directed at Josephine and not at her. Anyone who could run

Josephine out of town was a staunch ally in Mistinguett's camp. Josephine's position was somewhat different. If she wasn't careful, her precarious role as America's attaché of black culture could quite easily be seized from right under her nose.

BONJOUR PARÉE!

When Leslie announced that *Blackbirds* would travel to Paris to perform a limited engagement at the prestigious Moulin Rouge, there was much excitement amongst the cast. It was the first time a Broadway revue had been booked to appear at the music hall and as such generated enormous interest.

To celebrate the show's departure, George Gershwin threw a lavish party to bid the cast farewell. He held the affair at his smart Riverside Drive penthouse on Manhattan's West Side. As well as inviting the entire cast of *Blackbirds* the guest list read like a who's who of American showbiz and literary society. Regular guests at Gershwin's parties included such luminaries as Scott and Zelda Fitzgerald, Edmund Wilson, Langston Hughes, James Weldon Johnson, Carl Van Vechten and Fanny Brice, to name but a few.

By the time Adelaide arrived at the apartment, the party was in full swing. In the far corner of the palatial reception room sat Gershwin at his famous Steinway grand piano. The room was dominated by a long panoramic picture window and the view across the Hudson River out towards the Palisades of New Jersey was spectacular. His large collection of French oil paintings and African sculptures decorated the walls and gave one the impression of entering a private art gallery. Nothing gave Gershwin greater pleasure than to play his latest compositions to a devoted audience and in the course of the evening he hosted the whole party sitting in front of the keyboard.

When Adelaide entered the room, Gershwin beckoned her over. He presented her with a small parting gift. A wooden musical box in the shape of a miniature grand piano. The piano was hand-crafted to the finest detail, complete with ebony and ivory keys, a sheet music stand and a piano lid that lifted to reveal wire strings inside. It was a perfect copy of his prized Steinway.

As the evening progressed and the guests became noticeably inebriated on Gershwin's generosity, the party's course took on a wilder, more spontaneous atmosphere. Much to the delight of all those present, many of the guests took turns to perform a song. To thank her host for his hospitality and parting gift, Adelaide sang "I Can't Give You Anything But Love, Baby" whilst perched on top of Gershwin's grand piano. In New York, Gershwin's parties were renowned for lasting well into the night. At nine the following morning when the housemaid arrived to clean the apartment, she unlocked the front door to find the party still in full swing.

On Friday May 24, the big day finally arrived and everybody who knew anybody in *Blackbirds* cast came down to the quayside to wave goodbye.[2] The whole length of Pier 9 was buzzing with activity. Leslie arranged for a jazz band to entertain the crowds of well-wishers and Gershwin sent numerous crates of champagne along to toast the cast's departure in style. It seemed like every relative, friend and neighbor that the cast had ever known was present and that didn't include the media and press photographers that turned up. Adelaide's arrival by limousine caused great excitement. As it came to an abrupt halt outside the dock's main gate the vehicle was instantly mobbed. Her only route of escape was directly through the horde of fans that blocked the roadway. It took her fifteen minutes to be guided through the throng before she eventually reached the gangplank. At the foot of the platform she waved her final goodbyes. Her hand-blown kisses blew across every face in sight. Then, holding the rail to steady herself, she walked up the steep gangplank to board the SS *Ile de France*. At the top, she turned around for one more glance, then called out her last farewell to the crowds, "Good-bye America, I'll miss you."[3]

It was the era of the great ocean liner, the golden age of transatlantic travel when the affluent gave as much thought to crossing the ocean as they gave to crossing the street. The liners that sailed this route were built like floating palaces and the *Ile de France* was the pride of the French shipping line. If you were sailing first class, no expense was spared to accommodate your comfort. The luxury and extravagance bestowed upon such passengers was seen as an essential part of the voyage. In the center of the ship stood a magnificent beige-colored marble staircase, whose obtrusive descent between each deck ended with a grand flourish as it swept into the opulent first-class dining room. It was ideal for making grand entrances and during the voyage was used very effectively by many of the wealthy ladies aboard.

The chief purser escorted Adelaide and Bert to their deluxe cabin on A-Deck. The passage was Adelaide's first break in nearly two years and she fully intended enjoying every minute of it. That evening, they were invited to take dinner at the captain's table. During the meal he asked if the cast of *Blackbirds* might like to stage a benefit show to aid the sailors' benevolent fund. Their efforts raised over $2,000 and more than a few eyebrows along the way.

Seven days later, the *Ile de France* entered the warmer waters of the English Channel and glided majestically into the Baie de la Seine off the

Direct from Broadway

French coast. Here the ship dropped anchor and moored restfully for the night. Outlined in the distance, and clearly visible from the ship's decks, shone the glistening lights of the French coastline, etched like an expensive string of pearls hung around an old lady's craggy neck. At the break of dawn, a fleet of tenders scurried along the starboard side of the ship to transport the passengers and their luggage ashore. As they excitedly stepped down the gangplank towards Le Havre jetty, Lew Leslie, who had sailed ahead of the cast, was waiting to greet them at the quayside. In a brief welcoming speech Leslie informed the cast that they would be making the rest of the journey to Paris by train. He would drive ahead by car and meet them upon their arrival at Gare St. Lazare.

The Moulin Rouge had enjoyed continuous success over the previous few years with its Jacques Charles revues starring the reigning queen of the music hall, Mistinguett. At the end of 1928 Mistinguett deserted the Moulin Rouge for greener pastures, leaving the directors Marcel Foucret and Edmond Sayag in a quandary both financially and artistically. Enticing a relatively unknown actress called Elsie Janis to star in their next revue proved to be a fatal mistake. Within a week of opening, the show prematurely closed when Miss Janis contracted pneumonia. After her recovery the show re-opened but the public had lost interest in the actress and within three weeks the revue ended for good. With the show's failure came the end of the theater's long-standing collaboration with Jacques Charles.

Without the pulling power of Mistinguett and the writing talents of Jacques Charles the magic had gone and the music hall seemed doomed to become yet another cinema house. It was a fortuitous stroke of luck for Foucret and Sayag when Lew Leslie contacted them with the proposition of installing *Blackbirds* at the theater. The proposal came as a lifeline and Foucret jumped at the offer. Little did Leslie, Adelaide and the rest of the *Blackbirds'* cast realize just how much the directors of the Moulin Rouge were depending on the show's success. If the revue failed to attract the public the theater would have to be sold for redevelopment. Without the faintest idea of what they were letting themselves in for, *Blackbirds'* cast arrived in Paris with a guillotine hovering perilously above their heads.

Oblivious of the artistic dilemma her so-called rival Josephine was now confronting, Adelaide entered Paris amidst mild scenes of hysteria.[4] As she and her *Blackbirds* troupe disembarked from the boat train at Gare St. Lazare the reception that greeted them was astounding. A mass of press and public well-wishers surged forward to catch their first glimpse of America's hottest Broadway export. Leslie had co-ordinated the affair to capture as much publicity as possible. Not since Charlie Chaplin's visit two years earlier had Paris turned out in such force to welcome a visiting celebrity.

Bonjour Parée! Adelaide arriving at Gare St. Lazare, Paris. (Photograph courtesy of Keystone-F.S. Pictures)

Emerging from her railroad coach, visibly overwhelmed by the sheer size of the reception, Adelaide stood mesmerized at the top of the carriage steps and waved appreciatively towards the flashing cameras. From her expression of disbelief it was obvious she had not expected such a warm welcome and was totally unprepared for it. To be confronted by such genuine enthusiasm in a country she knew little about gave her a compelling desire to express her gratitude in the native tongue.

"Bonjour Parée" were the only French words she could think of, and Adelaide repeated them to every person she met. Leslie stood to one side of the platform looking totally smug about the whole affair and speculated upon how many column inches of newspaper coverage he had achieved. The cast shuffled endlessly amongst the reporters like a pack of playing cards and posed in every conceivable angle—in front of a Pullman carriage, together with the railroad porters, shaking hands with well-wishers; it seemed as if everybody wanted to be photographed with a blackbird on their shoulder.

Various dignitaries were introduced to Adelaide on the station concourse. Like a visiting head of state she politely moved along the line shaking hands with each person she was presented to: the Mayor of Paris, various Town Hall officials, prominent theater directors and, finally, her host, the Director of the Moulin Rouge, Marcel Foucret, who promptly kissed her twice on both cheeks.

It was Foucret who had arranged for a fleet of automobiles to ferry the cast to Montmartre, their hotel and the most famous red windmill in the world.

A fashion studio portrait of Adelaide taken in 1929 prior to her trip to Paris.

The arrival of the *Blackbirds* troupe at the Gare St. Lazare from Le Havre on
May 31, 1929. Marcel Foucret (Director of the Moulin Rouge) escorts Adelaide
to a waiting limousine. Aida Ward is already seated in the front of the automobile and one of the Berry Brothers, seated on a running-board, waves to the
crowds of onlookers. (Photograph courtesy of Keystone-F.S. Pictures)

DIRECT FROM BROADWAY

If Berlin had liberated Adelaide, then Paris reaffirmed her belief in humanity and threw open the doors to her heart. Driving through the streets in an open-topped automobile on a warm summer's afternoon showed off the intense beauty of the city's architecture to its fullest and most dramatic effect. Foucret had arranged with the automobile firm Donnet-Zédel for a chauffeur-driven limousine to be at Adelaide's disposal throughout her entire stay in Paris. He had also promised a big surprise would be awaiting her arrival at Montmartre but gave no hint as to how big the surprise would be.

Erected outside the front entrance of the Moulin Rouge, rising over four stories high, stood a wooden facsimile of Adelaide dressed in her feathered "Diga Diga Do" costume. The hoarding had been constructed to publicize the show. With arms akimbo and legs spread open wide, her image peered out over the rooftops of Pigalle like an enormous beacon that could be seen for miles around. At nightfall thousands of tiny light bulbs illuminated the figure. Even Broadway hadn't witnessed a spectacle such as this before. Since its erection, the structure had become quite a tourist attraction.

The shock of confronting her own partially naked image left Adelaide speechless. For a moment she just stood transfixed on the sidewalk and stared up at herself with wide-eyed amazement. For the first time in her life it suddenly dawned upon her exactly how famous she had become. Despite feeling both flattered and a little embarrassed by all the attention, for once she found herself truly lost for words.

For Bert, the impact clearly had the opposite effect. Enraged by what he saw as a vulgar and cheap publicity gimmick, he angrily attacked the hoarding.

"Lord have mercy, for I cannot believe what I am seeing." He then turned to face Adelaide.

"Would you take a look at that, honey, the customers are walking in and out between your legs."

For a moment Adelaide saw the humorous side to it and burst into a fit of laughter.

"If that's what they call show business, then you can stuff it. I'm out of here." He paused for a second whilst deciding which direction to take, then grabbed hold of Adelaide's arm . . . "And so are you, honey."

Pushing through the crowd of onlookers Bert hurriedly led Adelaide away from the offending spectacle along boulevard Clichy towards rue Fromentin and their hotel, the aptly named Mont Joli—Happy Mountain!

Back in their hotel suite Bert's temper finally simmered down. His self-opinionated and puritanical behavior had done little to dissuade Adelaide, Lew Leslie or Foucret that the hoarding should be removed. This was Paris, after all, home of the Folies-Bergère where nudity and art went hand in hand. Here it was accepted practice for an attractive woman to reveal her most coveted assets, especially in front of an audience. In the eyes of the Parisians a beautiful body should be worshiped and admired, not hidden away under layers of stuffy clothing, a philosophy Josephine Baker had discovered at her Paris debut and used greatly to her advantage ever since.

"Bert will just have to get used to the idea. The hoarding stays!" These were the last words on the matter from Foucret.

The Hotel Mont Joli was situated at 8 rue Fromentin on a quiet back street just around the corner from Place Pigalle. Typically French in a modest style, it was small, cosy and built around a neat, cobbled courtyard, in which blossomed a large magnolia tree. The establishment was owned and efficiently run by Madame Au Clair, as she liked to be known, a stout short motherly woman whose husband had died during the war. Its homely style appealed to many Americans. For a short period Josephine had been a resident there when she first arrived in Paris. Foucret had booked the whole cast of *Blackbirds* into the hotel primarily because of its location; it was literally two blocks away from the Moulin Rouge. As the cast soon discovered, rue Fromentin was also conveniently sited for the famous rue Pigalle where most of Montmartre's notorious bars and nightclubs operated, including Bricktop's club, the Grand Duc.

Leslie was convinced the glamour and prestige associated with performing at the Moulin Rouge would bring a new dimension to *Blackbirds'* success story. In just under a week the show had to be rehearsed and adapted to suit the Parisian stage. As usual such rehearsals were intense and lengthy and strictly surveyed by Leslie. Any prying journalists who might try sneaking in to witness the proceedings were dealt a heavy blow. However, after pressure from Foucret, Leslie relented during one afternoon session and eased his ban to allow a gifted young artist called Paul Colin entrance. Colin's dynamic images drew heavily on jazz for inspiration. Foucret had commissioned Colin to sketch members of the cast for a poster to publicize the show. To meet the printer's deadline, Colin had been given only one day to complete his *affiche*.

It was particularly warm that afternoon and many of the cast were dressed in simple slacks and cotton undershirts. Colin sat quietly on his own, unnoticed by the cast, towards the rear of the hall at one side. With his large sketchpad resting upon his lap he drew as many of the performers as he could in quick succession. Out of costume and from a distance many of the cast looked similar. This greatly annoyed him. Colin was known for using vibrant colors in his drawings. He complained to Foucret that the lighting was wrong. Irritated by his interruption Foucret replied that this was not a dress rehearsal and he must do the best he could. Colin was not inspired by what he saw, that was until Adelaide arrived on stage. Colin's eyes immediately lit up. He stopped sketching, placed his pencil and pad to one side and simply watched as Adelaide ran through her number. What he saw mesmerized him. Like the powerful aroma from incense Adelaide's aura spilled out across the stage footlights and filled the whole auditorium. Her sweet fragrance intoxicated Colin's imagination.

Colin instantly recognized in Adelaide the model he had been searching for, his "Dame aux Camellias," the inspiration behind his continual quest for perfection. His thoughts ran back to the first glimpse he caught of Josephine Baker rehearsing at the Théâtre des Champs-Élysées in 1925. The comparisons were similar, yet polarized. Whereas Josephine's appearance had intrigued him, Adelaide's presence excited him beyond belief. Like the racing effects of a hallucinatory drug, a sudden rush of adrenaline ran through his veins. He felt a compelling desire to watch every movement she made, as if he were in a trance, yet simultaneously felt totally unable to keep his own body static. He frantically sketched her image upon his pad. With her arms outstretched in an angular fashion and legs kicking in all directions her long lithe body immediately came to life on his page.

After the rehearsal had concluded Colin gathered up his few belongings and went backstage. With his portfolio of sketches tucked underneath his arm he introduced himself to the vision of his dreams.

"Bonjour Mademoiselle Hall, je suis Paul Colin, et je suis un artiste."

Colin spoke little English; Adelaide spoke even less French.

"Parlez-vous français?" he inquired hesitantly.

Adelaide understood enough to reply "Non."

"Mademoiselle, un instant s'il vous plaît, pendant que je vous montre mes dessins." Colin walked across the room to her dressing table where he unfolded his sketchpad and displayed the splendid images he had captured that afternoon during rehearsal. "Voici, voilà," he announced, then proudly stood back, allowing Adelaide to view his work. From her reaction, Colin immediately saw she was impressed.

"These drawings are very good, Monsieur Colin, you certainly know how to flatter a woman," confessed Adelaide rather coyly.

Colin pointed to her body then pretended to draw around her image in the air "J'aimerais beaucoup que vous posiez pour moi demain." He opened his wallet then took out his *carte-de-visite* and handed it to her.

"Je voudrais bien vous inviter à mon atelier pour vous dessiner comme il faut, j'adore votre corps." Pointing to the address on the card, he then wrote down the hour, 12 p.m.

"Veuillez-vous venir à mon atelier demain?" insisted Colin.

The day's hectic schedule had been long and tiring. Adelaide felt the desperate need for a solitary break. In order to get Colin out of her dressing room she readily agreed to his request. "Yes, Monsieur Colin, as a fellow artist I should be delighted for you to draw me," then, as an afterthought quickly added, "although as a wife, I'm not so sure my husband would be that pleased." Without fully understanding what it was she had consented to, Adelaide bid Colin farewell as he gathered up his belongings and made his exit.

Adelaide's agreement to pose for Colin was not the innocent sitting she had believed it to be. At his studio he begged her to pose naked. Although she felt highly flattered by his request, his plea went unrequited. Adelaide flatly refused to pose naked for someone she hardly knew. Instead of discouraging him, her modesty inspired him to push even further with his request. In a fit of desperation he drew her naked as he imagined she looked and then proudly presented her with the sketch.

Adelaide looked startled at the image he had drawn. The confrontation of Colin's vivid glorification of her naked body suddenly left her feeling vulnerable and uncomfortable in his presence. She felt angry that her privacy had been violated and immediately told him so.

"Your imagination works like a powerful aphrodisiac, Monsieur Colin. Now you must understand why I won't pose naked for you."

A look of arrogant disappointment flashed across Colin's face. Adelaide realized that she had unintentionally offended him. As Colin continued to sketch her in silence, she began to feel uneasy sitting in his studio. To alleviate the awkwardness of the situation, she tried making polite conversation, not easy when neither person could speak the other's language.

Adelaide's rebuttal did little to dispel Colin's infatuation with her. Pouring cold water on his priapic advances only made the chase that much more exciting for the hot-blooded French man. Her feet had only trodden French soil for a few days and already Adelaide was forming the distinct impression that most Parisian men would rather see her body naked than clothed. She had yet to discover that in Paris even art has its pimps.

Born in Nancy, Paul Colin studied graphic art at the city's Collège de Beaux-Arts and only moved to Paris to seek work. Desperate to make a living from his craft, he took the first job that was offered to him, designing posters for the Théâtre des Champs-Élysées. His first commission was to publicize the American imported *Revue Nègre*. The success of his poster soon established Colin as one of the city's leading graphic illustrators. He was now earning a healthy living designing posters and stage sets for many of the important theaters and music halls in Paris.

The star of the *Revue Nègre*, Maud de Forest, had left Colin artistically cold and uninspired. He described her as "resembling an elderly oriental carpet seller." His description was in no way a criticism of her talent; it was just that, in his eyes, she lacked the mystique and beauty he was looking for. On his poster for *Revue Nègre*, Colin cleverly featured the misshapen, liquorice body of an unknown female dancer from the chorus and in doing so, successfully captured an image that evoked the soul of Harlem. The poster not only fired the imagination of the French public but also Maud de Forest from her leading role in the revue. The unknown dancer Colin had chosen to feature in the poster was Josephine Baker.

The meeting of Baker and Colin turned out to be a fortuitous one for them both. Not only did it help propel Colin's art into the mainstream, but Josephine also found a supportive friend who taught her the etiquette of French society thereby opening up a world of opportunity to her. Colin seduced her with his knowledge of the arts and in return Josephine became his lover. Although their affair was fiery and short-lived, their friendship remained lifelong.

Colin's comical caricatures of Josephine purveyed an almost innocent, if not naïve eroticism that left little to tickle the imagination. Yet still, the general public found reason to be shocked by his blatant fascination with Baker's black flesh. No matter how one viewed the drawings, Colin's pictures purposely provoked interest and certainly helped pack the theaters where Josephine was performing. They weren't in the least bit complimentary, but then he never set out to compliment her. He drew exactly what he saw and, in their simple, fluid manner, the drawings are quite endearing to the viewer and not in the least bit offensive.

Paul Colin's interest in Josephine diminished greatly as soon as she began appearing at the Folies-Bergère parading on stage like a mannequin. Her act was aimed specifically at the cabaret market. In Colin's eyes her parody of Mistinguett was a big mistake. He accused her of forfeiting her primitive creativity in order to gain mass acceptance as just another Parisian showgirl. When he discovered that she had been scrubbing herself with lemon juice, in the misguided belief that it would lighten her skin coloring, he felt sickened by her behavior. Sadly, even within the black community the shade of one's skin was a terribly important factor. Unlike a chameleon, Josephine did not possess the power to change the color of her epidermis to suit her surroundings. Her desperate attempts to conceal her true identity discarded the one thing Colin found intriguing, her individuality.

Colin's *affiche* for *Blackbirds* that was plastered on every Morris pillar across Paris captured Adelaide in an intriguing pose, although it's left to the viewer's imagination to work out if she's in full song, seducing the onlooker or simply smiling.[1] Her long-lashed ebony eyes sparkle as they peer out coyly from the center of the poster encouraging one to stop and take a second look. Upon closer inspection, two mean-looking, burly individuals confront the viewer. They act like bodyguards and help shield Adelaide from further public scrutiny. Adelaide appears totally at ease, dressed in a flimsy, white satin, low-necked gown with a red and black bonnet cocked up on one side of her forehead. The beholder's attention is then slowly drawn down towards the luxurious expanse of cleavage that Colin has endowed her with. She oozes sex appeal but not in the vulgar sense of the word; more in a refined seductive manner. Any man viewing the poster would willingly have left the girl next door safely tucked up in bed at night just to spend an evening in Adelaide's company. The poster worked well. It cleverly revealed as much as was necessary in order to get the punter to part with his francs and buy a ticket to see the hottest new show in town, direct from Broadway . . . *Les Oiseaux Noirs*.

LES OISEAUX NOIRS

Accolades for Adelaide
On Friday June 7, one day behind schedule, *Blackbirds* held its grand gala opening at the Moulin Rouge. By all accounts it was a star-studded affair attended by the glitterati of Paris. Tickets for the event were disposed of

Paul Colin's *affiche* for *Blackbirds* was plastered on every Morris pillar across Paris. (© ADAGP, Paris and DACS, London 2001)

way in advance and on the evening the management was forced to enlist the aid of the Gendarmerie to help keep out the large and insistent crowd of gatecrashers.[2] Mistinguett arrived with her dance partner and lover Earl Leslie.[3] To quell gossip Maurice Chevalier came on his own. To fuel gossip Boris Kochno, the artistic director of Sergei Diaghilev's *Ballet Russe*, arrived flaunting his handsome French boyfriend, the artist Christian Bérard. Checking out the competition were Paul Derval, director of the Folies-Bergère, and Henri Varna, producer of the Casino de Paris. Also in attendance were some of the most glamorous stars of the French music hall including Grock, Jean Gabin and Barbette. The preshow reception in the theater's opulent foyer attracted the highest turnout of American and European society seen in many a year. To the beleaguered bar staff and waiters it seemed as if the whole of Paris was clambering to take advantage of Lew Leslie's complimentary champagne.

As usual, Mistinguett's arrival was timed to cause the maximum amount of fuss and had the theater management rushing around like a flotilla of barges attending to her majesty's every wish. With all the fresh young talent invading what she deemed to be rightfully her territory, her fear that the public's eye might catch the tell-tale signs of aging meant her image was paramount at all times. As she gracefully alighted from her chauffeur-driven automobile, her outfit, which was totally covered in shimmering silver beads, dazzled even the hardest theater critic who witnessed her entrance.

At such gala events Leslie always took command of the baton and conducted the orchestra himself. From the pit he felt in control and would put the fear of god into any performer who might slacken the pace of the show. Having the boss peering up at them all night certainly kept the cast on their toes. The program that evening ran fueled with adrenaline.

The sensation that Josephine had created back in 1926 when she appeared at the Folies-Bergère naked, except for a skirt of yellow silk bananas hung freely around her waist, was to be eclipsed by Adelaide's volcanic appearance at the Moulin Rouge with her performance of "Diga Diga Do."

The song appeared third in the running order of the show and supposedly transported the audience to a jungle on the Polynesian island of Samoa, where Adelaide recounts a tale of uninhibited native lust. On a bare stage, she made her entrance in total darkness. An orchestral accompaniment repeatedly played the song's introduction as she positioned herself in the center, directly in line with the main spotlight. Attached to the rear of her costume hung the famous thick plumage of fluffy white ostrich feathers. From either side entered a flock of 24 identically dressed dancers who formed a chorus line immediately behind her. Stretching her legs apart, Adelaide adopted the stance of the hoarding that adorned the façade of the theater. When the lighting technician hit the switch Adelaide looked out directly at the audience and, for a moment, posed in perfect stillness. Then slowly she peered down in-between her legs, before looking back up with an enormous grin across her face. Turning her body sideways, she then brought her legs together and bent them slightly at the knee. With both hands resting upon her right calf she gently pushed her stomach in and lifted her backside up as far as it would go.

The movement was wildly erotic yet at the same time outrageously camp. As members of the public simultaneously jumped up from their seats to applaud, the chorus line leapt straight into their dance routine. Viewed from the side, apart from her plumage of ostrich feathers cascading down like a waterfall, to the human eye Adelaide appeared to be naked. In fact it was a trick of the light that bleached out her costume. From that moment on, she held the audience in the palm of her hand. To those who knew her it seemed that Adelaide had already adopted the idiom of her host country.

Accepting the fact that French tastes were more sophisticated than American ones and fearing Broadway censorship might seem old-hat in Paris, Adelaide's white "Diga Diga Do" costume had been modified and retailored to suit French taste. Both the bikini shorts and brassiere were remade in a lighter flesh-colored material. Although Bert initially objected to having the costume altered, the effect worked brilliantly and revealed no more of Adelaide's modesty than had already been aired in public.

Strutting across the stage like a proud peacock, with her hips swinging provocatively in time to the infectious rhythm, Adelaide stormed into the song: "Com'on, girls, let's show 'em what we're made of."

> Now there's a spot I know a
> Place they call Samoa, by the sea,
> Talking there is not the mode
> They palaver in a code . . .

When the chorus hit, Adelaide raised her feathered fan behind her to create a half-moon effect that rose just above her head.

> Zulu man is feeling blue, hear his heart beat a little tattoo,
> Diga Diga do, Diga do do,
> Diga Diga do, Diga do.
> You love me and I love you, and when you love it's natural to
> Diga Diga do, Diga do do,
> Diga Diga do, Diga do.
> So let those funny people smile, how could there be a Virgin Isle, with
> Diga Diga do, Diga do do.
> Diga Diga do, Diga do.

The song was so contagious that by the second verse it felt as if the whole theater had been transported to Samoa and contracted a strain of jungle fever.

> Everything they've got they quiver, from the ankle to the liver,
> And they make the island shiver, yelling Diga Diga do . . .
> Now I know why 50,000 Frenchman can't be wrong.

Even if the audience couldn't understand the song's lyrical content, they knew exactly what the dancers were insinuating every time they accompanied Adelaide's "Diga Diga Do" lyric with rapid hip shaking. It was tremendous fun and whipped the audience into a frenzy, so much so that at the end of the song they demanded encore after encore. For fear of overrunning the tight schedule, Leslie promptly led the orchestra into the opening bars of the next number, "Je ne peux vous donner que mon amour," providing Adelaide with the perfect break to lead her blackbird troupe off stage. "I Can't Give You Anything But Love, Baby" saw Aida Ward coupled with Lewis Cole in a duet. After a quick costume change Adelaide returned on stage to join them in an extended reprise. The show was packed full of punches: "Bandanna Babies," "Porgy" and "I Must Have That Man." The hit songs kept rolling out. No matter how quick-paced the performance, the stubborn persistence of the audience requesting encores stretched the running time way over schedule. By the finale the show had overrun by almost 45 minutes.

The media's summary of the evening was unified. Never before in the history of Parisian theater could they remember a more sensational opening night. Theatrical agents across Europe, including Berlin and London, could hardly wait for the finale to end before storming Leslie with demands to present the show in their respective countries. Even though Leslie's future plans were still unfinalized, Charles B. Cochran— Britain's equivalent to Broadway's bigwig producer Florenz Ziegfeld —insisted London be the next stop on the itinerary. As the title to one of the sketches in the show exclaimed, "Quelle nuit!"

Europe had no Prohibition and backstage after the performance Adelaide's dressing room resembled an overcrowded speakeasy. Brimming with revelry, well-wishers jostled and pushed and blocked the corridor to her room in a vain attempt to toast the hottest new star in Paris. To commemorate the occasion Foucret presented her with a special memento, a Louis Vuitton crocodile-skin vanity case. Inside it were an array of crystal perfume bottles and various cosmetics, some of which had the Moulin Rouge monogram embossed upon them.

From the theater, the celebrations continued around the corner at Bricktop's club in rue Pigalle. Here, the champagne flowed freely all night as the cast taught the French how Americans party.

The following day, Adelaide and Bert awoke around lunchtime. A light breakfast was taken in bed. Foucret had thoughtfully had the morning newspapers delivered to their suite. However, there was one small problem—neither Adelaide nor Bert could read French. Bert rang down to reception and spoke to the hotel owner, Madame Au Clair. Five minutes later she arrived outside their door clutching her reading glasses.

"Bonjour, I hope you both slept well last night," inquired the hotel owner.

"Yes . . . exceptionally well," yawned Bert as he welcomed her into their suite. Madame Au Clair picked up the pile of newspapers and seated herself down comfortably on the long sofa by the window. Opening *Le Figaro,* she quickly flicked through the pages until she arrived at the entertainment section.

"Mademoiselle Adelaide is mentioned in all the best papers," she declared rather haughtily whilst peering over the rim of her spectacles, "and also in some of the not-so-good ones," she added jokingly as an afterthought.

"Oh good . . . read the disreputable ones first," laughed Adelaide impatiently from her armchair.

Over the coming weeks many articles appeared in the French press, most of which were unanimous in their praise for both the artists and the show.[4] Even Lew Leslie, with his tendency for over-exaggeration, could not have dreamt up such accolades. As the main focus of the show, much mention was made of Adelaide's beauty as well as her talent. Comparisons to Josephine were made but these only added weight to Adelaide's individuality.

Jacques Patin in *Le Figaro* blessed her with the look of a "lightly bronzed Venus with large eye pupils of jet."

In *Paris-Midi,* Louis Léon-Martin concentrated more on her physique and proclaimed she possessed "a body without fault."

Henri-Jaunet, in his account, declared her to be "an astonishing woman. She dances to perfection," and one clearly smitten critic reported her triumph a little more eloquently, "Last night Paris witnessed a bright new star in its constellation."

After brief comparisons to *Revue Nègre, Le Figaro* admitted the success of *Les Oiseaux Noirs* was "grander, more brilliant and more justified. Adelaide Hall is to the show . . . what the sparkle is to champagne. Those birds are going to spend not only summer in Paris, but the winter as well." *Le Journal* professed Adelaide to be "the Josephine Baker of the show. She is graceful, of an animal suppleness, very seductive and has perfect aestheticism," whilst *L'Intransigeant,* after lamenting the invasion of the French music hall by so many foreign artists, informed its readers reassuringly, "Here at last is the pearl of the season . . . *Les Oiseaux Noirs.*"

Théophile Gautier, editor of *Le Figaro,* wrote in his poetical appraisal of the cast: "These beautiful dancers are not black. They have flesh the color of tea, mastic and of sand in the sun. Their limbs are perfect; their bodies supple and fine . . . as supple as foliage. Their movements are so quick they make the earth turn faster beneath one's feet. When they sing, their voices are vibrant and accentuated." As most of the artists in the show were singled out for praise somewhere amongst the reviews, no one in the cast felt left out. Perhaps one of the most interesting accounts of Adelaide's performance, which could only have been written by a French man, should not be taken too seriously. "Watching Adelaide perform is like making love to a goddess; it makes one feel inadequate during the event."

Josephine's unannounced visit to see *Blackbirds* occurred a few days later. Accompanied by Pepito she slipped warily into the music hall only seconds before the curtain rose, with the sole intention of disguising her presence. The couple were swiftly directed to a private box where they remained seated throughout the duration of the show.

When the final curtain descended, Josephine hurriedly vacated her seat and scurried out of the building as fast as her lizard-skin shoes could carry her. In doing so she made no attempt to acknowledge greetings from well-wishers and snubbed anyone who approached her. However, her rapid escape was unexpectedly foiled at the exit, where she was pounced upon by a pack of hungry journalists. Someone had tipped them off.

Eager for a story, the press swooped upon their prey. With an appetite for gossip that would normally devour a helpless victim, they attacked Josephine for her comments on the show. This was exactly what Pepito had wanted to avoid, a confrontation with the press. Without a brief, Josephine's tongue chattered like a live wire on a telegraph pole. She said what she felt and suffered the consequences later. Like a hunted tigress, Josephine was cornered.

"No comment," complained Pepito bitterly as he tried shielding Josephine from their barrage of questions.

"No comment, s'il vous plaît." But still the newsmen insisted.

Pepito whispered quickly into Josephine's ear, "Just tell them you enjoyed the show and then we can all go home . . . you understand?"

Josephine smiled a wicked look of mischief back into Pepito's fiery eyes as she slowly eased the collar of her coat away from her neck.

Turning to face the pack of wolves she lifted her head, gritted her teeth and allowed the words to tumble out. As her speech rapidly descended into mockery Pepito abruptly halted the proceedings by covering her mouth with his hand.

"As you just heard, Josephine thoroughly enjoyed the evening and now we must depart. Thank you for your consideration. Now if you'll just step to one side, we'll be off."

Josephine's words were as sharp as lemon juice and just as bitter on the tongue. If her career was to progress, Pepito knew full well that the time had come to banish her string of wilting bananas from her stage trunk forever and replace them with a more sophisticated string of pearls.

Little did Josephine realize at the time that her taut expression spoke a thousand words to the journalists who witnessed her hasty departure. Like a rejected wire coat hanger in a crowded wardrobe Josephine felt exposed. In some respects Mistinguett and Josephine were sisters. They both found it impossible to accept another person's success gracefully if that glory directly threatened to eclipse their own.

Having purposely set out to seduce the press, Adelaide now found herself in the enviable position of being courted by them. By crowning her the new jazz laureate, they automatically labeled her public property.

Amused and humbled by all the attention, Adelaide made a great effort to develop a personal relationship with the French public. Their endless appetite for the smallest details regarding her life meant these were wildly exaggerated when translated into tabloid news. Pictures of her and other cast members taken around town appeared daily and gossip columns regularly reported the night-time antics of some of the more spirited members of the troupe.

Eager to capitalize on the free publicity, Leslie took full advantage of the situation, arranging photocalls and interviews at regular intervals. This was his way of keeping the public's interest alive. Unwittingly, Adelaide's triumph shifted the focus of attention away from *Blackbirds* as the product and put the spotlight directly on her as an artist. This swift shift of emphasis gave her role in the show a totally new dimension.

On Broadway, *Blackbirds* had been a musical phenomenon that Leslie had controlled autocratically. In Paris, he now found himself losing grip. As far as the French public were concerned, Adelaide was the main reason they flocked in droves to the Moulin Rouge. She was the star. The show had merely become the vehicle in which she was being driven. To those around her it appeared that Adelaide's personal success was about to eclipse *Blackbirds'* reputation. That the raw talented teenager from Brooklyn had finally blossomed into a ravishing sophisticated chantreuse could only in all honesty have been credited to Leslie's astute foresight. Unluckily for him, unlike his previous protégée, Florence Mills, whom he fortunately managed, Adelaide was only under contract to Leslie for the duration of the show.

One event that created quite a splash in the French newspapers occurred on Sunday June 28, at Tourelles in the northeastern suburb of Paris.[5] The annual swimming championships were being held in aid of charity. To attract a large attendance, the organizers of the event invited stars and actresses from the Paris music halls to partake in a beauty contest. The pageant took place along the edge of the Waterdrome, the largest open-air swimming pool in the city, and there were various prizes up for grabs—including the crowning of that year's beauty queen.

The organizers' trick worked and on the day the celebrities attracted a huge turnout. As the stars mounted the catwalk to parade their outfits, polite cheers from the spectators helped them along their way. When Adelaide appeared, dressed in a patriotic red, white and blue striped bathing suit, little did she dream of having any chance of winning one of the prizes. As far as she was concerned just being asked to represent the Moulin Rouge was in itself an honor. However, her appearance caused quite a sensation and generated the loudest applause of the day. One reporter went so far as to quote that they were the wildest scenes of enthusiasm he had witnessed since Lindbergh's landing at Le Bourget. It was probably fair to say that many of the public present had never seen a black female before, let alone one that was partially naked.

In contrast, the response Adelaide received from one of France's leading actresses of the day, Mlle. Diana, who was also a participant, was colder than the water in the outdoor pool. Mlle. Diana had clearly expected to win the beauty contest hands down and hadn't banked on Adelaide creating the wave of support she received. When it came to judging, the organizers had a problem of diplomatic proportions. Should they crown Adelaide the beauty queen—she was obviously the crowd's favorite—or should they bow to pressure from certain biased officials and give the prize to Mlle. Diana? As the audience grew more restless by the minute, the judges came to a hasty compromise. They announced a tie. Mlle. Diana was crowned "winner with the best costume" and Adelaide was crowned (with the same crown) "winner with best form and originality." Their attempt to keep the peace fell flat with the press. In the following day's papers, reporters cruelly mentioned that Mlle. Diana's fiancé had been one of the judges and wondered if this had possibly swayed voting in her favor. Whatever the outcome, the event had been staged for charity so should have been taken more lightheartedly by certain contestants. That a black girl from Harlem could beat the French in a beauty contest, right under their nose, *C'est magnifique!*

Publicity from the event sent demand for tickets to see *Blackbirds* soaring.

Not surprisingly, Adelaide found life in Paris far more congenial than she had imagined. Her daily routine took on a regular, if somewhat irregular, pattern. She slept until noon, ate breakfast for lunch, spent afternoons shopping, took tea whilst bathing and arrived at the Moulin Rouge around six to prepare for that evening's show. Dinner was always eaten after a performance followed by the customary late night on the town, sampling the boundless delights of French hospitality.

BUCKIN' THE DICE

The summer of 1929 was an exceptionally long and hot affair and Paris blossomed in its glow. Despite the heat, which was no worse than that of a New York summer, the *Blackbirds* cast knuckled down to their three-month engagement inside their temporary nest at Montmartre's old red windmill and became the hit of the season.

Before a performance, Adelaide invariably became impatient and slightly irritable. Over the years, Bert had wisely learnt that it was best to leave her alone at such times. On these occasions Bert would occupy himself by organizing an impromptu card game with whoever was to hand and could be persuaded to play.

Bert loved playing cards, especially blackjack, and always carried his favorite pack of playing cards inside his jacket pocket. They were the sort you could pick up in a souk in any foreign port and had risqué pictures of naked women posing as pin-up girls on the reverse side. These were his lucky cards, or so he bragged, and whenever he got the opportunity to test his luck, out came the cards and a game of blackjack would ensue. These games would occupy many hours of waiting around, especially backstage during a show.

Having joined the cast in Paris, the Berry Brothers, Ananias and James, who were young and impressionable and knew little about the ways of gambling, soon became hooked on the game. Each day, in-between performances, they would sit on wooden crates in the wings playing Blackjack with Bert. Filled with the confidence of youth, the brothers thought they were top-notch players; that was until Mr. Hicks, as the brothers called him, kept winning. More often than not the brothers lost all their weekly spending money at the game at which point Adelaide would intervene and scold the boys for being so stupid with their hard-earned cash.

"Now you've lost all your money," Bert would tease, "I suppose you'll be asking me for a sub." He would then lend the boys some cash so they could try winning back what they had lost. Surprisingly, they always managed to do so, as unbeknown to the youngsters, this time Bert would allow them to win. After the success of winning their money back, the brothers would dance around backstage like lunatics escaped from an asylum chanting, "We've beat Mr. Hicks, Blackjack is our latest trick!" The boys never did wise up.

The Berry Brothers were hugely talented and inventive dancers for their age and stole many a curtain call from some of the more established acts on the bill. Bert took a shine to them and became their unofficial chaperon during their residence in Paris. He unconsciously molly-coddled them, as if they were his own sons, and went to great lengths to ensure their stay was a memorable one. Paris became one big adventure for the brothers, who were away from home for the first time, and Bert had more than his hands full just trying to keep them out of trouble.

One of the funniest sketches in *Blackbirds* revolved around a crooked four-hand poker game in which the actors—although the audience was oblivious of it because of the many crossfire quips and wisecracks—really dealt, drew and bet on the result once during every performance of the skit. After almost playing a royal flush one night, Tim Moore, the double-dealing con man of the four players, was heard to ad lib, "I've come to the conclusion that a straight flush is as rare on the face of a girl as it is in a poker game."

Back home in America, the black press watched *Blackbirds'* progress avidly. News from Paris filtered through regularly from various foreign correspondents, including members of the cast.[6] On July 31, in the *New York Amsterdam News,* the paper went to town and proudly proclaimed in bold headlines, "Adelaide Hall now new Parisian idol."[7] In a full-page feature they detailed her remarkable success with meritorious pride. "Adelaide takes Paris by storm," "*Blackbirds* hold their own," "Adelaide Hall's popularity growing with leaps and bounds." The paper covered practically every angle in documenting her acclaim. In a glowing report, J. A. Rogers explained why the Parisians' love affair with Adelaide had now reached fever pitch:

> *Blackbirds* continue to be the sensation of the season. Already their ten-week engagement has been extended to fourteen. In spite of the warm weather the Moulin Rouge is crowded at all performances. Adelaide Hall's popularity continues to increase. She's hailed by many of the French papers as being superior to Josephine Baker. Josephine came at a time when the Negro dancer was still a novelty in Paris. Her wild primitiveness and superb body flashing nude swept her into fame. Later Miss Baker was content to rest upon her laurels and when we saw her in May 1927, her performance was poor and lamentable. Adelaide Hall is full of vim and snap. She is vivacious, fascinating, very good-natured and unaffected—the sign of a real artist, which she is. Her eyes reflect unlimited reserves of nervous energy, and her shapely legs and body could well be the dream of some master sculptor. Comparisons are odious but sometimes they can't be avoided. As a dancer or as an artist Miss Baker simply cannot be mentioned in the same breath with Adelaide Hall. We saw Miss Hall for the second time last week and she was so excellent that we shall certainly go to see her again and again. As to her singing certainly we have never heard any human sing in so many voices at one time. What a jazz band does for music, Miss Hall with her single voice does for singing. She is distinctive and merits the generous applause and encores she receives. Miss Hall has youth, beauty and talent in abundance.

> She is not the star of a day or a season . . . she possesses variety
> of talent, the lack of which causes many actors to last but a
> season. Already she is the most talked about actress of her genre
> in Paris. All that she needs now to boost her fame is a clever
> press agent.

From his honeyed report the reader might easily form the view that Mr. Rogers was indeed touting for the job as Adelaide's press agent but in all fairness his account was sweetened by a genuine respect and admiration of the artist's talent. Even taking into consideration the fact that racial attitudes in Paris were amongst the most relaxed in Europe, the show and its cast had still achieved a tremendous amount and had a lot to be proud about. America's ostensibly biased entertainment bible, *Billboard*, also drew the same comparisons and conceded that *Blackbirds* was "the outstanding revue hit of the year. The colored troupe scores a knock-out with the cosmopolitan audience at the Montmartre music hall."[8]

~~~

Paris had an exhilarating effect upon Adelaide. Ever since stepping off the boat train at Gare St. Lazare she had felt an instant affinity with the city. For some inexplicable reason she sensed that she was staring destiny straight in the face. The memorable events that enlivened her visit over the next months only helped strengthen her initial impressions.

The ornate beauty of the city and the elegance of its people charmed her. She discovered a new phrase, *laissez-aller*—unconstrained freedom— and on several occasions found herself crying uncontrollable tears of joy. She couldn't remember ever having felt this happy before. It was as if she had been waiting for this moment to arrive all her life. Now that it had, she had no intention of letting go.

It wasn't *déjà vu*. It was more akin to a strong sense of foreseeing her fate. In the back of her mind she had already accepted that her lifestyle must change. Just how dramatic that change would be she had yet to find out. Secretly she promised herself that someday she would return to Paris, not just to visit but to live. For once, the thought of living out of a suitcase held a fascinating appeal.

Each day Adelaide grew more accustomed to the French lifestyle. She made a great effort to learn and speak the language and even incorporated certain phrases into her performance. With practice she became *au fait* with French mannerisms, although at times their habits did appear quaint and unusual. It didn't take her long to realize just how wide the distinction between America and Europe was. It wasn't just the Atlantic Ocean that separated the two cultures; the French had a totally different perspective on life from the Americans. Her observations left an indelible impression upon her. Adelaide had already convinced herself that Paris would provide the perfect refuge should they ever wish to leave America. All she had to do now was convince Bert.

In return for the enthusiasm Adelaide displayed for Paris, its citizens

"Adelaide Hall is to the show . . . what the sparkle is to champagne." (Photograph by Paul Walery, Paris 1929)

bestowed an adoration upon her unseen since Josephine's baptism in 1925. During the previous year the Parisians' love affair with Josephine had clearly waned. In Adelaide they saw her natural successor. With her simple charm and native beauty she captivated everyone. The warm reception she received during a chance encounter with the fashion designer Coco Chanel was indicative of the affection she attracted from total strangers. At her salon in rue Cambon, Chanel was so thrilled to meet Adelaide she promptly presented her with the largest bottle of perfume in the shop. The perfume, called Cuir de Russie, was inspired by the recent visit of another troupe of dancers to the city, Diaghilev's *Ballet Russe*.

"The scent of one genius is passed to another," declared Chanel rather grandly as she handed Adelaide the gift. Humbled by her generosity, Adelaide's quick response came spontaneously, "From now on Cuir de Russie will be the only thing I shall be seen wearing when I go out," to which Chanel nodded her approval before making a loud tut-tutting sound.

"If you don't mind me saying, Mademoiselle Hall, I think even in Paris we are not yet that uninhibited. We expect a beautiful young girl to wear a little more than just perfume."

Paris fashion houses and art galleries were experiencing a cultural insurgence against all things European and had acquired a great passion for everything Negroid. Amongst the many ethnic influences that seeped into daily life, brightly dyed silk turbans, African shawls and ivory and wooden bracelets had become *de rigueur*. Even the home began to take on a vague African look when Banbangi masks, leopard skins and wicker artifacts were introduced to decorate walls. Literary sources dubbed this eclectic period "Le Tumulte Noir" and Paul Colin published a book of inspired lithographs to celebrate African influence upon art.

In the eyes of the American public you were black or white, inferior or superior and there were no shades of gray in-between. In Europe this all changed. Noir, Zwart, Schwarz, Preto, Maypo, no matter what language it was translated into, black stars were recognized for their talent not their skin color and their names were celebrated in lights, something white Americans were still reluctant to do. Here black performers were lionized both socially and professionally and treated like true artists. They merited the respect and privileges that were bestowed upon their white counter-parts. At first this shift in opinion came as a culture shock to the cast who were used to a segregated existence. In Europe they discovered enthusi-asm for their work and freedom from racial pressure.

Adelaide's joy at discovering such liberality was carefully expressed during an impromptu interview with a persistent reporter who had been stalking her during an afternoon shopping expedition:

> The Parisian public aren't afraid to applaud us or mix with us in the street, yet in America, especially in the Southern States, they still show the same mistrust and disgust in the face of colored folk.

Then, as if to acknowledge her fortunate circumstances, she warmly announced, "Paris is the perfect town for artists."

Certainly, by the late Twenties, Paris had become a magnet for free-thinkers and freelovers from around the globe. In a bid for recognition a steady stream of black entertainers crossed the ocean and headed straight for Montmartre. At times Paris appeared to be so crowded with fellow Yanks, it became a joke that the city had become the third largest in the U.S.A.

However, not all Parisians gave blacks the red-carpet treatment. A certain fraction of the community complained bitterly to local authorities that the sudden influx of Senegalese into the city had caused a worrying increase in burglaries and disease.

Blackbirds attracted many famous personalities during its residency at the Moulin Rouge. Picasso brought his much-painted mistress of the moment, Marie Thérèse, and Cole Porter, Ethel Waters and Valaida Snow all visited the show during their European vacations. Nancy Cunard, heiress to a British shipping fortune, who was then living with her black lover in the city, became a regular attendee.

Adelaide became the darling not only of the French press; artists and photographers constantly feted her as a model. Fuziek followed Paul Colin's example and drew a series of lively caricatures depicting her in various jazz dance poses, and the noted photographers Paul Walery and Manual Freres captured her portrait on film. Cecil Beaton also took

"Adelaide Hall now new Parisian idol." (Photograph by Paul Walery, Paris 1929. Courtesy of Hulton Images)

inspiration from the show for a series of photographs he later produced.

Meanwhile, Josephine Baker's expedition to South America did not fare as well as she had hoped.[9] News bulletins from Argentina charting the erratic progress of her tour arrived regularly in Paris. Billed as the "Black Venus," her pre-publicity hype failed to capture the public's imagination and attendance figures at her Buenos Aires shows dwindled daily. A further setback came when, in an endeavor to maintain public decency, President Hipólito Irigoyen ordered Josephine to put more clothes on or "no more shows." In a brave attempt to save face, thousands of free tickets were distributed to drum up interest in her show.

"A body without fault." Adelaide, as photographed by Paul Walery, Paris 1929. (Courtesy of Hulton Images)

The *Blackbirds'* cast were not just famous for their performances on stage; they acquired quite a reputation for their antics off the boards. They may have been called blackbirds, but at nightfall they turned into owls. At the end of an evening's performance they thought nothing of spending the rest of the night partying like animals until dawn. Many clubs they visited expected spontaneous performances from the cast, who obliged no matter how inebriated they were.

Earl "Snakehips" Tucker, who had taken over Bojangles' role in the show, was certainly on everybody's party list. He had created such a sensation for wiggling parts of his anatomy in directions most people thought were impossible that the French press nicknamed him the "shivering dancer." So fluid and slippery were his body movements that he could easily have been mistaken for a rattlesnake. He was an odd character, brawny, yet trim, with a squat face that made him look like a boxer. For him Paris was like playing on home territory. He was able to whisk an audience into frenzy, as easily as tossing a salad. When he danced his famous hip dance, muscles miraculously appeared on his physique from nowhere like molluscs surfacing on a deserted beach after the tide had gone out. His shins were so hardened from dancing that French women referred to them as "frog's legs." They found him irresistible and he loved it.

Paris society welcomed the cast with open arms. Party invitations to some of the most fashionable addresses in town arrived daily.[10] No soirée seemed complete without at least one member of *Blackbirds'* troupe in attendance. One such memorable affair took place in an aspiring artist's studio over an art school in Montmartre. The party was thrown in honor of the black writer Claude McKay. Unfortunately for the hostess, many of the guests were stifled by good manners and protocol. Although the champagne flowed freely, the hostess feared nothing would enliven the frosty atmosphere. She clearly had not encountered the cast of *Blackbirds* before. Shortly after midnight, a fleet of taxis screeched to a halt outside the school and out stepped every shade of skin imaginable. Like an aphrodisiac the arrival of the *Blackbirds* troupe brought an instant pep to the party. The cast was so full of gaiety and laughter that you would never have guessed they had just performed a strenuous two-hour show. At the far end of the room, surrounded by a crowd of handsome men, Adelaide held court from a makeshift throne. Peg Leg Bates and Snakehips took turns to dance with the ladies whilst the rest of the cast overwhelmed the pianist with song requests. At one point the merriment became so riotous that nobody noticed a raging thunderstorm had developed outside. At six in the morning the gale died down, as did the party. Those who still had any reserves of energy headed off to the Coupole Restaurant for breakfast before retiring to their beds for a well-earned sleep.

No sooner had Leslie announced to the press that *Blackbirds* would be heading directly to London after its Paris engagement, to replace *Wake Up and Dream* at London's Pavilion Theatre, than he changed his mind and decided to head back to the States.[11] Realistically, the logistics of touring with a cast of 150 across Europe posed too much of a headache to be feasible. Since many of the performers had commitments back home it seemed a more sensible plan to regroup the company in New York and head out on an American road tour.

On August 7, Leslie sailed back to New York to commence rehearsals on his next production, *International Revue*, which was to have an all-white cast.[12] Once more the songwriting talents of Fields and McHugh were commissioned to write the score and a Broadway premiere was planned for October. The revue was Leslie's most expensive project to date. After *Blackbirds'* Broadway run had reportedly netted him over a million dollars' profit, he could now afford to splash out a little.

Sadly, even the profitable run of *Blackbirds* couldn't help save the Moulin Rouge from the developer's hammer.[13] Foucret announced that at the beginning of September the music hall would close for major renovations and re-open at the end of the year showing motion pictures. At the expense of Parisian culture the momentum of the talking movie claimed yet another casualty.

Summer was practically over and the vacation season was drawing to an end. Leaving Paris with such fond memories and so many new friends made parting much more difficult to contemplate. On September 9, having previously said their farewells in private, Adelaide and Bert caught the boat train at Gare St. Lazare and traveled to Le Havre. They spent that evening at a small hotel in the center of town before boarding the SS *Ile de France* the following day. After a lengthy delay, blamed on severe weather conditions, the majestic liner finally left French waters on September 11 in the early hours of the morning.

Once more a call from America beckoned.

Adelaide's arrival at New York harbor on September 17 was met with the customary press reception. Unfortunately for the impatient media, Adelaide's appearance was somewhat delayed. The customs shed ran the entire length of Pier 92 and was crowded to capacity with weary passengers, all queuing in line under the appropriate initial of their surname. If any person felt unsure about where to stand, overhead a large sign hung that bore that particular letter of the alphabet. As a celebrity, Adelaide was given priority treatment but even so, having arrived home with twice the amount of luggage that she had left with, customs inspectors took longer than usual to clear her belongings.

When first they inquired, "Miss Hall, have you anything to declare?", Bert came to the rescue with a carefully prepared three-page declaration that read like an inventory from a house clearance. After meticulously inspecting her baggage a different picture emerged.

"They're mostly gifts," explained Adelaide embarrassed, as an array of unspecified artifacts surfaced from the depths of her trunks. Unfortunately for Bert's wallet, Adelaide's oversight taught him a costly lesson—that being famous doesn't give one automatic exemption from paying duty.

Blackbirds immediately hit the road on a national tour.[14] Although her triumphs in America and Paris had brought her mass public attention, Adelaide felt cornered by Leslie's increasing demands. Her discontent slowly began to manifest itself in her mood swings. She now wanted more than Leslie was prepared to give. It had reached the point where if her nerves didn't crack something else would.

Blackbirds' 1929 road tour

Week commencing: Sept. 30: Newark, New Jersey
Oct. 14: Pittsburgh, Pennsylvania
Oct. 28: Cleveland, Ohio
Nov. 4: Detroit, Michigan
Nov. 26: Chicago, Illinois

MY FATE IS IN YOUR HANDS

Blackbirds, *Adelphi Theater, November 26, 1929, Chicago, Illinois*
For obvious reasons gangster-ridden Chicago was not one of the most favored cities for an artist to perform in. On the circuit it had a reputation for being a hard nut to crack. A city that had all the glitz and razzmatazz of

Broadway yet lived on the wrong side of the dividing line called law. It was also known to be bitterly cold.

No opening night in Chicago would be complete without its gangsters and gangsters' molls in attendance. *Blackbirds*' first-night gala at the Adelphi Theater was no exception.[15] The show was booked solid for a twelve-week run. Billed as "The fastest, funniest, most tuneful musical revue ever presented, and the sensation of two continents," Leslie's elaborate pre-publicity campaign had the city clamoring for tickets. The term "black market" took on a new meaning as touts profiteered from a roaring trade. Not only did *Blackbirds* arrive with an element of prestige attached to it, but Chicago's newspapers billed Adelaide as "The greatest female star of her race."[16]

In the *Chicago Defender*, Leslie announced that *Blackbirds* would become a yearly event. "Broadway has been looking forward to an annual race revue for years. Only now am I in a position to promise playgoers an annual edition."[17] When asked why he had used white songwriters he confessed regretfully that he was forced to use Dorothy Fields and Jimmy McHugh because he could find no suitable material written by black songwriters.

During their stint in Chicago, many party invitations arrived for Adelaide and Bert to attend. One of the more interesting affairs requested their presence at a dinner-dance to be given by the famous movie star Gloria Swanson.[18] The soirée was held in a grand mansion on South Parkway. For the occasion the ballroom had been effectively festooned with pea-green and pink decorations complemented by huge floral arrangements of crimson rose buds. Guests were treated to an extensive buffet and entertained by a particularly good jazz band.

Adelaide and Bert arrived late, after *Blackbirds*' evening performance. They were presented to their famous host in the glamorous setting of the ballroom. Considering the invitation had stated dinner attire, Miss Swanson appeared oddly overdressed for the occasion, dripping in jewels and wearing a loud sequin and feathered gown that trailed lazily upon the floor behind her.

"Good evening, Miss Hall, I'm honored to meet you and so pleased that you could attend my little soirée. May I say how enchanting you look tonight."

Adelaide accepted the compliment gracefully, thanked Miss Swanson for the kind invitation, then introduced Bert.

"I've seen your performance in *Blackbirds* on numerous occasions both on Broadway and in Chicago and I'm a big fan. What I wouldn't do for a voice like yours," continued the throaty Miss Swanson, intermittently punctuating her words with large sweeping hand movements.

"I too am a great fan of yours, Miss Swanson . . . I especially enjoyed your performance in *The Trespasser*. I thought you sang 'Love, Your Magic Spell Is Everywhere' with great emotion."

"Oh! . . . you're far too kind, Miss Hall. My singing voice is not my best asset . . . but the studio did insist."

The stilted conversation continued with the exchange of mutual compliments until Miss Swanson politely excused herself to attend to her other guests. The meeting had been short but extraordinary. Both Adelaide and Bert had been amused by Miss Swanson's deep, raspy and sometimes masculine-sounding voice and agreed that her use of over-flamboyant hand gestures was totally out of character at such an affair. Adelaide dismissed it as theatrical eccentricity although Bert was not convinced. The evening continued pleasantly enough if uneventfully and during the latter part of the affair Miss Swanson made an impromptu speech to thank her guests for attending. Before her departure Adelaide was presented with a small parting gift, a silver visiting-card holder in remembrance of the evening.

At the theater the following day Gloria Swanson's party was the talk of the cast. Adelaide relayed the story with great excitement and little restraint, graphically accounting how masculine Miss Swanson's voice had sounded and how melodramatic she appeared in real life.

It was a few more days before Adelaide finally discovered the truth behind the whole affair. An actor, a very talented female impersonator who called himself Gloria Swanson, had staged the event. So clever, in fact, was his disguise that many people found it impossible to tell the real Miss Swanson apart from the impostor. After discovering the truth Adelaide inspected the gift she had been presented with a little more closely. Removing the rectangular white card that was placed inside the silver holder, she re-read the dedication:

With love, Gloria Swanson

Only then, after turning the card over, did she notice a smaller inscription written in the bottom right-hand corner:

Walter Winston . . . Female Impersonator

Even though Al Capone was out of town, temporarily residing in a Philadelphia prison after his arrest and prosecution for the possession of an illegal firearm, his entertainment establishments in Chicago were still open for business. To help launch his latest revue at the Cotton Club in Cicero, which was managed by Capone's brother Ralph, Adelaide and the cast of *Blackbirds* were invited to the premiere.[19] Whereas Adelaide— accompanied by Lew Leslie—did accept his offer and attend, either fear or sheer cowardice caused many of the cast to decline.

For some reason Chicago always brings out the best and the worst in a person's character. The highly charged city encourages the two traits to run perilously close to one another, at times too close, like the two sides of a fault in the earth's crust, forever anticipating disaster. At this point in the tour it seemed like an opportune moment for one blackbird to start planning her migration.

Leslie's autocratic behavior coupled with Adelaide's growing resentment over his manipulative hold over her career came to a head during the company's stormy engagement in Chicago. For reasons known only to Leslie, he adamantly refused to advertise Adelaide's name in lights outside the theater.[20]

When challenged, Leslie was known for his fiery rhetoric. Although a confrontation with him seemed unavoidable, Adelaide had no intentions of being drawn into a slanging match. Bert came prepared. He opened the *New York Times* and recited a list as long as his arm of every star performer on Broadway whose name was displayed in lights outside the theater they were appearing at. It was ludicrous that Adelaide should be treated differently. Bert read the list aloud like a mantra but Leslie refused to change his decision.

Adelaide's cage had been rattled. No matter what the outcome she was determined to battle out their differences. She threatened that unless

Leslie agreed to her demand she would walk out of the show there and then. To his cost Leslie treated her threat as idle and scoffed at it. His arrogance and audacity astounded her. If nothing else, Adelaide's resolve should have forewarned him that this time she meant business. Like an *agent provocateur*, Leslie called her bluff.

"Be my guest, walk out . . . the show goes on with or without you."

Although in jest, his words were spoken with venom. He genuinely believed Adelaide would retract her statement.

Ever since her return from Paris, Adelaide had known she had outgrown the show. For a while she had been patiently treading water, waiting for the right opportunity to arise before making her next move. The time to hang up her feathers had arrived. Although distraught, her sudden exit was tinged with both sadness and anger. After all the success they had achieved together Adelaide was sad to leave on such a sour note, yet angry at the way Leslie had mistreated her. No matter how distressed she felt at leaving, she could never have known her departure would signal the inevitable downfall of Leslie's empire.[21]

Having unexpectedly flown the nest, Adelaide's future suddenly looked less than certain. Back at their hotel suite later that evening, the full impact of the situation hit home. Bert's gut reaction was to call Bojangles and explain the circumstances they now found themselves in.

"Get the hell out of Chicago and head straight back to New York," came Bojangles' sage advice. "As soon as you arrive, give me a call and I'll set up a meeting with my manager. Now that Addie's free from her contract there's no reason why she and I couldn't do another show together, that's if she'll have me back."

These were the words of encouragement Adelaide had been waiting to hear.

"I suppose it's time to pack up and hit the road again," sighed Adelaide despondently.

"You bet, honey . . . time to hit the trail, but not until you and I have eaten the best meal in Chicago. Come on, babe . . . let's paint the town," came Bert's reply.

UNEASY LIES THE HEAD THAT WEARS A CROWN

Adelaide had performed continuously in *Blackbirds* for two years, giving almost a thousand performances. Throughout its entire run, only once— at the insistence of her irate mother—did she miss a show, rendering her understudy's role obsolete. Within one month of her departure *Blackbirds* folded and the cast disbanded, leaving Leslie to retreat to New York licking his wounds.

Only one fact is certain in the entertainment industry—success is fickle. It offers no security for the future.

Uneasy lies the head that wears a crown. Had she made the right decision to quit? Over the following weeks, this question played havoc upon Adelaide's mind. The thought of failure cast a long shadow of doubt. Perhaps she had forgotten the golden rule?—"After success, don't ever look back"; no one can take the past away from you.

With hindsight she need not have worried. Over the next few days she soon discovered who her real friends were and how her fears had been totally unfounded. As a graduate from Lew Leslie's stable of artists, Adelaide's qualifications were impeccable and held her in good stead for any future career move. In some ways, pursuing a solo career would be her ultimate challenge. New beginnings induce a fresh surge of energy, revitalized by necessity. However one viewed her situation, it was hardly as precarious as Adelaide and Bert had first thought.

Back in Harlem, in a well-organized and highly publicized event, Adelaide gave her first performance since leaving *Blackbirds*. The *New York Amsterdam News* staged a Christmas Charity Dance at the newly renovated Rockland Palace in aid of Christmas baskets for the poor of Harlem and the Bronx.[22] On the day the benefit was announced over 500 requests for baskets arrived at the newspaper's offices. On December 20, Harlemites turned out in their thousands and broke all attendance figures at the venue. Adelaide, accompanied by Fletcher Henderson's band, headlined the show and all the entertainers donated their services free. The function proved without doubt the immense pulling power of Adelaide's name and gave her a much needed lifeline and platform from which to launch her solo career.[23]

As the last days of the decade drew to a close, the disastrous effects of October's Wall Street Crash continued to register. In a matter of hours, "Black Tuesday" had seen $18 billion evaporate into thin air. The stock market had become a battleground of corporate greed and the casualties were left to either pick up or pack up. Like a horse toppling at the last fence in a race, no one could have predicted the market's downfall but, unlike the horse, the animals in this particular race had never worn blinkers. Stocks and bonds that had once been priceless were now viewed as worthless pieces of paper with imaginary figures written upon them.

It seemed inevitable that Broadway would take the full impact of the collapse in the economy, but how badly was anyone's guess.

Like the end of an all-night party, the unwelcome glare of the bright morning sunlight woke everyone up on New Year's Day with a hangover. The end of Harlem's liberation was in sight.

PART III

AND THE MONEY CAME ROLLING IN

1930–35

WHERE TO NOW?

1930

No matter who you were, or how important you might be, the stark reality of the Depression brought everybody back down to earth with a sobering thud. Unlike other performers, Adelaide had had the good foresight to invest in her career, not stocks and shares.

"And where to now?" spoke a quiet voice within. The closing of one door invariably means the opening of another.

Adelaide and Bert arrived early at Marty Forkins' plush Broadway office. They sat in reception for a few minutes before his secretary escorted them through into an adjoining room. Their meeting was calm, direct and controlled. As with his favorite drink, vodka, which Forkins drank neat, he wasn't one to mix his words with tonic. He knew show business inside out and the business knew him. He spoke the truth and never made false promises. His candor was both impressive and reassuring. The meeting went well.

Forkins mentioned that he had recently received a script entitled *Brown Buddies*, which he hoped to adapt into a musical and present on Broadway later on in the year starring Bojangles. Although the show was still in its early stages he thought the female lead would be ideal for Adelaide.

In the meantime, to capitalize on her Broadway popularity, Bert suggested a solo tour might be a wise move. Forkins agreed and recommended the RKO circuit. Not only would such a tour reach a wide audience, but the power of RKO's publicity machine would bring Adelaide's name to the attention of every important agent and director in America. He also suggested that Webber-Simon might be the right booking agency to handle the tour. They represented the biggest vaudeville acts in the country.

Bert contacted Nicholas Gyory at Webber-Simon and arranged an appointment. This meeting was not as decisive as he had hoped.

"Now listen here!" Bert's raised voice suddenly took control of the conversation.

"She's the biggest black female star on Broadway. Of course she'll sell. I'll lay down any amount of money on it, and if Broadway producers don't have the wherewithal to promote her, then I'll take the whole show out on the road myself. The audience will love her!"

Gyory's concerns, that a white vaudeville audience was totally different from a Broadway audience, made for his hesitancy. However, he acknowledged Adelaide's appeal and agreed to arrange a short tour to test the reaction.[1]

Blackbirds of 1928 had played to over a million paying customers on Broadway and become the longest-running all-black revue in history. The touring company almost doubled the show's attendance figures. In the wallets of Broadway producers, Adelaide was a bankable asset. In vaudeville she was an unknown quantity.

REACH FOR THE MOON

At New York's RKO Palace Theater, Bojangles was treated like a king. He had played there so many times that he joked he could walk from the stage back to his dressing room blindfolded. If his name was on the bill, the show would be an instant sellout. Over the years, Bojangles had learnt exactly how to manipulate this particularly tough audience and could hold them spellbound in the palm of his hand. His popularity created a headache for the theater's manager who found Bojangles a nuisance. His routine would stop the show and nobody would want to follow him, which is why he was invariably billed as the last act of the evening.

On February 8, Adelaide made her debut at the Palace. Of course she was nervous. Who wouldn't have been? This was the big crunch. If she could make it here, not only would it increase her salary potential, but the doors to every white vaudeville theater in the States would be opened for her. She knew it, Bert knew it, Bojangles knew it and, more worryingly, the RKO bosses knew it.

The Palace was the most renowned variety theater in the world. There were usually eight acts on the bill, three headliners to pull in the punters and five specialty features that could range from trapeze artists to animal acts. Sometimes, if the audience liked a particular turn, they would sit in the theater all day just to catch it again. It was vital for Adelaide's future in show business to make a good impression from the start.

Backstage was buzzing with excitement and some of the biggest names in the entertainment world.

"No need to be nervous, honey, just go out there and reach for the moon. They'll love ya." Somehow, in the midst of all the hullabaloo that surrounded her, Bojangles' words of encouragement dissipated into oblivion. In their place the dichotomy of no fear and total fear took effect. Every pulse point in her body sharpened and, no matter how she viewed her situation, she felt sick with worry.

Adelaide might have been a nervous wreck but when she walked out on stage that night to face the vast auditorium, she had confidence in her smile.

It was Bert's idea to have two pianists—Putney Dandridge and Carrol Tate—accompany her on stage. This was highly effective musically, and added greatly to the spectacle of the performance. She made her entrance in between the two pianos and used them as props throughout her act. Imitators were quick to follow, including "big-voiced" Ethel Merman, who used a similar outfit for her performance at the Palace a few months later.

Adelaide need not have worried. Her act literally stopped the show, and she shared top credits with Fanny Brice and Phil Baker. The *New York Times* called the bill "the pleasantest entertainment purchasable."[2] The review claimed Adelaide's performance proved without doubt that she was one of the best vocalists in the business, and *Billboard* named her "the dusky satellite" and "one of the big hits of the show."[3]

Adelaide's name in lights outside Broadway's RKO Palace Theater.

Her performance was delivered via four complete wardrobe changes, in a cycle of numbers intermingled with dance routines. She even managed to play the ukulele. Some die-hard critics felt her act was tailored to suit a white audience and would have much preferred more of a jungle setting. In fact this was intentional. Her crossover, from black novelty act to a sophisticated chanteuse, was carefully choreographed to gain mass appeal, something no black female artist had ever attempted before.

Towards the end of her program, Adelaide suddenly announced Bojangles was in the audience, which met with loud cheers of approval. She invited him up on stage, and in an impromptu skit they danced a duet to rapturous applause. The number was so well received that the management invited them to star as a headlining double act later in the year.

In her dressing room after the show, Nicholas Gyory confirmed her performance had been a revelation and had, without any shadow of doubt, established her name in variety.[4] Like the last kiss of the decade, that moment would remain sacred in her memory for ever.

Over the next three years, Adelaide set a record by starring at the

Palace Theater on seven separate occasions, more than any other black female vocalist.

RKO's head office was located in Times Square over the Palace Theater at 1560–1564 Broadway and from here the company governed their vast network. As well as owning scores of theaters across the country they had over twenty situated in and around New York. To compete with the cinemas most ran double bills with movies. Only the Palace, as America's sole surviving straight vaudeville house, refused to show movies apart from newsreels.

Contracts were consigned to a performer a few weeks in advance of each engagement. These would be agreed, signed and then returned to head office, so the agent could pay the artist at the conclusion of each engagement.

Rehearsal hours at RKO's New York and Brooklyn theaters started ridiculously early, 8 a.m. at Jefferson's on 14th Street and 9:30 a.m. at Broadway's Palace.[5] With as many as four shows crammed into a day, this left little time for the artists to recuperate from tiredness. At the bottom of each contract, a rider, typed in bold red letters, forewarned of the consequences should the artist arrive late for rehearsals: "Don't travel by motor. Late arrival at the theater will result in a salary reduction." The fine was usually one-third of a week's salary. Failure to report at all would bring indefinite cancelation.

As the snowballing effect of the Wall Street Crash gained momentum, a deepening depression took hold of America's financial institutions and unemployment spiraled out of control. Cumulative debts brought a tidal wave of chaos and panic for millions of investors who now viewed their stocks and shares as worthless pieces of paper.

The entertainment industry was viewed as a luxury commodity and, as such, one of the first casualties of the ailing economy. Where queues had once formed daily outside theaters to obtain tickets, they now appeared alongside the Church and Salvation Halls in the hope of receiving food. The promise of free "soup, soap and salvation," was too tempting to miss. For the recipients, any thoughts of sitting on a plush velvet seat watching a Broadway show was the last thing on their mind.

Many legitimate theater owners found they were unable to weather the storm, either financially or creatively, and, rather than incur more debt, allowed their theaters to fall dark. In the process, Broadway's golden era of musical revue drew to a close. One by one the bright lights on Broadway's canopies were unceremoniously extinguished. It was as if someone had unwittingly yanked the plug out of the electricity generator and plunged half of the theater district into darkness. One worried journalist likened the desertion to a plague: "It's as if they'd fallen ill with a mysterious virus."

If the critics' reviews were mediocre, the safest option for a producer was to hedge his bets and close immediately, thereby avoiding any further loss of money. He could always re-open the following week with a brand new show.

Only the fittest productions survived and, in a last-minute endeavor to keep ailing shows alive, anxious theater owners tried to persuade their performers to take salary reductions. Even Broadway's biggest superstars had their wings clipped. Rather than be unemployed, some graciously agreed to have their salaries cut whilst others, who believed in their own pulling power, adamantly refused. Many entrepreneurs were unwilling to put up with such idiosyncratic and greedy behavior and refused point blank to hire such artists, no matter how big a draw they were. Those who blessed the credulous fools that believed in their own invincibility were just as much to blame for many of the shows' closures. For some performers any job seemed better than no job at all and working for peanuts became their only option. Their desperation took away the agents' power of negotiation.

Like an overworked chorus line, dragging its heels at the thought of yet another reprise, the big lavish musicals of yesteryear began to look jaded. Audiences were complaining that they had seen it all before and they probably had. In a sad twist of fate, a rush of lavish Hollywood screen musicals that endured the public's affections took their place. This conjuncture threw Broadway completely off balance.

Since the mid-Twenties, Hollywood's movie industry had steadily taken control of many vaudeville houses, stripping out the stage and replacing it with a large, blank movie screen. The battle for survival for those theaters that continued to show live productions grew more difficult by the day. In the producer's eye, the movie industry had become a license to print money. Now everybody wanted to be in on the act. Florenz Ziegfeld and Busby Berkeley were both poached away from Broadway to produce movies for Hollywood. Actors and songwriters quickly followed suit and headed out to Los Angeles in droves, hoping to grab the rich pickings that were on offer.

Even Duke Ellington felt tempted to try his luck in front of the camera lens. Not satisfied with his outstanding success at Harlem's Cotton Club, he made the long trek across the States to the West Coast. He appeared in the film *Check and Double Check*, featuring the hugely popular comic duo Amos 'n' Andy. Hollywood had yet to view black women as leading lady material and still preferred to cast them in menial supporting roles, such as maids and house servants.

If the Twenties roared with riotous behavior, the Thirties were captured by Hollywood's "Depression" movies. In the smash-hit film *42nd Street*, Ruby Keeler sang "yenom eht ni er'eW"—"We're In The Money"— backwards. Her tongue-in-cheek satire typified the "Let's put on a show, right here" nothing to lose attitude which had now become prevalent on Broadway.

Extravagantly styled, with oversized props, lavish costumes and endless, finely choreographed dance routines, such movies offered people a welcome escape from their own mundane existence. The camera captured parades of dazzlingly beautiful young girls, all dressed identically, in much more detail than they could ever have been seen on the stage. In these "feel good" movies audiences found a ray of hope for the future and left the cinema feeling a hell of a lot better than when they went in.

Life in the Leslie organization was also rapidly beginning to fall apart. Rumors were rife that he had accepted an offer to film the entire *Black-birds of 1928* revue.[6] In the contract, the production company stipulated that the original cast would be required to participate in the making of the movie. Unwisely, Leslie signed the contract at the end of December 1929, knowing full well that he couldn't fulfill his obligations. His deception resulted in the production company filing a lawsuit against him.

At the beginning of 1930 Dorothy Fields and Jimmy McHugh signed a contract with Metro for a weekly salary of $500 and a royalty guarantee of $2,000 a week.[7] Their song "I Can't Give You Anything But Love, Baby" had become the most sensational hit of the last five years.[8] Worldwide, phonograph and sheet music sales were the highest the industry had ever known, justifying Leslie's claim that he would make the song into the biggest hit in the country.

Later that year, Fields and McHugh also issued Leslie with a writ for unpaid royalties on songs they had written for *International Revue*. Leslie's response to the writ was one of contempt. He issued a press statement announcing that he was broke, having lost $300,000 on the production, his first major flop.[9]

Jobs may have been scarce and money even scarcer but the public still tried to put on a brave face. In Times Square pitching pennies became a popular pastime, anything to try and make a buck. Those down on their luck gambled their last coins by throwing them at a chalk line. The closest to the line cleaned up. In a sense, the "what the heck" attitude of the players typified the mood of the nation: "If it's a gamble, it's a gamble."

As the dust from the stampede to sell people's assets began to settle and the bankruptcy files had been lodged, life in Harlem resumed a hint of normality once more. People still needed to escape the drudgery of daily life and, during the past decade, Harlem had become highly proficient in catering for such distractions. Although an air of pessimism prevailed, some club owners were heard to exclaim, "Depression! What Depression?"

In May, Adelaide returned to Harlem and starred in *Lucky Sambo* at the Lafayette.[10] Billed as "Broadway's Colored Idol," her name carried the entire production. The show did little to further her career. It acted more as a stopgap in her itinerary but the overwhelming reception she received confirmed her popularity as America's No. 1 black female star.

In July, Marty Forkins made a surprise announcement to the media.[11] Bojangles had turned down a lucrative offer to star in Florenz Ziegfeld's next presentation, *1930's Follies*, and would instead open on Broadway within the next few months in the musical *Brown Buddies*, alongside Adelaide.

Remarkably, Broadway's Palace Theater was having its most profitable year since it was built nearly twenty years earlier, averaging a weekly gross of $27,000.[12] Adelaide's return to the Palace in August saw her partnered with Bojangles.[13] The show was perfectly timed to publicize their forthcoming Broadway musical, *Brown Buddies*, which had now commenced rehearsals.

On Friday August 29, the NBC Radio Network transmitted *Harlem on the Air*, a tribute to the white comedy duo Amos 'n' Andy who, at that time, were America's biggest radio act.[14] The show was transmitted live from New York at 10:30 p.m. and broadcast across the States to hundreds of thousands of listeners. The bill had an impressive array of black stars including Cab Calloway and his Missourians, Aida Ward, Shelton Brooks and James Lilliard. Bojangles compered the program and Adelaide headlined. The show gave *Brown Buddies* a tremendous plug and the audience figures peaked at the highest level the radio station had ever known.

During the broadcast, Adelaide sang two numbers, "What's The Use?" and George Gershwin's "Maybe," accompanied by Cab Calloway's orchestra. In the latter song she strummed her famed ukulele as Bojangles provided rhythmic accompaniment by tap dancing.

BROWN BUDDIES

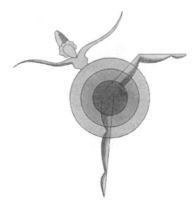

Adelaide and Bill, Bojangles and Hall, Adelaide Hall and Bill "Bojangles" Robinson, however the press billed them, they were still dubbed the black equivalent to Fred and Adele Astaire. For Marty Forkins it was the first show he had produced on Broadway and both he and Bojangles invested a considerable amount of money in the production.

Unusually for a black musical, *Brown Buddies* had a complex story line. It revolved around a company of black soldiers from East St. Louis, who leave their homeland to fight in the muddy trenches of France during the early stages of America's participation in the First World War. To help morale, the soldiers are followed by a troupe of YMCA entertainers, who also hail from East St. Louis. As in all good musicals, a romance develops. The top sergeant of the regiment, Sam Wilson, played by Bojangles, falls head-over-heels for the pretty young star of the YMCA troupe, Betty Lou Johnson, who was played by Adelaide.

Their love affair gains momentum across the dug-up fields of Flanders and through the horrors of a heartbreaking battle scene. Adelaide's yearning lament in "Give Me A Man Like That" only adds to the expectancy that something awful will happen in the finale. At a time when money was too scarce to mention, at great expense the show bravely depicted a full battle scene with cannon explosions, wounded officers dripping blood and dramatic lighting and sound effects, much to the horror of the audience sitting in the front row.

The first scene is set in the mud flats of East St. Louis during the summer of 1917. The next act swiftly transports the audience to France and the army barracks. The date is spring 1918. Most of the following scenes take place in the trenches or in some other war-related location in France. The final two scenes return to East St. Louis, where everything comes out to form on Armistice Day.

With a cast of 60, rehearsals commenced mid-August. To regain her svelte figure, Adelaide leapt into a rigid routine of exercise and diet. On September 15, the show opened at Nixon's Apollo Theater in Atlantic City.[15] The following week, it played Baltimore and then traveled to Pittsburgh for a final tryout before its Broadway premiere.[16]

On Sunday October 5, just before their departure from Pittsburgh, disaster struck. Bojangles was shot and wounded by a police officer, who mistook him for a thief.[17] As he left Bailey's Hotel to hail a taxi to the Pennsylvania railroad station he witnessed the robbery of a white woman by a black youth. Hearing her screams, Bojangles dropped his bags on the sidewalk and gave chase to the fleeing youth, in an attempt to recover the woman's snatched purse. In the course of the pursuit, Bojangles drew his gold gun, presented to him by the New York Police Department, and fired into the air. A local patrol cop, seeing the revolver and hearing the shot, mistook Bojangles for the thief and fired, wounding him in the arm. He fell to the ground and the real culprit escaped. The bullet entered Bojangles' upper left arm and lodged in his biceps. After hospital treatment, where the slug was removed and his arm bandaged in a sling, Bojangles was discharged to continue his journey back to New York. The police officer in question later explained his error, "All black men look alike to me."

News of the shooting hit the front page of many national papers and gave *Brown Buddies'* publicity campaign the biggest boost it could ever have wished for. In true theatrical style, Bojangles vowed that the show must go on. When he arrived back in Harlem, he released a dramatic statement to the press. He would appear on stage at the premiere "even if it meant his death."

Brown Buddies opened on Broadway on October 7 at the Liberty Theater, which was, by coincidence, where *Blackbirds of 1928* had originally enjoyed some of its long run. Despite his wounded arm, Bojangles took to the stage on opening night and gave a brave performance. Although they found it difficult to cuddle, the customary love duet between Adelaide and Bojangles still took place during the number "Happy." Bojangles was fifty-two but on stage he appeared twenty years younger and when he danced with Adelaide he made every man in the house wish that they were in his shoes. Towards the end of the evening, the pain in his left arm became so excruciating that he missed the finale and took no curtain calls, choosing to remain in his dressing room in order to rest his maimed limb.

On the whole, the show drew good press notices with few dissenters.[18] Walter Winchell in the *Daily Mirror* said, "One of the best song and dance shows in town. There is nothing like it for speed, pep and zip!" "We've had a lot of Negro shows which tried to be white . . . this one is true to its color. It has the honesty of its own humor," wrote Charles Darnton in the *New York Evening World,* "*Brown Buddies* is a war play of entertainment. Nobody is killed and everybody is happy." Considering the amount of all-black shows Broadway had savored over the previous decade, the *New York Times* praised it highly: "Whether the performers enjoy *Brown Buddies* more than the audience would be difficult to say, since both appear to be having an uncommonly good time."

Bojangles was hailed as the gallant hero, no doubt his bandaged arm fitted nicely into the plot, and Adelaide, "Grinning with pleasure, turned music into exclamation. 'Give Me A Man Like That,' she shouts, making wicked eyes."

Reading the reviews, one can't help but think the show must have been a real heart-warming treat, the kind of show where the audience feels reluctant to leave at the end. On stage, the chemistry between Adelaide and Bojangles generated magic. They genuinely adored each other and it showed through their repartee.

Although the story line was thought to be flimsy the song and dance routines that accompanied the plot more than made up for its weaknesses. "No anatomical displays or Harlem vulgarity to be found," *Billboard* assured its readers. "*Brown Buddies* is entertainment for children and the children inside of grown-ups." That statement alone could never have been made ten years earlier, which showed how far black musicals had progressed. Marty Forkins must have been wildly pleased with the notices. To celebrate, he threw a lavish party and invited all of Broadway's bigwig producers, agents and stars to the affair.[19]

Forkins took a leaf out of Lew Leslie's book by ensuring Adelaide's input was continual throughout the show's run.[20] She created a new dance routine, which was promptly inserted into the plot, and named it the "Darky Rhythm," for which Joe Young and Peter Tinturin wrote an accompanying song.[21] It was described as having a "low down" suggestion, furnished and inspired by Bojangles. The routine was said to be so suggestive that it set the pulse beat of Pike Davis and his Brown Buddies Orchestra racing so fast that they were unable to assist Adelaide with musical accompaniment. "It's too hot for the orchestra to play and still keep their minds on their work," claimed Marty Forkins. A solo accompaniment by Putney Dandridge on piano was used instead. In December, to keep the show fresh, Adelaide added another number to her performance, "I Hate Myself For Falling In Love With You," which was specially written for her by Abner Silver and Dave Oppenheim.[22]

During the show's Broadway run, Bojangles conducted a dance class on stage at the theater after each Wednesday and Saturday matinée.[23] Members of both the public and theatrical profession attended. Even the film star Ruby Keeler was spotted at one session. Bojangles would slowly talk his way

Adelaide serenades
Bojangles in *Brown Buddies.*

through various steps and explain how there were at least four ways to do every tap step, sometimes as many as eight, and then perform a routine that included them all. Adelaide occasionally joined in the class and confessed to the pupils that she had had no idea that she was performing one step four different ways until Bojangles had pointed it out to her. The classes were a good exercise in public relations and gave the hands-on approach, enabling the audience to meet the stars in a relaxed environment.

Bojangles was famous for his congenial and humorous personality. He was also known to be a strong administrator and believer in equality for all races and noted for his quick temper if anyone offended him.[24] He would act before thinking a situation through and would often bring his gold gun out of his pocket and start waving it about to make sure the other person got the message. When the tryout tour played in Baltimore, various fellow cast members visited a café next door to the theater to purchase a nickel cup of coffee. The owner of the establishment charged the actors a dollar for each drink. After inquiring why they were being overcharged for a nickel cup of coffee the owner acidly replied, "Because you are what you are." After returning to their backstage dressing room at the theater, the actors relayed the incident to Bojangles. Without uttering a word, Bojangles picked up his jacket and immediately stormed round to the café to purchase a nickel cup of coffee for himself. Whilst the proprietor's back was turned, Bojangles quietly removed his famous gold pistol from inside his jacket pocket and placed it on the counter, pointing directly at the owner.

"How much will that be?" Bojangles inquired politely.

Viewing the pistol on the counter with startled horror, the proprietor gulped before replying nervously, "Five cents."

After Adelaide's abrupt departure from *Blackbirds*, Leslie tried to rekindle public interest in the show by associating her biggest rival Ethel Waters' name to it. His ploy didn't work. *Blackbirds of 1930* bombed dismally. Leslie had failed to recognize that since the onset of the Depression the public's taste had become more discerning. They now wanted a change. Unfortunately for Miss Waters, once again incompetent management saw her career thrown off course. Bad luck and misfortune had a habit of following her around like the smell of rotten eggs.

Benefit shows for the unemployed were now becoming a regular occurrence and most of Broadway's big stars and theater owners gave their services to such events free. Such concerts were indicative of the worsening economic climate which was becoming more worrying by the day.[25]

In a cunning twist to the Leslie saga, a special midnight gala was presented at the Lafayette Theater on Sunday November 23 to aid Harlem's Co-operative Committee for Relief and Unemployment. The show attracted tremendous interest from the black community, not least because of the number of celebrities who were involved in the affair. Ironically, in the heavens that night not a single star was in sight. Only the majestic full moon gave out any light as it sailed alone across an empty sky. To the ticketless crowds trying to gain entrance to the show, the only place stars were shining that evening was on stage at the Lafayette.

The first half of the program contained excerpts from Leslie's latest edition of *Blackbirds*, which had Ethel Waters heading the cast. After the interval, the full company of *Brown Buddies* occupied the stage. Even though Adelaide and Miss Waters were best friends, the fact that Lew Leslie was involved in the affair brought out the worst in Adelaide's character. She had every intention of showing him just how foolish he had been. During the opening bars of her first song "Happy," Adelaide spoke briefly to the packed house of her concerns for the unemployed and of ruthless company bosses who were exploiting the current situation by paying ridiculously low wages to the already badly paid workers.

"I have, after all, had first-hand experience of a ruthless manager profiteering from my own talent." The audience rose to their feet in support of her.

A look of anger flashed across the face of her former Svengali, Lew Leslie, who was seated in the front row of the audience. His only acknowledgment of her remark was to turn his head away from the stage in disgust.

Adelaide learnt a lot during her two-year residency in *Blackbirds of 1928*, not least that the rewards of success could be translated into many currencies. The cost of admission to the upper echelons of society lay in the volume of ticket sales you generated as an artist. As long as you remained big news and sold theater tickets by the lorry load, your name would appear on every important party invitation and guest list in town. Bert had every intention of converting that privilege into "readies."

Brown Buddies, with its universal certificate, played on Broadway for an impressive fourteen weeks to moderate but profitable business. Even though attendance figures were higher than any other black show at the time, competition from movies and the huge popularity of radio saw the show reluctantly close at the end of January 1931. Whereas a revue is easy for an audience to navigate around, a musical has a story line and asks for more of the viewer's attention. Some felt the story line held the performance back, preventing any instinctive ad-libs or audience participation. Forkins suggested editing the show to a revue and taking it on tour to play the movie houses. As the architect of Adelaide's future, Bert had other plans on the drawing board. After *Brown Buddies*' closure, it was agreed her next career move must capitalize financially from the stature of her popularity. Already, the Broadway producer Earl Carroll, of *Vanities* fame, had approached her to star in his next revue and offers from Europe were arriving with encouraging regularity.

Under Forkins' direction, Adelaide's salary had risen to over $2,500 a week.[26] Her successful transition into vaudeville earlier on in the year generated an exciting offer from her new agent, Nicholas Gyory, who confirmed RKO were now keen to talk business. He proposed a major American coast to coast concert tour, playing all the major cities *en route*. The proposition was too good to refuse.

1930 RKO Dates

Feb. 1–7 Central Theater, Jersey City, New Jersey
8–14 Palace Theater, Broadway, New York

Mar. 8–14 Earle, Philadelphia, Pennsylvania
22–28 Palace Theater, Chicago, Illinois
28 Hippodrome Circus, Chicago, Illinois
29–31 Palace Theater, Cleveland, Ohio

Apr. 1–4 Palace Theater, Cleveland, Ohio

Aug. 9–15 Palace Theater, Broadway, New York

Benefit concert (possibly) held on November 30, 1930 at Broadway's Waldorf Theater. The concert was organized to benefit the NAACP. Interestingly, not only does this picture show some of the most important figures of the Harlem Renaissance, but it is also the only known photograph in existence of Adelaide and Duke Ellington together.

Front row from left to right: Sonny Greer, Ivie Anderson, Duke Ellington, "Snakehips", Adelaide, Bill "Bojangles" Robinson, unknown, Ethel Waters.

Back row from left to right: Aida Ward, Buck, Edith Wilson, Bubbles.

RKO, COAST TO COAST

ADELAIDE HALL

1931

As if to verify the fact to himself, F. Scott Fitzgerald wrote to a friend in May 1931, "The 'Jazz Age' is over." After christening the era and mythologizing it in several novels, it seemed only fitting that he should announce its dissolution. Without so much as a farewell wave the liberating Twenties, with their emancipating ideals, gave way to the bread-and-butter Thirties. On Broadway, shows were closing as quick as lightning, some before they had even opened. Overnight the overwhelming sense of optimism and promise that was prevalent in the Twenties simply vanished.

After the closure of *Brown Buddies*, Adelaide had two choices: to continue working in musical theater or to kick off her Broadway shoes and head out on tour. Her impatience made the decision an easy one. In a climate where money was becoming decidedly more difficult to come by, the offer of regular hard currency was too good to miss.

Unlike most stars, who had taken the well-trodden path from vaudeville to Broadway, Adelaide had done the reverse. She had started her theatrical profession on Broadway and was now in the daunting position of packaging her act for the white vaudeville circuit. This transition altered the direction of her career for ever and the next two years proved to be her most lucrative to date.

RKO publicized her concert tour as the biggest ever undertaken by a black female performer. In large advertisements in the trade papers they proudly announced, "Adelaide Hall booked solid through to August 1932." Her contract exploited her popularity to the full. Throughout the tour, she performed over 1,000 concerts. The press hailed her as a stylist, an innovator and an inspiration to her race. Her success paved the way for fellow black artists to follow. She did what she did best: sing. Gone were the complicated dance routines with a troupe of chorus girls backing her. She now concentrated on projecting herself as a vocalist and the rhythm of Harlem traveled with her.

Billed as the "Crooning Blackbird," her itinerary stretched the length and breadth of America, crossed over into Canada and, for the first time, saw her visiting Britain. Like a songbird in flight, most of the dates were booked back to back. Her schedule showed little opportunity for rest periods.

The organization and preparation for such a tour was immense. In the space of two weeks, musicians had to be hired, a new wardrobe of costumes designed and intensive rehearsals undertaken. Miraculously, the deadline was met and the show hit the road as planned. As a considerable amount of time would be spent traveling, Bert employed a full-time maid to assist Adelaide. Her name was Minnie and she accompanied Adelaide constantly.

Minnie had only recently arrived in New York from the West Indies. She had originally intended to explore the States before settling into a full-time job but her money had run out so her plan had temporarily been put on hold. Her employment with Adelaide allowed her to work her passage across America. Even though she enjoyed her job, was reliable and possessed a wicked sense of humor—an invaluable asset on tour—Minnie always had a miserable look on her face. No matter how much make-up she applied or how colorful her clothes were, she always looked doleful. It wasn't that she was ugly or particularly unhappy; she just

Publicity still, inscribed to Ruth during Adelaide's visit to Cleveland in March 1931. (Photograph courtesy of the B.F.I.)

happened to possess a permanently sad facial expression. However, beneath this anguished exterior lived a heart of gold that could be called upon at any time of the day. Though her salary was meager, her loyalty and hard work were rewarded with a ticket to see the world. Her contentment and good-humored disposition afforded Minnie many years of service in Adelaide's household.

For most of the tour Adelaide traveled from one engagement to the next overnight by train, escorted by her maid. This ensured her prompt arrival at each destination. Bert journeyed ahead by automobile. Sometimes, if the schedule permitted, the two pianists accompanied him. This arrangement helped cut expenses, and gave Bert time to prepare for Adelaide's visit before she arrived.

The itinerary kicked off in Cincinnati on February 28 with Alex Hill and Joe Turner as her piano accompanists. The week before she left,

Adelaide appeared at Broadway's Palace Theater as a surprise guest during Noble Sissle's act, by way of thanking him for her first theatrical break in the musical *Shuffle Along*.[1]

CHICAGO

March 7, 1931, Palace Theater, Chicago
When he arrived at Chicago's Palace Theater, Bert asked the backstage doorman for permission to park his Buick in the side alleyway during performances, so that he could escort Adelaide from the theater without incident. The doorman explained that such authority was not his to give and that he would have to consult a higher official. Later that evening a sealed envelope was delivered to Adelaide's dressing room. Addressed to Mr. Hall, the short note read as follows: "Dear Mr. Hall, please feel free to park your car in the backstage alleyway at all times during your wife's engagement at the Palace Theater." The note was left unsigned.

After the show that evening, as they were leaving the theater, Bert made a point of thanking the doorman for his assistance. "You don't have to thank me, Mr. Hall," replied the bemused doorman. "It's Mr. Capone you want to thank."

In certain cities, especially those with a large black population, the fans' persistence at trying to get Adelaide's autograph became such a worry that Bert began to fear for her safety. To try and avoid the opportunity for such confrontations he devised an alternative procedure of evacuating her from the theater at the end of a performance. Rather than have her leave the building through the main backstage exit, Bert arranged in advance for his car to be parked in a side alley, by an unmarked exit. After the audience had cleared the theater, her escape would then be unobstructed. Once safely inside the car, Adelaide would lie across the back seat with a blanket over her, until the vehicle had driven a safe distance away from the theater. Although the trick worked undetected most nights, there were occasions when the more fanatical members of her fan club realized what was going on.

Chicago was one city where Adelaide had a particularly avid and loyal following, who at times went to ridiculous extremes to meet their idol. One besotted, very wealthy, white gentleman, who sat in the same front-row seat every night, showered her daily with bouquets of red roses. His chauffeur-driven limousine was permanently parked outside the theater at her disposal. Each day his gifts grew more extravagant, until Bert, exasperated, forbade Adelaide to accept any more and promptly ordered the delivery boy to return them. Needless to say, from that night onwards, the gentleman in question was no longer seen occupying his front-row seat in the orchestra stalls.

Another fan spent a whole night locked inside the theater in the hope of being able to meet Adelaide the following day. After gaining access backstage he hid in her dressing room where he lay in wait. When Adelaide arrived the next day she found the young man fast asleep inside her dressing room wardrobe.

"Stop pacing the room, honey," complained Adelaide, "either sit down or leave . . . you're making me nervous."

Bert's impatience irritated her beyond belief.

For a moment, he stood still by the open window and peered down at the deserted alleyway below. The cool evening air blew gently across his face. It helped him to relax a little. All kinds of crazy thoughts were running through his mind.

Adelaide rarely got nervous, and neither did he—but then, how often did an invitation to sing for Al Capone arrive at your dressing room door?

The theater was now completely empty; the audience had gone home long ago. Only the backstage doorman remained in the building.

Bert poured himself another scotch and knocked it back in one.

"You'd think they'd be here by now," he muttered under his breath whilst checking the time on his silver fob watch.

After inspecting her make-up in the large dressing-table mirror for the umpteenth time, Adelaide applied yet another layer of Estée Lauder deep-rouge lipstick. She mentally ran through her checklist and ticked each item off in her mind: costume, shoes, gloves, handkerchief, coat and, most importantly, her make-up bag. For some reason Adelaide felt sure she had forgotten to do something and spent the next few minutes trying to remember what it was. Her absent-mindedness annoyed her to the point of distraction.

Outside in the alley, the sound of cars arriving broke the silence.

"They're here," Bert shouted across the room in a panic.

Picking up her full-length mink coat and resting it comfortably upon her shoulders, Adelaide turned to face Bert. "How do I look, honey?"

For a brief moment Bert gazed admiringly at his wife and then, with a huge warm smile across his face, lovingly informed her, "Priceless, honey . . . must be a million dollars or more."

Together they walked along the maze of backstage corridors towards the metal stairs that led out on to the empty stage. The thought of what lay ahead became more daunting with each step. As they trod the boards Adelaide stopped for a brief moment to peer out across the footlights. She found it hard to believe that only an hour ago the deafening roar of 2,000 fans applauding her performance had echoed in her ears. In contrast, the quiet eeriness of the empty auditorium made her feel uneasy and sent a rush of cold shivers down her naked arms.

"Hurry up, darling, they're waiting for us outside in the street," sighed Bert impatiently as he ushered her on towards the exit.

"Good night, Miss Hall," bid the doorman as he held the stage door open. "You'd better wrap up, ma'am, it's damn chilly out there tonight."

Chicago's nickname, the Windy City, comes from its rapid drop in air temperature at nightfall. This sobering effect does, however, have an added advantage for its citizens: the devilishly cold breeze that howls in from Lake Michigan keeps the city's streets relatively clear of undesirable characters.

Conspicuous by their sudden arrival, the two black limousines had parked in the alleyway alongside the theater. On the sidewalk, close to the first automobile, stood two burly but smartly dressed gentlemen.

The older, more sinister-looking member of the pair, whose wide-angled suit looked one size too big for him, stepped forward to welcome them. Holding his hand out, he bent slightly forward to acknowledge their arrival and in a deep, rough Italian accent offered his greetings. "Good evening, Miss Hall. Allow me to introduce myself. My name is Frankie, I'm here to take care of you. My companion will be your driver for the night. His English may be bad, but believe me when I tell you, he's one of the best drivers this side of the Alps."

Turning to face his colleague, who could barely have been out of his teens, Frankie continued his welcoming speech, "Hey, show some respect and say good evening to the young lady. Let me tell you, this is one very special passenger you'll be driving tonight. She's one of the biggest singing stars on Broadway, you must have heard of her, Miss Adelaide Hall."

With a look of youthful embarrassment written upon his flushed face, the driver stepped forward and offered to shake Adelaide's hand. He spoke in an even broader Italian accent, expressing as colorfully as he could, with added hand gestures thrown in, how happy he was to meet her and how privileged he was to be her driver for the night.

"Hey, that's enough. You'll smother the lady," interrupted Frankie.

"Allow me to introduce my husband and manager," responded Adelaide calmly. "Bertram Hicks, but you can call him Bert, everyone else does."

Both Frankie and the driver took turns to give Bert's hand a good shaking.

With the pleasantries over, Frankie motioned to his companion to return to his automobile. Holding the rear door of the second limousine open, Frankie invited Adelaide and Bert on to the white-leathered seat.

"I'll be in the front car," Frankie informed Bert, "escorting you to Cicero. Enjoy the drive, you'll find everything you need in the back."

The journey to Cicero took no time at all. At that hour of the night, the streets were clear of traffic. Adelaide's driver kept quietly to himself throughout the entire journey and concentrated on the road. He made sure he drove as close as he could behind Frankie's vehicle, even if that meant jumping the red lights.

The car's interior was luxuriously fitted and had a well-stocked cocktail cabinet which Bert made full use of. At the end of a long day, his vivid imagination had a tendency to work overtime. He was convinced Capone's men carried sub-machine guns but, as Adelaide kept pointing out, "If so, where do they conceal them?"

Bert's suspicions were uncalled for. As an invited guest of the Mafia, you were automatically given privileges that were usually only bestowed upon their immediate family and inner circle of friends. Adelaide and Bert's safety was guaranteed under Capone's direct orders. Like Adelaide, Capone had spent his childhood growing up in a multiracial neighborhood. He knew, first hand, how it felt to be discriminated against and all about racial warfare from the rival street gangs that terrorized Brooklyn.

Since his rebellious years as a teenager, Capone's tactics had matured and were now aimed more at confounding the authorities.

When the convoy reached East Cicero, the limousines turned left into a deserted alleyway and pulled up in front of what looked like the back of a disused factory. Frankie jumped out of his automobile and walked straight over to Adelaide's vehicle. Opening her door, he announced their arrival.

"If you'd like to follow me, it's this way."

A recess, concealed on the left side of the gloomy building, lit only by a dim light from above, housed the entrance to the club. In the center of the door, positioned at eye level, was a small square window, covered by a metal grille. Behind the window, which couldn't have been any larger than a face, was what looked like a wooden shutter.

Frankie knocked hard on the door, then stood back two paces and waited. In the interim, Adelaide fleetingly glanced behind her and noticed the two limousines had been parked at either end of the alley. Suddenly, the window's inside shutter levered open and out through the grille peered an indistinguishable face.

"Who is it?" rasped a husky voice from within.

"Hey, it's Frankie. Let me in. I've got the famous jazz singer Miss Adelaide Hall with me."

The shutter closed as quickly as it had opened. Silence followed. Frankie turned round to Bert and nodded a smile, as if to reassure him all was well. The scraping of what sounded like a metal bolt broke the silence and the shutter was flung open once more.

"Welcome to Cicero, Miss Hall," proclaimed a voice from inside. Then, a hand came out through the small window. Frankie stepped to one side as he motioned Adelaide to move forward. Adelaide took hold of the hand and shook it.

"Thank you for inviting me."

"No," replied the voice, "I must thank you for accepting my invitation and at such short notice. As my guests tonight, please don't hesitate to ask for anything you require. My hospitality is at your disposal."

Finally the hand let go of Adelaide's and retracted through the metal grille. The shutter closed. Adelaide looked anxiously at Frankie. In a low voice, Frankie then explained Al Capone had just welcomed them to his party.

The invitation to sing for Capone had arrived in Adelaide's dressing room at the Palace Theater late that afternoon attached to an enormous bouquet of flowers. The theater management politely advised her that it would be wise to accept the request. "No one ever says 'no' to Capone and, if they do, they don't get to see the sunrise the following morning." Adelaide's concert that evening was her last in Chicago before leaving for Cleveland, Ohio, a city she particularly wanted to visit.[2] In a sense, Capone's invitation seemed like a fitting farewell to the city of broad shoulders.

Yet again, Capone had been headline news in all the papers that day. After two years' deliberation, the Grand Jury at the Federal Court building had finally issued an indictment upon him for tax evasion between the years of 1925 and 1929.

That afternoon, as Capone left the courtroom fighting his way through crowds of well-wishers, he laughed the accusations off and flippantly told news reporters, "I ain't worrying about a cell, I'm not there yet. There are other courts." His spirit of rebellion was indicative of his contemptuous feelings towards the law. "I'm a fighter to the end," he firmly declared. In response to his plight, various sections of Chicago rallied round to support him by adopting him as their unofficial second Mayor. In reality he already held more power than the official one.

Capone's way of showing his rivals that he wasn't going to worry about an indictment was to throw a party and a lively affair it was. Suspicions in the underworld were already rife that this time he was truly cornered for good. If nothing else the party would act as a good public relations exercise to help ward off rumors that he was a broken man. As the most celebrated singer in town, it seemed only fitting Adelaide should attend, especially as their paths had crossed briefly in the past.

Cicero is situated in a quiet suburb of Chicago. Any outsider visiting the neighborhood for the first time would have had no idea that most of the area was owned and controlled by Capone and his Mafia organization. His headquarters were certainly based here, concealed behind the façade of an ugly and purposely uninteresting building named the Hawthorne Inn, chosen so as not to attract unnecessary attention. Inside, behind bulletproof shuttered windows, Capone meticulously planned and built his empire. He reputedly earned over a hundred million dollars a year from illegal operations. Not only was the taxman after a share of the booty, so were his competitors.

Capone's control of Chicago's nightlife gave him an interesting sideline as an entrepreneur. This job he greatly enjoyed and by all accounts took very seriously. Although he was known to favor grand opera, he soon learnt how to satisfy his customers' fashionable taste for jazz. He employed a platoon of black musicians and distributed them throughout his numerous clubs and restaurants. Many musicians complained they were cajoled into working at his establishments. In order to retain an element of peace and the musicians' services, he cunningly rewarded their loyalty handsomely with ever larger pay-checks.

Indirectly, Capone's role as the patron saint of Chicago jazz helped redeem his image as a man of the people.

Adelaide and Bert were shown directly to a dressing room. It turned out to be a small suite comprising a lounge, kitchen and bedroom with an adjoining bathroom. Each room had a large arrangement of fresh flowers. On a long console table stood a bottle of chilled vintage champagne in a silver ice bucket. Bert looked warily around the room, then leant over and whispered slowly in Adelaide's ear, "Just remember, honey. If walls have ears, then mirrors have eyes."

A thorough inspection of the suite found nothing more alarming than several lines of cocaine neatly laid out along the glass vanity top in the bathroom. Bert popped open the champagne, poured Adelaide a drink, then took a long swig from the bottle. The alcohol helped lower his defenses a little. "You've got a long night ahead of you, honey, try and relax a little," encouraged Bert as he passed Adelaide the glass.

For some reason Adelaide suddenly recalled what Ethel Waters had told her many moons ago at Edmond's Cellar Bar in Harlem.

"If the Mafia like you, they go out of their way to show it, and shower you with generosity and support." That part was OK. The thing that worried her was what Ethel had failed to tell her. What happened if they didn't like you?

The club had gaming tables, a bar, no stage and a small wooden dais on which the band performed. The place was packed with guests from the underworld. Adelaide's eyes moved inquisitively from face to face around the room. She tried hard to recognize anyone who might seem familiar. It wasn't easy. The fractured light and shade made it impossible to distinguish anyone clearly. The air reeked of cigar smoke and the gambling tables, placed sporadically around the bar, were crowded with players.

Singing to such an audience of hardened gangsters and criminals gave Adelaide's performance an edge that evening. When she announced, "I Can't Give You Anything But Love, Baby" and dedicated the song to her host, a hail of cheers and cat whistles shouted their approval. She purposely pulled out all the stops and, given the circumstances, gave one of the smoothest performances she could remember.

Capone was renowned for giving big tips. He always carried a thick wad of hundred dollar bills in his pocket and thought nothing of rolling off a few thousand to show his appreciation. When Adelaide returned to the dressing room after her performance, she found a thickly stuffed brown envelope on the console table. Needless to say, the contents were discreetly credited to her private bank account the following day.

In contrast to her worst fears, the Mafia treated Adelaide with courtesy and respect and made her feel welcome and at ease in a strange world that bore no resemblance to her own. After her act, Adelaide and Bert were escorted back to their limousine and the sobriety of their Chicago hotel.

The journey back was comparatively uneventful. During the drive Bert gazed reflectively out of the automobile window as Adelaide sank into the seat's soft leather upholstery and gently dozed. Though she felt physically exhausted, her mind was still buzzing. In her thoughts she flitted from scene to scene, recounting what she had witnessed at the party. Suddenly, she remembered what had been niggling her earlier that evening at the theater. So as not to attract the driver's attention, she leant over and whispered in Bert's ear, "I knew there was something I'd forgotten to do."

"And what was that, honey?"

"I haven't written out a will."

"What on earth made you think about that, tonight?"

"Well . . .You know! . . . Just in case our luck ran out."

On October 24, 1931, Capone's luck finally ran out. The Grand Jury found him guilty of tax evasion and the judge sentenced him to eleven years' imprisonment, most of which he served, in the formidable bastion named Alcatraz.

In 1931, Adelaide performed at almost every RKO vaudeville house in New York in a series of concerts spanning more than twenty weeks.[3] She starred at Broadway's Palace Theater four times, a record that year for any vocalist, and became the highest-earning black female entertainer in American show business. Her repertoire changed regularly taking in blues, jazz, torch songs, hits from the previous shows she had appeared in, and songs especially written for her by various composers including Mack Gordon and Harry Revel.

CROSSING BORDERS

Crossing the border via Buffalo, the tour entered Canada. First port of call was Shea's vast Hippodrome Theater in Toronto. By coincidence, Duke Ellington and his orchestra were also in town, appearing at the Imperial. The occasion seemed too good an opportunity for the media to miss. The press had a field day pairing the two jazz greats together in numerous articles.

"This week is one not to be missed by lovers of modern music," proclaimed the *Evening Telegram*.[4] In the same article Adelaide was hailed as "The finest female artist of her race the world has ever known. One moment she gives her all to the hottest, maddest jazz, then a crooning melody filled with heart throbs. A glorious, golden voice that makes you close your eyes, and dream of your heart's desire." The *Toronto Star* felt she, "epitomized the spirit of jazz."[5]

Bert encouraged Adelaide to befriend the press and in each city in which she appeared she would make a point of introducing herself at the local newspaper offices.

"Let folks know who you are, honey!" Bert kept reminding her.

On June 3, at 9:25 p.m., Toronto's Radio CFCA broadcast Adelaide's performance live from the Hippodrome stage.[6] The program gave Canadians their first real taste of a sophisticated black jazz chanteuse.

It was to be expected at some point during Adelaide's visit that after her Hippodrome performance she would make the quick journey across town to catch Ellington's show at the Imperial. How many excursions were made is not documented but Adelaide certainly rose to the occasion and gave Ellington and his audience at least one surprise call. Her unannounced arrival backstage created quite a stir. When the clarinetist played the haunting introduction to "Creole Love Call," Adelaide joined in and began to sing the counter-melody. Immediately recognizing her voice, Ellington rushed into the wings and invited her on stage to perform the song.

At various stages throughout the tour, Adelaide employed different pianists, including Alex Hill, Joe Turner, Francis J. Carter, Bennie Payne, Art Tatum and Bernard S. Addison. Each had his own style and each brought a different flavor to her performance.

RKO made it a firm practice to book only one black act on each bill. Strangely enough, blacks never questioned RKO's theory that a white man's concentration would lapse into boredom if he were submitted to too much Negro entertainment. It was the agent who was responsible for booking a balanced, family-orientated variety show that appealed to the masses. At the end of the day, many black acts just felt lucky to be included. Being the star made it vitally important that Adelaide's act was tailored specifically to such an audience.

Like a butterfly escaping its chrysalis, Adelaide's metamorphosis began to take shape. Since her crossover to the RKO circuit she had purposely incorporated certain nuances and props into her performance that were now identified as hers. Bert encouraged her to elaborate upon them. The holding of a silk handkerchief in her left hand became a trademark, as were the heavy diamanté bracelets worn upon her wrists.

Fashion always had played an important role in Adelaide's life. On stage she was determined to be the best-dressed woman in the house. Her act included several costume changes, which, although in later years they hotly denied it, gave her pianists the opportunity to perform at least one solo number during the show.

Thankfully, wherever Adelaide performed, the kudos of *Blackbirds* stood her in good stead. The show became her calling card and its songs, "I Can't Give You Anything But Love, Baby" and "I Must Have That Man," the most requested in her repertoire.

AND THE MONEY CAME ROLLING IN

Torch songs were songs about separation and longings sung from the heart. They epitomized the mood of the Depression, the heartache and yearning for a better life. The Wall Street Crash had seen many industrial cities grind to a halt. Unemployment spiraled. Henry Ford closed his automobile production plant in Detroit—if he couldn't sell the cars, there was no point in producing them. The city was paying out more in relief than any other in U.S. history. Toledo had 80 percent of its population jobless, the highest in America. Ethnic communities in such cities were hit the hardest and for many immigrants their only way of survival was to return to their homeland.

It's not an exaggeration to state that throughout the Depression Adelaide earned a fortune. In later years, when asked about this period, she would often respond, "In the Depression, was I depressed? No way! For the first time in my life I felt rich."

At the end of June, the tour returned to New York. Once again Adelaide topped the bill at the Palace, this time with Lou Holtz and Vic Oliver.[7] The show was a real money-spinner and box office receipts skyrocketed, almost doubling on the previous week's takings. Adelaide opened in dynamic manner, impressing even the hardened management, who, in vain, tried to hold her over for another week. Their last-minute attempts to reschedule failed because Ethel Merman, who was contracted to appear the following week, refused to amend her itinerary. Even Adelaide's pianists, Alex Hill and Joe Turner, received a worthy mention in *Variety*: "The colored boys are solid musical support and delivered a real hot medley for solo."[8]

Shortly after the Palace performance Alex Hill left the duo. Due to his addiction to alcohol his behavior had become increasingly erratic and unpredictable and as a result he was fired. Joe Turner recruited his buddy, Francis J. Carter, to replace him.

Without having the commercial appeal of either Adelaide or Bojangles' name attached to his shows, Lew Leslie was finding it increasingly difficult to produce another Broadway hit. With *Rhapsody in Black* he changed his artistic direction. He decided to promote the Negro as a serious artist. The show inclined to the form of a recital, with no spoken line, comedy skit or monolog included throughout, and relied on neither chorus nor fancy scenery. With Ethel Waters, the Berry Brothers and Valaida Snow on the bill, Leslie hoped to attract a large audience.

The revue opened on April 4, at the Sam Harris Theater, to admirable notices but only managed a ten-week run before it closed. Leslie relaunched the production, only this time he decided he needed a star that could be relied upon to attract a larger audience.

Eating humble pie, he telephoned Adelaide's booking agent, Nicholas Gyory, and put forward a proposition for her to star in *Rhapsody in Black*. Gyory informed Leslie rather awkwardly that Adelaide was in the middle of an extensive tour but that she would be returning to New York for a couple of weeks at the end of August to prepare for her trip to Britain.

Although their friendship had at best been described as a love–hate relationship, since their acrimonious split in Chicago Adelaide had been adamant that she would not forgive Leslie for his disdainful behavior. They were as stubborn as each other and neither party was prepared to patch the rift, only this time Leslie knew he was cornered. He needed Adelaide's services more than she needed him, so somehow he had to convince her that he was sorry.

When Adelaide returned to New York, Leslie phoned Bert and invited him over to his office. Bert immediately turned down any suggestion of Adelaide starring in *Rhapsody in Black* and informed Leslie that she was already committed to a lengthy tour. Leslie was not that easily dissuaded. He was determined to try and have Adelaide's name associated with the production. Leslie then suggested that perhaps Adelaide could appear as a special guest during the revue's relaunch at Harlem's Lafayette Theater. Behind closed doors the pair hammered out a financial agreement that would, hopefully, benefit both parties. Bert agreed to nothing, but did promise he would discuss the proposal with Adelaide.

As was to be expected, Adelaide did not take kindly to Leslie's proposal nor did she like the fact that Bert had gone behind her back to visit him. "An apology would not have gone amiss," Adelaide shouted abruptly, as if Bert were hard of hearing.

Bert chose the words of his reply carefully, "Lew told me that he regrets the past and the ill-feeling between you and wishes there'd never been a split."

"Well, he would, wouldn't he," smirked Adelaide in defense. "He's bankrupt."

"Lew sincerely wishes to patch up any bitterness that exists between you and, by way of proving his good intentions, is prepared to offer you a substantial fee for one week's work."

"Well, so he should . . . but it's not the money . . . it's him. He's a monster to work for, as well you know."

To help pacify the situation Bert explained that he hadn't promised Leslie anything other than that he would speak to her.

Adelaide's final decision was not an easy one to make. Her acceptance may have been a benign gesture at reconciliation but there still remained one major obstacle to overcome: which artist received top billing. Ethel refused to have her name removed from the top and Adelaide refused to take a supporting role. The dilemma caused Leslie a huge headache. How could he appease both artists without offending either one of them? Like jigsaw pieces, he rearranged his options until he finally arrived at an amicable solution. Both artists would have equal-sized lettering, but Ethel would remain the show's star. Adelaide would be billed as a "Special Added Attraction."

On August 29, under the grand title, "World premiere of Lew Leslie's new edition of *Rhapsody in Black*, which will open on Broadway soon," the Lafayette flung its doors open to the public. With Adelaide's name on the bill, as Leslie predicted, the show created an unprecedented scramble for tickets. Within hours the theater sold all its seats for the entire week. "Lafayette continues to turn away thousands anxious to get in," reported the *New York Amsterdam News*. "Theatrical history is being made in Harlem."[9] Due to unparalleled demand, the show's run at the Lafayette was extended although without Adelaide's inclusion. If Leslie could have convinced Adelaide to remain in the show, he would have, but even he knew that after their previous estrangement the chance of such a miracle happening was slim.

Even though Adelaide was only contracted to appear in the production for one week, such was her pulling power, Ethel felt threatened and complained bitterly to Leslie that her name would be undermined by Adelaide's presence. Unless he made it clear to the public that she was the star, Ethel threatened to sue him for breach of contract. Not wanting to cause more outrage in his ranks, Leslie's hand was forced. In an extraordinary move he placed a large advertisement in the *New York Amsterdam News* to clarify the situation:

"ADELAIDE HALL is now appearing as a Special Added Attraction with Lew Leslie's new edition of *Rhapsody in Black* of which ETHEL WATERS is the star."[10] In retrospect, it was a bad move for Adelaide. She should never have allowed herself to be used as bait.

The show's title was a pun on Gershwin's piano concerto "Rhapsody in Blue." The program did in fact feature part of this piece, performed by Pike Davis' Continental Orchestra, with Valaida Snow conducting. Leslie was determined to get his money's worth from his stars. Not only did Adelaide perform three solo numbers, but in a surprising move, for the first time she sang a duet on stage with Ethel Waters. In the *Amsterdam News*, the editor wrote how the audience was quick to sense that in this duet they were witnessing a historical moment. "The reception that greets them is thunderous."[11]

Rhapsody in Black steered Ethel Waters in a completely new direction and promoted her as a first-class, all-round, wholesome entertainer. The show lifted her from the emotional doldrums she was in and helped clear some of her heavy financial debts. Secretly, Leslie had every intention of using Ethel to undermine Adelaide's popularity in America.

ADELAIDE HALL

"THE CROONING BLACKBIRD"
Opens Week of September 21, 1931
PALLADIUM, LONDON
Booked Solid R-K-O Until August, 1932
Late Star Lew Leslie's "Blackbirds"
Headliner R-K-O
Victor Records
Radio

Booked Thru Weber-Simon
NICHOLAS GYORY
Personal Manager

HELLO LONDON

Since the mid-Twenties, Europe's interest in American music had greatly increased in popularity. Authentic jazz, performed by real black Americans, appeared much more exotic to European tastes than listening to their own home-grown white imitators.

It was Adelaide's first visit to Britain. Her arrival was to herald a minor influx of American jazz performers, before the British musicians union stepped in to outlaw foreign competition. Adelaide and Bert, accompanied by her two pianists, Francis J. Carter and Joe Turner, departed from New York on September 8. Once again Adelaide crossed the Atlantic in style onboard her beloved liner *SS Ile de France* and once more she and Bert received all the comforts and attention a first-class passenger expects. For some unexplained reason, when the ship docked at Plymouth, Adelaide altered her age on her port registration documents to 26, the age her deceased sister Evelyn would have been if she had still been alive.

Her arrival in London was announced with a photo call in Regent's Park, just around the corner from where she was staying.[12] Adelaide's British debut took place on September 21. After ten years as a performer she was now headlining the London Palladium, an achievement even Josephine Baker had yet to accomplish. The Palladium was the premier and most prestigious variety theater in Britain. For a foreign artist to command top billing, they had to be a crowd-puller.

In a concerted bid to attract more custom away from cinemas, the Palladium's owners had recently spent a fortune on refurbishing the interior of the theater in the latest futuristic Art Deco style. The management had also drastically altered their entertainment policy, to include a more varied and international program.

Since leaving *Blackbirds* Adelaide's stage routine had evolved into a highly polished and sophisticated act. Bert's idea of having two pianists accompany her on stage had been hugely effective. At the Palladium she specifically requested two white grand pianos and for contrast had her accompanists Carter and Turner wear black tuxedos with bright yellow neckties.

The British music fraternity, steeped in classical tradition, showed little enthusiasm for jazz music. They referred to it as a novelty and dismissed it flippantly as fashionable and faddish. Few people in Britain had ever heard real live jazz so they really didn't know what to expect from a performer such as Adelaide. English critics fully expected her act to be vaudeville. How wrong could they have been? Some accused her of ultimately selling out to commercialism. Although such criticism hurt, Adelaide had learnt that whatever approach she chose, in the opinion of cynics, it seemed she could do nothing right.

The Palladium audience was greeted with an apogee of refined professionalism, sleeker than that of any other black artist who had graced a London stage before her. Gone were the jungle looks of grass skirts and feathered bikinis. Her native outfits were replaced with elegant flowing gowns, epitomizing the height of Parisian fashion. On stage she appeared natural and relaxed without the slightest hint of pretense. When she stripped down to her shorts during "Red Hot From Harlem" the sight of her long lithe legs and midriff raised more than a few conservative eyebrows in the house. In America, Adelaide's sophisticated style had become her trademark and many of her contemporaries were already imitating it. In Britain, for obvious reasons, she was not thought to be so fashionable. "A veneer of high culture" was how one critic described her image.

Most of the audience had never heard a true jazz vocalist before, let alone experience the subtlety of scat singing. Adelaide's program, culled from her RKO tour, included hits from *Blackbirds* and a selection of popular songs from composers she admired. Some critics thought her performance too commercial and over-rehearsed. Others reveled in her originality and praised the intensity of emotion she displayed. However, her improvised scat vocalizing did, at times, seem to go above the audience's heads.

Her reviews were noteworthy for one reason: the wide spectrum of opinion they covered. Some papers, most notably *The Times*, chose to ignore her visit completely. Presumably, they found her too controversial. The *Stage* claimed Adelaide justified almost all that had been said about her: "She croons, sings and dances and has a vivid personality," but then, as a postscript, added "but she is not a Florence Mills."[13] On the other hand, in the *Evening Standard* Philip Page wrote "As a dancer and a singer she is certainly an acquisition and full of personality" and noted that she was "more emphatic than Florence Mills."[14] No matter what Adelaide did, it was inevitable she would be compared with Florence somewhere along the line.

Perhaps the critique given by the Guyanese musician and conductor Rudolph Dunbar, who was in the first-night audience, sums up the consensus about her performance. He later professed to Adelaide that her "Impressionistic" act was "superb, but too much in advance of that period."

Whatever the critics thought, the public were genuinely excited by her presence in London and her twice-nightly shows at the Palladium were well attended, although business was not as brisk as the theater's management had anticipated. In general, Adelaide found her British fans extremely well mannered. She was astonished to find autograph hunters stood in an orderly queue at the stage door and found most of the public just wanted to get a closer look at her. However, there was one incident that caused a little concern, when an over-zealous fan clung on to her limousine as she was driven away. Such hysterical scenes were unusual for a black celebrity.

Her visit was feted with the full-scale celebrity treatment. A run of elaborate parties was thrown in her honor and her attendance was noted in society gossip columns. The famous bandleader Jack Hylton threw a swish cocktail party for her at his grand house in Mayfair and invited over 300 guests, including members of European royalty.

Considering variety shows in Britain were full of brash bawdy humor, Adelaide's act must have been quite an innovation. A good night out for the majority of the British public was more akin to a knees-up down at the pub. Perhaps her critics expected too little of Adelaide's performance and found to their surprise that they were confronted with an intelligence they found threatening. Maybe they were expecting a Josephine Baker clone, all sequins, naked flesh and feather boas. Whatever their preconceptions, Adelaide certainly gave the Palladium audience more than they had paid for.

To commemorate her visit, Oriole Record Company invited Adelaide to cut several tracks. In all eight songs were mastered including Cab Calloway's recent hit "Minnie The Moocher," which contained his memorable catchphrase "hi-de-ho" in the lyric. As most people in Britain had no idea what a "Moocher" was, at the start of the recording Adelaide informs the listener that the term is in fact "American slang for a young girl that's out stealing other girls' sweethearts." The sessions took place at Maurice Levy's Studios in Soho, with Carter and Turner providing piano accompaniment. At one session, Turner complained of a stomach upset and the pianist Bennie Payne took his place.[15] The recordings reveal a flawless, relaxed vocal technique and are a fine example of her style at that period.

Whilst in London, Adelaide and Bert stayed in a magnificent Georgian townhouse at 17 Regent's Park Road as guests of the well-known philanthropist Lady Cook. She shared her home with her black protégé, American baritone John C. Payne. He had previously lived in Harlem and arrived in Britain with the Southern Syncopated Orchestra. He liked the English way of life so stayed on and tried his luck in the theater. Modest success in various West End musicals and regular classical recitals at the Wigmore Hall gave him an air of distinction. In later years, he became known as the "Dean" of London blacks on account of his continual support in promoting awareness of African culture.

The British attitude towards blacks was less stringent than in the States. Mixed-race couples were accepted and there was less fear of segregation in public places. Nevertheless, there were certain hotels that still refused entry to black clientele. To avoid this embarrassment, Lady Cook invited visiting black stars to stay at her elegant home in Regent's Park. Those who had previously experienced her hospitality included Ethel Waters, Alberta Hunter, Paul Robeson and Eubie Blake.

Payne dealt with the day-to-day running of the household including the cooking and organizing of any house parties. He was an excellent chef and put his skills to practice each Sunday when Lady Cook threw regular soirées for her friends. The guest list usually included any black celebrities who were in London at the time. The house was large, had numerous floors and was tastefully decorated with antiques. Lady Cook was regarded as the perfect hostess amongst London's rich social set. Her warm hospitality was renowned and invitations to her house parties were much in demand. After-dinner recitals at which Payne sang light operetta were the highlight of the evening. As a courtesy to the hostess, performances were also expected from any celebrities attending.

Adelaide and Bert thoroughly enjoyed their stay at Lady Cook's house. When I questioned her about the hospitality she received and the relationship between her hostess and John C. Payne, Adelaide chose her words carefully, "The house was so full of love and affection that it was difficult not to enjoy my stay. There was certainly somebody liking somebody else a lot, of that I'm sure."

Francis J. Carter and Joe Turner were not so lucky with their accommodation during their stay in London. They shared an apartment at 2 Torrington Square, which by all accounts was dirty, smelly and far too noisy at night to sleep in. As the premises were leased on a short-term let, their complaints to the landlord fell on deaf ears.

In the midst of her hectic schedule Adelaide managed to double in cabaret for four nights at the Café de Paris, a swanky supper club in Piccadilly.[16] At the management's request, she included the Harry Akst song "Dinah" in her program. Originally written for Ethel Waters, the number was popularized in one of Lew Leslie's revues at the Plantation Café. "Dinah" had only recently become a favorite of the British public and it scored such a big hit with the audience that it remained in Adelaide's repertoire from then on.

At one performance, a note arrived on stage requesting she sing "I Can't Give You Anything But Love, Baby" for a special guest in the audience. The guest turned out to be Edward, the Prince of Wales—the future king of England. Many years later, Lena Horne revealed in her autobiography, *Lena*, that it was rumored the Prince had pursued Adelaide during her visit to Europe.[17]

Adelaide's last performance before returning to America was given at a special late-night gala at the fashionable Berkeley Hotel in Mayfair, another favored haunt of the rich and titled socialites.[18]

Although the trip to London hadn't been the undeniable success Adelaide had hoped and a certain element of the British press had been indifferent or hostile towards her, the visit was invaluable in spreading the popularity of American jazz. Her performance helped clear the path for future black artists to follow.

Apart from Adelaide, no other black artist of significance visited Britain during 1931. There had been a steady growth of complaints from members of the musician's union regarding the right of foreign musicians to work in the country. These objections finally led to a total ban on foreign musicians, which lasted nearly twenty years. Luckily for Britain, before the act was enforced, Louis Armstrong visited in 1932, Duke Ellington toured in 1933 and Cab Calloway brought his orchestra over in 1934, which all helped significantly in widening the demand for jazz music.

On October 7, longing for home, Adelaide and Bert sailed from Plymouth harbor onboard the transatlantic liner *De-Grasse* bound for New York.[19]

As soon as she got back to New York, Adelaide's tour resumed with the lightning speed of an express train and rattled on its unstoppable course, zigzagging across State borders, through sweltering deserts and rain sodden plains, from city to city across the length and breadth of America. Already audience attendance figures had skyrocketed, totaling almost half a million to date. Eager to capitalize on Adelaide's overwhelming popularity, RKO announced a string of extra dates and slotted them into her already vigorous itinerary. The tour was a sell-out almost everywhere it played . . . and the money came rolling in.

Cracks were beginning to appear in Adelaide's make-up. The thrill of living out of a suitcase had lost its appeal. Tedium and the monotony of a daily routine had taken its place. After ten continual months on the road, fatigue had begun to set in and she was still only halfway through the tour. The strain of early morning rehearsals and performing as many as four shows a day had begun to drain her energies.

At night she found it difficult to sleep. This triggered anxiety attacks which her doctor assured her would pass. To try and help relieve her tiredness, she took to catnapping, an art she perfected in-between performances. Her secret eating binges saw her weight increase. When she stripped down to her shorts on stage, the press noticed the added pounds and cruelly commented upon it.[20] Her mood swings became more frequent and, in an attempt to conceal them, she began distancing herself from people around her. During one temperamental outburst, she insisted that from now on her pianists refrain from using her christian name and refer to her at all times as Miss Hall. Some likened her behavior to that of a prima donna and found her attitude difficult to accept. One such person, pianist Joe Turner, found the situation stifling and concocted an excuse to break his contract and quit the tour.

To help quell increasing rumors of her irrationality, at the end of November Bert placed a large notice in *Billboard* to thank all those involved with her tour for their untiring efforts on her behalf. He then, rather grandly, extended Adelaide's "Season's Greetings to the Entire World."[21]

ADELAIDE HALL

EXTENDS

Season's Greetings to the Entire World

Many Thanks to RKO Executives, Bookers, Theater Attaches and Others for Their Untiring Efforts on My Behalf.

Opening on RKO INTACT ROUTE Week Nov. 28

Direction—WEBER-SIMON AGENCY

THE ART OF TATUM

Toledo, Ohio, January 16, 1932

Adelaide had previously visited Ohio with *Blackbirds* back in 1929 and at the beginning of her RKO tour in March 1931. Her return in January 1932 brought an unexpected discovery.[22]

Art Tatum was born in Toledo on October 13, 1909 and had lived there ever since. Born with milk cataracts in both eyes, he was almost totally blind. As with many handicapped people, the loss of one sense sharpened the others. His genius as a pianist was recognized at an early age. As he grew older it seemed likely that he would leave the confines of a small town to enter the big world of show business. His only obstacle was his overprotective mother. Adelaide's original account of how she first met Tatum was as follows:

I was playing on the RKO circuit. Art came over to the theater in Cleveland one morning and we ran through some numbers. His playing was out of this world. One of my pianists was leaving so I hired him on the spot. Jazz historians say I was instrumental in giving Tatum his first break. I suppose I was. It's difficult to remember. So much has happened since then.

Although her account seemed concise, I felt the actual events surrounding Tatum's discovery were not so straightforward or correctly chronicled. After sifting through heaps of newspapers and books I managed to piece together the majority of Adelaide's RKO tour itinerary, which clearly dates exactly when and where she appeared in Ohio. Armed with my discovery, I put this information to her. At first she was amazed that I had gone to so much trouble to unearth the facts. Fortunately, my efforts were rewarded as they did help jog her memory.

As was usual on a lengthy tour, Adelaide and Bert stayed with friends whenever possible. In Toledo, they were house guests of William and Ella Stewart at their large comfortable home on the corner of City Center Street and Indiana Avenue. The Stewarts' home played host to many visiting black stars. Two autographed publicity stills of Adelaide, signed to the Stewarts and dated January 21, 1932, still survive. Facsimiles appear on the cover of Art Tatum's Collectors' Items Album "Strange As It Seems."[23]

Over the years many people have claimed credit for discovering Tatum including Adelaide's former pianists, Joe Turner and Francis J. Carter. After talking through the events that led up to her concerts in Ohio, Adelaide's memory suddenly became a lot clearer and she admitted that it probably was in Toledo and not Cleveland that she first met Tatum. This is the story she recounted, following my discoveries. It was almost as if she could still hear the noisy workmen in the theater banging their hammers.

By the time the tour hit Toledo, Joe Turner was looking for a way out of his contract. He claimed to have family problems back home but later it transpired that disagreements with Adelaide prompted his resignation. It was Ella Stewart, who lived close to the Tatum residence, who suggested Art as a temporary replacement. The following morning, Bert drove round to the Tatum house, collected Art and brought him to the Rivoli Theater for an audition. The auditorium was undergoing renovations. Workmen were hammering and banging so loudly that it was difficult to think. When Tatum began playing the piano the theater went silent—the effect was instant. Adelaide offered Tatum the job on the spot and he accepted. His only concern was what his mother might say. Bert promptly stepped in and told him not to worry; he would have words with Mrs. Tatum.

Tatum was hired and played on stage opposite Francis J. Carter. Initially he only agreed to accompany Adelaide for two weeks, during her shows in Toledo and Milwaukee. Whilst in Toledo, he returned each night after the show to honor his job at the basement bar where he held a residency. When the tour left Toledo, Tatum's mother, whom Adelaide remembered as being very strong-willed, insisted he return home within the month.

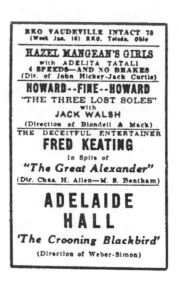

RKO tour, week commencing January 16, 1932, Toledo, Ohio.

At the end of the second week, Bert drove back to Toledo. He approached Tatum's mother warily with the request to employ Art for the remainder of the tour which would culminate in New York at Broadway's Palace Theater. Mrs. Tatum was not convinced her son would be as well looked after on tour as he was at home. After much persuasion, she finally agreed to allow Art to carry on with the tour with the proviso that Adelaide promised to look after him as if he were her own son. Much to his annoyance, as Art would later recall, "Adelaide was worse than six mothers." Fortunately for Art, Adelaide retired to bed around midnight, giving him the opportunity to slip out of the lodgings wearing his suit over his pajamas to indulge in extra-curricular night activities.

Art Tatum had never lived away from home before. In fact he'd never traveled out of Ohio. At the age of 22 he was still very much tied to his mother's apron strings. He was painfully shy and only loosened up after drinking a few beers. Once on stage, it immediately became apparent that he was far too good a pianist to be an accompanist. Sometimes, in the middle of a song, Adelaide would stop singing to marvel at what he was playing behind her. This became a regular high point in her act, during which the audience would wildly applaud Tatum's solos.

Tatum stuck with the tour for one reason only, to reach New York. Adelaide was his calling card to a brighter future. In New York he intended to plan his own agenda.

From Ohio across to the roaring Pacific, the tour played every major city in its path. As part of the route crossed the desolate Midwestern States, for security purposes Adelaide's booking agent, Nicholas Gyory, suggested Bert purchase a dog. Rex, a huge Belgian Alsatian, was a fully trained guard dog. He had spent his working life attached to the narcotics squad of a New York police department but due to an injury had been forced into early retirement. The hound came highly recommended as the perfect traveling companion. More worryingly, Bert was also advised by Gyory to arm himself with a gun and learn how to use it.

On tour, time discarded any resemblance of normality. Routine grew disorderly, Monday became Friday and the rush to repack trunks, bid farewell and journey to the next State took on a harrowing weekly recurrence.

Bert drove until fatigue set in, at which point Carter took over the wheel. Traveling by road, especially across the dusty plains of Middle America, was known to be hazardous if you were black. In the course of the tour Bert encountered many racial attacks. Just eating and going to the restroom became two of the most difficult daily procedures. Many of the restrooms were signposted "Whites Only" and most of the restaurants and roadside cafés refused point blank to serve Negros. Some of the towns in the outback were so poor and out of touch with the twentieth century that you could smell the poverty. No matter how fast Bert drove, life in the sticks ran at a much slower pace.

During one particularly long stretch of road, Bert became really hungry. Seeing the welcoming lights of a roadside café, he pulled in to purchase a take-away. Outside the café's entrance, on a narrow wooden veranda that ran the entire length of the building, sat the meanest looking dog Bert had ever seen. As he approached, the dog bolted upright and began to snarl menacingly at him. With each step Bert made to approach the door, the dog's glazed eyes stared more piercingly. Fearing for his life, Bert froze at the foot of the steps that led up to the entrance. It was at that precise moment that the café's screen door swung open. In the doorway stood the proprietor, a tall, grossly overweight character with a grubby stained apron tied around his waist. In one hand he brandished a long kitchen knife, in the other a half-smoked cigarette.

"Can't you read the sign, it sez no Niggers allowed."

Bert hadn't even noticed the sign let alone read it. "I don't want to eat inside, I just want to buy a take-away. We've been driving all day without food and yours is the first café we've come across."

After an uneasy pause, during which the proprietor smoked what was left of his cigarette whilst scrutinizing Bert's car and its occupants, he took a few paces forward to face Bert.

"Wait there, Nigger . . . and don't come any closer, unless you fancy being a lump of dog meat." He then went back inside the café leaving the screen door swinging to a halt behind him. The dog stood guard in his absence with saliva, growing longer by the second, dribbling from his jaw. Bert remained at the foot of the steps and waited nervously in silence. After a short while the proprietor reappeared with a large brown paper bag.

"There's enough in the bag for the three of you." Without moving a step he threw the bag over to Bert. "That's three dollars you owe me, Nigger."

Bert opened his wallet and found he only had five-dollar bills. He removed one and held it out to pay.

"Leave it on the step, Nigger," motioned the proprietor.

"Don't worry about the change," Bert replied impatiently, in a half-hearted gesture of gratitude.

As the proprietor bent down to pick up the five-dollar bill, Bert caught a glimpse of the guy's filthy hands. They looked so disgusting, the sight made Bert's stomach churn.

Back in the car, Bert opened the brown paper bag with apprehension and removed the grubby looking packages that were inside. The food had been wrapped in dirty old newspaper. The meal comprised dried-up, wrinkled, partly eaten chicken legs, stale clumps of moldy potato bread and burnt cobs of blackened corn. The food was stone cold and was clearly other people's leftovers that had been reclaimed from the garbage bin. With hesitation, Bert offered the food round, but neither he nor the others had the stomach to eat it. Everyone's appetite suddenly appeared to vanish. Even the dog turned his nose up at it.

Bert started the engine and slowly reversed the car until it was directly opposite the café entrance. He then wound down his side window and with an almighty thrust threw the whole food parcel out of the car on to the café veranda. The food spewed out across the decking and hit the guard dog as it fell.

Without hanging around to witness the outcome, Bert slammed his foot down on the gas and sped off into the night, "It's better to eat a dry crust of bread with peace of mind, boys, than to have a banquet in a house full of trouble."

That evening, they arrived late at the theater, tired and hungry from the day's long journey. Adelaide was in her dressing room, already made up and waiting to perform. Bert apologized profusely for being late and tried briefly to explain why. As there was no time to eat before the show commenced, Adelaide suggested they dine after.

"How about ordering a take-away, so we can eat in the dressing room?" proposed Adelaide thoughtfully.

Bert and the boys went deadly silent and stared aghast at one another.

"I think we'll skip the take-away tonight, honey," replied Bert tactfully. "Let's eat back at the hotel instead."

Bert's attitude to racism was cut and dried. Either ignore it or try and work round it. He believed that battling against bigots only lowered his intelligence to their level. If a hotel refused him entrance, why force the issue; it was much easier to walk out. It was common practice amongst black stars to boycott hotels with a racist policy. Instead, many stayed with friends but sometimes there just weren't enough friends to go around. On such occasions, Adelaide's pianists would often find them-selves sleeping rough, on the back seat of the car with only the dog for protection. Any hotel that did allow black entertainers admittance usually insisted they use the service elevator, so as not to upset the white guests.

By the time the tour reached the East Coast, Adelaide had been traveling for almost fourteen months. Frustration and tiredness had taken its toll on her nerves. In a life where anything seemed possible, suddenly the thought of failure and rejection began to play upon her mind. Somehow she had to escape from the continual pressure she was under.

"How many more days in the week do you expect me to work? I'm already working seven!" Bert registered her anger. "You look tired, honey."

"I am tired," snapped Adelaide. "I'm tired of this job. I'm tired of living out of a suitcase and, most of all, I'm tired of never knowing where I am from day to day. Bert . . . I want to go home. I want to sleep in the same bed every night, in our bed, and I want to wake up in the morning with my own belongings around me. For God's sake, even a gypsy has a caravan."

. . . and the money came rolling in. (Publicity still taken by White's Studio)

San Francisco, with its mild-mannered lifestyle, came as a pleasant respite in the itinerary. Under the warm, spring coastal skies the pace slowed down a little and Adelaide began to relax once more.

"The greatest colored singer since Florence Mills," cried the San Francisco *Chronicle*.[24] Adelaide proved her worth yet again with a resounding series of shows. Her presentation at the Golden Gate Theater was said to be "in excellent taste," even down to her costumes. The reviewer, Katherine Hill, found her renditions of "River, Stay Away From My Door" and "I Must Have That Man" outstanding but couldn't help mentioning how her act, as a *chanteuse du jazz*, bordered on the refined. Miss Hill's choice of words clearly indicated she had expected a more "Sophie Tucker" approach.

Further down the coastline, at the RKO Theater in Los Angeles, Adelaide performed to numerous legends from the silver screen. The city was alive with talent. Every night there seemed to be at least one important movie star hosting a party. Her good friend Al Jolson was in town and a lavish bash was thrown in his honor. It was held at Mary Pickford and Douglas Fairbanks' stylish Beverly Hills mansion, Pickfair, and Adelaide was invited to sing.

At the party, she was introduced to a casting director from Paramount Studios who invited her to sit for a screen test. "We might just have a small part for you in a future production," added the director encouragingly, "as a siren of the night. It'll be a good opportunity to break into the movies." Nothing materialized from the shoot but Adelaide had great fun observing how the inside of a major film studio operated.

If Hollywood brought a temporary hiatus in her tiring schedule, it was short-lived. The tour soon resumed its jagged course. Understandably, there were times when Adelaide found herself wondering if life would ever return to normality. Harlem seemed like a thousand miles away. It was. She was homesick and, more than anything else in the world, wanted desperately to see her mother again.

By the end of the tour Adelaide was physically and mentally exhausted. Her return to New York brought instant deliverance from her anxieties. At first, just the comparative luxury of waking up in the same bed each morning seemed novel. Then reality hit her. Life in the city had changed dramatically since they left it. The spiraling effects of the recession had cut deep into the pockets of everyone they knew.

Adelaide was ecstatic to see her mother again. Her mother was just relieved to see her daughter home safely.

"Was it worth the wait?" inquired Elizabeth.

"You bet," came back Adelaide's immediate response. "Worth the wait in gold."

It was estimated that Adelaide performed to over a million people throughout the tour. By way of celebration, her return to Harlem was welcomed with a week's engagement at the Lafayette. Over a year had passed since she had performed there. Her homecoming turned into a momentous event and created quite a commotion in the jazz world.

On July 3, Adelaide breezed into Harlem's Lafayette Theater accompanied by Francis J. Carter and the unknown Art Tatum. As if anyone might have doubted it, "Harlem still likes Adelaide," yelled the *New York Amsterdam News*, "just being her own sweet self."[25] It felt good to be home and Adelaide had every intention of enjoying her reception.

Tatum's arrival stirred much interest amongst New York's jazz musicians. Many came to the Lafayette to hear the wonder kid play. Within days his name could be heard in all the bars and clubs up and down Seventh Avenue. His nimble fingers and innovative ideas in harmonic progression had the best jazz pianists in town talking. As was to be expected, it wasn't too long before Fats Waller called backstage at the theater to see what all the fuss was about. His visit, though friendly, took on a more competitive stance. He invited the youngster to a night on the town with a few buddies, for a cutting contest. The evening ended at Morgan's, a bootleg joint with a good piano. On stage with Adelaide, Tatum played mostly background chords. At Morgan's he had every intention of showing Fats exactly what he could do. With effortless grace he cut into Vincent Youman's "Tea for Two" and played it as if every note on the keyboard was written in the melody. His right hand played phrases no one knew existed, whilst his left held down a solid beat, interspersed with endless arpeggios that would normally have required two hands to play. His performance stunned Fats who instantly recognized the guy was a genius. The contest proved Tatum's skill in front of the best jazz pianists in the business. His future was sealed. For many years after the event, that evening in Morgan's remained one of the most talked about in Harlem.

Tatum's technique terrified his contemporaries. He wasn't just good, he was bloody good. The speed of his fingers was unequaled by any other jazz pianist around and matched only by the speed of his mind. His virtuosity seemed inherent yet spontaneous. In all honesty he was far too good to be an accompanist, and he knew it.

On August 5, Adelaide's musical union with Tatum was captured for posterity on two tracks for the Victor label, the first recordings he ever made. Charlie Teagarden, Jimmy Dorsey and Dick McDonough were hired as session musicians. The group assembled at studios in New York and recorded "I'll Never Be The Same" and Fats Waller's "Strange As It Seems." Both titles were cut in the one day. Victor were so pleased with the result they commissioned two more tracks. On the following Wednesday, as a trio, Tatum and Carter backed Adelaide on "You Gave Me Everything But Love" and the haunting "This Time It's Love."

Acclaimed in future years as one of the greatest individualists in jazz, Tatum's influence on other musicians was immense. Revered by all of his contemporaries, he sadly never became as successful as most of them and, at times, appeared bitter at the lack of recognition the public gave him. Soon after his recordings with Adelaide, Tatum's own agenda took over. With help from the English composer Spike Hughes and millionaire record producer John Hammond, Tatum secured his own recording contract with Brunswick.[26] He also received an offer of regular work at New York's Onyx Club that doubled his salary.

Adelaide urged him to take it. "I couldn't possibly have afforded to pay him such a salary." The rest is history.[27]

In the days when flying was still regarded a novelty, the immensity of America made touring a backbreaking challenge. Even hardened vaudeville acts found the going tough. Although Adelaide moaned continually about the workload, ambition drove her on. Her fear of failure grew obsessive and, as more concert engagements flooded in she found it increasingly difficult to refuse them.

Her workload took its toll upon her health. After eighteen months of relentless touring the itinerant lifestyle had worn her nerves down to a frazzle. Her body had little energy left to give and she was desperately in need of a break. The triumph of success now seemed too little a reason for careering towards a breakdown. It was time to take stock of her life.

Bert's camomile suggestion of a relaxing break made little impression upon her. She had never had a real vacation and knew nothing about the rejuvenating effects of such a custom. In her mind, a holiday would just prolong her absence from home, which, at this point in her life, was clearly the only place she wanted to be.

"It's not easy being an entertainer. Having to smile, look bright and cheerful and keep oneself looking pretty all the time, especially when you really can't be bothered. It's one hell of an ordeal, honey. You should try it sometime."

As usual, Bert switched off the receiver in his inner ear and listened to her moans without actually hearing a word she said. By now he had learnt exactly when to remain silent. His ears were for acknowledging her grievances, not necessarily accepting them. Bert's attention had wandered on to more pressing matters, closer to home.

Adelaide yearned for a house of her own, somewhere she could feel proud of, that reflected her hard work, wealth and position in society. Her financiers agreed that a large investment in property would be a wise move.

In July Adelaide went shopping with a bulging bank balance to purchase her dream home.

THE LARK ON LARCHMONT HILL

The idea of investing a large amount of money in real estate had initially come from Adelaide's accountant. He discussed the matter with her in depth, and in principle she agreed. Since returning to New York Adelaide had acquired a second dog and her apartment on Seventh Avenue was far too cramped to accommodate both animals. Bert thought a modern larger apartment in a newly built Manhattan block might be more suitable for their needs. Adelaide was not convinced. She preferred the idea of a house with a rambling garden, in which to keep her hounds happy. Bert was fully aware that a private garden in New York City was a luxury only the super-rich could afford. Although she was wealthy, Adelaide was not yet in that league.

They finally came to a compromise and settled upon the fashionable town of Larchmont in Westchester County. Situated within an hour's drive of Times Square, the location was ideal for commuting to and from the city.

Set back in a quiet cul-de-sac, 11 Kilmer Road was a recently built detached residence positioned in the affluent leafy backwoods of

Larchmont. The area originally took its name from a forest of coniferous trees that once grew upon the hill and Kilmer Road was named in remembrance of the young American poet Joyce Kilmer, who died tragically in the French trenches during the First World War. The particulars described it thus:

> A smart and secluded Tudor styled property with an imposing edifice, built from brownstone brick and topped with a half-timbered gable. The house has four bedrooms and a large garage with enough space for two cars. The garage doors operate electronically, enabling the driver to motor straight in without the bother of leaving his vehicle. At the front of the estate, the grounds are set off by expansive lawns, intersected by gravel walks and a curved driveway. Kilmer Road is viewed as the most prestigious and sought after thoroughfare of Westchester's ritziest community. Included in the lease is a private beach complete with a small wooden beach-chalet. The dwelling benefits from the latest in modern gadgetry and security devices.

The photograph of the house certainly made it look handsome and homely, and its comprehensive description sounded perfect. "A dream home . . . It sounds too good to be true," thought Adelaide, as she studied the details. More importantly, the price of the property seemed extremely reasonable and easily within their price range.

What the blurb failed to mention, however, was why such a fine house had remained unoccupied since it was built, four years previously. Its owner, Bernard K. Marcus, a former President of the Bank of the United States, had bought the holding as an investment for his retirement but had never moved in. After viewing the property it soon became apparent that certain renovations would be necessary in order to make it habitable. The interior decoration had not been completed and the unkempt gardens required extensive landscaping. In view of the fact it had been unoccupied for so long Mr. Marcus was fully aware that some superficial refurbishment was necessary and the cost of such work was reflected in the asking price.

Adelaide fell in love with the white house on Larchmont Hill on her first viewing. It was spacious, had style and tremendous potential, but more essentially, was secluded enough for privacy. At $35,000, it seemed a bargain.

Bert put in an offer that Marcus accepted. On July 18, a deposit of $4,500 was paid to their lawyer, Lawrence Mingey. Contracts were exchanged and August 20 earmarked as the date for completion.

With such a roomy house, Adelaide could easily accommodate both her mother and grandmother but, no matter how much she enthused, her excitement did little to persuade them to want to live there. Elizabeth was vehemently against the upheaval, "No way am I living in an overpriced white-man's suburb."

Adelaide had already made up her mind. She saw no reason to change it whatever her family's feelings. She and Bert were moving to Larchmont, and she hoped the rest of the family would follow. The property would comfortably house the whole family, including her disapproving mother, and there were servants' quarters for Minnie and a housekeeper. What's more, with two acres of land, the dogs would be thoroughly spoilt.

In the meantime Bert employed a housekeeper, Robert, to help run the property and Adelaide went shopping in search of antique furniture. Over the coming weeks, as the house was prepared for occupancy, the residents of Larchmont took more than a neighborly interest in their new arrivals. They secretly embarked upon a vicious smear campaign to remove them from the community.

Somehow, news of Adelaide's acquisition of 11 Kilmer Road was mysteriously leaked to the local press. The revelation provoked an immediate response from the townsfolk. Various articles appeared in the papers, some for and others against. Those in favor outlined Adelaide's achievements on stage and foresaw the arrival of such a celebrity as bringing luster to the area. Other reports were not so kind. In a bid to provoke opposition anonymous letters of protest began to arrive at the newspaper offices. A certain faction of the white community, who resented her living so close to their own dwellings, were behind them. The media, who can sniff a good story when they smell it, jumped on the bandwagon and published the letters, thereby fanning the flames of bigotry.

Within days, a campaign of hatred flared up across the neighborhood bringing anger and discord out on to the normally quiet streets of

Larchmont. The protesters' feelings were so heated that they decided to form a residents' fighting committee, the Kilmer Road Association. Led by Edward McConnell, of 19 Kilmer Road, they intended to lobby the local mayor and, if need be, take the matter to court. In a statement issued to the *Larchmont Times*, they announced their plan to seek an injunction against Miss Hall, preventing her from occupying her new home. At the end of the article the reporter, who clearly sympathized with their views, mentioned that such vitriolic behavior had never been seen before in the sleepy suburb of Westchester.

As if to provoke even more reaction, a few days later the *Larchmont Times* followed their report with a cautionary article. Under the curt headline "Adelaide Hall, colored actress, arrives at her Larchmont residence," the paper gave its readers a very direct view of the situation:

> Adelaide Hall, colored prima donna of such musicals as *Brown Buddies* and *Blackbirds*, paid her rambling home on Kilmer Road in Larchmont a tour of inspection last Saturday afternoon. Miss Hall is said to have procured the lease on the property and is expected to move into her new quarters this week. Furniture to adorn the new home of the famed Harlem singer has been arriving daily and it now seems only a short matter of time until she takes full possession of the house. Her mother, grandmother, husband and servants will occupy the residence with her.[1]

The publishing of the article was clearly timed to aggravate matters. If the local residents were to have any effect on Adelaide's decision to move into her home, then they must act promptly. Stern letters of complaint from the agitators were dispatched directly to Mayor Stiner.[2] In his role of office, as an impartial representative of the local community, he could offer neither support nor counsel to their requests. However, in his short reply the mayor did offer a glimmer of hope: "Perhaps pressure from theatrical circles in New York might make her get out?"

With little hope of finding alliance from the mayor, the Kilmer Road Association regrouped to discuss further tactics. Threats of a lawsuit were brandished in the air and calls to boycott all town merchants and local establishments that supplied Miss Hall with provisions were voted in.

Taking the mayor's advice literally, McConnell contacted Adelaide's friend, the lyricist Dorothy Fields. He appealed to her better judgment and asked her to intervene, by encouraging Adelaide to change her mind. Needless to say, Miss Fields had no intention of being roped into a race riot and declined to offer any assistance in the matter.

To help quell the furore, Adelaide's lawyer, Lawrence Mingey, issued a statement to the press. In it he curiously declared that in fact he was the new owner of the property and Adelaide had only leased the house from him for a period of ten years. He claimed he had purchased the property from the New York real-estate firm Fish and Marvin.

Smelling a rat, a news correspondent quickly traced the story through for verification and interviewed the real-estate agent's manager, Benedict McGrath. Predicting such a move, Mingey had already tipped him off. McGrath's story, though it differed slightly, tied in with Mingey's. He stated that Mingey had bought the property for himself, as a retirement home, and any talk of Adelaide Hall taking up residency was "merely manufactured gossip" and should be totally disregarded. McGrath's collaboration with Mingey only confused the journalist further and left him in more doubt as to what the truth behind the story really was. The plot thickened.

Adelaide's dream of settling in a peaceful community was not to be. Although she was fully aware that a certain faction of the townsfolk were in opposition to her presence, nothing could have prepared her for the scale of antagonism that greeted her on the day she moved into her new home. In the backwoods of Larchmont a heady storm was brewing, yet there wasn't a cloud in the sky to be seen.

AUGUST 20, 1932

Bert slowly drove round the corner and entered Kilmer Road. Further ahead, a large crowd of protesters blocked the roadway.

Drawing a long deep breath, Adelaide straightened her posture. "Just carry on driving, honey. Don't let them see we're upset."

Adelaide's two dogs had slept peacefully on the back seat of the car during the journey up from New York. When the muffled sound of distant shouts and jeers became audible, they soon roused from their slumber. The local police station had suspected such a confrontation might take place and had, accordingly, dispatched a small squad of officers to help maintain order. As the vehicle edged closer towards the demonstration, the dogs grew more agitated and began to bark. In an attempt to clear the road the officers hemmed the mob back on to the sidewalk.

Bert began to feel nervous. "Make sure your door's locked, and hold on to your seat. I ain't stopping for no one."

All of a sudden, a mass of protesters surged forward and broke free from behind the police cordon, then ran across the grass verge back on to the road. Screaming abuse, they charged defiantly towards the vehicle, waving clenched fists at its occupants. In a determined bid to halt the car, the demonstrators hurled themselves in its path. Fearing for someone's life, Bert slammed his foot on the brake. The vehicle screeched to a halt. The mob closed in on them from all sides. Someone bashed a stick against the rear window and the dogs went berserk. Like savage wolves they leapt uncontrollably across the backseat, howling at anyone that came close. In sheer panic, Bert froze. The sound of someone pounding heavily on the roof with his fists soon brought Bert back to his senses. In a flash he managed to restart the ignition and stamped his foot down on the accelerator. The car slowly began to move forward, only this time it was like driving through dense fog. A crowd of bodies blocked its path.

The police seemed incapable of regaining order. No matter how many people they pulled away, replacements took their place. In a brave attempt to free the vehicle, Bert swerved the car to the right and veered across the sidewalk on to the grass verge. With his foot flat down on the accelerator, the car sped violently across the lawn towards the driveway of 11 Kilmer Road.

At the back of the house, waiting by the open garage door stood Minnie and Robert. The car raced towards them. When it reached the house the vehicle skidded momentarily on the gravel before shooting into the garage like a bullet. Bert hit the brake and the car slammed to a halt in front of the rear wall. Without delay, Robert set the electronic security button and the garage door came tumbling down behind them.

It was a miracle nobody was killed.

Adelaide and Bert and their petrified dogs clambered out of the battered vehicle and ran like lightning up the inner staircase that led directly into the main lobby of the house. Only then, behind the relative safety of four walls, did the shock of their ordeal hit them.

For a moment neither Adelaide nor Bert could speak. They both felt as though the breath in their lungs had been forcibly kicked out of them. To stop herself shaking, Adelaide took hold of the long kitchen table and steadily lowered herself into a chair. Even though she was wearing a summer coat, her arms and legs felt unbelievably cold. At the base of her neck, just at the point where the spine meets the skull, her muscles had locked. Spasms of hot pain sent violent contractions through her body. She peered across the room but found it difficult to focus. Her stomach churned repeatedly, as if being wrung by a mangle and she felt violently sick.

Bert stood motionless, with his back towards her, crouched over the kitchen sink. In an effort to calm his nerves he turned the cold water faucet on and lowered his head under the running water.

Within seconds, Adelaide had collapsed across the kitchen table and burst into an uncontrollable fit of tears.

Bert yelled across the room at Robert, "Bob, get me a large scotch . . . No, forget that, just bring me the bottle."

Minnie tried her best to comfort Adelaide, who seemed inconsolable. Later that afternoon, the local doctor paid a visit. He diagnosed Adelaide as suffering from severe shock and prescribed a strong sedative coupled with a restful night's sleep.

Adelaide's mother had always been convinced such an attack might happen and had therefore decided to stay in Harlem. No matter how well guarded the property was, Elizabeth had no desire to live in Larchmont, sleeping with one eye open and one ear firmly placed against the floorboards. When news of the riot reached her, she pleaded with Adelaide to quit the place and return home immediately, whilst she was still in one piece.

Their first night at 11 Kilmer Road was not to be a restful one. Although they had been promised 24-hour police protection, Bert's sleep was broken by the sound of breaking glass. By the time he got downstairs to the hall, the dogs were barking hysterically in the kitchen. As he opened the kitchen door, they leapt out and pounced upon him. Bert lost his balance and fell to the ground hitting his head with an almighty thud on the wooden floor. The blow knocked him unconscious. At the far end of the house, Robert and Minnie were also awoken by the commotion. They rushed to the hallway and discovered Bert lying face down, like a cold stone slab, with a small pool of blood around his forehead. Broken glass from the windowpane in the front door lay scattered across the floor.

"Call the police!" screamed Minnie. "Immediately!"

Minnie ran to the kitchen to fetch a damp cloth, only to discover that one of the kitchen windows had also been smashed. For some reason the dogs kept growling and jumping at the internal door that led downstairs to the garage. It didn't take her long to put two and two together. Beneath her feet she could hear the muffled sounds of intruders. She rushed back to warn Robert.

"They've broken into the garage."

"Where are the dogs?" asked Robert urgently.

"They're standing guard behind the door that leads downstairs."

"Good . . . leave them. No one'll get through that door, unless they shoot the dogs first."

"What do we do now?" pleaded Minnie.

"I've called the police. They said to hang on, they'd be here straight away."

"I thought they were supposed to be outside already."

Robert shrugged his shoulders.

"What about Adelaide?" whispered Minnie.

"I went to check on her. She took a sedative so she's still fast asleep."

Minnie crouched down on the hall floor and gently lifted Bert's head upon her lap. The blood appeared to have stopped seeping from the gash across his forehead. Robert knelt directly opposite Minnie, with his back against the wall, gripping a baseball bat. All they could do now was wait. Wait and pray, and hope salvation arrived before the predators.

Suddenly a blinding flash of light shone through the broken windowpane in the front door.

"Is anybody in there?" hollered a deep voice.

Closing her eyes as tight as she possibly could, Minnie let out the loudest scream that any human being could possibly give. It seemed to last for ever.

The beam of light hit her startled face and then slowly moved down towards the floor until it reached Bert's body. Robert tried to push his back even tighter against the wall, to keep himself out of sight. Minnie went silent, petrified with fear. Then, without any warning, the front door crashed open like a thunderbolt. Minnie let out another almighty roar.

Outside stood a group of indistinguishable figures blackened by the glare from their own torches.

"It looks like somebody's injured in there!"

Although the police arrived just in the nick of time, their incorrect assessment of the situation gave rise to much criticism. Thankfully, Bert's wounds were found to be superficial but still the doctor ordered him to spend the next 48 hours resting. The neighbors' welcoming acts of violence and intimidation did little to weaken Adelaide's resolve. In the morning, after surveying the damage to her property, she vowed to remain at Larchmont even if it meant a battle in court.

The day took on a somewhat restless mood.

News of the incident saw a full corps of reporters mobilized and dispatched to Larchmont to cover the story.

That afternoon, Bert summoned Adelaide, Minnie and Robert into the dining room and sat them round the table for a meeting with a representative from the local police department. The officer spoke of his concerns for their safety and expressed his regrets for the senseless acts of violence that had occurred the previous night. He also explained that little else could have been done by the police to foresee or prevent such an incident from happening, especially as the property was situated on two acres of unfenced ground, accessible from all sides. He promised his department's full assistance in handling the investigation. Though his words sounded reassuring Bert still feared more attacks might take place. To help diffuse any future tension, the officer confirmed a 24-hour police guard would be stationed prominently on the roadway directly in front of the property, until further notice.

Bert wondered if such action might encourage more acrimony towards them and thumped his hand down heavily on the table to show his concern. "Surely we must stand our ground, be vigilant and show them we mean to stay."

"Quite," replied the police officer, startled by Bert's sudden aggression. "As long as you do it peacefully and within the limits of the law."

At the end of the meeting the officer reiterated to all those present that his station would be at their complete disposal if and whenever it was necessary.

"It might be a good idea if Miss Hall were to give the waiting press outside a brief interview. It might help clear them away for the day, if they can see your fighting spirit still intact."

A worried frown appeared across Adelaide's brow.

"Do I really have to, Bert? Can't we just issue a written statement and have it delivered?"

Bert thought hard for a moment before answering her question.

"No! I think we should take the advice of the officer, darling. It'll look far better if they see we mean business."

As an afterthought, the officer suggested that it might be more appropriate if he announced her appearance to the press. He also recommended that Adelaide appear with her two dogs at her side. "Let them see the welcome they'd get. It's always a good deterrent."

Her appearance caused great excitement amongst the reporters who were now camped opposite the property. Eager to get her side of the story they dashed across the road and regrouped on the front lawn. At the top of the steps that led up to the front door of the house stood Adelaide. Given the circumstances, she looked relatively composed as she peered down at the gathered throng beneath her. It was a brilliant vantagepoint and one that could not have been better choreographed by a film director. She watched impatiently as the press corps fumbled for their pens and notepads and jostled for the best position. The sudden flurry of activity caused the dogs to become restless. Yanking their leads tight, Adelaide reined them in, close to her side. An air of expectancy prevailed. Her heart was pounding. A look of apprehension flashed visibly across her face.

"Tell us how you are, Miss Hall," came the first call from the crowd.

A measured silence followed.

Adelaide drew a long, defiant breath, before answering the question. "Thank you for your kind concern. I'm as well as can be expected under these unusual circumstances."

"We understand your husband's been injured, Miss Hall," inquired another reporter.

At the side window in the reception room, overseeing the proceedings, stood Bert.

Adelaide glanced briefly across at him, before making her reply.

"He's suffering from mild concussion and a few cuts and bruises, thankfully nothing too serious. Otherwise he's OK."

"Has anyone been arrested yet?" called out the next journalist.

At this point one of the police officers stepped forward and took control of the meeting.

"Such questions will have to be directed to the Superintendent in charge of the investigation. Miss Hall is not at liberty to answer police matters."

After dispensing with the pleasantries, the questioning proceeded on a more antagonistic course.

"Miss Hall, are you going to fight back or will you be moving back to live in Harlem?" Such a thoughtless question could only have provoked fury. Enraged by the reporter's impertinence, Adelaide instantly replied,

"This is my home and I intend to stay put. No one, and I repeat, NO ONE is going to evict me from my own property, and if they want a fight, I'll give them a battle." As if to verify her determination, she threw a sardonic smile at the photographers then waved a clenched fist in the air before continuing her speech matter-of-factly.

"I'm a true American with American Indian blood in my veins. If there's going to be any court action, I'm just waiting to put some of the new-rich residents of Larchmont on to the witness stand to ask them how their grandfathers spelt their surnames."

A rush of adrenaline swept through the gathering as an outburst of flashguns exploded, giving the whole affair the transitory appearance of a firework display. Even Adelaide was taken aback with the effect.

Sensing the interview had reached its conclusion, the officer in charge stepped forward and called a halt to the proceedings.

"Thank you, everybody, that'll be all for today," shouted the officer as the police began slowly to push the crowd back towards the road.

"Could you all now please be kind enough to leave Miss Hall's property."

"Miss Hall. Excuse me, Miss Hall," called out an insistent journalist at the front of the crowd. Adelaide turned around and looked across the lawn to see who was calling her name.

"Before you go, Miss Hall, would it be possible to have just one more picture. Maybe sitting down on the front steps?"

By now Adelaide knew the procedure inside out; she had heard it all before. Just one more picture, just one more interview. There was always one reporter who wanted a different angle, more exclusive than the others. She had also learnt from past experience that if she didn't oblige more often than not he would write a stinking article about her.

"OK, just one more picture," sighed Adelaide wearily. "I'll sit down here, on the top step . . . with my two dogs."

ADELAIDE HALL, AMERICA

The ordeal had been worth her effort. The press reported the story in depth. Most of the coverage, especially in the black papers, was sensitively written and sympathetic. Only extreme right-wing publications carried indifferent formal reports of the riotous events.

Rallying to her defense, the *New York Amsterdam News* plastered the headline "Adelaide Hall moves in bag and baggage" across its front page.[3] The accompanying story showed three photographs depicting Adelaide in fighting spirit, standing obstinately on the front steps of her new home. Her cause had now taken on the banner of a crusade and the screaming caption did little to calm the situation. In a scathing counter-article entitled "Grave catastrophe befalls the town of Larchmont," the editor spoke of his genuine sorrow for white people: "In their fear of the Negro, they reveal the most astounding ignorance. It's when this fear is real that we are tempted to feel sorry. Sometimes the white man's fear of the Negro borders on insanity, and the insane of any race should have our sympathy." He condemned the local media coverage and accused them of inciting a riot. "Few people—black or white—would have known that Miss Hall lived in Larchmont if the daily press, by making the fact known, had not sneakily suggested to her neighbors that they should object to her presence."

Hearing of Adelaide's plight, the National Association for the Advancement of Colored People stepped in and offered all its resources to help assist her case. Letters of support began to arrive daily at her home. Some were simply addressed "Adelaide Hall, Larchmont, America." It was as if,

by writing, the sender had wanted to reinforce their belief in the constitutional right of every American citizen:

> We the people of the United States, in order to form a more
> perfect union, establish justice, insure domestic tranquillity,
> provide for the common defense, promote the general welfare,
> and secure the blessings of liberty to ourselves and our posterity,
> do ordain and establish this Constitution for the United States of
> America.[4]

Adelaide's brave stand against bigotry and her belief in equality for one
and all, no matter what color their skin, touched the very core of
American democracy. If American citizens couldn't feel safe and secure in
their own homes then how could they be expected to feel proud of their
country and its people? Even New York's Mayor, James J. Walker, who was
a close friend of Bert's, offered his assistance in helping to resolve the
matter.[5] To substantiate his support and give weight to her cause he personally issued Adelaide with his Badge of Office which granted her all the
privileged facilities his title and position held. Eleanor Roosevelt, wife of
the future President, who was known to be a passionate campaigner and
advocate for black equality, also willingly lent her name to the case. Even
with such influential backing, death threats and letters of condemnation
continued to arrive with alarming regularity.

Meanwhile, daily routine at the house took on a peculiar procedure of
its own. Fortunately, Adelaide and Bert could come and go safely by car
without having to confront either the reporters or neighbors face to face.
Gradually, tension eased a little and life took on a semblance of normality.
Finding there was little more they could do in the present circumstances,
the local residents retreated, leaving Adelaide to roost in the isolation of
her fortified nest.

No police charges were ever filed against the perpetrators of the
violence. The reporters soon grew bored of waiting for a circus that never
happened and the 24-hour police guard was lifted. Adelaide returned to
the one thing she knew best, work, and the household went about its daily
chores unchallenged. During the following months, there can't have been
a single person in Westchester who, at some point during his or her daily

procedure, didn't travel by 11 Kilmer Road just to take a look at Adelaide Hall's famous residence. Ironically, it seemed that Bert's philosophy, "Confuse them, then they won't know what to think," had, for the moment, done just that.

Ever since the Ancient Greeks voted "Yes" with a white pebble and "No" with a black one, the stigma attached to the color black has existed. Following the liberation of African culture in the Twenties, America witnessed a racial backlash during the Thirties, especially out in the sticks. Hopes of integration were fast becoming idle promises written on the wind.

Throughout the controversy Adelaide's name was repeatedly slandered. On the streets of Larchmont she found herself openly reviled by her neighbors who, sarcastically, twisted her stage persona as the "Crooning Blackbird," by referring to her as the "Lark on Larchmont Hill." A lark sings continuously whilst soaring up into the sky and Adelaide had every intention of adopting the same attitude. She was determined not to let the disruption affect her career.

Since her well-publicized brush with racism during *Blackbirds*, Adelaide had learnt that the media's attention was a necessary tool for promoting one's beliefs. She was adamant that no one was going to tell her where she could or could not live and issued a further press release which mirrored the statement she had made on the front steps of her home:

> I'm a true American with American Indian blood in my veins. If
> there's going to be any court action, I'm just waiting to put some
> of the new-rich residents of Larchmont on to the witness stand
> to ask them how their grandfathers spelt their surnames.

She was, of course, referring to her mother's relatives who descended from the Indian Shinnecock tribe of Southampton on Long Island. In the opinion of her neighbors, such Indians should still be living in hogans.

An encampment of Shinnecock Indians had lived on Long Island since records began. It was only after the arrival of European travelers along the island's northeastern coastline in the early sixteenth century that any

The songwriters Dorothy Fields and Jimmy McHugh pose with Adelaide in the grounds of her Larchmont estate, during a weekend stay.

reference to the "friendly" natives was noted. These "friendly" Indians welcomed the newcomers with apprehension. Nevertheless, they helped the settlers build their first town, Southampton, on Little Peconic Bay. They willingly shared their skills and taught them how to trap game, dig clams, cultivate the land, and grow crops of corn fertilized with dried fish, and even how to cook the local dish of wholesome porridge called samp.

Unfortunately, in helping the new settlers the Indians signed their own death warrant. Within a relatively short space of time, many Shinnecock tribes had been displaced from the land. Following the arrival of the Dutch, large areas of the island were purchased in exchange for cheap trade items such as kitchen utensils, cloth and farming tools. Those who resisted such sales were often murderously killed. For the sake of acquiring a few acres of land, generations of Indians were decimated. Any who escaped fled west to settle in Pennsylvania. In 1626, New York, which was then the Dutch colony of New Amsterdam, introduced slavery. It wasn't abolished until 1827, by which time Long Island's indigenous community had almost disappeared.

The Shinnecock tribe is first mentioned in the Indian Deed of Southampton. Compiled in 1640, the document states, "The above named Indians shall have liberty to break up ground for their use to the westward of the creek on the West Side of Shinnecock Plain." The name Shinnecock is derived from the Indian word meaning to "level land" or "flatten ground." Ironically, there's an old saying in Indian folklore that the worst insult one Indian can give to another is to call them an "Apple," red on the outside and white in the middle.

The fate of the Shinnecock Indian tribe was a classic example of the white settlers' ruthless determination to gain supremacy regardless of cost or human suffering. Adelaide's stand against discrimination proved the fighting spirit of her forebears' lineage was still intact. She had made her point and she knew she had no option but to see it through to the end. She also knew she couldn't win whatever the outcome: she would be damned if she succeeded with her cause and damned if she lost.

In order to live in harmony one must first alleviate the build-up of dissension that surrounds you. By virtue of her skin color being darker than her neighbors', Adelaide's presence in Larchmont was seen as a direct threat to their quiet genteel community. As a police officer quite rightly pointed out, such incandescent rage was not manufactured; it was deep-rooted, inbred through generations and such discrimination was not going to vanish overnight.

THROUGH NO FAULT OF HER OWN

Lew Leslie had tried every possible way to induce Adelaide back into his fold. He now falsely announced to the press that she would be starring in his next revue, *Pie Pie Blackbird*, which he planned to put together in the fall.[6] The show was also to feature Hollywood film actress, Nina Mae McKinney. His scheming never ceased to amaze. The show never materialized but Leslie's determination to acquire Adelaide's skills led to another offer which did temporarily see her back on his pay-roll.

On August 28, Leslie's latest production, *Dixie to Broadway*, a revamped edition of *Rhapsody in Black*, arrived at the Paramount Theater in New York's Times Square for a week's engagement, before heading off on a provincial tour.[7] The show starred Ethel Waters and the Mills Brothers. Once again, Leslie was up to his old tricks. Ethel's continual wrangling over her salary had created bitterness between her and Leslie and he was now looking for a way of totally removing her from the cast before the show's Broadway opening.

After secret negotiations with Bert, an arrangement was reached whereby Adelaide would take over the starring role in *Dixie to Broadway*. With Adelaide signed up, Leslie saw no reason to pay top whack for two stars to head the bill and had Ethel's contract terminated.

Ethel immediately contacted her lawyer. To play Leslie at his own game her agent arranged a tour that ran in direct opposition to *Dixie to Broadway*. Leslie was trapped. Ethel had become too big a draw to ignore. With his finances in such a precarious state the competition was too risky. His hand was forced. Leslie retracted his dismissal and renegotiated her contract. Unbeknown to Adelaide, Ethel was re-instated in the show.

So as not to offend Adelaide, Leslie billed Ethel as an "Extra Added Attraction." Although in real life they were great friends, the stars were in direct competition with each other. Such was their rivalry, an unbearable atmosphere developed between them backstage and their friendship began to suffer. After its initial six-week run, Adelaide quit, allowing Miss Waters to head the production. This time, Adelaide's resignation sealed her fate with Leslie for ever.

December 21, 1932
Broadway had recently seen an excellent revival of Jerome Kern and Oscar Hammerstein's rousing musical *Show Boat,* which included one of Jack Kapp's favorite scores. Kapp was Brunswick Records' highly respected artist and recording manager and it was his idea to produce a selection of songs from the musical to make into an abbreviated cast album, something that had never been attempted before with one show. The result—a boxed set of four 78-rpm records—sold like hot cakes at a jamboree.

The album's success encouraged Kapp to record the full score from one of his all-time favorite revues, *Blackbirds of 1928.* As the show had by then disbanded, the task of arranging the production turned out to be a huge undertaking. This time Kapp wanted to record the whole score using the greatest array of black talent that had ever been grouped together on one album. Without Lew Leslie's interference, Kapp's job was made a lot easier. He could choose the musicians and artists whom he felt would best carry the songs.

Duke Ellington with his eponymous orchestra was contracted to record five of the most popular numbers from the score, including a *Blackbirds* medley, in conjunction with various vocalists. Adelaide, Ethel Waters and the Mills Brothers were the chosen artists. By coincidence all three had just appeared together in Leslie's *Dixie to Broadway*.

"Diga Diga Do" went to the Mills Brothers and Ethel had the privilege of singing "I Can't Give You Anything But Love, Baby" and "Porgy," but once again Adelaide was summoned to record "I Must Have That Man" and the song Lew Leslie originally discarded, "Baby."

Adelaide was not happy with the choice of songs she was given. She had already made successful recordings of the same two numbers with the Blackbirds Orchestra in a Kapp production back in 1928.

Before signing her contract Adelaide asked Kapp to explain why she couldn't record "Diga Diga Do" or "I Can't Give You Anything But Love, Baby," especially as the public identified both of these songs with her. Kapp's reply came as a double-edged compliment. He felt most of the songs from *Blackbirds* were easy for a vocalist to interpret but argued strongly that no other artist alive could sing "I Must Have That Man" with the same yearnful conviction that Adelaide portrayed. Any other rendition would be second best. As for "Baby," because the song had originally been written for her, he felt it belonged to her, and no one else.

The whole concept of the album was to record each song with the best artist. Kapp clearly had a difficult task in deciding who should sing which song. In retrospect, choosing the Mills Brothers to sing "Diga Diga Do" was absurd. Of all the songs in *Blackbirds*, this was the one that Adelaide was most closely associated with. Without being in the least bit detrimental to the Mills Brothers' rendition, it was like giving the queen's crown to a distant relative to wear.

Due to each performer's professional commitments the album took two months to complete. Bojangles, Cab Calloway and Cecil Mack's Choir laid down the remaining numbers from the score with Don Redman's Orchestra. Although the album could not be termed an original cast recording the final product did produce the first complete recording of a Broadway musical. As a publicity gimmick, when the boxed set of six 78s was released, Kapp sent an amusing "exploitation record" to all the dealers in the trade. It contained his own voice extolling the genius of Fields and McHugh as songwriters.

The project received tremendous praise and sales far exceeded Brunswick's expectations. One reviewer, in summing up the intensity of Adelaide's vocal on "I Must Have That Man," clearly recognized her attachment to the lyric: "No-one could put more into or get more out of a song, than Adelaide Hall."

The following year saw little change in Adelaide's predicament at Larchmont. Only the seasons brought a different outlook. Her mother and grandmother remained in Harlem. Even their rare visits to the house were short and uncomfortable. The aftermath of the events at Kilmer Road plagued Adelaide sorely. To some, it appeared her black heart was getting whiter by the day.

Even though the tension eased, bitter animosity remained. The escalating effects of the Depression saw many of her neighbors redundant. The fact that Adelaide's earning potential was far greater than most of theirs only added more wind to the storm. Adelaide appeared to have the world on a string. Not only did she own a beautiful house, drive a luxurious car and wear expensive jewelry and furs; her bank account was stashed with cash. She had been ostracized for her ancestry; now she was condemned for her success. Through hard labor she had built a distinguished career and her marriage was considerably more stable than most but, like the shifting silt that flows unnoticed along a riverbed, she felt her life drifting helplessly out of control through no fault of her own.

LENOX AVENUE BLUES

1933

At the beginning of the year Adelaide starred at Harlem's Opera House in an oddly named production—*Moments of Song, Beauty and Grace*.[1] It was a brave change of direction for her. The program contained classical, blues and gospel songs with new material especially written and featured an all-star cast, although no supporting names were advertised. Nor was any of its content documented in the press. Despite the show's lack of media coverage, it appears to have been well received by the public and played a short run on the vaudeville circuit.

Her next presentation, which had its premiere at Harlem's Lafayette, had no title and simply went under the banner of her own name. The large cast included the eccentric, one-legged dancer Peg Leg Bates, the comedian Marshall Rogers and Hy Clark's Missourian Orchestra under the direction of Joe Jordan. The revue was tailor-made to display Adelaide's various talents—she even choreographed some of the dance routines—and for the first time Bert took production credits.

When the show opened on May 20 the audience didn't know what to expect. A shock announcement in the *New York Amsterdam News* reported it to be "Adelaide's farewell appearance." However, on scrutinizing the article the statement became somewhat clearer. In fact, it would only be her farewell appearance that year in Harlem, as she would be away on tour for the rest of the year.

Bert's decision to produce and part-finance the show was a gamble that paid handsome dividends. *New York Amsterdam News* called it "Excellent" and RKO booked the complete production for a tour, including a week at Broadway's Palace Theater commencing June 17.[2] Never before had a black star compiled and toured in her own revue. The concept set a precedent many white producers found worrying. *Variety* reviewed her Palace performance as "straight and controlled . . . very much in the prima donna mold," which clearly indicates the extent of Bert's involvement with the direction.[3]

Included in Adelaide's act were Harold Arlen's recently penned "Stormy Weather" and Irving Berlin's minor-keyed lament "Blue Skies." Bert was clever to spot the potential of "Stormy Weather" before it became an international hit and turning point in Ethel Waters' career. The song was originally written for the Cotton Club's 22nd edition in which Ethel was starring. The show had only recently had its premiere and was playing to packed sittings three times a night. Already, Ethel's impassioned rendition of "Stormy Weather" was attracting tremendous interest. However, because the number emotionally drained her, Ethel only sang "Stormy Weather" once each evening. In an unusual move, Bert sought permission from both the club's management and Harold Arlen to include the song in Adelaide's show.[4] Remarkably, permission was granted as it was felt Adelaide's enormous popularity would help generate custom for the club.

Historically, "Stormy Weather's" success is only attributed to Ethel's performance at the Cotton Club but, in truth, Adelaide was also instrumental in promoting the song, a fact she has never been accredited with. Moreover, Arlen was so impressed with her rendition that in September, at the end of Ethel's contract, he requested Adelaide be given the leading role in the touring production, the first and only time an original Cotton Club revue hit the road.[5] Irving Mills sponsored the plan and notified the press that he intended to give theater patrons in various Midwestern, Southern and Northern cities the rare opportunity to see an original Harlem cabaret.

With her new contract signed, Adelaide's itinerary was rescheduled. Helped no end by regular radio broadcasts, the Cotton Club tour drew record attendance figures. Its popularity even attracted an offer from London to play in Europe, although the proposal was never taken up. The

show returned triumphantly to New York in December and performed at the Rochester Palace and Harlem's Lafayette. To capitalize on her success, Adelaide released two songs on the Victor label: "Reachin' For The Cotton Moon" and Ellington's "Drop Me Off In Harlem." Accompanied by the Mills Blue Rhythm Band, the disc captured a little of the Cotton Club magic for posterity. The tour lasted almost six months and played in accordance with the RKO circuit in such cities as Washington, D.C., Cleveland, Detroit, Cincinnati and Chicago and directly brought about Adelaide's starring role at Harlem's Cotton Club in March 1934.

I think it's fair to say that 1933 was a turning point in Adelaide's career. Her domination as America's foremost black female entertainer took a worrying nudge from her friend and arch-rival Ethel Waters. Already well known in New York, Ethel's appearance at the Cotton Club, via the ubiquitous ear of its regular live transcontinental radio program, turned her into a household name across America. At the end of her engagement at the Cotton Club, Ethel sailed effortlessly on to Broadway in Irving Berlin's *As Thousands Cheer* and became a star all over again. After years of toil and disappointment she finally established herself on the Great White Way.

To add to Adelaide's worries, on September 26, an indictment against her former lawyer, Lawrence Mingey—preferred against him by Adelaide—was heard at Jefferson Crown Court.[6] Once again the house at Larchmont stirred both local and national media interest.

After signing a check over to Mingey on July 18, 1932 for $4,500, on the understanding that he would purchase real estate on her behalf, Adelaide claimed she had never received the property deeds and that Mingey did not return the money. The magistrate, William Farrell, called for the hearing to take place the following day.

Charged with suspicion of grand larceny, Mingey pleaded not guilty. At the end of the sitting no conclusion was reached and Judge Farrell ordered the accused be held in jail without bail to await a further hearing. Although the publicity kept Adelaide's name in the headlines the delay in the trial was not good news.

On October 27, Adelaide and Bert jointly filed a suit in the County Court seeking immediate title to 11 Kilmer Road, the property they believed they had purchased in good faith from Bernard K. Marcus. The Hicks named as defendants their former lawyer, Lawrence P. Mingey, their realty agent, Stephen R. Tobin, and Mingey's housekeeper, Ellen H. Sutherland, who was said to have withheld evidence regarding certain key facts relating to the case. They alleged that Mingey misrepresented himself as an attorney and was unlawfully withholding funds entrusted to him aggregating $4,500, which was made as a deposit for the purchase of the Marcus' home.

During the case, certain revelations regarding the sale of the property were disclosed. It transpired that after neighbors inundated Mingey with letters objecting to the sale of the property to Negro buyers, Adelaide and Bert had secretly allowed Mingey to acquire title to the estate, on the understanding that he would then sign it over to them. Adelaide claimed Mingey then double-crossed them and, instead, for an undisclosed sum signed the deeds over to Mr. Tobin. Adelaide's counsel argued that Mingey, a former New York attorney, had misrepresented himself to his clients by acting as their attorney when, in fact, he had been disbarred from the profession in 1906. The Hicks also asked for an accounting of all funds that were given to Mingey. As with all cases of litigation, the courts proceeded at a snail's pace.

The outcome of the case was finally settled satisfactorily in the Hicks' favor. Mingey was found guilty of larceny and charged with gross misconduct. The title deeds to the property were reverted to their rightful owners and court costs and compensation awarded. Although Adelaide won the lawsuit, the trial left a bittersweet after-taste to her victory.

Some felt the Government gave America the best Christmas present ever when Franklin D. Roosevelt announced the repeal of Prohibition on December 5, 1933. The manufacture, sale and possession of alcohol was no longer illegal and the intoxication that followed was best described as a temporary blur in most people's memory. Like the highly addictive alcoholic drink absinthe, whose potent after-effect can cause dementia, the repeal of Prohibition held hidden consequences. Clearly, such sobering news was devastating for the racketeers who operated illegal breweries.

THE APOLLO, HARLEM, JANUARY 1934

There was great excitement in Harlem when the Apollo Theater opened on January 26, 1934.[7] It had previously operated as a burlesque house known as Hurtig and Seamon's and practiced a strict "Whites Only" door policy. Frank Schulman, owner of the famous Lafayette and Lincoln Theaters, purchased the building for a snip after it had fallen into disrepair. Following lavish renovations, including the installation of high-fidelity RCA sound equipment identical to that used at Radio City Music Hall, the theater re-opened to exclusively showcase black entertainment. To guarantee top-quality revues Clarence Robinson was engaged as in-house producer. For the gala opening Schulman sought a top box-office draw. With no expense spared, his list of potential acts looked like a producer's dream bill. The fact that most of the artists were already booked to appear elsewhere rapidly whittled the list down. However, after rescheduling her itinerary he finally managed to secure ex-Blackbird Aida Ward.

On February 16, Adelaide starred in Clarence Robinson's first full-length revue at the venue entitled *Chocolate Soldiers*. Coincidentally, Sam Wooding's Orchestra was contracted to provide musical accompaniment. Adelaide and Wooding had last appeared together back in 1925 during the *Chocolate Kiddies* tour of Europe from which Wooding had only recently returned having carved a profitable career for himself on the Continent. Perhaps the reuniting of two former *Kiddies* stars gave Robinson the inspiration for naming his revue? The show ran for a limited engagement, was highly praised by the black press and helped establish the Apollo as Harlem's premier black theater. Its success would eventually lead to the Lafayette's closure.

THE HOUSE THAT JACK BUILT

> Gradually, as the voodoo took control,
> the lyrics' wild sexual innuendoes emerged
> and off came the layers of lace, one by one . . .

Cotton Club Parade, *March 11, 1934*
Harlem's Cotton Club had enjoyed unparalleled custom since opening its doors to the public in the fall of 1923. Known, in the words of Lady Mountbatten, as "The Aristocrat of Harlem," the club was renowned for

its dazzling stage show, gastronomic menu and homemade illicit booze named Madden's No. 1. The building was situated on the northeast corner of 142nd Street and Lenox Avenue. It originally housed a casino and vaudeville theater. Their failure prompted Jack Johnson—a former black heavyweight boxing champion—to lease the premises in 1922 and convert the place into a supper club.[8] Johnson only owned it for a few months before he sold it to the Mafia.

A syndicate of gangsters led by Owen "Owney" Madden bought the club. For obvious reasons Madden kept a low profile and allowed one of his henchmen, Harry Block, to front it. Unlike his fellow associates, Madden did not fit the stereotype image of a hard-nosed Mafia figure. Small and softly spoken with gentle blue eyes, his manners were impeccable. Nonetheless, in his role as boss, he was ruthless and was said to have killed several men in cold blood before reaching the end of his teens. He fought hard to attain his position in the underworld and, as such, commanded huge respect as one of New York's most important godfathers. One of Madden's close friends, the actress Mae West, humorously nicknamed him the "clay pigeon," because he was shot at so many times. "Comes with the business" was how he would nonchalantly shrug off such acts of violence.

Harry Block hired the staff and supervised the daily running of the establishment and was ably assisted by Herman Stark, a former machine gunner, who took his job as stage manager very seriously. In 1925, Block was found guilty of selling illicit alcohol on the premises. He was fined and a three-month closure was enforced upon the.club. Ironically, it was his astute management techniques that caused his downfall. In retaliation for having a rival club wrecked, Block's body was found bullet-ridden in the elevator of his own apartment building. His death saw Stark take control and under his guidance the club climbed to even greater heights.

Despite its owners' dubious origins the Cotton Club gave off an air of respectability. If violence occurred on the premises it was shielded from both the guests and backstage artists. After viewing Francis Coppola's 1984 movie about the club, Adelaide felt the violence portrayed in it was glorified for the screen: "We knew nothing about the shootings and killings. We wouldn't have stayed if we did. It may have been run by the mob but we had no dealings with them. We just did our job and got paid."

Lew Leslie was hired to produce the first Cotton Club revues and Jimmy McHugh wrote the scores. Their top-class entertainment helped the club's reputation grow rapidly. Customers from downtown were captivated by its ambiance and jungle décor—false palm trees with dangling coconuts—and found the black waiters positively polite. The interior was laid out in the shape of a horseshoe. From the middle of the shoe projected an extended proscenium around which tables were arranged in tiers on three sides, with the orchestra positioned at the rear of the stage. Along the walls, individual booths allowed those guests who wished to remain anonymous to enjoy a more intimate supper. When the club re-opened at the end of 1925, Stark fired Leslie as producer and hired Dan Healy to take over.

Known for operating a "Jim Crow" policy that catered for rich white folk, it seemed odd that such an establishment was situated in the very heart of the largest black community in America. The management was fully aware of local discontent over this issue but insisted they were creating worthwhile jobs for Negroes which would not otherwise be available. In any case the club was far too expensive for a black man's pocket—unless you happened to be Bojangles.

Despite its high entrance fee and costly menu, the place was packed to the seams nightly. Its continuous popularity enabled Healy to afford increasingly more lavish stage shows on a par with any Broadway musical and to hire the biggest black stars of the day to perform in them.

At the peak of its success the Cotton Club revue was as feted as any hit Broadway show. As it commenced late enough for theatrical folk to visit after their own performance downtown, it wasn't unusual to see a selection of top-class stars and celebrities enjoying the entertainment. During a visit to the club one columnist noted that as well as spotting various minor celebrities, Tallulah Bankhead, Eleanor Powell, the Marx Brothers and Al Jolson were all in attendance, seated with separate parties throughout the audience. Surprisingly, as head of the FBI, J. Edgar Hoover, who had been appointed to solve the increase in Mafia dealings, frequently patronized the club, often accompanied by a male companion.

Two revues were produced each year and referred to as editions. The second revue commenced rehearsal during the last month's run of the previous edition. This maintained continuity, preventing the necessity to close the club. The show was performed as many as three times a night, depending on reservations, and the venue remained open until dawn, which invariably meant the cast never got home before 7 a.m.

Harlem's nightlife had changed considerably since the early Twenties, when the area's ethnic charm first attracted the attention of white downtown New Yorkers. Little of the neighborhood's untamed character remained. Sophisticated cabarets and tourist dives now predominated. Adelaide's headlining revue at the Cotton Club in March 1934, the first after Prohibition had been lifted, witnessed the release of the stranglehold such Mafia-owned establishments held. With its well-earned reputation for staging the most lavish revues off-Broadway, their 24th edition—*Cotton Club Parade*—lived up to the public's expectations.[9]

The show was a huge financial success and ran for eight months attracting over 600,000 paying customers, proving Adelaide's pulling power was still intact. Its premiere on March 11 drew a hotchpotch of notable and distinguished guests.[10] The reservation list read like the credits on a Hollywood blockbuster and included Paul Whiteman, Sam Goldwyn and his wife, Abe Lyman, Vincent Lopez, Harold Stern, Jack Little, Fred Waring, Jack Denny, Glen Gray, Ozzie Nelson, Marilyn Miller, Miriam Hopkins, Margaret Livingston, Gregory Ratoff, Irving and Ellin Berlin, Lee Shubert, George White, Jimmy Durante, Lillian Roth, Gene Buck, Ben Pollack, Victor Moore, Jo Frisco, Peggy Hopkins Joyce and Harriet Hilliard. The fact that Sam Goldwyn attended is interesting, for he was known to admire colored artists greatly. His friend King Vidor, who had previously worked for him, had made the movie *Hallelujah* using an all-black cast. The picture was one of Goldwyn's favorites.

The 24th edition blew in another score by Harold Arlen and Ted Koehler. It was to be their last joint work of standing for many years. The score turned out to be Adelaide's most memorable since *Blackbirds of 1928*.

It's impossible to imagine American popular music without Harold Arlen. His ability to write an unforgettable tune was surpassed only by George Gershwin and Cole Porter. Such was his influence that it was considered a great honor to have a song especially written for you by the maestro. Not only did Adelaide have that privilege bestowed upon her; she had a whole show composed around her. After the huge success of

"Stormy Weather" the songwriter hoped to duplicate its popularity with the meteorological sequel "Ill Wind." The song never did achieve parallel sales but, to this day, is still regarded as one of his best. Arlen believed emphatically in divine inspiration. After composing a tune he would stand in the corner of the room and thank "him upstairs" for the melody and pray for the next one. The inspiration behind "Ill Wind" was reported to have been nurtured in this manner. It was said that when Arlen heard Adelaide perform the song for the first time at a rehearsal, he burst into tears. Her chilling interpretation rendered him speechless for the remainder of the afternoon.

In view of the limited size of the proscenium, the sets were elaborate and detailed. Forever wanting to be one jump ahead of his competitors, producer Dan Healy experimented with dramatic lighting, spectacular outfits and the latest mechanical devices. For this production he pulled out all the stops. To complement the female chorus line, he introduced a male equivalent. To give "Ill Wind" authenticity, he had a specially designed set built and used a dry-ice machine to create a fog effect, the first time such equipment had been used on stage. At rehearsals the smog caused more than a few coughs and worried frowns from the local fire department, which was concerned that the smoke might cause panic and disorientation amongst the revelers.

Dubbed "Mistress of the lyric," the revue centered on Adelaide and ran for 90 minutes—much longer if the encores got out of hand. No matter how many ballads or swing numbers were incorporated, Cotton Club audiences always expected a wild jungle number, so on went the grass skirts, ivory bangles and tooth necklaces. The management called it "Jungle Music" and promoted Adelaide as an African Diva.[11] In this particular edition such native abandon was amply illustrated in "Primitive Prima Donna" during which Adelaide stirred the whole club into a frenzied cocktail. Her arrival on stage in a brilliantly colorful outfit comprising numerous layers of lace and satin belied the sassiness of the number. The flow of the fabric cleverly accentuated the luscious curves of her body and left little to the imagination. Gradually, as the voodoo took control, the lyrics' wild sexual innuendoes emerged and off came the layers of lace, one by one. Pace, and more pace, was the routine's chief ingredient adeptly choreographed by Elida Webb, displayed to the rhythmic prowess of Jimmie Lunceford's orchestration. By the end of the song, Adelaide had indeed transformed herself into a primitive prima donna.

Over the years the club had been a springboard to fame for many gifted artists including Cab Calloway, Duke Ellington, the Nicholas Brothers, Ethel Waters, Lucky Millinder and Edith Wilson. Waiting in the wings of this edition was another hopeful, somewhat younger than the rest but just as talented—Miss Lena Horne.

Every show had its chorus line of bronze-legged beauties. Some were hand-picked solely for their good looks, pale skin and body form; others, called "ponies," actually did something. Lena Horne was one such pony. Aged only sixteen, her entry into show business literally occurred via the back door of the Cotton Club.

Her first job, in the 23rd edition, could not have occurred without external intervention. As an under-age teenager, by law she still required a school education. As the principal breadwinner in her family, Lena's truant officer took pity on her and turned a blind eye, reporting her missing—whereabouts unknown. As it happened, daily life in the club was an education in itself and taught Lena enough to carry herself confidently in the society in which she was now mixing.

Lena's beauty was unquestionably breathtaking and overshadowed all the other girls in the chorus. One couldn't help but notice her. Even though she was only a dancer, when she was on stage all eyes focused upon her. She sparkled like a yellow diamond in a jasper setting. Such was her attraction, the management fought tooth and dagger to retain her for the 24th edition and even offered to employ a private tutor. Lena went one better and employed a singing coach. The lessons paid off. In this revue she got to sing a duet, "As Long as I Live," with Avon Long. To guard her reputation should any guy get too interested in Lena's affections, whether out-front or backstage, she came chaperoned at all times by her overprotective mother.

In Lena's eyes Adelaide arrived at the Cotton Club as the Queen of Harlem. She was by far the most celebrated black female star in America and held all the trappings that wealth and fame could bestow upon her. Having been courted by celebrities and European royalty, she truly was the local girl made good and as such Lena was in awe of her presence.

Lena soon learnt that Adelaide was just as approachable as the next person, if not more so. Gradually, a great friendship, which remained life-long, evolved between them. Adelaide, whom Lena affectionately nicknamed "Auntie," was to have a profound influence upon the young teenager's career. During Adelaide's apprenticeship, when she was a chorine in the musical *Shuffle Along*, she set her sights on one day becoming the star of such a show. At the Cotton Club Lena lived the same scenario. Watching the acclaim Adelaide received each night helped Lena focus clearly upon her own future aspirations.

Considering the club claimed to be so exclusive, its backstage dressing room was probably the worst a performer could ever encounter—a long corridor, divided in two by a pole over which a curtain was draped. Men dressed on one side and women on the other. If they got bored they talked to each other over the top of the rail. A narrow staircase, one body wide, led down from the room directly into the wings. During the show, when the stairs got busy, you couldn't change your mind halfway down and decide to go back up. Only the main star and bandleader had their own personal dressing room, located beneath the staircase. The artists knew the conditions when they accepted their contract so had little comeback if they complained.

"We knew we were being paid by the mob, but we never really got that close to them," declared Adelaide nonchalantly when I questioned her about the working conditions at the club. "On Saturday evening Elida Webb, the show's choreographer and manager, came backstage with a wicker tray stacked with brown envelopes, one for each artist, containing that week's wages in cash. After Sunday night's show we'd then be off until the following Tuesday evening when the next week's run commenced."

During Duke Ellington's initial residency at the Cotton Club, WABC introduced nightly radio broadcasts from the premises, which helped promote jazz music nationally. The program, which still ran regularly, opened up a world that was otherwise alien to most suburban Americans and gave them a fascinating glimpse inside the nation's most famous nightclub. The broadcasts also helped spread the fame of its stars. After Ellington left for Hollywood, Cab Calloway took over as bandleader, although not in his footsteps. His whirling antics on stage brought him equal recognition. Calloway's role as a bandleader gave him the perfect platform to display his extrovert personality and the Cotton Club gave him the audience to lavish it upon.

The 24th edition was the first time Jimmie Lunceford and his orchestra had played at the Cotton Club.[12] Unfortunately, Lunceford's assignment did not run as smoothly as those of his predecessors. In May, after a dispute over salary, he severed all connection with his agent (Mills Artists) who, in retaliation, maliciously pulled him out of the prestigious engagement.[13] The Fletcher Henderson Band, which Mills Artists conveniently handled, was their immediate replacement.

No matter how elaborate the revue, the Cotton Club's glamour always had hidden dirt around its collar. It was rumored that the management expected the chorus girls to make themselves available to rich punters, should the interest arise. How specifically they were pressured into doing so is questionable, but certainly many of the girls took advantage of their position to line their own pockets. Duke Ellington's views on the matter were well known; he found the situation both degrading and humiliating for the girls.

At the end of an evening many of the cast hit the Nest, a local black after-hours drinking club that never appeared to close. Those who frequented the joint used the term "slumming it" liberally, for the place had little space and even littler charm. Its appeal came from the show-people that frequented it—such stars as Fanny Brice, Bojangles and Helen Morgan were regulars. The club's lack of pretense made it a comfortable watering spot to unwind in before heading home.

It was at the Nest that Bert first met Captain Gordon Halsey. Tall and debonair with the obligatory Englishman's moustache, Halsey owned the smart Florida Club in London's Mayfair. He was visiting New York scouting talent for his next floorshow. Bert was keen to establish Adelaide in Britain and felt the Captain might be a useful contact for the future. The impression Halsey painted of the Florida Club convinced Bert that the establishment held great potential for staging a black revue in the style of the Cotton Club. As a way of introducing Bert to the London scene Halsey invited him to Britain for a short stay as his houseguest. He suggested his visit coincide with a Champagne Birthday Ball he was hosting at the Dorchester Hotel on May 31, followed by cabaret and a Mermaid Competition at the Florida Club.

Bert did visit Britain alone as Halsey's guest to attend the ball and during his stay established an important link that in later years led to him purchasing the Florida Club thereby giving Adelaide her first London nightclub.

A certain prestige came with working at the Cotton Club. It created great demand for the star and attracted lucrative spin-offs, radio appearances and solo concerts. These events were usually slotted in before the midnight performance commenced at the club. During one week in July, as well as appearing at the Cotton Club Adelaide doubled for six nights at the Harlem Opera House, appeared in a benefit show for underprivileged children alongside Al Jolson and Bojangles at the Apollo and headed the bill in a surprise Duke Ellington homecoming concert at Broadway's Capitol Theater.[14]

During her residency at the Cotton Club, Adelaide commuted from her home at Larchmont. Although the intrusion into her private affairs was less turbulent, her daily life in the community had taken on an air of solitary confinement. As she had little contact with her neighbors, Adelaide now found her isolation created an unforeseen effect. The resulting tranquility brought a welcome respite from her hectic lifestyle. She also discovered that the luxury of having one's own beach had its rewards. Here, she could dance on the sand to her heart's content without fear of harassment.[15]

With three guest bedrooms in the house, Adelaide often invited friends over to stay at the weekend. Many noticed an unusual calm prevailed upon the dwelling, as if it were being watched by binoculars from all angles. If it hadn't been for the anonymous death threats that arrived in the mail with alarming regularity the absurdity of the situation would have made it laughable. Over the previous three years Adelaide's battle to secure a better lifestyle had played an emotional tug-of-war on her nerves. No matter how hard she tried to integrate within the local community it seemed that her efforts were repeatedly dashed. Clearly such tension could not continue without repercussions.

There was, however, a glimmer of encouragement when, after performing

Adelaide, her mother Elizabeth (during one of her rare visits) and Adelaide's pet dog Rex, at 11 Kilmer Road, Larchmont.

at a concert to benefit a nearby charity, an element of local press coverage became noticeably more deferential towards her.

Disregarding its racial stance, the Cotton Club holds a unique position in the history of traditional American entertainment. It promoted a prodigious array of talent on a par with any Broadway production leaving behind a legacy that, to this day, enriches popular music.

Whereas the club paid its stars generously it was a totally different story for the black waiters and kitchen staff. Their salaries were deemed to be as low as a limbo dancer's tight rope. Some reckoned that if it hadn't have been for the tips, which were considerable, the staff would have had little reason to remain. By the end of 1935, the club was no longer the most fashionable nightspot in Harlem and attendance figures had fallen dramatically. Fewer customers meant fewer tips, and amid growing disquiet the waiters staged a strike. A statement issued to the press by an anonymous steward implied they received no salary at all and were expected to pay the busboys 25 cents a day and buy their own uniforms costing $17.50 from their tips.[16] Such revelations of slave labor had a disastrous effect on the club's reputation. Deepening resentment from the local community forced the club's owners into taking action. On February 16, 1936 the Cotton Club finally closed its doors, signaling the end of an era. Herman Stark took heed of local bitterness and relocated the premises in a more acceptable area, downtown on the corner of 48th Street and Broadway in the heart of the theater district.

To add further injury to Harlem's renown, the Depression had brought a startling increase in robberies and violence to its streets. After the Cotton Club's closure the rising crime rate brought a further reduction in the number of revelers who would risk the trip uptown after dark. New York's "Mink Set," who once found the area exciting and liberating, now viewed its earthier realities as seedy and unsafe. Harlem's Renaissance was truly over.

When Adelaide's residency at the Cotton Club ended in December 1934 she could hardly have known the engagement would be her last American "hurrah to the big time."

IF THINGS GO ON THE WAY THEY ARE

1935

When Roosevelt's administration took power in 1933 the U.S. economy was in dire straits. Unfortunately for the country, even the election of a new President couldn't help soften the hardening effects of the Depression. At a time when the majority of American families were living frugally on less than $2,000 a year, Adelaide's salary was almost double that a week. Inevitably, at some point her bubble would burst. Her gradual descent in popularity took place in 1935.

Although jazz had once defied convention, it was now an accepted part of American mainstream entertainment. Writers, musicians and film directors from all creeds had dipped into black culture for inspiration. Its mass appeal had diluted its impact on the public's hungry imagination. They now sought more stimulating alternatives.

Record sales had overtaken sheet music as the most profitable division of the music industry and record companies were frantically searching for new stars to push profits even higher. The gradual demise of the jazz boom created fresh opportunities for talented newcomers. The Depression had cultivated a generation of youngsters seeking a musical identity they could consider their own. With his unique interpretation of free form jazz, which he named Swing, Benny Goodman and his Band filled that void admirably. If jazz had been the product of a restless age then Swing, born of poverty, would find its audience relatively tame. The time to move forward had arrived but, unfortunately for jazz stars, the direction was not that clearly signposted.

For the past fourteen years Adelaide had toured endlessly throughout America. The ritual had now become tedious, as boring as breathing in air, yet just as necessary. She had exhausted the theater circuit and, in the process, depleted both her energy and enthusiasm. As if to signal a change was on the horizon, Broadway's Palace Theater made the transition from exclusively showing vaudeville to becoming a movie house. It could no longer compete with Hollywood's movie personalities and radio's hugely popular stars. Variety now looked destined to take a supporting role.

In Europe, black artists commanded higher fees and earned more respect. Many African-American performers followed this route. It seemed highly probable that Adelaide would join their numbers.

A further setback came in the Hall household when the *New York Amsterdam News* announced Ethel Waters' popularity, after her notable Broadway success in Irving Berlin's *As Thousands Cheer*, had now eclipsed that of Adelaide's, making her America's highest-paid black female entertainer.[17] With her role in *As Thousands Cheer* Ethel achieved star billing in a white show, something Adelaide had yet to accomplish.

With quality work becoming increasingly more difficult to find, Bert's manipulative hold on Adelaide's career now pushed his all-embracing sense of commercialism to new heights of suspicion. If 1931 represented the apex of her career, allowing her to clean up both financially and artistically, then 1935 saw the antithesis—a definite downward tilt. In a bid to reclaim her identity on Broadway, Adelaide returned to what she knew best, the stage, and at the end of spring began rehearsals on a new production. The show *Smile At Me* had financial backing but lacked strong direction and, in Adelaide's opinion . . . hit songs. As rehearsals progressed, the revue looked more blunt and pointless by the day. Like a worn-down pencil, it clearly needed sharpening.

Before its tryout tour commenced, Adelaide withdrew from the cast, disassociating herself from what she termed "an amateur production." Avis Andrews took over her role and the show opened at Broadway's Fulton Theater only to close a few days later after a slating from the critics. Thankfully, Adelaide's judgment was proved correct and saved her the indignity of being associated with a flop.

Despite the fact that Adelaide had already shot several film tests, Hollywood still showed little interest in her and movie directors did not view her as a leading lady. Their indifference was a bitter pill to swallow. What made the issue even more frustrating was noting how smoothly Bojangles' career had progressed into movies. Hollywood's flirting interest in the Negro saw him coaching and starring with the industry's youngest rebel, child star Shirley Temple. Perhaps the moguls in power viewed Adelaide as trouble they could do without. Whatever their opinion, the message was obvious. Hollywood had no room for a black diva.

Even if Hollywood didn't beckon, Adelaide did at least get to make a movie-short for Vitaphone, directed by Roy Mack. *All Colored Vaudeville Show* (later renamed *Dixieland Jamboree*) was released in 1935 and co-starred the diamond-toed Nicholas Brothers.[18] Perhaps Sam Goldwyn's visit to the Cotton Club to catch Adelaide's performance helped her secure the contract. As its name implies, the movie was structured around a variety show and was actually filmed on stage at Warner Brothers Theater in Brooklyn. With pianist Joe Turner and the full throttle of an orchestral accompaniment, Adelaide performed the uptempo ballad "To Have You, To Hold You" in dynamic form. Dressed in a long sleeveless gown and clutching her trademark silk handkerchief in one hand, she commences the number rather sedately, giving little indication as to what will follow. Her arm movements beautifully express the lyric without appearing trite. However, towards the end of the third chorus she calmly descends a short staircase. At the bottom she lets rip, yanks up her gown to reveal her long legs, and charges frantically into a buck-and-wing dance routine wearing, unbelievably, *high-heeled* shoes. The energy she exerts leaves the viewer almost panting for breath; heaven knows what Adelaide must have felt executing it. At the culmination of her dance, Joe Turner returns with a reprise of the chorus thereby rescuing Adelaide from imminent exhaustion at the end of which she concludes the song as she commenced, as posed as a rose in a vase. The movie played across America on variety bills doubling with live vaudeville shows.

During a brief summer RKO tour on the Southeastern circuit, Bert and

Adelaide confronted yet more racism.[19] The incident occurred whilst driving to a week's engagement in Atlanta, Georgia. As the two pianists were making their own way by train, Adelaide and her maid, Minnie, decided to keep Bert and the dogs company in the car. After a couple of hours driving along a clear stretch of road in South Carolina, Bert pulled into a gas station to refill the tank. From the outside the station looked deserted. The white owner had recognized the occupants of the car were black and had gone into hiding.

If Bert predicted trouble, he used to disguise his African origins with a Spanish accent and pretend to be South American. Though he didn't look particularly Hispanic the accent did sometimes fool rednecks into believing he was. The trick worked and the attendant finally appeared although he still refused to serve them, claiming the pumps were shut as they had run out of gas. Bert knew he was lying.

When Bert got back to the car Adelaide could tell from his glazed expression that something was wrong. Without uttering a word, he switched on the ignition, eased his foot down on the clutch and slid the gear stick into reverse, then revved the engine and released the hand brake. The vehicle shot backwards, straight into a gasoline pump, knocking it to the ground. With tyres screeching, Bert then made a hasty getaway, as fast as he could drive down the dusty road to Atlanta. Bert never did apologize to Adelaide for his headstrong act of vengeance. Under the circumstances he felt no need.

For the remainder of the summer Adelaide appeared at New York's Kit Kat Club on 53rd Street near Fifth Avenue, a swanky downtown supper club patronized by movie stars. Valaida Snow and Louise Cook joined her on the bill. The restaurant was famous for having telephones on its tables, a large opaque-tiled dance floor and one of the most expensive menus in town. The revolving stage housed a huge orchestra and a whole platoon of waiters monitored the guests' every move. Like the Cotton Club, it also operated a strict "Whites Only" policy, although it was never seen to advertise the fact. Judy Podell, impresario at the club, was known for her elaborate use of white drapes and oversized stage props, extensively copied and used to great effect in such Hollywood movies as *Gold Diggers of 1933*. To add contrast to the décor, she liked nothing better than dressing black performers in white, and white performers in black to compliment their looks. If nothing else, the engagement gave Adelaide the time to tread water until she decided in which direction her future path lay.

FULL MOON IN AN EMPTY SKY

Ever since her childhood visits to Coney Island, Adelaide had felt drawn to the sea. When the family moved to Harlem, the Hudson River continued her fascination with water. Whenever she sought refuge or time to think, she would wander down to Riverside Drive. Here, sitting alone by the water's edge, she would happily watch the ships pass slowly by and allow her fertile imagination to explore the endless possibilities life had to offer. It was at the tranquil water's edge she felt her calmest, without any pressure to be anyone other than who she really was.

One evening when Adelaide went down to the Hudson, it looked particularly magical as the full moon cast its long reflection across the entire width of the river towards New Jersey on the opposite side. The water gently glistened, as if covered in thin slivers of silver. Oddly enough, there were no ships passing that night and the piers, extending into the distance like fingers pointing out towards the sea, showed no sign of life.

Before the current on a tidal river changes direction, the water suddenly stops flowing altogether and stands motionless, like a stagnant pond. It's a strange moment to witness, quite eerie, when for a few minutes any sign of life on the river vanishes. Even the seagulls become disorientated and swoop down to find land, as if in transit, to wait for the phenomenon to pass. It was at that particular moment Adelaide gazed at the moon's luminous glow, effortlessly gliding across the still surface of the water. Its path, like a bridge, seemed to beckon her over to the other side. With each second the urge to cross grew stronger.

Like the flow on a tidal river, there comes a point in one's life when suddenly you realize you've run as far as you can go. When that moment arrives, no matter how forceful the current may have been, instinctively you know it's time to change direction. In her heart Adelaide knew that moment had arrived.

Even though tensions had eased slightly at Larchmont, the pleasures of domesticity never did take root. The four walls she called home were nothing short of a prison. She felt trapped and claustrophobic yet saw withdrawal as a denial of her human rights. She was resident in a bourgeois dormitory town, surrounded by narrow-minded bigots, with a career that had peaked and was now in decline, typecast by the shade of her skin in a role she couldn't escape. What hope had she of building a future in a country that still found her color and race threatening?

That evening by the water's edge Adelaide made a promise to herself, a promise she would move mountains to keep. No longer was she content to sit and watch the tidal flow. She had waited long enough. She wanted to move as far away as possible from the chaos that had hijacked her life to a place where she had freedom of choice without loss of identity, but more importantly where she was beholden to no one. Like the river . . . her course was about to change direction.

Adelaide was well aware on which side her bread was buttered, only the challenge to fight was no longer there. Like a worn-out blade on a carving knife, her nerves were blunt with exhaustion. It was time to do something radical with her life and Europe's attraction was undeniable.

Financially, she was solvent. The thought of devaluing the currency of her name seemed ludicrous. "The more you look at something the cheaper it becomes"—such philosophy held an element of truth. Hard work and astute management had rewarded Adelaide substantially. She had become one of the wealthiest black stars in America. If she couldn't afford to take life a little easier now, when could she?

As the "Crooning Blackbird," Adelaide had inspired a whole generation of black female vocalists. New singers of great artistry such as Ella Fitzgerald, Billie Holiday and the young Lena Horne were now beginning to gain commercial recognition. Adelaide had broken the stereotypical image white Americans held of Negro performers and in doing so pioneered new ground. She became the template from which black female vocalists now fashioned their act. That, in itself, could only be regarded as a compliment.

On September 19, Adelaide returned to Chicago to honor a contract at the ultra-chic, mob-owned Grand Terrace Café.[20] The club was Chicago's equivalent to Harlem's Cotton Club and its revues held just as much weight. The establishment had been closed for several months, undergoing extensive refurbishment. Its reopening was the talk of the town. The program had a full company with no expense spared on production. For Adelaide it was to be a particularly good engagement, Earl Hines' Orchestra was on the bill. She received tremendous press notices and her four-week residency was extended by a further six weeks. Regular radio broadcasts, as many as three a night, were transmitted from the café and attracted huge audience figures. Although she wasn't aware of it at the time, this would be Adelaide's last ever engagement in Chicago.

Numerous celebrities visited the show including Paul Robeson, in town to promote his latest movie *Sanders of the River*, the heavyweight champion boxer Joe Louis, on a self-imposed alcohol-free one o'clock curfew due to his impending fight, and two of her previous pianists, Art Tatum and Joe Turner, who were performing elsewhere in the city.[21] To publicize her visit, on October 14 the *Chicago Defender* invited Adelaide into its offices, to help edit the newspaper's stage, screen and drama pages.[22] Not only did she become editor for the day, but she also got the run of the office and invited one of her close friends from New York, the singer Josephine Hall, along for the occasion. Needless to say Adelaide was heavily featured in that week's edition. So much so, the articles about her totally overshadowed news of Josephine Baker's sudden arrival in town. Her feature was relegated to the back pages; Adelaide obviously thought its newsworthiness held limited appeal.

Josephine was on a brief visit to Chicago catching up with friends, before a reunion with her mother in East St. Louis. She was staying as houseguest of Mr. R. Abbott, editor of the *Chicago Defender*.

A few evenings later, Adelaide had a surprise guest in her audience. With Mr. and Mrs. Abbott in tow, Josephine dined at the Grand Terrace Café. Her presence sent the management and staff into a panic and caused Adelaide to suffer an anxiety attack. Adelaide need not have worried. Her performance that evening was exemplary. As also was Josephine Baker's. Worried that she might not shine under Adelaide's light, Josephine tried every trick possible to distract the patrons' attention during Adelaide's performance. From the merest flick of an arm to repeatedly calling the waiter's attention, she fought desperately for the diners' attention. Of course all eyes in the restaurant were already discreetly focused upon her. It was the thought that they might not be that put Josephine in a state.

Confirmation of Adelaide's European tour was given the go-ahead and her extension at the Grand Terrace Café cut short.[23] It had always been Bert's goal to establish Adelaide's career on the Continent and the offer to appear at the Alhambra Theater in Paris seemed like a godsend and too good an opportunity to miss. Adelaide returned to New York at the beginning of November to prepare for her departure.

The big news in Harlem centered on Josephine Baker's return from the Continent where she had been resident for the past ten years. Josephine was back in New York to clinch her aging dream of becoming a Broadway star. She had been contracted to feature in Ziegfeld's latest production of *Follies* and was busy undertaking extensive rehearsals under the guidance of ballet master George Balanchine. Ironically, as if it were choreographed, once again Adelaide and Josephine briefly rubbed shoulders in the departure hall.

At this stage in Josephine's life, her lot was not a happy one. Since she had left America a lot of soul-searching had taken place. Her relationship with Count Pepito Abatino—her manager and purported husband—was strained to breaking point and momentum in her career had temporarily floundered. She was desperate to try her luck on Broadway again. Unfortunately, her unreasonable demands put a lot of people's backs up. When Josephine was in town everyone switched to red alert. She had a crafty way of monopolizing one's time without giving the slightest consideration for the inconvenience it caused. Her refusal to perform in Harlem and preference for eating in downtown white restaurants made her presence unwelcome in the black community.

Josephine had fully expected New York to fall at her feet as Paris had done. This was not to be. Parading on stage with rhinoceros tusks protruding from her costume meant the critics and Broadway audiences never took her act seriously and treated her instead as a comedian. Deeply hurt by their disfavor, she had Pepito running in circles, like a dog on a lead, blaming him for her failure. The indignity of traveling all the way back home to face the reality of her shortcomings in public was too humiliating to contemplate. The truth of the matter was much simpler: her act was banal and out of date. She had lost touch and it showed.

With their relationship in tatters, Pepito returned to Paris, leaving Josephine to soldier on alone.

With jobs on Broadway and nightclub work becoming increasingly more difficult to find, many black artists now appeared to be "resting" longer than they were in employment. One particularly snooty actress adamantly refused to use the term "resting," arguing that it implied she was incapacitated, and much preferred to inform people that her career was having a "short commercial break." Sadly, for many performers the "short commercial break" took on epic proportions.

On a pleasanter note, New Yorkers took out their bunting and streamers and honored Bojangles for his tireless services to the black community by electing him Mayor of Harlem, a badge he wore with great pride.[24] His role, as an ambassador of black culture, was now firmly secured in black American history.

HEAVEN LOOKED DOWN IN WONDER

Memories of Paris kept flooding back. Fond recollections of tolerance and understanding, where no one kept reminding Adelaide who she was and what she could or could not do. Perhaps they were purely romantic visions. She couldn't tell any more, for she had reached a point in her life where she could no longer differentiate between fantasy and reality. "Sometimes I look in the mirror and don't recognize myself any more."

Adelaide had been courting the idea of moving to Europe ever since her triumph at the Moulin Rouge in 1929. Only her commitments at home had held her back. Like the interest on her savings account, those commitments had now become flexible. In her present incarnation Adelaide had gone about as far as she could. Many artists confirm that the happiest point in their career is just before fame strikes. Adelaide had that feeling. Something good lay around the corner, only this time that corner lay over 3,000 miles away.

At precisely two minutes to midnight the stately liner SS *Normandie* pulled out of New York's harbor bound for Europe. This time there were no crowds of cheering fans and gaping onlookers to wave Adelaide goodbye. Not even her mother braved the cold weather. Like the chill wind that blew sharply across the ship's deck, their absence made her departure painful. She could never have guessed that it would be over ten years before she would see Harlem again. If her fans had known, perhaps some would have made the effort to bid her farewell.

By the time Manhattan's skyline sank into the horizon, Adelaide and Bert were already settled snugly into their first-class cabin. Only their maid, Minnie, who was accompanying them to Paris, bothered to stay up and watch the Big Apple fall from sight.

On November 23, in mid-Atlantic, Adelaide received a wireless telegram from her anxious mother that read simply: "God Bless You Darling."

One can only assume from those four words that Elizabeth had finally accepted that her daughter's destiny lay across the ocean. Adelaide's decision to leave America was not hers to question. Under the circumstances it seemed only natural that Elizabeth should view her offspring's departure with bated breath, as heaven looked down in wonder.

PART IV

SOMEONE'S SITTING ON MY CLOUD

1936–38

PARIS MATCH

Paris, where so many butterflies have burnt their wings, only offers success with all its accoutrements to the lucky few. Those that attain such distinction are held firmly against her bosom for life.

After six years' absence, Adelaide's return to Paris felt surprisingly good, like visiting an old acquaintance. This time she and Bert arrived at Gare St. Lazare with less of a fanfare. A taxi, sent especially by Madame Au Clair, whisked them off to the Hotel Mont Joli in Montmartre where the best suite in the house had been reserved for their stay.

That evening, Bricktop hosted a surprise welcoming party at her smart nightclub, Bricktop's, on rue Pigalle. Many old friends and a scattering of new ones were invited to the occasion. As with all parties in Paris it commenced at midnight, after the music halls had shut, and lasted until the early hours of the morning.

Bricktop's closest friend was Mabel Mercer, an English vaudeville singer who had arrived in France penniless back in 1931. Taking Mabel under her wing, Bricktop offered her a residency at Bricktop's and it was here that Mabel carved a comfortable living for herself. Her performance technique, in the half-spoken half-sung tradition of French *diseuse*, was perfect in the intimate surroundings of a *boîte*. It was Mabel who organized the extraordinary cabaret for Adelaide's surprise party which included an exotic acrobatic troupe from the cast of the Folies-Bergère.

Everyone knew Bricktop, or so they claimed, and at times it seemed as if everyone did. Christened Ada Beatrice Queen Victoria Louise Virginia Smith—as her mother didn't want to offend the neighbors who all wanted to name her—Bricktop was short in stature, had fine reddish hair, hence her strange nickname, and a face full of freckles. She possessed the ideal personality for a hostess—courteous yet discreet, spontaneous yet measured—and was gifted with a tremendously perceptive sense of humor. She never claimed to be a singer, "I'm a performer and saloon-keeper" was how she preferred to describe her profession, but if a customer insisted she sang, she would usually reply, "You'll be sorry," a remark that belittled her exceptional talent.[1]

To the outside world Bricktop was everybody's friend, but inside she was nobody's fool. Having just turned 40 she still possessed a heart as frivolous as a teenager's yet her demeanor appeared many years older in experience. Her extraordinary lifestyle bestowed upon her a goldmine of knowledge, which she used wisely. Friends and diplomats alike sought her valued advice on all manner of subjects. Her social life revolved around a continual whirl of cocktail parties, functions and dinner invitations.

She had arrived in Paris ten years earlier from New York's Connie's Inn expecting a ballroom to work in only to be confronted with a run down café the size of a parlor room. Through sheer slog and tenacity she transformed the place into the hottest square foot of dance floor in Montmartre and in the process evolved into the doyen of Paris nightclub culture. Shrewd planning brought her her own *boîte* in larger premises further up rue Pigalle. It was here she reaped the rewards for all her hard work and amassed a small fortune. An evening out wasn't complete without calling in to say *bonsoir* at Bricktop's.

Her club became a magnet for visiting Americans, a home from home where they were assured of a friendly welcome. She referred to the joint as a "combination club," for it was used not only as a meeting place, but also as a maildrop, an out-of-hours bank and, at times, a refuge for the homeless and stranded. During her time in Paris, Bricktop had witnessed all manner of misconduct and misdemeanors and could now barely be bothered to lift an eyebrow upon hearing the latest bit of scandal. "Nothing surprises me anymore!"

Situated at République in the tenth arrondissement, the 2,500 seater Alhambra Theater was known to be a cold and difficult venue to sell out. Adelaide's engagement commenced on December 6 and ran for two weeks, playing two performances a day. Also on the bill was the French star Armand Bernard.[2] The promoter promised an elaborate presentation and at huge expense secured the Willie Lewis Orchestra to accompany Adelaide.[3] They were reckoned to be the best American jazz orchestra in Europe. Fortunately for the promoter's pocket, ticket sales were extremely healthy.

On December 12, during a live interview on the Paris broadcasting station Radio Cité, Adelaide enthused about how happy she was to be back in the city and how warmly she had been received at the Alhambra. She also informed listeners that it was her intention to stay on in Europe for the foreseeable future. To show her appreciation she sang one song in French, the first time she had ever sung in a foreign language over the airwaves.

Soon after her arrival in Paris Adelaide met up with her former pianist Joe Turner who was momentarily resident in the city.[4] Now back in her good books, Turner keenly accepted Adelaide's offer to join her on stage at the Alhambra. They even recorded together for Ultraphone—two tracks, "Truckin'" and "I'm In The Mood For Love," as a duo and two more, "East Of The Sun And West Of The Moon" and "Solitude," with added accompaniment from John Ellsworth's Orchestra. The featured violinist for the session was Stephane Grappelli.

Although Turner had his own expressive style of playing, when listening to him perform one was constantly reminded of Art Tatum and Fats Waller, such were their influence on jazz pianists of that period. Since his arrival in the country, Turner's love affair with Paris and the French lifestyle had been instantaneous. No matter how hard Adelaide pushed, the thought of touring Europe with her did not appeal to his romantic nature. He was hooked on Montmartre and adamant that his stay in the city would be permanent.[5]

For a brief period in the early Thirties, the Truckin' dance swept America as the hottest craze. By taking her tapping mat into the recording studio Adelaide hoped to introduce it to Europe. Its invention can be pin-pointed directly to Bojangles, for it was during his role in *Brown Buddies* that he presented Truckin' to the public for the first time.

The inspiration behind the dance came from a job Bojangles held during the First World War.[6] With money hard to come by and vaudeville theaters closed, Bojangles took temporary work as a packer in a Chicago stockyard. Part of his duties involved pushing an overladen truck from a lorry to the depot. It was tough labor but Bojangles made light of it. He figured that if a fake circus strong man could carry a two-ton weight, he could balance his cargo to seem lighter. His deduction led him to place packages in a certain way so the weight became balanced and shifted the load from the truck handles. In doing so he managed to carry twice the amount of boxes as his co-workers. His initiative caught the boss's eye and Bojangles was promptly promoted to foreman. At the end of the war his job in the stockyard came to an end. Vaudeville houses reopened and Bojangles returned to the stage.

The motion of transferring weight from one side to the other inspired Bojangles to create the Truckin' dance. The dance involves shifting the body's weight from one shoulder to the other whilst swaying the hips from side to side, giving a sexual rhythm to the upper part of the body. The feet perform short, forward shuffle steps and, after each one, the heel is turned in. During the routine the dancer wiggles an index finger above their shoulder to attract a partner.

Adelaide introduced Paris to Truckin' at the Alhambra. During the number she would invite members of the audience to join her on stage to participate. As with all practical tutorials, the results were often quite hilarious. Overenthusiastic members of the public would sometimes try the dance themselves and consequently take over the spotlight, Truckin' nonstop up and down the aisles of the theater. As one can imagine, the act literally brought the show to a standstill.[7]

After the Alhambra concerts, Adelaide prepared to fly to London where she had been contracted to appear for the Christmas festivities. Before her departure, she agreed to perform at *A Night of Stars* benefit at the chic Les Ambassadeurs supper club to aid the Paris poor.[8] It was the biggest and most elaborate showbiz charity event of the year and attracted the free participation of all the biggest names in French entertainment. Tickets, upwards from 300 francs, included dinner, a show, an auction and the chance to mingle with the Paris élite.

Mistinguett helped co-ordinate the show and, accompanied by Maurice Chevalier, headed the list of performers. As usual Mistinguett's decision, as to who could or could not appear on the program, was strictly adhered to. Fortunately for Josephine Baker, her absence from the country prevented any sticky confrontations. Adelaide was invited to participate as a guest of honor. ("No competition there," thought Mistinguett.) An invitation Adelaide felt duty bound to accept if she was to remain in Mistinguett's good books during her stay in the country.

The evening was nothing short of spectacular and many prominent political figures, European aristocracy, and famous sports and show business personalities were in attendance. Over a million francs were raised from the affair, the majority of which came from the auction in which all stars were asked to donate an item. Adelaide gave a chunky silver diamanté bracelet; Mistinguett went one better and threw in a pair of real diamond earrings. Not wanting to feel left out of the occasion Josephine Baker had her housemaid deliver a jeroboam of vintage pink champagne to which a sealed envelope was attached. When the lucky bidder opened the envelope, inside were found two front-row tickets to see Ziegfeld's *Follies* on Broadway, the show Josephine was currently featured in. Josephine felt quite rightly that anybody who could afford to bid for the champagne could easily afford the passage to America. The lucky bidder turned out to be Mistinguett; pink champagne was known to be her favorite tipple. Needless to say her trip to the States was never booked.

Adelaide's tremendous reception at the Alhambra generated many propositions for her to tour. An invitation arrived to visit the Soviet Union with the Willie Lewis Orchestra.[9] The promoter offered to pay 180,000 French francs a month. Adelaide jumped at the offer. With the contract signed and an advance wired for travel expenses she rushed out and bought a new mink coat to take with her. On January 21, her two-month European visa expired so the trip gave her the perfect excuse to renew it. In preparation for the tour she opened an account at the "House of Alix" and consulted the salon's chief fashion designer, Madame Gres, on a whole new wardrobe of costumes. Unfortunately, due to a fuel shortage, the trip was canceled at the last moment but as the contract had already been signed Adelaide got to keep her fur coat, which she claimed as traveling expenses.

Having missed out on one snow-bound country, the mink coat came in very useful when, in February, Adelaide's hastily arranged European tour commenced in Switzerland.[10] In an unusual change of direction she starred in the *Black and White Revue* with Albert Gaubiers' Ballet Company. Whilst Adelaide was in Switzerland she learnt to ski, a sport she took a keen interest in thereafter.

The tour continued at a leisurely pace for the majority of the year calling at Belgium, Holland, Spain, Italy, Germany and the South of France. Her performances took place within various guises—a circus, in cabaret, revue and in concert. For the more prestigious engagements the Willie Lewis Orchestra accompanied her. For the smaller venues she used a five-piece band comprising Benny Payton on drums, Joe Turner on piano (after Bert increased his fee), Frank Ethridge on guitar, Harry Cooper on trumpet and Bricktop's ex-husband Peter Ducongé on clarinet. Touring helped solve the strict labor permit complications that affected foreigners who wished to work in Europe over lengthy periods. This way they could flit in and out of countries unrestricted.

Every Saturday night, Willie Lewis hosted a 90-minute music program on Paris' Radio Cité. Adelaide regularly featured as a guest artist.[11] Whilst the exposure was brilliant, her contract with the network company created quite a headache if she was scheduled to perform in another country later that evening. As the program was transmitted live, directly after her session there would be a mad dash to the railroad station in order to get her across the border.

Europe gave Adelaide freedom. It broke the chains she had been shackled to and restored her *joie de vivre*. Like a holiday in the sun, the salutary effects were instant. For Bert, just seeing her look happy again shed a multitude of worries from his shoulders.

EACH NIGHT BRINGS FORTH A NEW DAY

Disturbing news from America arrived by overseas telegram:

HOUSE AT LARCHMONT BROKEN INTO.
PLEASE CONTACT YOUR LAWYER DIRECTLY.
MUCH LOVE MOTHER.

Since Bert and Adelaide left America, the house at Larchmont had remained unoccupied. Both Adelaide's mother and grandmother still categorically refused to move there and continued to live in Harlem. Of the household staff, only Robert the housekeeper had been retained. Even Adelaide's beloved dogs had been kenneled. It was Robert who discovered the break-in and brutal vandalization of the property. The intruders cleverly forced entry through the rear kitchen door thereby leaving no visible trace of their violation at the front of the property. Inside the house, Robert found the destructive work of madmen. Each room revealed a catalog of damage. Expensive antique furniture lay strewn across the reception room smashed like broken matchsticks beyond repair. Authentic Persian rugs were daubed with paint and heavy damask curtains, still dangling from their rails, had been ripped to tatters. Little had been left untouched by their venomous hands. Even the garage had been broken into and Bert's most prized possession, his beautiful black and silver Packard convertible, wrecked.

More upsetting was the discovery of graffiti scrawled across the walls in animal's blood, "GO HOME NIGGER SCUM," written as a final vindictive warning before the bigots fled.

When questioned by the police the neighbors were unified in their agreement as to having heard or noticed nothing suspicious at the property. As if to exonerate the community's involvement, the police noted in their report, "Larchmont is a quiet, respectable neighborhood and such violent acts of behavior are totally out of character with its residents."

Without delay, Bert contacted his lawyer in New York. When the full extent of the damage became apparent, Bert had no hesitation in instructing his lawyer to sell the property forthwith. He then arranged for

Minnie's swift return to the States to help organize the packing and storage of their personal belongings. Any furniture and chattels that remained intact were to be sold at auction. Insurance covered the monetary loss of wrecked items, including the trashed Packard automobile, but no insurance claim could ever compensate the deep feelings of hurt and regret Adelaide and Bert experienced. Once again the hand of destiny appeared to be pointing its finger in a new direction. In later years Adelaide admitted "a certain numbness surrounded the whole episode," but she felt the sale of Larchmont removed a lot of superfluous clutter both mentally and materialistically.

Each night brings forth a new day and with it new horizons. When one door slams shut, a whole archway of doors open. The alienation America conferred upon her brought about Adelaide's determination to remain in Europe where, hopefully, she could rebuild her life away from prying eyes. That one senseless act of vengeance should leaven the good her fourteen-year career had fostered seemed preposterous. Perhaps her residency at Larchmont had been an enormous folly, or maybe it had been the wisest move she had ever made. Whatever, the exercise had been costly both financially and emotionally.

Following Minnie's sudden departure Adelaide employed a new personal assistant, Maude Rumford, a fellow American now resident in Paris who acted more as a secretary and interpreter than as a maid.[12] This greatly eased the burden of replying to correspondence. She also accompanied Adelaide to interviews and meetings where a translator was necessary.

With Adelaide's engagement diary looking fuller by the day Bert felt more confident about renting a permanent residence. The reverent rewards Europe bestowed upon foreign artists attracted many to take such sanctuary. It was agreed Paris should be their base and where better to set up house than in Montmartre.

After spending the whole afternoon viewing prospective properties they eventually arrived at their last port of call, a top floor apartment on the steeply twisting rue Lepic. By now it was early evening and the city was cloaked in twilight. The apartment's large airy rooms were arranged in a sweeping line from end to end. Not surprisingly, its previous tenant had been an artist. In the bedroom Adelaide flung open the shuttered windows to reveal the most breathtaking view she had ever witnessed. It must have stretched almost 20 miles. The panorama clinched it. Adelaide instantly fell in love with the sight. "It was as if a million electric light bulbs had been switched on to welcome us." For the next three years their haven, perched high upon Montmartre, became home from home.

Bert was an incredible cook and Adelaide willingly allowed him to rule the kitchen. His preferred style of cooking was Creole at which he was a very able and knowledgeable chef. To prepare Creole food one must heat the ingredients without water thereby intensifying the taste. Creole Jambalaya, Creole cabbage and sauce and Creole cakes were some of his specialties.

If Bert's cooking expertise was commendable his linguistic skills were questionable. Adelaide's command of French was even worse. Her accent was so bad, Maurice Chevalier repeatedly made fun of it. Adelaide blamed the French for conversing too quickly for her to understand. However, she did persevere and gradually began to introduce the language into her stage performance, although sometimes with hilarious consequences. Strangely, she found it much easier to sing in French than to carry out a conversation. Despite carrying a pocket-sized translation manual with her wherever she went, her brave attempts at stringing sentences together were usually a disaster. Much to her dismay, shop assistants would recognize her American accent and reply in English, defeating the object of the whole exercise.

Montmartre still had a distinct flavor of Harlem about it, albeit not as concentrated as in the Twenties. Back in New York, Bert was known as a snappy dresser. In Paris, he and Adelaide could indulge their keenness for fashion to their hearts' content. The *haute couture* salons along rue du Faubourg St. Honoré became familiar haunts. Schiaparelli, Dior and Chanel gowns were now an added necessity in Adelaide's ever-expanding wardrobe. Unlike many Caucasians, colored folk aren't embarrassed about dressing up and enjoying themselves and the city's bustling streets basked in their spontaneous gaiety. Bert and Adelaide soon became recognized as the most exotic couple around town. No party was complete without an appearance from them, and party they did, until dawn.

After a late night on the tiles it was customary for revelers to have breakfast before heading home. At the top of rue Pigalle in the local food market, Adelaide discovered a wonderful all-night café that served the best homemade bouillabaisse in Paris. Cooked from an old Provençal recipe, the fish stew came thick with prawns, mussels and crabmeat, all freshly delivered early each morning. The dish arrived at your table with the pinkest prawns you've ever seen, neatly arranged around the rim of the soup tureen. As with all French meals it came served with a fresh baguette, straight out of the oven. By the time Adelaide and Bert hit bed the daily onslaught of tourists had commenced. During summer's long hot months, this was how the natives spent life in Montmartre, endlessly recovering from the previous night's excesses.

Paris without Josephine seemed unusually quiet and sane. Her plan to conquer Broadway had backfired and since leaving Paris her faithful manager and confidant Pepito had died from cancer. After a disastrously short run, Ziegfeld's *Follies* closed and Josephine fled New York, wounded but nursing a clearer perspective of what she wanted from life. Europe was that vision. Over the previous few years her ubiquitous presence on the Continent had taken its toll on her popularity and things had quietened a little. Though still a forceful personality, the rage in her soul had simmered down. Her naked ambition had now become costumed with Parisian designer labels and, as the wise aphorism states, "There's always a price tag attached to everything."

Josephine arrived back in Paris towards the end of June to face a new, if somewhat uncertain, future.[13] To help soften the blow of Pepito's death she flung herself immediately into rehearsals at the Folies-Bergère. Once again, in true music hall fashion, she recaptured the hearts and fat wallets of the French public. Having endured the humility of her American defeat, the warm affection Paris bestowed upon her gave her back the self-confidence she had temporarily mislaid.

Adelaide's settlement in the city obviously aroused Josephine's suspicions. Her predatory instincts were easily aroused. She need not have worried. Adelaide had no intention of imitating her antics at the Folies-Bergère or indeed following her footsteps into music hall. Their respective arts were poles apart and as such created no infringement but still Josephine feared Adelaide's beam might eclipse hers.

Interestingly, even though Josephine had lived in Paris for ten years,

Mistinguett still found her presence threatening. Although with age they had begun to show less vitriol towards each other their rivalry reached new heights of absurdity. When Mistinguett posed naked in a bath of feathers Josephine went one better and strolled down the Champs-Élysées with her pet leopard Chiquita. As if that weren't striking enough, she attached a $10,000 diamond studded collar to the feline's neck.

Paris attracted a large number of black celebrities, many of whom were personal friends of Adelaide's. In spring her buddy Alberta Hunter arrived in town from Athens where she had just completed a cabaret engagement. The pianist Garland Wilson was frequently noted around town and Leslie Hutchinson popped over regularly from London to perform on variety bills. The opera singer Caterino Jarboro, who had recently found fame at La Scala in Milan, was happily ensconced in her new Parisian home and Hollywood film star Nina Mae McKinney was now spending much of her free time in Europe and could often be spotted shopping in the city's smart fashion houses.

In a surprise announcement the *Chicago Defender* claimed Adelaide had at last succumbed to Lew Leslie's continual pestering to rejoin *Blackbirds* and would be starring in his next edition, planned to open in London in May.[14] Once again the report was mere conjecture. Adelaide had agreed to hold preliminary meetings with Leslie in London during which she would view the show in rehearsal. Her final decision depended on the quality of material she was expected to perform. However, Adelaide never did make the trip across the Channel. Leslie's magic had finally lost its spell.

In-between her European dates Adelaide returned to Paris as often as her itinerary allowed. Not one to sit around idle, she regularly performed at venues across the city. Various cinemas, including the Empire and redeveloped Moulin Rouge (both of which Adelaide appeared at), still adopted a vaudeville policy before the main feature film. A return engagement at the Alhambra in *Harlem Parade* paired her with the singer Leslie Hutchinson. Once again the press threw superlatives at her performance: "Grande, forte, extraordinairement, dynamique—ne fait-elle pas des claquettes tout en chantant?—Adelaide Hall a."[15] In the eyes of the discerning French critics it seemed she could do no wrong.

During the summer, France transmitted its first live television

Adelaide with the bandleader Willie Lewis and his wife Jeanne on the celebration of their two-year marriage. Chez Florence nightclub, Paris, July 10, 1936. *Left to right:* (unknown), Adelaide, Carol King, Willie Lewis, Jeanne Lewis, (unknown).

program—*Paris Soir*—which was broadcast simultaneously across the airwaves. This historic occasion saw an array of music hall stars headed by Maurice Chevalier and Mistinguett. Adelaide too was invited to participate in this momentous landmark in French entertainment. Unfortunately, as hardly anybody in the country owned a television set most of the French public were totally ignorant of the fact that the broadcast had taken place.

Adelaide's tour resumed in Belgium at the northeastern town of Knokke.[16] The beach-resort was considered the most exclusive on Belgium's coastline. A bad summer season, attributed to foul weather and the ailing economy, had seen the local tourist trade scuppered and wealthy Europeans, who normally spent vacations in Flanders, had deserted their splendid white villas and headed to the warmer climate of the Mediterranean.

It was hoped Adelaide's appearance at the town's famous casino with the Willie Lewis Orchestra would attract custom. Built in the over-indulgent Twenties, its walls were lined with tapestries and original oil paintings. In the foyer hung the largest Venetian crystal chandelier in

Europe, under which, it was said, many a romantic encounter had been forged. So grandly decorated was the interior of the casino that many likened it to a palace. Business was so slack that on occasions the staff outnumbered the gamblers. To prevent having to close the casino down for the season the management desperately sought ways to cut costs. As their biggest expense, the show was axed. Early dismissal saw Adelaide's speedy return to Paris. With few commitments in her engagement diary until fall, the sudden freedom gave her time to relax and explore the new city she called home.

In the long shade of a late afternoon, when the sun's heat has simmered to a warm glow, the magic of Paris is at its most intense and exquisitely beautiful. It was on such days, at such times that the simple pleasures of life seemed priceless, when any thought of returning to New York became only a remote possibility. Once again, Adelaide found herself challenged by an irresistible force, only this time, for the first time in her life, she felt in total control of her own destiny. It was a feeling she felt good about and one she intended never to lose sight of in the future.

Bert (right) in Brussels with his friend Harry Fairley, from Edinburgh, Scotland.

Publicity photograph of Adelaide taken in Germany, 1936.

THE QUEEN OF MONTMARTRE, MR. HALL AND THE DUKES OF DECEPTION

High upon the hill of Montmartre, known locally as "La Butte," stands the misplaced Byzantine cathedral Sacré-Coeur. From its imposing northerly vantagepoint, the church looks out like a stately watchtower across the breathtaking panorama of Paris that lies below. In the pale blue haze of dusk, an air of ethereal serenity cloaks its many awkwardly shaped cupolas, giving it the surreal appearance of an over-decorated wedding cake. At the foot of the hill, amongst tightly packed cobbled lanes and neatly kept squares, sits the exotic area of Pigalle. Here, through night and day, sleaze and culture warmly embrace, frowned upon disapprovingly by the basilica's saintly statues.

With its colorful pavement cafés, ivy-clad artists' studios and all-night bars, Montmartre holds a romantic attraction for the tourist. In the Place de Tertre, struggling artists find lucrative pickings from the constant stream of sightseers who roam the area daily. Forever willing to part with cash for a small reminder of their visit, they awkwardly sit and pose for their prized souvenir. In the evening, crowded into their favorite haunt—Auberge de la Bonne Franquette—the artisans gaily drink away their day's profit.

In its heyday the area boasted over 30 windmills. Many of the surviving ones are converted into cabaret clubs where the French love of *risqué* revues caters for the locals and tourists alike. The most celebrated and largest, the Moulin Rouge, inspired many of Toulouse-Lautrec's Epicurean paintings. Serving like an artery, meandering from the top of "La Butte" to Place Blanche on Boulevard de Clichy, winds the main thoroughfare, rue Lepic. At nightfall, strains of carefree laughter mingled with hot jazz riffs constantly drift out from the numerous crowded bars along its route.

Most foreign visitors to Paris make time to explore Montmartre's picturesque streets, if only to sample its bohemian atmosphere and catch a fascinating glimpse inside one of the infamous playgrounds of the privileged élite. Despite the fact that many of its clubs were uncomfortably intimate and held as few as a hundred people, all featured live jazz, where musicians worked continuously throughout the night often skipping from venue to venue.

In 1936, one such visitor was American businessman George Gibson.[1] Working for an American engineering company, he had been dispatched to Paris to negotiate the sale of equipment to the Vacuum Oil Company—later taken over by Mobil—for their two French refineries. A condition in the contract stipulated that the manufacture of the equipment should take place in France and a representative of the American company should be available to inspect and oversee all steps of the operation, including its construction, installation and test trials.

With his original task completed, George cabled his boss in America to inquire whom they would be sending to supervise the project.

"You are there, so you are he," came back the reply.

What was to have been a short trip to France for George turned into a lengthy stay of around twelve months.

As his office was in central Paris, the pleasures of Montmartre were hard to resist. One warm summer evening, having little to do and feeling tired of using his secondary-school French, George headed for Pigalle. There, he knew a café where the bartender, who had previously worked in the States, spoke fluent English. After a couple of drinks the place began to fill. Noticing George was still unaccompanied, the bartender leant over the counter and thoughtfully inquired if he would be interested in meeting an American girl he knew. Pointing to an attractive young lady sat on her own at the far end of the bar, George approvingly agreed.

"I'd be glad of the company."

Her hair was tinted a bright shade of blonde and her skin lightly tanned, far lighter than the color achieved after a season in the sun.

Introducing himself as a fellow American, George invited the young lady to join him for a drink.

"OK. If you don't mind drinking with a Jigaboo," came back her curious reply.

It was the first time George had heard this particular derogatory term used to describe a person of African ancestry.

Carol King was her name, a pseudonym she had concocted in Paris for the stage, suggested by the notoriety of Romania's King Carol who was a regular visitor to Pigalle. Carol's real name was Charlotte Lewis. Her family hailed from Detroit, Michigan, where her father, as leader of a jazz band, had become a local celebrity. His death led to her mother moving the family to live in New York so they could be closer to relatives. It was in New York that Carol entered the theatrical profession.

Carol had arrived in Paris as a chorus girl in the cast of *Blackbirds* back in 1929. She found the French way of life irresistible. At the end of the show's engagement, instead of returning to the States with the rest of the troupe, she stayed on to try her luck in Europe. Her temperament—she was pretty, with a warm personality and her shortcomings were shorter than most—assured her regular work. A severe illness hospitalized her for a lengthy period and saw her savings dwindle. She now existed on occasional nightclub bookings and the generosity of a few close friends. One such friend happened to be Adelaide.

As the evening unfolded, Carol suggested they call in at a nearby club where Adelaide was performing, to catch the tail end of her set. It was a slack night and the club was almost deserted.

Adelaide was ready to quit for the evening and proposed supper at a local Chinese restaurant on rue Colisée. Towards the end of the meal the restaurant's proprietor joined their table for drinks, which he considerately provided on the house.

After consuming numerous bottles of champagne, the group moved on to Melody's, an all-night drinking bar in Montmartre and favorite haunt of jazz musicians and actors. Inside, the place was jumping. Several friends joined the party, including the well-known contortionist Jigsaw "Breakback" Jackson, who was featured in the current Folies-Bergère revue. As was usual during an evening at Melody's, its celebrity clientele gave impromptu performances, much to the delight of all those present.

It was dawn before the crowded bar began to thin out, and dawn in Paris is never early. Only the diehards were left hanging on to close the place. At this point, feeling tired and ready to quit, George bid farewell and made his way home, back down the meandering rue Pigalle.

If Paris is said to be the city of many colors, then Pigalle has all the shades of a rainbow. With so many late-night drinking bars to choose from, catering to all eclectic tastes, the reveler is spoilt for choice and often spends the whole night flitting from one to the next. Equally as popular as Melody's were Bricktop's, L'Enfer, Cabaine Cuban, Gavarnies' and the rowdy Boudon's Café, where black musicians frequently ate in-between work engagements.

Throughout that summer, George met Adelaide on several occasions, always at Carol's suggestion and always in her company. During one such invitation, Carol insisted George accompany her and Adelaide to the Sphinx, a famous bordello in Montmartre. At that time, brothels, where boys rush in and men walk out, were still legal in France and the Sphinx gained quite a reputation as a tourist attraction. For obvious reasons, Adelaide could not be seen entering such an establishment without a male escort.

The club occupied the entire building and was run by an elderly Madam who greeted the clientele at the door. To judge by its façade, the house looked as respectable as all the other residences in the street and gave no indication of the nature of its business. The main reception room had a small bar along the length of one wall at which several attractive *danseuses* were seated, all dressed seductively to accentuate their fine figures. Many were professional dancers down on their luck trying to make a few extra bucks. Primarily, their job was to persuade punters to order expensive champagne by the bottle, from which they earned a commission. Any additional services were provided at their discretion.

Heavy velvet drapes and thick carpet cushions gave one the immediate impression that you were entering an Eastern harem. Dim lighting gave the room a warm appearance. In the far right-hand corner lay a small wooden dance floor around which circular tables were positioned allowing a suggestion of privacy for the more bashful guests. These tables were specifically reserved for the wealthier clientele. Drinks were served by the *danseuse* of your choice and, if you so requested, for a pre-arranged fee she would join you at your table. To the left of the room a curved staircase mysteriously crept upstairs to the various playrooms.

One such boudoir had a specially constructed chair, rumored to have been commissioned for King Edward VII after he had become so portly he could no longer enjoy sex in the normal position. During the course of the evening a steady stream of visitors nimbly climbed the stairs to partake in the more pleasurable pursuits on offer. At weekends, a three-piece band performed in the main reception room, playing popular tunes and requests, and guests were openly encouraged to dance with the escorts.

Adelaide's group spent the early part of their soirée discreetly seated in a corner, drinking champagne, enjoying one another's company. As the evening progressed, Carol noticed an attractive black girl and invited her over to join them at their table. It turned out she came from the French West Indies island of Martinique and had only been resident in Paris for a short time. Armed with the only advice her mother thought beneficial for her daughter's survival, "You're sitting on a gold-mine girl. Make sure dem men dig deep into their wallets before you let 'em strike it rich," she had found steady employment at the Sphinx. Several drinks later, Carol expressed a wish to talk more intimately with the girl and found George's presence inhibiting.

It was suggested George invite a girl to join him upstairs where the rooms for the normal business of the house were located. Embarrassed by this sudden proposal and its implications, George politely refused but offered to compromise and instead asked a girl to dance.

"Have you ever danced closely with an erotically charged woman, clad only in a string of beads and a pair of high-heeled shoes?" was how George later recounted his liaison at the Sphinx to his friends back home in America.

Carol and Adelaide never did reveal to George what the mystery girl from Martinique taught them that evening at the bordello, and George was far too much of a gentleman ever to ask.

At the end of George's assignment in Paris Adelaide made one request to him before he departed for the States, to deliver a small gift to her mother in Harlem and to assure her of her daughter's good health and happiness.

The last days of summer hung around like overfamiliar friends, not knowing when to make their excuses to leave. The tourist season was drawing to a close and Montmartre was slowly reverting to its quiet village-like atmosphere once more. As the days turned into weeks and the weeks into months the thought of leaving Paris became more and more distant in Adelaide's mind. In letters she wrote to her mother she found herself referring to the city as home and even invited her to spend a vacation with them in France, an offer Elizabeth politely declined. She had no intention of leaving Harlem. Perhaps the money orders Adelaide sent home regularly made her feel too independent? Anyhow, she loved the place too much and positively hated the thought of traveling so far away from her friends.

When autumn finally arrived, a noticeable calm descended upon Montmartre. Paris without tourists brought an uncustomary loneliness to the city. Its empty streets, washed in drizzle, give one too much time to think. "October must have been the dullest month of our lives," wrote Adelaide rather surprisingly in her diary. "Nothing happened. No one called and no one appeared to be in town." The onset of cooler weather seemed an opportune time to take a trip and a good excuse to follow the warm autumn sun.

For the next eight weeks, Adelaide toured the French and Italian Riviera performing at some of the most famous and prestigious casinos along its coastline. Accompanied by her secretary, she first took a short skiing trip in Biarritz where she met up with friends from America. Bert followed her theatrical luggage south and joined them later in Nice. Smart vacations were all the rage and the rich and titled flocked in droves to lap up the pleasant congeniality that awaited them in such resorts as Monte Carlo, Cannes, Cap Farret and San Remo. To be seen mixing in such circles added greatly to an artist's prestige, but more importantly for Adelaide, the excursion introduced her to European society. Nowhere on the Continent does money talk more loudly than on the Riviera's talcum powder beaches.

***

Since the early Thirties Europe had witnessed a tremendous political upsurge. In 1933, the leader of the Nazi party, Adolf Hitler, had seized power in Germany. His radical views against minority groups, such as Jews, blacks and homosexuals, had yet to manifest themselves in the gruesome atrocities that would later alter mankind's belief in humanity. In May 1936, after Mussolini's troops captured Addis Ababa, Vittorio Emanuele was proclaimed Emperor of Ethiopia. It was a triumphant end to the war for the Italian dictator, who had already been in power for fifteen years and now looked invincible. After his victory an unparalleled wave of Fascism swept Italy and at one stage Adelaide's tour to the country was in doubt. As Mussolini's government had already banned Josephine Baker from performing, it now seemed highly probable that Adelaide would be the next casualty of his regime. In July, Franco's revolt against the Republican Government turned the Spanish Civil War into revolution. Like the winds of change, Europe's political powers were shifting strongholds with alarming speed. Time for gaiety and carefree pursuits was being strangled by the season.

In the summer of 1936, most of the Nations of the World convened on Berlin for the 11th International Olympics. Berlin was by then a police state and troops patrolled the city with a fearsome grip. The Games' opening ceremony was a carefully staged show of propaganda to enhance Hitler's status. By reaching out for respectability in the eyes of the world's media, he hoped to charm his many adversaries.

Black athletes, especially America's Jesse Owens, posed a serious threat to the German Aryan race and its beliefs. Their success in sport was difficult to comprehend, especially as they were regarded as inferior human beings. As if to prophesy what the future held for such minorities under Hitler's regime, the German contender Max Schmeling beat America's heavyweight boxing champion Joe Louis—the "Brown Bomber"—to pulp. To the Americans, Louis was a sporting hero and a symbol of all that was brave and courageous; to the German race Schmeling became his equivalent. At the end of the games, if only for a short while, Hitler basked in his country's new-found glory. Germany's winning Olympic gold image did not last long, however, before the tarnished realities of Hitler's doctrines became evident.

Undeterred by Mussolini's threats, on October 19, Adelaide stormed into Italy and placed herself at the mercy of her host country. She commenced her tour at San Remo's luxurious beachfront Casino Municipale and headed the bill of *Spettacoli Di Varietà*. As was to be expected the opening gala was charged with adrenaline but not necessarily for all the right reasons. Although Adelaide's presence posed no threat to Fascism, her defiance as a black artist did. Adelaide was too important a star to be ignored and the authorities were well aware of her stance. Her stay at the resort was monitored meticulously. Should she wish to venture anywhere, a police escort accompanied her for her own safety, which gave her numerous shopping trips in town inflated importance. Owing to extensive media coverage, bookings were heavy and her itinerary extended. At the end of the trip, Bert, Adelaide and her accompanying secretary were driven under police escort to the Italian border where they were safely delivered back into France.

Her triumphant return to Paris was marked with a welcome back party thrown by her good friend Maurice Chevalier. To celebrate, she bought an expensive new gown from Schiaparelli. Josephine Baker's attendance was noted to be curiously subdued. She noticeably kept her distance from Adelaide throughout the evening. Adelaide always had detected a certain prickliness in Josephine's company but for some reason that evening Josephine looked vulnerable and lost. It was as if more than anything else in the world she needed a friend, someone she could trust and lean upon. Pepito's death had clearly knocked her for six.

In December, the black American boxer John Henry Lewis arrived in Paris celebrating his recent victory.[2] After successfully defending his title as the world's light heavyweight champion in London he was now traveling around Europe with his manager on a short vacation before returning to the States. Upon his arrival at Paris Gare du Nord the conquering hero was given a huge ovation and besieged by autograph hunters. Wherever he appeared in town, crowds gathered. His movements were monitored like a visiting President. As his visit was brief, to help save time it was suggested he employ a guide to show him the city's sights.

Having met Lewis on numerous occasions in Chicago, Adelaide contacted him at his hotel to offer her congratulations and invited him out for a wild night on the tiles. The evening commenced at one of the top restaurants in Paris followed by best seats at the Folies-Bergère to see Josephine Baker. Included in the party were Bert, Lewis's manager, his wife and his personal trainer. After the show they went backstage to meet Josephine who, reportedly, was still mourning Pepito's death. On the contrary, they found her full of vim and she appeared to have forgotten all about her sorrows. The reason for Josephine's sudden transformation was her attachment to a new lover, Paul Meeres. Josephine and her beau, along with another black cast member, boneless dancer "Jigsaw" Jackson, promptly joined the group and headed off to the Bal Tabarin music hall. Here, they met bandleader Willie Lewis (no relation) and his wife. At 2 a.m., noticeably merry but still raring to party, they headed off to Bricktop's new *boîte* in Montparnasse. They finally quit her premises around dawn. The evening must have been memorable; reports of their riotous behavior received newspaper coverage as far away as New York and Chicago.

Adelaide's visit to the Folies-Bergère had been a revelation. She was stunned to see how much of a pineapple Josephine had become. Gone were the grass skirts and hula-hoops; she now paraded on stage like a cheap courtesan in a royal pageant, wearing headdresses that doubled her height and gowns that flowed longer than the River Seine. The French public had placed her on a pedestal and worshiped her like a goddess, and whatever price such adulation cost, Josephine had willingly paid it at the expense of losing her credibility. Though their art was poles apart, Josephine had no intention of being toppled by anyone, least of all Adelaide.

1937

The opportunity for Bert to open a nightclub in Paris came by accident although the idea had been floating around in his mind ever since his arrival in the city.[3] A commercial proposition from a silent partner procuring him a half-interest in the venture gave Bert the financial backing to proceed with the project. The chosen venue (possibly the Lido, renamed the Paris Plage) was spectacularly located on the Avenue des Champs-Élysées and was aimed at the more affluent end of the market.[4] As well as a candle-lit dinner and a full floorshow, the club held a daily afternoon tea dance. It was a huge undertaking and from the outset a financial risk, especially as tourists to the city had noticeably dwindled during the previous season. To welcome the New Year the nitery opened on January 1 and drew a brilliant crowd to the occasion. Adelaide headed the revue, which featured the phenomenal dancer "Jigsaw" Jackson, Paul Meeres (Josephine Baker's current dance partner and lover) who performed "Truckin'" with Adelaide, Edith Cue from New York's Cotton Club and the dance team Cook and Brown. Amongst the many notable guests at the opening were various American friends and acquaintances including Valaida Snow with her fiancé Earl Lutcliffe, Josephine Baker who was keeping a tag on her beau and, rather surprisingly, Lew Leslie— in town seeking a theater to stage his recent edition of *Blackbirds*.[5] The night proved a splendid success drawing many customers away from both Bricktop's club and Josephine Baker's recently opened nitery sited close-by off the Champs-Élysées in rue François Premier.

After encouraging business during its initial weeks of opening the club looked set to take Paris by storm. That was until the owners of the building demanded an outrageous rent increase. With city economists predicting an uncertain future, rather than take the brunt of the financial increase himself Bert cut his losses and backed down from the venture and withdrew his capital. Without sufficient funding, the club was forced to close.[6] If nothing else the club's short-lived prosperity only served to whet Bert's appetite even further. He was now even more determined to open his own establishment.

Meanwhile, Adelaide received an offer to star in a long engagement at New York's Cotton Club with a scheduled spring premiere.[7] The club, having recently moved premises downtown near Times Square, was once again attracting great business from the after-dinner theater crowd. Bojangles and Cab Calloway had headlined its first revue at the new location and the club's manager, Herman Stark, was after equally big name draws for its second. Ellington and his band had already been contracted to appear but Stark felt a female lead was required to complement the bill. At great expense he offered to ship Adelaide and her belongings back to America. Though the offer was tempting, the thought of returning to her former life with all its limitations was not. The invitation was courteously declined and Ethel Waters took her place. The show went on to be a smash hit, breaking Adelaide's previous club record for attendance figures.

There followed a return visit to the South of France where Adelaide starred at the tropically themed Club O'Rio in Cannes. With its honey-colored villas, azure skies and temperate climate, the resort held an ongoing attraction, which Adelaide found irresistible.

The words "lavish" and "extravagant" instantly spring to mind when describing the revues that were staged at this particular venue. They had to be good: the club was regarded as one of the best along the coastline. In a community which relies solely upon its trade from tourism, competition from rival establishments was fierce, and in a tactical bid to attract custom away from the O'Rio, one of its competitors, George Cavalli, installed Valaida Snow at his club The Dolphin. Having two Harlem top-notchers in the resort at the same time was considered unusual, to say the least. With both singers justifying respect from the press, loyalties from hotel and casino concierges, who were often expected to recommend entertainment to their guests, were divided, depending on the size of back-handers given in advance. The situation must have been contentious, as it even warranted a mention in the *Chicago Defender* under the sparring headline "Valaida vs. Adelaide in Cannes' best niteries."[8]

One Paris nightclub always worth visiting was Le Bœuf sur le Toit. Its literal translation—the Ox on the Roof—caused many tourists to strain their necks as they scoured its weathered slates for a bull. The club's interior was best described as looking elegantly "Queenie" and as such attracted a loyal, although not exclusive, homosexual following. The writer and director Jean Cocteau spent many an evening there; in fact the club's name came from the title of a ballet he had devised. As with any place that has a fashionable tag attached to it, performing at such a venue adds great luster to an artist's reputation. Upon her return from Cannes, Adelaide received an offer to star at the club during May.[9] Although the fee was way below her asking price, Bert thought it prudent to accept.

Thankfully the summer of 1937 saw a welcome influx of visitors to Paris. The capital was chosen to host a Colonial Exposition opening in May to run for six months, the largest event of its kind seen in Europe for many years. The exhibition would, hopefully, bring salvation to the ailing economy which was seriously confronting the effects of the world recession. It would attract hundreds of thousands of tourists to the city who would have to be housed, fed and entertained, so its announcement brought a new wave of optimism to the Parisian public.

Preparations for the event kept the city's merchants frantically busy, none more so than Bert who immediately saw the potential to profit from it. He decided to invest capital in a new Montmartre nightclub called the Cotton Club, which was loosely based upon the famous New York supper club.[10] The club's director was Monsieur Dajou and other financial backers included the musician Freddie Taylor and ex-bantamweight world champion boxer Al Brown. Initially Dajou had difficulty in finding suitable premises, thereby delaying its opening. However, it did eventually commence trading on May 22, just in time for the Exposition's opening on May 24. Though the club was on a much smaller scale than its namesake in New York, the premises were large enough to hold a fourteen-piece orchestra and present a modest revue.

The club was sited at Place Pigalle two doors away from Bricktop's. Leon Abbey and his Orchestra were flown back from Bombay in India especially to play on the first night.[11] To comply with strict French labor laws, Monsieur Dajou had to employ as many French musicians as foreigners, thus creating an enormous headache for the revue's producer.

The gala opening attracted a capacity crowd but the event was marred by an unfortunate incident that sent the black community in Montmartre reeling.[12] At approximately 2:30 a.m., two colored musicians Cle Saddler and Herbert Robinson with their white female companions entered the premises. A corner table was designated to them but before they had time to seat themselves the headwaiter, Monsieur Henri, appeared, expressing his regrets for being unable to serve them as the party was for invitation holders only. Feeling they were being ridiculed, the foursome insisted on staying put.

Some time later the two couples began dancing to Leon Abbey's Orchestra but were abruptly interrupted on the dance floor, again by the headwaiter, who advised them to stop. They refused. Monsieur Henri then threatened police intervention. Sensing the atmosphere to be racially motivated, Saddler and Robinson decided to test the waiter's reaction when they danced with colored females. By coincidence, Adelaide was seated nearby enjoying the company of a white girlfriend. Saddler approached Adelaide for a dance. Unaware of the altercation, she accepted and they danced several numbers together. During their dance Saddler informed Adelaide of the ill-treatment he and his party were receiving. Shocked by his revelations, Adelaide offered to help discreetly by informing her husband who had a stake in the enterprise.

Saddler then complained to the barman that the two bottles of champagne they had ordered never arrived at their table, to which he replied, "For you, nothing doing." Feeling totally fed up with their hostile reception, the foursome finally quit the premises and popped into Bricktop's next door. After a few beers the two couples left her establishment and headed down rue Pigalle. At the first street corner, Saddler crossed over to ask directions, leaving the remaining members of the party on the sidewalk, about twenty yards from the Cotton Club. Upon his return, to his horror he found his friends sprawled prostrate on the sidewalk having been severely beaten about the face and body. Glancing further along the road he spotted those who he presumed were the culprits, charging away from the incident.

Horrified and stunned by what he saw, Saddler yelled for assistance. His shouts were answered by a taxi driver who promptly stopped his cab to help. Together they hauled the bloodied bodies onto the back seat of the taxi. A waiter from Bricktop's phoned for the Gendarmerie and within minutes the riot squad arrived at the scene. Assuming Saddler and his party to be among the troublemakers, they immediately apprehended them and escorted them to the police station, along with one of the fleeing attackers. There, the French assailant did all the talking. The officer in charge listened cautiously, then rather suspiciously released him. Saddler, who had escaped the street brawl, was then taken to a cell where he was set upon by six policemen and brutally pounded. His girl-friend's screams for compassion went unheeded. She too received a beating for her protest. The foursome were then detained in a cell for a further eight hours without medical attention before their release the following afternoon. No explanation was ever given by the Gendarmerie for their vicious behavior.

After hospital treatment, Saddler made an official complaint to the Foreign Office. He claimed he recognized one of the assailants as a Cotton Club employee and believed the club's proprietor engineered the attack, but unfortunately did not have enough evidence to file a lawsuit.

News of the assault raced through Montmartre. Soon every black person in the community was up in arms. Both the British and American Embassies and the French Foreign Office were inundated with protests and calls for an official inquiry. Leon Abbey and his orchestra refused to continue their engagement at the club and black citizens boycotted the premises.

A committee was set up to investigate the allegations. When the director of the Cotton Club, Monsieur Dajou, was interviewed he insisted no "Jim Crow" policy was exercised and stated, "Whatever happens outside my club is not my affair." The outcome of the inquiry was undecided but many held Dajou responsible. As stakeholders in the operation, this left Bert and Adelaide in an awkward situation. Clearly there was no alternative but for Bert to withdraw their investment.

In Rotterdam on August 23, Adelaide acquired her first British passport, number 45435, from the British Consulate General. Inside, on page one, her National status was given as British subject by marriage, to a British subject by birth. Her permanent residence was declared as Paris and she signed her signature Adelaide Hall-Hicks. Dressed in felt hat, silk scarf and a gabardine jacket her passport photograph reveals her looking

Adelaide's British passport photo 1937.

relaxed and continental, not in the least bit like the celebrated American entertainer she was. Perhaps, due to the extensive traveling she undertook and the present political turmoil in Eastern Europe, the British Embassy had advised her that it would be wiser, if she were to continue touring, to acquire her own British passport should she wish to remain in Europe.

When the Paris Exposition came to an end, so did the mass invasion of visitors. As the turnstiles ground to a halt, the heady days of profiteering fizzled away quicker than a burnt down sparkler. Halcyon days were to follow.

With such an unhealthy economy, some people thought Bert's plan to open his own nightclub ill-judged and foolish. Without customers, Montmartre's nightlife couldn't survive the winter. To save face, many proprietors pasted "Closed for the Season" notices across their front doors, laid off waiters and chefs indefinitely and tightly bolted the premise's quaint green window shutters. For those clubs that did remain open, the going was tough. At dusk the area took on an uncanny silence. Only the locals and the odd tourist wandered the cobbled streets. Even Bricktop, who knew more about Parisian club culture than the French, had to face up to reality. At her new establishment, business was so bad the staff outnumbered the clientele. In a brave bid to bail herself out of debt, she sold her country house and sank the money into her business. Sadly, all to no avail. She too stuck "Closed for the Season" across her club's entrance, although in her heart she knew it would probably be for much longer.

Undiscouraged, Bert ploughed ahead with his plans. With little competition from similar establishments, he thought it an opportune time to open such a concern. What Bert had waiting in the wings that other proprietors hadn't was Adelaide, and could she pull a crowd! When Hetty Flacks, a wealthy Jewess from England, offered to invest capital in the venture the project took a giant leap forward.

In the eyes of the public, Bert had spent the past fourteen years living life as Mr. Hall. The time had finally come for him to stamp his mark on their marriage. By establishing his own enterprise, he hoped to reclaim his identity as Mr. Hicks.

Bert and Hetty had spent the whole afternoon walking the rain-sodden streets of Montmartre surveying what real-estate agents termed "suitable premises." Much to their annoyance, most of the property they viewed turned out to be of the unsuitable variety. However, there was one establishment that Bert thought had potential. Located at 73 rue Pigalle, at the top end of the road by Place Pigalle, it had previously operated under Bricktop's guidance as a supper club but, due to the waning tourist trade, had been forced to close.

Paris nightclubs were known to be small and intimate, sometimes consisting of only one room furnished with tiny tables placed close together, where a four-piece jazz band would be tightly squeezed into a corner and the dance floor would be overcrowded if a dozen couples gyrated at the same time. They catered for the rich and celebrated rather than the locals, who had their own backstreet haunts to frequent. The property Bert was interested in looked different. Its main reception room was larger than usual. It housed a good-sized parquet dance floor, and held two bars and a small raised stage to seat a music combo. These were the good points. In Bert's estimation its disadvantages were minor: bad lighting, tacky décor, an under-equipped kitchen and no dressing room for the performers. At a cost, he thought the place had great potential. Hetty was not so enthusiastic.

"Perhaps we should first find out what Adelaide thinks before we make any decision," said Hetty warily, unconvinced by Bert's worrying optimism.

The following day Adelaide viewed the establishment. Her impression was similar to that of Hetty's . . . unfavorable. After inspecting the premises a look of doubt crossed her face.

"Without a dressing room how can I be expected to make an entrance, let alone a change of costume," asked Adelaide sarcastically, "and how can I perform under stark houselights? Where's the illusion going to come from?"

"Don't worry about the technicalities," insisted Bert, agitated by her cold dismissal. "Does the place feel right?"

"In a word . . . no!" replied Adelaide bluntly.

"What do you mean, no! Where's your imagination?" sighed Bert, who was rapidly losing patience with his two female partners.

"Look, which part of NO don't you understand, the N . . . or the O?" retorted Adelaide as she kicked up her heels and headed for the door with Hetty in tow.

In past revues, Adelaide had been accustomed to a full orchestral accompaniment, a chorus line of nubile dancers to complement her dance routines and amber spotlights and special lighting effects to enhance her image. How could she be expected to trail her expensive Paris gowns along a stage no larger than a bar-counter?

Outside on the sidewalk, Adelaide stood back and glared gloomily at the premises. In her opinion, Bert's proposal was ludicrous.

"I don't know!" Adelaide moaned, "I really don't know. It looks all wrong to me."

Unbeknown to Adelaide, later that afternoon Bert signed the lease for the premises and presented the documents to her the following morning on her breakfast tray.

"All you need worry about now darling is what name to call the club." Comely, Jewish and wealthy was how Adelaide remembered Hetty Flacks. She hailed from Manchester in northern England, had ordinary looks and an ordinary life to go with them. In the back of her mind she was forever seeking adventure and wishing for a more romantic existence. Only her strict upbringing had held her back from accomplishing the things she so desired. She was a well-respected, congenial, family-orientated woman with little hope of reaching her full potential in life without drastic outside intervention. As it was, Hetty was left forever looking for a way out of her humdrum existence.

Having no previous connections with show business, she was the sort of person who bought *Variety* religiously each week just to keep track of the stars that appeared in it. She devoured the showbiz gossip columns and went to extraordinary lengths to satisfy her appetite for tittle-tattle. She was what one can only term "star struck" and worshiped the whole ethos of the celebrity bandwagon. When the opportunity arose to invest capital in the opening of a nightclub hosted by Adelaide Hall, what else could Hetty do but jump at the chance?

Bert set to work renovating the old building. His idea—to present a glimpse of sophisticated Harlem in the midst of bohemian Montmartre—did not come cheap. He installed low-level lighting, stocked the cellars with fine wines and vintage champagne, re-equipped the kitchens and bars and compiled an authentic Creole menu. His theory, that people didn't just want to visit nightclubs to drink, they also wanted to eat, brought a Jamaican flavor to the place. Creole food was a whole new experience for the French and Bert fully intended to educate their taste buds with Southern fried chicken, waffles, pancakes and rice cooked as in the Tropics. The use of claret-colored fabrics and mahogany furnishings gave the interior class without appearing ostentatious. Four huge designs of a luscious rosy apple and three life-size oil paintings of a brown-skin girl wearing a sunbonnet adorned the walls. The girl in the picture was captured mid-flight demonstrating the Big Apple dance. Bert auditioned acts for the floor show, hired two small orchestras, employed kitchen, bar and waiting staff and brought in a Senegalese doorman called Joseph to front the establishment. In all, the refurbishment took six weeks to complete.

Bert solved the dressing room problem rather ingeniously. In the loft, housed directly over the Grand Salon, was a small storeroom reached only by a wooden ladder through a trapdoor above the stage. The storeroom was used for stockpiling canned food, kitchen products and mineral drinks. With imagination Bert reckoned he could adapt the space into a makeshift dressing room cum store. His plan took him to a run-down eighteenth-century chateau near Rambouillet where he purchased an old iron spiral staircase. This was transported to Montmartre by truck and installed beneath the storeroom's trapdoor. Once secured to the ceiling the stairs led directly on to the stage. Not only did it solve the dressing room problem; it created a wonderful prop from which Adelaide could make her entrance. To compensate for the cramped conditions she would have to endure, Bert painted a bright silver star on the storeroom door.

In the interim, Adelaide resumed her tour and headed for the cooler regions of Scandinavia. In Copenhagen she performed at the National Scala Theater with Denmark's premier dance-band, the Kai Ewans Orchestra. The show, *Midnight Follies*, incorporated acrobats, comedians, instrumentalists and an oddly named vocal group Kvartetten Synkopen. Before leaving the country, Ewans and Adelaide recorded four tracks together including the suitably titled "Stormy Weather" and even more aptly titled "There's A Lull In My Life."

From Denmark she traveled to Sweden. At Stockholm's massive Scala Theater she received unprecedented reviews for a solo performer. She was acclaimed "the greatest stage sensation ever to have appeared in the town."[13] No wonder she found it difficult to sit idly at home. She returned to Paris, cheered by her Scandinavian reception, to prepare for her new nightclub's opening gala.

Adelaide didn't have to think hard about what name to choose for her club. She christened it the Big Apple, after the first bar Bert had managed in Harlem. In a sense the name conjured up the whole spirit of New York: huge . . . colorful . . . and agreeably piquant. When Hetty asked why she had named it after a fruit, Adelaide replied dreamily, "Because Bert makes the best apple pie this side of the Atlantic."

Like the last starburst in a dying firework display, the Big Apple exploded on Montmartre with a bang. On opening night the place was packed to the rafters.[14]

Considering the limited size of the stage, the revue ran without a hitch. When the compere finally announced the star of the show, the audience rose to their feet in anticipation: "Mesdames et Messieurs, from Broadway, via various European cities, please put your hands together and warmly welcome Miss ADELAIDE HALL."

As the orchestra reached a rousing crescendo the stage suddenly went dark and the whole place came to a halt. Like a shooting comet, a lone spotlight hit the top rung of the spiral staircase. As if floating upon an invisible cloud, a foot dressed in a satin shoe appeared from nowhere. To the sound of deafening cheers, Adelaide's slow descent commenced.

LA GROSSE POMME PIE

December 9, 1937, the Big Apple opening gala
Each night, at that precise moment when Adelaide made her entrance down the spiral staircase, the same wave of thunderous applause greeted her. Little did the audience know that the cloud she had just descended from was a cluttered storeroom no bigger than a wardrobe stacked to the ceiling with crates of wine and boxes of canned food. Whatever hardships Adelaide had to encounter to accomplish the effect, the illusion worked a dream. Unfortunately, as there was no dressing room for the rest of the performers, they were expected to arrive already made-up in costume for their stage entrance via the club's less impressive rear door.

New York had already had its season of dancing the Big Apple earlier on in the year.[15] Reports of balconies and wooden dance floors collapsing under the weight of folks doing the dance had resulted in many nightclubs banning it. Adelaide introduced the dance, with a slight variation, for the French palate and renamed it the Canned Apple.

The Big Apple dance was said to have originated on the burning sand beaches of Pauley's Island in South Carolina where the natives performed it barefoot under the moonlight. The dance is formed from various steps taken from the Charleston, the Suzie-Q, Truckin' and Praise Allah. To enact it, a group gathers in a circle, someone calls out the steps as in old-time square dancing and the Big Apple starts. Several variations of it existed including the Round Apple, the Red Apple and the Dixie Apple. As well as the shakes, shrugs and stomping of the original dance,

Adelaide's version included high kicks, splits and gyrations from the French Can-Can. When questioned by a bewildered journalist why the dance had so many different steps, Adelaide simply explained, "Parisians have been accustomed to the Can-Can for more than fifty years so I had to make the Canned Apple more difficult."[16] To accompany the dance Maceo Jefferson wrote "The Big Apple" song, which figured prominently in the evening's entertainment.

The club comfortably accommodated around 250 guests. As there were two floorshows, when customers left, new ones were admitted thereby doubling the evening's attendance figures. Two bands entertained the guests. In the Grand Salon, Havana Casino played solely calypso music and in the bar The Black Diamonds performed popular hits of the day. As one band faded out the other struck up, ensuring the club never lapsed into a moment of silence. The frontman and guitarist in Havana Casino was Maceo Jefferson, a highly respected musician from America who had arrived in Paris in 1926 with Lew Leslie's Plantation Orchestra. He had remained in Europe ever since. Django Reinhardt visited the club regularly to catch Jefferson's set and it was during one of his visits that Bert approached Django with the proposal of hiring his Quintette du Hot Club de France for a residency at the Big Apple.

Despite such a splendid opening party, it has to be admitted that the club did have its initial teething problems.[17] For the first two weeks the Big Apple struggled to attract customers. With a half-empty till each morning, it was reported that both Adelaide and Hetty pawned or sold jewelry and furs to pay the bills and wages of the staff. Many competitors booed the club, claiming it would turn into apple sauce by the end of its third week. The fact is it didn't. Through hard slog and focused determination they baked the most scrumptious apple pie in the city and everybody wanted a bite. Aided by the Christmas and New Year crowds, a crisis was averted. During the notoriously dull month of January, just as Bert had predicted, Adelaide's slick performance attracted punters by the score and, before long, roped barriers along the sidewalk were herding the public into lengthy queues. Bert's two-year wait to establish his own professional enterprise had finally begun to pay dividends.

On the narrow sidewalk outside the club's entrance stood Joseph, the handsome Senegalese doorman. As an ex-soldier, his tall athletic figure, resplendent in a lizard-green tailored uniform, attracted much attention from passers-by. To protect himself from the cold, he wore a long, pleated frock coat adorned with gold buttons and plaited chevrons. A matching peaked cap and spotlessly white gloves completed his outfit. Amidst the cheap hookers and gigolos, unkempt artisans, transvestites and eccentric bohemians that inhabited Pigalle, his appearance added a much-needed touch of respectability to the streetlife. Braving all kinds of weather, he stood steadfast at his post, meeting and greeting the guests, many of whom he welcomed by name.

As the club's popularity grew, rue Pigalle came alive once more and took on a carnival atmosphere as partygoers flocked to the Big Apple. At nightfall a steady flow of cars slowly wound their way up the narrow cobbled street. One after the other, limousines and Rolls Royces arrived. No sooner did one pull away than another would pull in. Joseph's expertise at opening car doors to help their occupants out was renowned and earned him generous tips. Only he had the authority to admit or refuse entrance to the club. He chose wisely. Only the rich and famous, or those that looked as if they had spending power, entered. If you were ordered to queue, this invariably meant you would not be viewing the interior of the establishment. "Pas possible" was how Joseph usually greeted the unlucky ones before ordering them to join the back of the line. Some would offer him backhanders to which he would reply indignantly, "If I could get you a table, you'd be the first to know." Although he was strict and orderly like a sergeant major, he had a dry sense of humor, which charmed everyone who met him. To liven up the proceedings, he would occasionally take off his white gloves and start directing the passing traffic, much to the customers' amusement, who would roar with laughter.

Within a relatively short space of time, the Big Apple had attained the unique distinction of becoming the most chic and talked about nightclub in Paris. Although it was advertised as "Adelaide Hall's Big Apple," behind the scenes Bert was most definitely the boss. He hired and fired and ran the establishment with an eagle eye. Adelaide never got involved in that side of the business. Her job was to pull in the punters, and pull she did with gravitational force.

As proprietor of the Big Apple, Bert gained his own identity and, more importantly, respect. He favored conducting business by gentleman's

Adelaide rehearsing with The Black Diamonds inside the Big Apple nightclub.

agreement. During their residence in Europe, many of Adelaide's concert engagements were negotiated in this manner, sealed only with a handshake. With a staff totaling almost 40 employees, Bert's integrity was often pushed to the limit.

Not everybody welcomed the Big Apple's success. With so many night-clubs vying for business all concentrated within such a small radius, it was inevitable that further closures would follow. Bricktop's unannounced departure for London could hardly have been a coincidence. With her hold as the doyen of Parisian nightclubs relinquished, her presence in Paris seemed superfluous. The embarrassment of witnessing a friend succeed where she had fallen was too humiliating to contemplate. She wasn't prepared to play second fiddle to anyone. Similarly, Monsieur Dajou's Cotton Club, situated two doors away from the Big Apple, experi-enced a dramatic cut in business and promptly closed, as did the famous Chez Florence where the rich and titled had once flocked.

After Bricktop's hasty departure, her close friend Mabel Mercer, for want of anything better to do, often accompanied Adelaide to the Big Apple in the evening. She and Adelaide were great friends and Mabel was wonderfully amusing company. As Mabel no longer had regular employment, Adelaide sometimes invited her to sing at the club. On occasions when Mabel had a singing engagement elsewhere, Adelaide would return the favor and accompany her for the evening.

Although living in a foreign city was exciting, it did create certain problems for blacks, but these were usually only minor inconveniences such as the lack of hairdressers that knew how to style Negro hair. Unfortunately for Mabel, the lack of such hairdressers created enormous difficulty in her life. Mabel was very light skinned with extremely short, fine wiry hair that just wouldn't grow. She always complained about it and spent hours in front of the mirror trying to fashion it into the latest style. So paranoid was she about her hair, or lack of it, that when they arrived together outside a club where she was to perform, Mabel would wait on the sidewalk and send Adelaide in before her, to see who was inside. Whilst Adelaide was gone, Mabel would briefly open the door just enough to peep in, before closing it quickly so no one saw her. If Adelaide returned and said the place was crowded, Mabel would run up and down the sidewalk in a panic shouting, "There's too many people in there, it's packed. What about my hair, why won't it grow?" To aggravate the situation, Adelaide would burst out laughing hysterically. "Don't worry about your hair, gal. They're coming to hear your voice," she would cruelly jest, to which Mabel would reply in a fluster, "What voice? I haven't got one."

Directly opposite the Big Apple on the corner of Place Pigalle stood a famous lesbian theater, which attracted custom by the tram load. Paris had a strong lesbian set and Lulu, the owner of the place, was a pivotal figure of the community. She would regularly pop into the Big Apple during the course of an evening to have a chat. Known as a butch bitch with a masculine build, her look was so convincing female customers often mistook her for a man. Blessed with a voice that could outshine a town-crier's, she was hopeless at keeping secrets and whenever a famous personality arrived at the theater Lulu took to her post and made sure the news ricocheted around the area quicker than an echo.

As a hostess, Adelaide's new role propelled her into a totally different limelight. The press dubbed her the "Queen of Montmartre" and hailed the club as the most fashionable in the city.[18] With little competition from the few remaining niteries that could still afford to operate, the city's *beau monde* flocked to gain entrance. The club became a magnet to statesmen, millionaires, diplomats, theatrical celebrities, the nobility and titled royalty including the Duke and Duchess of Windsor whenever they passed through the capital. *Habitués* included actor Charles Boyer, Maurice Chevalier, Mistinguett, Josephine Baker and her new husband bandleader Jean Lyon, Al Brown, Leslie Howard, Roland Toutan, music-hall star Lucienne Boyer (no relation) of "Parlez-moi d'amour" fame and heiress Barbara Hutton during her frequent extravagant shopping trips, often accompanied by her handsome young cousin Jimmy Donohue. Its clientele would not have looked amiss in "Who's Who."[19] During one par-ticularly busy evening, the guest list included Prince Aly Khan, the English composer and conductor Constant Lambert, Burgess Meredith, President Roosevelt's son on honeymoon with his new bride and a party of Indian princes of whom there were far too many to name.

"Just about everybody came to the Big Apple at one time or another," recounted Stephane Grappelli. "One night a customer came up to me after we'd played 'In The Still of The Night' and told me he'd written the song. It was of course Cole Porter."[20]

When Adelaide sang, people listened, be it in a smoke-filled nightclub or a marbled concert hall. On stage she could alternate her personality at the click of a finger, from crooner to vamp, be as composed as a swan or as fierce as a tiger. During her varied career in show business, there was little she hadn't learnt and her act was as polished and prized as a gold ingot. The radiance of her smile could change the mood of a room as soon as she stepped into it and in the confined space of a cabaret club her charisma worked magic. With elegant insouciance she'd table hop like a bee in search of pollen, mingling with ease amongst the clientele. She became so much of a draw that if her name wasn't billed to appear, customers openly complained. Some even threatened to go elsewhere, causing Bert to take stock of his investment and cut down her touring.

Maurice Chevalier claimed his excuse for visiting the club so regularly was to hear Adelaide's cute French accent. His presence always attracted much attention and throughout the evening his table was guaranteed to

The Queen of Montmartre: Adelaide entertaining Maurice Chevalier at the Big Apple nightclub.
Left to right seated around the table: Adelaide (2nd), Hetty Flacks (3rd).
Maurice Chevalier is in the center of the group surrounded by pretty female fans.
On the far right of the picture is the Duc de Verduro.

be full of the most glamorous females in the establishment.

One song Adelaide had frequent requests to sing in French was "My Symphony." Knowing her grasp of the French language to be far from good, at the beginning of the number she had perfected a build-up routine where she deliberately sang in bad French to cover up her poor translations. Then her contagious giggle came to the rescue. She laughed, then the audience laughed in response and soon the whole club was in on the joke.

Chevalier was a good friend of Marlene Dietrich and it was through him that Adelaide first met her. The encounter took place at the Bois de Boulogne one warm spring afternoon. Chevalier invited Adelaide to go horse riding in the park. She had little experience of the sport but her keenness to learn encouraged Chevalier to offer to teach her. After the first lesson, Chevalier asked her to join him for afternoon tea at the park's Pavilion where he had arranged to meet someone. As usual, his friend was late arriving.

Halfway through tea, a taxi pulled up outside the café entrance. Out stepped an immaculately dressed woman wearing a close-fitting light-mauve suit with matching suede shoes and a floppy silk hat. It could only have been Marlene Dietrich. Miss Dietrich was in the city recovering from a hectic film schedule. "In Paris you can rest and let the world pursue its own mad course," she declared with an air of confidence. Tea progressed into cocktails after which Adelaide made her apologies and departed, but not before inviting Miss Dietrich to spend an evening in Montmartre as her guest at the Big Apple.

If commitments allowed, Adelaide and Chevalier often went horse riding together. She also featured on his popular *Paris Soir* radio program during which, in fun, he regularly commented upon her cute accent.

As a nightclub proprietor Bert excelled. In the after-hours world of insalubrious living, he was in his element. His discretion guaranteed the concealment of a multitude of habits and foibles many of his customers would rather the outside world did not know about. From drug addiction to sexual deviations, from the conducting of illicit affairs to high-class prostitution, all manner of indiscretions were witnessed with nonjudg-mental vision. Bert made sure the secret lives of his customers were kept safely guarded away from prying journalists. Such activities came hand in glove with such an establishment; it was Bert's job to keep the joint respectable and in doing so maintain the club and its clientele's reputa-tion intact. He had no qualms about ejecting anyone, no matter how wealthy or influential, who overstepped the mark.

Bert's jovial personality and generosity created many a headache for both Adelaide and their accountant. Certain guests saw him as a soft touch and ran up extensive bar tabs which they had no intention of ever paying. When the heavies were dispatched to collect payment, to prevent any affront Bert would retire to the downstairs kitchen away from the embarrassing affray that inevitably followed.

MAISON DE CUBA

Adelaide rehearsing with Havana Casino at the Big Apple nightclub. Playing guitar on the far right of the picture is Maceo Jefferson.

The Big Apple took on a momentum of its own. As a pun on Paris fashion houses, Bert dubbed it "The House of Cuba" and shipped in regular supplies of Havana cigars. The music was blisteringly hot, arguably the best outside of America, and any black musicians in town would make a beeline to the venue to jam with the combo. The night Fats Waller paid a call created huge excitement in rue Pigalle.[21] As always, after a few warm-up drinks, Fats was persuaded to play the piano, which finished with an hour-long duet with Adelaide. The extra publicity his visit generated brought in thousands of dollars' worth of additional business the following week.

As with reputable supper clubs in the States, a live radio broadcast was transmitted directly from the premises, which further helped spread its reputation. Every Saturday night on a Continental hook-up the program was beamed to millions of listeners. Unexpectedly, the show's huge popularity encouraged countless foreign tourists to arrive on the establishment's doorstep at all hours of the day demanding entrance.

The term "poor little rich girl" was penned by Noël Coward to describe "Hutton-Tott," as she was known amongst her family and close friends in New York. As the only offspring of an American multi-millionaire industrialist, Barbara Hutton led a charmed, if somewhat isolated, childhood. Doted upon by her father, who found it impossible not to give his little princess whatever she desired, in the eyes of the working class her life took on the role of adopted royalty.

On her twenty-first birthday, she received a check from her father for one million dollars. Two years later, after his death, she inherited his considerable fortune, which included the Woolworth chain of department stores. The newspapers now dubbed her the "world's richest heiress" and her wealth inspired the songwriters Billy Rose and Mort Dixon to pen "I Found A Million-Dollar Baby, In A Five And Ten Cent Store." Not only was she the most traveled lady in New York society, she was also the most talked about.

After her disastrous first marriage had been annulled, news of her betrothal to Count Cort Haugwitz-Revenlow of Denmark filled the tabloids. The couple's arrival in Paris was celebrated with a lavish reception. Invitations were prized and feted like a trophy. The hottest gossip on everyone's lips concerned who was or wasn't invited. The American hostess Elsa Maxwell, whose unconventional parties were all the rage in Paris, was hired to organize the affair. Known for throwing wildly extravagant functions with no expense spared, especially when someone else was footing the bill, Elsa had a knack of getting exactly what she wanted. Unfashionably plump, with large lustrous eyes, she carried her best friend—a small pet boxer-dog named Saga—around with her in a wicker shopping bag everywhere she went.

Elsa much admired Django Reinhardt and his combo Le Quintette du Hot Club de France. Although she thought the group ideal for such an event, Miss Hutton specifically requested the hiring of a vocalist. When Elsa explained her predicament to the group's bassist, Louis Vola, he came up with a solution. If she were to hire a vocalist such as Adelaide Hall for the evening then his quintet could accompany her.

Louis looked back in astonishment when Miss Maxwell agreed. "Madame, the services of Adelaide Hall do not come cheap."

Elsa seemed unruffled by Louis' remark. "Then I should have thought that was more of a reason for hiring her."

It was at Barbara Hutton's reception that Adelaide first performed on stage with Stephane Grappelli and Django Reinhardt and it was rumored in the press that she received a staggering fee of $5,000 for her appearance.

The party proved to be a vulgar affair from all accounts even though it had the best of everything money could buy. It appeared that Miss Hutton's willingness to throw cash around so freely at people she hardly knew bought her little respect in return.

For many years, her marriages, divorces and overindulgence fueled reporters' pens with gossip on an almost daily basis. Even though royalty, movie stars and celebrities courted her, she found little solace in her relationships. Many of her so-called friends and lovers were in fact nothing more than money-grabbers. Throughout her recklessly extravagant life much of her lawyer's advice went unheeded. She spent her fortune almost as quickly as she acquired it, and on her deathbed ended up with little more than the expensive gowns in her closet.

It was said that Django Reinhardt's intuitive understanding of music prevented him from ever either playing out of tune or the wrong note. To him playing his guitar was as instinctive as talking; he always had something interesting to communicate. His residency at the Big Apple with Le Quintette du Hot Club de France gave him a welcome base for

The Big Apple nightclub at 73 rue Pigalle, Paris. Django
Reinhardt and Stephane Grappelli are advertised above the
entrance. On duty outside is Joseph the doorman.

several months. As well as providing backing for featured artists, the
group performed their own set. They were without question the hottest
band in Paris, if not the whole of Europe, and securing their services was
seen as a real coup for Bert. Undoubtedly, their association with the club
helped spread both their own and the club's fame. The band comprised
three guitars, violin and bass, an odd combination for a jazz band, but
nevertheless the combo created a sensation wherever they performed.
Led by Stephane Grappelli and Django, their appreciation of each other's
talent has since been widely documented in print, as has their rivalry.

During a live transatlantic radio broadcast from the Big Apple to the
United States, for the CBS *Saturday Night Swing Show*, Grappelli and
Django's seasoned bickering flared up into an embarrassing altercation
which took everyone by surprise. Apart from the prestige of performing on
such a network, it was the first time a French band had been invited on
the program. The show was to be aired in conjunction with broadcasts
from similar clubs across America. It was a highly organized affair and
timing was of the essence. All afternoon, technicians fussed around the
futuristic-looking radio van, parked directly outside the club, monitoring

the various microphones which were positioned around the premises to enhance the live atmosphere. When the big moment arrived everyone was on tenterhooks. As the announcer was given the count down he leapt into his introduction, "Bonsoir from Paris," to which the audience responded with a vociferous cheer. "And now," he continued, "Stephane Grappelli and his Hot Four." For contractual reasons certain recordings by the group had been released in America under the name of Stephane Grappelli and the Hot Four. It was this that had led to the announcer's confusion over the band's identity.

Furious that the announcer had implied the band was Grappelli's, Django rose to his feet and fled the stage leaving the band in silent bewilderment. Hot on his heels ran the producer pleading that it had been a genuine mistake and he would make amends further on in the program. With little except nervous silence being transmitted, frantic signals from the technicians implored the band to commence performing without him. Fortunately, they agreed and the broadcast ran without Django, who adamantly refused to play until he had been introduced to the American public.

Although it had truthfully not been Grappelli's mistake, Django was convinced he had pre-arranged the mix-up. His moment of fame had been discourteously snatched away from him. Now there was a score to be settled. Django remained true to his gypsy fraternity heritage and never settled a grudge without getting even first. After the broadcast had finished he refused to speak to Grappelli for several weeks. Many of his close friends claimed he bore his resentment until his dying days.

Apart from this incident, both Grappelli and Django agreed in their respective biographies that their tenure at the Big Apple was the longest and happiest engagement in the group's career.

SAME LOVE, DIFFERENT LOCATION

Marriage proposals from young men about town arrived regularly. It was part and parcel of Adelaide's job. A signed photograph would usually suffice in satisfying the most enamored male suitor. However, some were more persistent than others.

One night at the Big Apple, Adelaide was introduced to an important

duke. In his mind, their meeting took on an immediate romantic attraction. Though his title was impressive, Europe was full of nobility, both
genuine and bogus. Josephine Baker's former manager, Pepito—Count
Giuseppe Abatino—had in reality been a humble stonemason from
Palermo. Such figures were commonplace in nightclub circles and not
seen as unusual.

Tall and slender with deep-set eyes and a torrent of jet-black hair, the
duke's appeal wasn't easy to ignore. As is characteristic with amorous
European men, his advances were openly displayed and, for a woman of
integrity, difficult to ignore. Quite simply, he fell head over heels in love
with Adelaide and set out on a determined path to win her affections.
Large bouquets of red roses, expensive gifts and invitations to dine arrived
frequently. As much as Adelaide was flattered by his displays of generosity
and charmed by his genteel personality, his persistence became an
unnerving irritant in her life.

He would lavishly entertain his many influential friends at the Big
Apple and gave enormous tips to the waiters. Admittedly, his presence
was good for business but, as the intensity of his advances increased, the
fear attached to them grew. Adelaide was never comfortable in his
presence and no matter how diplomatically she declined his offers, the
duke refused to take "Non" for an answer. Her rejection pushed his determination to the limit. Though his intentions were said to be honorable, in
reality he was a Duke of Deception. There reaches a point in the sanity of
a stalker where reasoning loses all perspective and the subject of their
obsession becomes the hunted.

Late one evening, just before closing time at the club, the chase took
on a frightening turn of events. In a final impassioned declaration of
devotion the duke declared he could no longer live without the love of his
life at his side and in a drunken stupor threatened to commit suicide
there and then but not before first taking Adelaide's life in the process. If
he couldn't have her as his wife, then nobody could. In the eye of an
obsessed madman such crimes of passion are the ultimate sacrifice and
unquestionable proof of their undying affection. A scuffle followed and
the duke, wielding a knife, lunged towards Adelaide's table only to be
apprehended mid-flight by a nearby guest who flung him to the floor.
Thankfully, before harm was inflicted on either party the disturbance was

calmed and the duke swiftly evicted from the premises.

To keep the incident out of the gossip columns the affair was hushed up. The police were notified and the duke was discreetly warned to keep his distance from Adelaide. He was temporarily banned from the Big Apple, but the thought that he might be lurking around the next corner remained a constant fear in the back of Adelaide's mind.

Sometimes the past has an uncanny habit of revisiting one, just when you least expect it. Late one evening, the English stage producer Basil Dean arrived at the club. His sole objective was to catch Adelaide's performance. After the show he introduced himself and explained why he had made the mad dash across the Channel from London to catch her act. He was there on behalf of the theatrical entrepreneur Charles B. Cochran to offer her a starring role in his next production, *The Sun Never Sets*, to be presented at London's Theatre Royal, Drury Lane. The musical was based on the famous African stories of Edgar Wallace and would be Cochran's most costly and elaborate presentation to date. He believed he had the perfect role in which Adelaide could make her West End debut . . . as the hot jungle Queen, Fitema.

A CALL FROM C. B.

MAY 1938

Adelaide departed from Paris Orly airport on a twin-engined DeHavilland aircraft bound for Croydon, London. Little did she know that the wind beneath her wings was blowing her in a totally new direction.

Charles B. Cochran's interest in Adelaide was first aroused in 1929, when he saw her perform in *Blackbirds* at the Moulin Rouge in Paris. He was so enamored by her personality that he pleaded with Lew Leslie to allow him to transport the whole show over to London's West End. It was only the colossal finances involved in staging such a production that prevented him from achieving his wish. Cochran had kept her in mind ever since and when the part of Fitema in *The Sun Never Sets* arrived she was his first choice.

Adelaide held a genuine affection for London. Her previous whirlwind visit in 1931, when she had starred for two weeks at the Palladium, had all been rather chaotic and exciting. Things had calmed down a little since her heady days of mass adulation but her desire to make it big in Britain was still as strong as ever.

From inside her cozy Covent Garden hotel suite, London appeared warm and inviting. Outdoors, the climate was not so kind. A chill spring breeze blew with full force along the neighborhood's tightly knit streets, dashing any hopes of clement weather.

In France it's considered bad form to arrive on time for anything. To be early is deemed unforgivable. How late one arrives depends upon the importance of the person, from a few minutes for a mere mortal, to a couple of hours for a notable celebrity. Adelaide somehow managed to turn up late at the first day's rehearsal. No matter how important her social standing, the show's producer, Basil Dean, was not impressed. The reason she arrived late was because she had altered the time on her watch incorrectly to compensate for the Continental time difference.[1] In England, being late is deemed the height of bad manners. Adelaide had a lot to learn about the English, their stiff social customs and, more to the point, how strictly Dean conducted rehearsals.

Cochran had assembled an impressive cast. The movie star Leslie Banks and the pretty English actress Edna Best had secured leading roles and the American baritone Todd Duncan and a handsome young actor named James Stewart were featured in the supporting cast.

Stewart's theatrical roles to date had been few and unimpressive. An American actor with the same name had recently risen to prominence, so Stewart was now left with the annoying task of having to find himself a new stage pseudonym. His procrastination over choosing a name forced Cochran to bully him into making a decision. Cochran refused to mention him in the theater program, claiming that he would miss the printer's deadline if he waited any longer. With time against him Stewart turned to Adelaide for help. Together they put their thinking caps on and later that afternoon James Stewart stepped out of Adelaide's dressing room re-christened Stewart Granger.

Todd Duncan, who taught as a professor of music at Howard University in Washington, D.C., had taken leave to appear in the show. He had previously played the lead in the original Broadway production of Gershwin's Negro opera *Porgy and Bess* for which his acting skills garnered huge praise from both the composer and critics alike.

Although Adelaide was desperate to make a name for herself on London's West End stage, her role as Queen Fitema in *The Sun Never Sets* was not the way she had imagined making her debut. In truth, the part was not particularly demanding and typecast her yet again as another jungle-bunny. She had abandoned such roles years ago and was now very reluctant to play them but the part did get her from A to B or, in this case, from Paris to London.

The plot, albeit simple, was faithfully adapted from Edgar Wallace's famous story *Sanders of the River* and set in the deepest African jungle. As Commissioner of a colony, Sanders—played by Leslie Banks—was deemed to have been too strict with his regime and thereby suspended from office by three busybodies in Westminster. When the Leopard Men from the local Ochori Tribe discover Sanders' iron hand of justice has been removed, the natives lay siege to the Commissioner's residence and kidnap the leader of the British troops. Away flees Sanders on a puffing steamboat only to be upstaged by the sudden appearance of an airplane piloted by the intrepid Edna Best—whose character is loosely based on Britain's record-breaking aviator Amy Johnson—streaking across the African sky before crashing into a swamp. Out of the jungle rush the sinister warrior Leopard Men who pounce and capture both her and her mechanic, then march them off to the Temple of the Moon Goddess. Here, they are tortured and terrorized and bound to the pillars of the Temple to await execution. Needless to say, Sanders, aided by a full battalion of British soldiers, sets out to rescue them. In the midst of the melodrama the good natives arrive, led by King Bosambo and his beautiful Queen, Fitema. The Temple, containing most of the wicked natives, is subsequently blown up, the hostages are freed and all return safely to the residency of the British Administration for Christmas dinner celebrations. The script was likened to a comic-book story line aimed at adventuresome adolescents rather than highbrow entertainment for serious theatergoers.

For the next five weeks the cast worked hard and diligently under Dean's direction in the cold dank conditions of the badly heated theater. Long arduous hours away from fresh air and daylight reduced everyone to a state of nervous exhaustion. Tempers flared and tears were shed. The show had to be tight. With so many dangerous stunts, electrical effects and dramatic changes of scenery, if any members of the cast missed a cue they were at risk of being injured. During one rehearsal, Miss Best, who first appears piloting an airplane, missed her entrance and ended up being knocked unconscious by a piece of flying scenery. After medical attention, she promptly returned on stage—sporting a bandaged head—to bravely resume her role. As the show's premiere approached, tension mounted and the last few days of rehearsal were as feverish as a dose of malaria.

A whole tribe of African dancers was assembled and rigorously put through their steps and routines. None of the regular staff at the theater could ever remember seeing such military precision. At night, after the weary cast had left for home, a small army of backstage technicians and craftsmen stayed behind to build the sets. In the morning, when the rested cast reappeared they marveled at the latest piece of scenery to be constructed. The colonial Ambassador's residence, dense foliage, exotic trees, log canoes, distant mountains, a blood-red sunset, a moonlit tropical swamp, a steamship, an airplane that flew, native huts, the magnificent Temple of the Moon Goddess, a rapid river, a thrashing waterfall; the crew worked ceaselessly to create an authentic African landscape.

With songs composed by Cole Porter and Kenneth Leslie-Smith, the score had substance and melody. Porter was known to be highly critical of the way his songs were interpreted and, it was said, wrote nasty letters to those who took liberties with his lyrics or tunes. When he heard certain lines were to be cut from one of his numbers, Porter promptly dispatched a letter of disapproval to Dean. The lyric was reinstated without further ado.

Much to the cast's relief, the self-contained imprisonment of rehearsals came to an end on June 6 when the show commenced previews.[2] Four days later, *The Sun Never Sets* officially opened.[3]

Dean's strenuous drilling paid off. The majority of the critics loved it. Real escapist stuff as is portrayed in cartoons was the consensus. The final scene, during which a recorded version of King George VI's Christmas message to the Empire was broadcast—the first time a reigning monarch's voice had ever been incorporated into a play—was said to be "sensationally spectacular, even for Drury Lane standards," and praised as "one of the most impressive scenes ever produced in a theatre."[4] One appraisal described Adelaide as "vital and attractive, superbly built, an ebony Venus and an embodiment of vibrant life"—not bad going for a girl from the tough side of Brooklyn.

With such approval, all benefactors confidently expected a lengthy West End run. So positive were London's ticket agencies that Keith

Prowse bought £25,000 worth of tickets in advance.[5] The production was said to be Cochran's most extravagant to date with figures of £250,000 brandished in the air. Certainly the sets and costumes were stunning and executed on a grand scale. The cast totaled over a hundred, with half as many technicians employed backstage. Just to break even, the show had to sell out continuously for six months before there was any profit to be had.[6] Considering Britain's depressed economy, it was an extremely risky undertaking by anybody's standards.

Adelaide's main number came during a ceremonial "Wedding Journey" in which she sang "My Love Is Like A River" to her betrothed, Todd Duncan. Whilst perched upon his knee she lovingly serenades him as the wooden honeymoon canoe they're sitting in gently glides down a river shaded by giant overhanging trees. With both actors wearing little beneath their smiles except a shammy loincloth, the number saw more hot steam rising from the audience than from the brewing tea-turns in the interval bars.

When Adelaide signed her contract with Cochran she had originally thought she would be able to commute back to Paris every weekend. In practice, this proved impossible due to an erratic flight timetable. She did, however, manage to return to Montmartre every fourth weekend where she would take to the stage at the Big Apple.[7] Her rendition of "My Love Is Like A River," during which she would suddenly pull out an imaginary paddle to row her illusory canoe, sent the Parisians reeling with laughter.

Whenever he was able, Bert would hop over from Paris to keep her company. It was during these occasional visits to London that Bert began searching for premises, with the idea of opening a new nightclub.

By coincidence, fate once again threw Adelaide and Josephine Baker's careers into alignment. On June 27, for one week, Josephine topped the variety bill at London's Palladium, the first time she had appeared at the prestigious venue.[8] It was sixteen years since their first acquaintance in Boston in the higgledy-piggledy chorus line of *Shuffle Along*. A lot of water had flown under the bridge since then, yet here they were, both still attracting accolades for their craft.

Adelaide's stay in London was not as enjoyable as she had hoped. Compared to New York and Paris the city seemed positively dull and the people were far too reserved for her liking. Nightlife shut incredibly early and the few supper clubs that did exist had the most amateur floorshows she had ever seen. She found British people cold and hesitant and difficult to befriend. At social parties, people very rarely came forward to introduce themselves, which gave Adelaide the impression she was being snubbed. Seldom had she felt so alienated. Fortunately, her work kept her mind occupied and the thought of returning to Montmartre kept her sane.

However well received the production may have been, unlike its title, the sun did set and the show closed abruptly on Saturday July 9. For all those involved, this unexpected development came as a bolt out of the blue. After only five weeks the plug was pulled. Although advance ticket sales were healthy, the main financial backer became increasingly concerned about the worsening economic and political situation in Europe and subsequently withdrew his investment. It had been a hugely expensive show to produce and without full monetary backing could not continue unaided until it broke even.

Directly after its closure, another financier, Tom Arnold, stepped forward. After lengthy discussions, Cochran decided to regroup the cast for a twenty-week British tour.[9] To help keep costs low, the cast was reduced and, apart from Adelaide and Todd Duncan, all principal members were replaced. Owing to the magnitude of the production, a whole fleet of trucks was hired to transport the 43 loads of scenery. The condensed version set out on its mammoth jaunt towards the end of summer and visited such London suburbs as Streatham and Wimbledon and the northern cities of Leeds, Manchester, Newcastle-upon-Tyne, Edinburgh and Glasgow.

ANOTHER TOUR, ANOTHER TOWN

In July 1938, Fats Waller arrived in Europe for a ten-week high profile tour of Britain and Scandinavia. His manager, Ed Kirkeby, arranged the visit to re-ignite interest in the pianist's career abroad. It was Fats' first tour in Europe and to celebrate the occasion he brought his wife over with him. The trip kicked off in Glasgow. Kirkeby's elaborate publicity preparations ensured the theater was packed on opening night. The reception Fats received was so overwhelming that at the end of the show the audience demanded ten curtain calls before they would leave the theater. By the time Fats arrived in London for his Palladium engagement his confidence that the British public hadn't forgotten who he was had been well and truly restored.

In the capital, Fats was reunited with his old buddy and previous writing partner Spencer Williams. Business at the Palladium was brisk and Fats' reviews were excellent. After each show friends and visitors crowded into his dressing room to congratulate him on his performance. In every town where Fats played, he made it a habit to sample the local nightlife. One place in London he regularly frequented was the Nest Club. Though small and rather run down, the club housed a hot resident jazz band that featured the highly talented Edmundo Ros on drums. After knocking back a few shots of bourbon, Fats could usually be talked into jamming with the band. It was at the Nest that Kirkeby had the idea of recording a commemorative album, celebrating Fats' first tour in Britain.

After discussing the venture with executives at HMV, the company agreed to the album but only on condition that Kirkeby organize a band for the sessions. As far as Kirkeby was concerned that wasn't a problem. The jazz musicians at the Nest Club were some of the most capable in Britain.

Two days were booked at Abbey Road Recording Studios in St. John's Wood, North London. During the first session on August 21, Fats recorded a few of his current favorites with the hired musicians—whom he later dubbed The Continental Rhythm Band. This set went without a hitch. For the second session on August 28, he chose to record solo, playing spirituals, which he specially adapted for the studio's recently installed Compton cinema organ.

Fats was very sensitive to the ambiance of his surroundings and liked to have familiar faces around him, especially when he was recording; it helped him relax. For his solo session he invited a few select friends along to the studio to keep him company. Included in the party were Adelaide and Spencer Williams.[10] In the middle of taping the last song, a touching rendition of "Sometimes I Feel Like A Motherless Child," Fats suddenly stopped playing. For a few seconds, he just sat still in front of the organ, in total silence, with his head cupped in his hands. Then, like a broken rag doll, he slowly leant forward and began to weep uncontrollably. Adelaide rushed down from the engineer's booth to comfort him. The song had brought back touching memories of his mother, Adeline, who had died when he was a teenager. The spiritual was one she had especially liked.

After a break, the engineer delicately inquired if he would like to try another take but Fats declined, saying the song made him feel too melancholy. However, he did suggest an alternative. For old times' sake, he fancied recording something a little livelier with Adelaide. This threw everyone into a panic. HMV had no contract with Adelaide. There had been no negotiation of royalties, no mention of advance payment and no guarantee of release. After realizing Fats had no intention of continuing the session without Adelaide's involvement, Kirkeby and HMV's executives came to a compromise. To calm the waters and complete the session, all parties agreed that the recording should go ahead. Two songs were taped.

Adelaide picked one of her favorite ballads, Sammy Fain and Lew Brown's "That Old Feeling," and Fats selected one of the songs that had made Adelaide famous, "I Can't Give You Anything But Love, Baby."[11]

It seemed ironic that Fats should choose "I Can't Give You Anything But Love, Baby" for old time's sake! Adelaide had made the song into an international hit ten years earlier, a fact that still made Fats' heart weep.

Back in the Twenties, when he was broke and naïve about the skull-duggery within the music industry, Fats was well known in Tin Pan Alley for peddling his own compositions to other songwriters for beer money. At the time, Fats had little faith in his talent as a writer and thought such deals were good value; that was until the songs became hits. One such composition he claimed to have written was "I Can't Give You Anything But Love, Baby," which he sold to Jimmy McHugh for a pittance. Ever since the song had become one of the biggest hits of the Twenties, Fats had banned it from being played in his presence. He also claimed McHugh bought "Sunny Side of the Street" from him for a paltry sum and accused both Fletcher Henderson and Irving Berlin of plagiarism. Sadly, because of Fats' habit of selling tunes for ready cash, historians find it impossible to compile a comprehensive register of his songwriting achievements, therefore such claims can never be confirmed.

This was to be Fats' first recording of the song he loved to hate and, if he really did compose it, Adelaide must have seemed the perfect vocalist to record it with. It certainly was a romantic ideal, uniting together at long last for posterity the song's true writer and the artist who secured its position in the Hall of Fame as one of the most successful standards in the history of popular music. Perhaps—it would be nice to think so—Fats had waited all those years for such an opportunity to arise.

Adelaide and Fats' friendship extended way back to their adolescence in Harlem. As teenagers, they grew up in the same neighborhood. The Waller family, who lived at 107 West 134th Street, were only a few blocks down from the Hall household and Fats was well known in the area for being a mischievous rascal. "If ever a devil was born without a pair of horns, it was he," claimed Adelaide, and how he enjoyed living up to his reputation. As teenagers, both attended Public School 89, although Adelaide's class was two grades above Fats'. They had the same music teacher, Miss Corlias, and were both chosen to play in the school orchestra, Fats on piano and Adelaide strumming the ukulele.

If Ed Kirkeby nicknamed Fats the "harmful little armful" then Adelaide likened him to a "big teddy bear." "You couldn't help but mother him," she recalled fondly, "he was as nutty as an almond tree, always had a big broad grin across his face and huge doleful eyes. He was loud and brash but always joyous to be with."[12]

In many ways Fats was at the peak of his prowess as a jazz pianist, as the recordings he made in Britain proved, even though they were played on an organ. During his takes with Adelaide, Fats interpolated humorous comments into the lyric whilst she was singing, breaking any semblance of order in the performance. Determined not to be put off by his mimicry, Adelaide held her own and joined in with Fats' teasing. During the second chorus of "I Can't Give You Anything But Love, Baby" Adelaide altered the line to "I can't give you anything but love, my little fat baby," to which Fats replied rather impatiently, "Oh, baby, don't talk like that."

In "That Old Feeling," Fats' happier mood can clearly be heard as he ad-libs a whole script of comical replies to Adelaide's sentimental lyric. When she sang "I got that old feeling the moment that you passed by," Fats called out laddishly from behind the Compton organ in defense, "I didn't pass by. I stopped."

During his visit to London, Adelaide accompanied Fats on various engagements including an autograph signing session at the Gramophone Shop in Sloane Street, Knightsbridge. They also spent a day at Sunbury-on-Thames—then a riverside village on the northern bank of the River Thames—as guests of Fats' old pal Spencer Williams.[13] In the evening they often visited Soho's Nest Club and it was here they met up with Django Reinhardt and Stephane Grappelli who were touring Britain with the Quintette du Hot Club de France. Fats lived life to the full and thought nothing of partying for several days at a time. When Adelaide invited him to join her on a lightning trip to Paris to call in on the Big Apple nightclub, he jumped at the opportunity.

At midday, on Friday September 9, Adelaide and Fats recorded an exclusive live BBC radio broadcast at St. George's Hall in London, which was later transmitted across the Atlantic to the United States via a Post Office telegraphy link. In the show, titled *Broadcast to America*, Fats accompanied Adelaide on the mammoth BBC theater organ. The program was relayed across America that evening at 00:45 a.m. (British time) by the NBC network. Adelaide sang "Ain't Misbehavin'," "I Can't Give You Anything But Love, Baby," "That Old Feeling" and "Flat Foot Floogee." As the schedule lasted a mere fifteen minutes, Fats only had time to include a couple of solo numbers.

The program received a warm response across the Atlantic. There was, however, one sour note to the whole affair. An account of the recording, written by a reporter named only as the "Detector" that appeared in Britain's highly respected music magazine *Melody Maker*, caused Adelaide tremendous hurt.[14] Unbeknown to her at the time, the essence of the commentary would be how certain critics would judge her artistry from now on. In a classic *faux pas*, the "Detector," who was one of a handful of privileged people permitted to sit in on the live recording, likened Adelaide's "sweetness of voice" to that of Ethel Waters, her "lyrical expression" to that of Mildred Bailey and her "originality and style of phrasing" to that of Ella Fitzgerald. To add further insult to injury he called her earlier recordings with such bandleaders as Ellington "amateurish and corny." Adelaide did not take kindly to his outspoken opinion. For the past seventeen years she had trodden her own path, without parallel. Now, for the first time in her career, a report indicated that her talent was not original. These were strong words for a prima donna to digest.

Although the "Detector" claimed to be impressed by her performance, he obviously had not done his homework and was not conversant with Adelaide's musical credentials. Like Django Reinhardt, there were times when Adelaide found it difficult to muster forgiveness. It was said that after this incident, for several years she declined invitations to meet the editor of *Melody Maker*.[15] For whatever reasons, the identity of the "Detector" remained shrouded in mystery.

Later that evening, after the recording had been completed, Adelaide rang her mother in Harlem to ask if she had listened to the broadcast. Although pleased to hear of her daughter's progress in Britain, Elizabeth did not sound happy. Concern for her offspring's safety in Europe overshadowed the conversation. When asked if she would be returning to America, Adelaide's vague reply received a frosty response. Her intentions were clearly not what Elizabeth wished them to be. In Elizabeth's eyes, the longer they were separated, the wider the divide grew between them. The call terminated on a caustic note.

Perhaps, if Charles Cochran hadn't enticed Adelaide to London, her future path may have taken a totally different course.

SOMEONE TO TAKE CARE OF ME

Throughout her lengthy engagement in Britain, Adelaide's return visits to Paris were short and intermittent. Like the moon that waxes and wanes every 28 days, they usually occurred about once a month, over a weekend. It was during one such visit that Adelaide made a startling discovery. Whilst emptying the pockets of one of Bert's jackets before sending it to the dry cleaners, she came across a hotel receipt. It was addressed to Monsieur et Madame Hicks. On the date in question Adelaide had been in London and Bert had supposedly spent the weekend with friends at a country farmhouse near Reims. In his wallet she then found a small photograph of a light-skinned child with fine hair. Adelaide held the picture away from her as if it were poisoned, stunned by what she saw. This time she had proof of Bert's infidelity and how the truth hurt.

Producing tears was not her style; the practice of splashing a few around for effect would not have altered the situation. If she could find any consolation from the bombshell, at least she now knew her suspicions were no longer based on hearsay. Her immediate reaction was to confront Bert with the evidence. Then, anger took control of her judgment.

Their relationship had become as unconventional as the lives they led. The idea of waiting around to watch their marriage crumble did not appeal to her self-esteem. When faced with an immovable obstacle, why confront the issue? It was far easier to look away, as she had done so often in the past. Life is full of unanswered questions—"Why do we kneel at the edge of a bed when we pray?"—and some are best left unanswered.

The bed in this case may well have still been warm, but the implications were painfully cold. Considering their relationship was wide open to misinterpretation, his adultery should not have shocked her, but it did. In the past, Bert's indiscretions had been simply that, but this time his clandestine ways had gone too far. In the back of her mind she had already made her decision. Either his misdemeanors stop or she would pack her bags and leave. The prospect of losing what they had built together and starting afresh was not a thought she relished. In the cruel light of day, Adelaide could make little sense of the trauma that now confronted her.

Late that afternoon she visited Sacré-Cœur Cathedral. Inside, she found the nave deserted and was taken aback by the holy quietness that prevailed. The church felt incredibly tranquil. The serenity calmed her and, between her thoughts, all she could hear was her heartbeat. It was as if the air had stood still to listen.

She knelt and prayed for forgiveness and guidance, not only for herself but also for Bert. In view of his actions she knew that wouldn't be easy. Like a recurring nightmare her thoughts kept focusing on the photograph she had discovered in his wallet. No matter how hard she tried to eradicate the picture, the image remained. It then suddenly occurred to her that the moment an image is captured on film, it ages. No matter what effects the photographer might apply, history steps in and takes control. With that philosophy in mind, Adelaide came to the conclusion that it was time she moved forward with her life, and let the past take care of itself.

When she left the cathedral, she crossed the street and stood at the top of the stone steps that lead down to Place St. Pierre. For a few minutes she stared at the spectacular view across Paris. In the late afternoon haze, the city looked desperately lovely. She then walked slowly along the cobbled streets towards Place du Tertre before returning to their apartment in rue Lepic.

As she began to climb the steps outside her apartment building, she heard someone call out her name, "Bonjour Addie."

Startled by the familiarity of the greeting Adelaide instantly turned around to see who had called. Recognizing the female to be an acquaintance of Bert's and not hers, her curt response came as a surprise.

"Sorry, have I met you before?"

"Non!" came back the baffled reply.

"Then kindly refrain from acting as if you have."

Adelaide stormed up the steps, unlocked the front door and slammed it behind her. She had now become suspicious of everyone.

No matter how she viewed the situation, in her heart she truly loved Bert. Admittedly, like every couple, they had their differences but they were good for each other, a great double act, and their bond was solid. When he laughed, she caught it. When she fell, he picked her up. She was strong-willed but easily swayed. He was a fast talker but nobody's fool. Their loyalty to one another demanded respect, if not from their friends then certainly from each other. However bizarre their marriage appeared to the outside world, for the moment, Adelaide's resolve to remain silent was her way of coping with the issue. She was, after all, an actress.

Saying goodbye is never easy. It becomes even more difficult when the parting is tainted with regret. After her short sojourn in Paris, Adelaide returned to Britain with a heavy heart.

Her tour of the British Isles with *The Sun Never Sets* resumed and gave her the perfect opportunity to focus all her attention on work. In the sanctuary of her dressing room Adelaide could peacefully retreat from prying eyes and view life through rose-colored spectacles without fear of criticism.

Since her arrival in Europe, Adelaide had suffered several deep bouts of homesickness. Her anger at having to leave a country she loved and her frustration at being separated from her mother had a profound effect on her emotional stability. Though worrying, her despair usually passed within days. However, during the following weeks her actions became noticeably irrational, confused and totally out of character.

〰

In Paris, Bricktop had never represented a threat to any visiting black artists from America. Even Josephine Baker understood that fact. Unfortunately for Adelaide, usurping Bricktop from her niche as the cultural doyen of Paris nightlife created untold tension between them. Bricktop had tried opening new clubs in Montparnasse, the South of France and London. All had failed. Her hasty return to Paris to try and salvage her career brought little comfort. Without funds or premises Bricktop was stranded. Even with her pedigree, in the present economic slump there was little chance of opening a new establishment in Montmartre.

With Adelaide away touring Britain for five months, Bert was left without a hostess to welcome customers at the Big Apple. When Bert offered Bricktop the job, he hoped it would help deflect some of the animosity in the air. Her bitterness was not sweetened that easily. Deputizing for Adelaide was not what Bricktop wanted. She was far too independent to work for anybody else. To be seen fronting a competitor's club was definitely a step down in her estimation. However, necessity needs where necessity must and, as a bankrupt with no income to rely upon, Bricktop's hand was forced. She accepted.

On August 4, Bricktop, with ever-faithful Mabel Mercer in tow, took over as temporary hostess at the Big Apple. Within five minutes of entering the premises, she physically aged 40 years. The humility of having to face guests whom she had once welcomed at her own establishment was an embarrassment she found incredibly belittling. Throughout her stormy tenure, her gilded smile became a constant reminder of the flippant remark she had used so often of others, "easy come, easy go," only this time it was Bricktop who was about to go.

As the shadow of impending war lengthened across Europe, it seemed only a matter of time before America sent an official recall declaration to all its citizens urging them to return home to the nest. On September 28, that news arrived. Under the martial direction of the American Embassy in Paris a somber letter of instruction was sent to all U.S. nationals registered in the city, which read:

> In view of the complicated situation prevailing in Europe, it is considered advisable to recommend that American citizens who have no compelling reason to continue their sojourn in Paris arrange to return to the U.S.

The revelry was over!

In October, Mabel Mercer booked her passage to New York. The worry of an uncertain future on both continents kept Bricktop soldiering on in Paris to the bitter end. Her attempts to salvage her reputation had become blighted by her own lack of vision. Now she could see no further than the front entrance of a nightclub. Her job, which in the past she had been passionate about, had become just that . . . a job. Bricktop was cornered.

During 1938 the Big Apple made a great deal of money for its owners. In late fall, when Bert decided to sell the majority of his holding in the venture, his initial investment had increased tenfold. As a prudent capitalist he still retained a small interest in the business. Owning a nightclub in Paris had added a certain cachet to Bert's standing in society. He now had the finance and credentials to open a new club in London. At his next establishment he planned to expand the artistic side of the operation and promote full-scale musical extravagances.

Bert's decision to sell the Big Apple came at precisely the right moment. No one could have forecast how quickly the drought would set in. The days of easy profits for Parisian nightclub proprietors were coming to an end. Gambling casinos along the French Riviera captured what custom remained. Only Pigalle's brothels and candle bars remained open for trade, and most of those were full of the homeless or loveless seeking a night's shelter. Clearly it was time to move on to pastures new, but no one seemed to know quite where that was.

Like the final curtain call, the heady days of Montmartre were drawing to a close. In the wake of the world economic slump, the famously wealthy found they could no longer afford to stay in Paris and without them the town seemed sober and deserted. Traveling with a large retinue of staff was no longer in style. Gershwin, Hemingway, Porter, Dietrich and Barbara Hutton all scampered home to replenish their bank accounts. Only the diehards, foolhardy or stone broke, remained.

By the end of fall, Montmartre was dead. A miserable forecast loomed. For those unfortunate Americans who were stranded, if they could have swum the distance, they would probably have headed straight back to their homeland under their own steam. As it was, if they continued to dismiss calls of repatriation, an unpredictable future lay ahead that could greatly endanger their lives.

TURN RIGHT AT MY HEART AND ENTER

Turn right at my heart and enter . . . were words Adelaide never expected to hear again.

Endless touring, the constant worry over her future and the continued separation from her husband had begun to play havoc with her health. Once again, Adelaide found herself emotionally exhausted. Like the female lead in a slushy romantic novel she had become vulnerable and weak, and in desperate need of compassion. In the fall of 1938, Adelaide became emotionally involved with a cast member from *The Sun Never Sets*. The affair was passionate, if brief, and stirred a barrel-load of emotions that hitherto had lain dormant for an age.

Life away from home had never been easy for her, especially when she traveled alone. Understandably, there were times when a little company was required, if only to see in the dawn. Unlike Bert's, her indiscretions were difficult to hide. Conveniently for Adelaide, on this occasion there stood between them the wide divide of the English Channel. Although the romance teetered on ecstasy, its cessation left a profound scar upon her mental stability. The affair was totally out of line with her character. She allowed herself to fall head over heels in love with the notion of falling in love. If the signposts were misguiding for her lover, loneliness is a strange affliction that's far too complex to explain during a passionate embrace.

To those around her, she had everything money could buy and a little bit more. Some said she had the world on loan. By continually dismissing her problems, she had never fully explored the inner tensions which gave rise to her melancholy. For far too long, denial had kept them well hidden behind the exterior of her public persona. It wasn't that she and Bert had made a conscious decision to lead separate lives; it was the demands of her career which had distanced them emotionally from each other.

The affair was an almighty disaster that plagued her with guilt lest she should be found out. The break-up left her shattered, to pick up the pieces of a marriage she had recklessly thrown aside. As each day passed, the daunting prospect of facing Bert weighed heavily upon her conscience. She desperately wanted time to be on her own, to rethink her life. The thought of sifting through fifteen years of rubble was too harrowing to contemplate.

If the signposts had been misleading for her lover, her intentions were not as selfish as one might think. Years of hiding from the truth had brought her to the brink of a nervous breakdown. In the harsh light of daybreak she now had to face up to reality. If their marriage was to continue both she and Bert had to reconcile their differences.

Turn left at my heart and leave . . . were words Adelaide had never expected to heed.

NOVEMBER 1938

Increasing concern over Adelaide's health prompted Charles Cochran to take the matter in hand. He firmly suggested she take a few days' leave and thought a short vacation might be beneficial to help ease the intense pressure she was under. Without consulting either Bert or any of her close friends in Paris, Adelaide agreed. The secret break took place at the beginning of November during which time an understudy took over Adelaide's role in *The Sun Never Sets*.

Adelaide flew to the Channel Islands where, under an alias, she booked into a Jersey hotel. Here, she spent a few days of restful calm, enjoying the fresh air, good food and the freedom of anonymity. On the day before she was due to leave she telephoned Cochran. During the conversation she gave him details of her return flight to England. Cochran asked her to contact him as soon as she arrived back in London.

> Beep, beep, beep, beep, beep, beeeeeeeep . . .
> This is the BBC World Service. The news will follow shortly.
> News has just been received of a serious air disaster that happened today in St. Helier on the Channel Island of Jersey. Two minutes after take-off, a Jersey Airline DeHavilland aircraft bound for Southampton crashed into a field. Local reports indicate fatalities are high.[1]

When Bert received the call from Charles Cochran regarding Adelaide's disappearance he immediately thought it was a hoax. It wasn't until Cochran had told him the full story that the seriousness of the situation sank in. Cochran said that early reports indicated there was a possibility Adelaide may have been booked on the doomed plane which crashed in St. Helier but, as yet, it wasn't confirmed.

For the next 48 hours, like rapid machine-gun fire, a continual succession of telephone calls ricocheted across the English Channel from Paris to London and back. No matter how many newspaper editors, news agencies, embassy officials or police stations Bert contacted, nobody held any information regarding Adelaide's whereabouts. Rumors of her suspected death spread through Montmartre like wildfire causing much excitement and concern amongst her grief-stricken friends and fans in the community. In true Agatha Christie fashion, her disappearance grew more mysterious by the hour.

Much as a cat sits by a mousehole, Bert remained day and night beside the telephone, awaiting news from England. By a strange coincidence, Alfred Hitchcock's latest movie *The Lady Vanishes* had just been released in Britain and was playing to packed houses in London.

Adelaide's brief sojourn in the Channel Islands had been arranged at the last minute. Though she had fully intended to fly to Southampton on the day of the fateful plane crash, at the last moment she altered her plans. On the night before her departure, she had retired to bed earlier than usual and slept deeply. Consequently, she slept through her early morning alarm call and awoke feeling unusually groggy. Thinking the brisk sea air would do her good, she canceled her flight and made a reservation on the more leisurely ferryboat. It was during the voyage that Adelaide first learnt of the plane crash on Jersey, although the report was sketchy and vague.

The ferry arrived in Portsmouth later that evening. As in Jersey, Adelaide booked herself incognito into the best hotel in town. Here, she spent the remainder of the evening quietly on her own, fully intending to complete her journey to London the next day. Once again she slept soundly.

The following morning, as Adelaide packed her luggage, she heard more information on the radio about the Jersey plane crash. The news report stunned her. The fatal flight had been the one she should have been on. Only then did it occur to her how lucky she was to be alive. In a strange way, she now felt as if she had been granted a new lease of life.

Adelaide didn't return to London that afternoon as she had planned. Instead, she remained in Portsmouth for another day. She spent much of that walking the windswept promenade talking to no one except herself. She took dinner alone and retired to bed soon afterwards. Unlike the previous few nights, that night she found it impossible to sleep.

The time on her small travel clock said midnight and still she was wide awake. She flicked through the glossy magazines she'd purchased on the boat but found little to interest her. Glancing across the room, she noticed her purse and slipped out of bed to fetch it. From inside the bag she pulled out a small, green, leather-bound address book. A friend had given it to her many moons ago. Written on the back page was a short poem. It was a poem she loved. It reminded her exactly why she strove so hard in life. She read the verse out slowly to herself, emphasizing each line with increasing empathy. As she reached the last two lines, her voice broke with emotion:

> Loving is a painful thrill, and not to love more painful still.
> But oh! It is the worst of pain, to love and not be loved again.

Her tears began to flow uncontrollably.

Those that deceive play hurtful games, not only with the victim but also with themselves. Adelaide knew this only too well from experience. Ironically, by choosing to believe only what she wanted to believe, her life had become twice as complicated. To be fair, Bert's impropriety was no less damaging to their relationship than hers was. They were both playing games and making the rules up as they went along. The time had finally come to face up to the truth and be honest.

Adelaide felt as if her whole life had been cut into small jigsaw pieces and now she had the unenviable task of putting them all together in order to create a clearer picture. In her fragile mental state, the challenge seemed insurmountable.

ONE HOUR LATER

Adelaide glanced across at the long gilt mirror that hung on the wall opposite. Without make-up, her face looked pallid and drawn. Her eyes were still sore from crying and all puffed up. A glazed expression of sorrow stared back at her. True, she felt hurt and betrayed by her so-called friends in Paris, but more than that she felt annoyed at her own stupidity. Not one of her friends had had the heart to tell her of Bert's affair. As Bricktop often said, "You don't sign the official secrets act unless you've got something to hide."

Adelaide took another look at herself in the mirror, then clicked open her purse. She rummaged around its contents until she found her favorite cinnamon-colored lipstick and then applied a thick layer across her upper lip. After pursing her lips together, as if one were kissing the other, she fleetingly looked back at her reflection in the mirror. To help steady her nerves, she took half-a-dozen long deep breaths, then walked over to the writing desk. Under the circumstances, she now felt as ready as she would ever be.

She sat down at the table, placed her gold Swan fountain pen to one side and laid out a clean sheet of writing paper in front of her. For a moment she just sat still and stared at the blank paper as she made herself feel comfortable with her thoughts. When at last she put pen to paper, the words flowed surprisingly easy.

"My dear darling Bert, for that is how I think of you . . ."

It was as if her whole life had now become a series of paragraphs each of which required an explanatory footnote attached to them. She was tired of making excuses for other people's behavior but more importantly she was desperate not to have to justify her own existence by making amends. As the pen reached the bottom of the page an overwhelming feeling of sadness and failure descended upon her which seemed to envelop her in a thick fog of despair. The feeling grew more profound by the second, until it reached a point where she could barely see the sheet of paper in front of her, rendering the words she'd just written illegible.

She had genuinely believed that by writing this letter she could rewrite the past. In a world where all things seem possible if you have a dream, it hadn't occurred to her that no one can rewrite the past. Not even Adelaide Hall could do that.

Without thinking what she was doing, Adelaide lifted the telephone receiver and dialed zero for the hotel's receptionist.

"Good evening, reception speaking. How can I be of assistance?"

"Hello. I'd like to make a call to France."

"One moment, please, I'll just connect you to the international operator."

Adelaide waited patiently whilst the connection was made.

"Hello, this is the international operator speaking. Which country, followed by city and number, do you wish to be connected to?"

"Paris in France. The number is Marcadet 36–59."

"One moment, please, whilst I connect you."

The phone rang and rang and rang. For some strange reason just listening to the gentle purring sound at the end of the line seemed comforting. As she waited, Adelaide held on to the receiver with such a forceful grip, her knuckles began to go white. Only then did the truth dawn. Deep down in her heart she was willing Bert to answer.

Bert awoke to the dull tone of the phone ringing on his bedside table. At first he just lay still, disorientated by the sound. "Merde! Who on earth could that be at this time of the night?" he mumbled to himself, then, realizing it might be a call from England wrenched the counterpane back and leapt out of bed.

"Allo, Marcadet trois, six, cinq, neuf."

For a moment Adelaide hesitated.

"Allo, Marcadet trois, six, cinq, neuf," repeated Bert, rather quicker the second time round.

"Hello, Bert . . . it's me . . . Addie," she sighed deeply. "Come and fetch me, honey. I want to come back home."

"Addie darling," yelled Bert in astonishment. "Thank God you're alive, we've been worried sick. Where are you?"

". . . I don't know!" came back her enigmatic reply.

"What do you mean you don't know!"

". . . I don't know . . . I just don't know where I am any more."

Adelaide broke off from the conversation, clearly too distressed to continue talking. In the background, all Bert could hear was her sobbing.

Without letting go of the receiver, he crossed the room towards the large picture window that gave an uninterrupted view across sleepy Paris. The full moon hung heavy in a starless sky.

"Listen, honey," said Bert softly, "go and stand by the window and take a look outside . . . tell me if you can see the moon."

Adelaide flung the curtains in her room wide open. There, high in the cloudless sky, shone the brightest full moon she had ever seen.

"Do you remember the words your father used to say?" Bert continued . . . "Sing to the moon and the stars will shine."

A short pause followed before Adelaide answered.

"Yes."

"Well, always remember this . . . as long as you sing . . . I'll know where to find you."

THE BIG APPLE

On December 10, 1938, exactly one year and a day after its opening, the Big Apple finally closed its doors to the public.[1] Hetty Flacks' husband, Louis Swirn, who helped run the club in its last weeks, declared that Bricktop had "messed them all up" by trying to freeze them out of business.[2] Her scheming failed, but ultimately led to her dismissal. The establishment was consequently sold to a French lady who struggled valiantly to keep the premises operating as a supper club only to be confronted in June 1940 by Hitler's troops invading the city.

To help quell rumors of Adelaide's troubled state of health, Bert released an official press statement regarding her disappearance.[3] In it he claimed reports of her death in an airplane crash were a hoax attributed to a sad prankster. Her disappearance was explained by claiming she had been staying in the English countryside, away from public view, rehearsing for a new London floorshow.

In 1939, Adelaide and Bert set up home in Britain. Their marriage, though it continued to have its ups-and-downs, lasted until Bert's death in 1963.

EPILOG

Many jazz historians place Adelaide's career on the periphery of jazz. I believe this occurs purely because they find it difficult to know exactly where else to place her. Although her public knew her as an all-round entertainer, as a jazz vocalist Adelaide was a pioneer. Her career was full of contradictions yet, throughout it, her abiding loyalty to jazz remained constant. Not only was she an innovator, she paved the way for her peers to follow. Unlike the American Indian who brushes his footprints out as he moves along, Adelaide left her legacy intact for future generations to discover and enjoy. I hope this book has finally lain to rest the misconceptions that surround Adelaide's career.

In 1939, Britain became Adelaide's permanent home. For the next twenty years her career blossomed. Through radio, television, concert tours, recordings, stage musicals and her own London nightclubs she established herself as one of Britain's highest earning entertainers. At the end of the Fifties, with the advent of rock and roll, in the eyes of the teenage beat generation Adelaide's style had become dated and unhip. Bert's death in 1963 pushed her career into a rapid spiral of mismanagement and the prospect of a forced retirement beckoned. In order to keep herself financially solvent she became indiscriminate about the work she accepted. Over the next twenty years her career nose-dived into a continual tour of nostalgia and Olde Tyme Music Hall appearances.

At the restful age of 83, Adelaide unexpectedly found her career re-ignited. With the release in 1984 of Francis Coppola's movie *The Cotton Club*, the world discovered a jazz legend. During the film, various scenes depict the club's stage revue. One of the characters portrayed in the revue is loosely based upon Adelaide. Two songs, her hit "Creole Love Call" and "Ill Wind", the number especially written for her appearance in the *Cotton Club Parade,* are featured.

Whilst he was making the movie, Coppola had no idea that Adelaide was still alive and resident in England. Just before its UK premiere the film's PR company stumbled across Adelaide's whereabouts and swiftly recruited her to help publicize its release. Not only did this massive publicity campaign reunite Adelaide with her past, it also helped regenerate the public's interest in her fascinating career and warranted her long overdue revival. She now found her "early" years giving warmth to her later ones.

Although in her latter years Adelaide's signature tune had become "Creole Love Call," her name will always be ineradicably associated with her classic hit from *Blackbirds of 1928* which, in a sense, neatly summed up her philosophy of life . . ."I Can't Give You Anything But Love, Baby."

On November 7, 1993, eighteen days after her 92nd birthday, Adelaide died peacefully in her much-loved adopted home of England. Her passing brought the end of an era and wrote the closing chapter to a remarkable period in America's black musical and social history.

On November 14, Adelaide's close friends Kate and Thomas Greer accompanied Adelaide's coffin to New York for burial. Her funeral service took place at the Cathedral of the Incarnation in Garden City on a miserable, gray, fall morning. Unlike her contemporaries, whose funerals attracted tens of thousands of mourners, Adelaide's final public appearance was a quiet affair, attended only by a handful of friends and relatives. She was buried alongside her mother, at Evergreen Cemetery in Brooklyn, not far from Steuben Street where she had lived as a child. Ironically, Evergreen Cemetery is located on the corner of Broadway Junction. After what must have seemed like a lifetime of separation, Adelaide was finally reunited, in peace, with her family once more.

I wrote and relived most of this book in my study at the back of my house in Notting Hill Gate. During tea breaks, which occurred regularly, I'd often peer out through the small rear window that looks down upon my overgrown and shamefully unkempt garden. Here, perched upon the withered branch of a dead almond tree, I frequently saw a beautiful solitary blackbird.

From her lonely perch, she'd cheerfully sing in a clear shrill voice and, seemingly, always stare across in my direction. From the time I started writing this book, she appeared routinely over many months of each year. On my final day's writing, purely from habit, I peered out through the rear window, down upon my still sorry-looking garden and immediately noticed the blackbird was nowhere to be seen. Since that day, the almond branch has remained empty and lifeless and the singing blackbird has never returned to my garden.

Upon reflection, I would like to think that the blackbird's departure was more than just a coincidence.

CONCLUSION

In writing this book I've traveled a long and fascinating journey, and witnessed an adventure I would not have missed for the world. Even Thomas Cook could not have sold me a more thrilling expedition.

Adelaide's theory as to why she remained so popular in show business for so long was simple: "Because I've kept my secrets to myself." I feel privileged to have been able to share a few with you.

In a sense, the feelings of fulfillment I hold at the culmination of this epic journey are intertwined with the hope that I have finally returned Adelaide Hall back home, where she truly belongs . . .

underneath a Harlem moon.

LETTER FROM H. D. ROTHSCHILD

It seems fitting to enclose a copy of a fan letter that was delivered backstage to Adelaide's dressing room at New York's Carnegie Hall before her last-ever American concert, on March 5, 1992.

1992

Dear Adelaide Hall,

A few roses from an aging admirer—though no stagedoor Johnny. Years ago in my late teens I saw you in *Blackbirds of 1928* and you gave one of the grandest performances in a revue or musical that I ever saw, and I've seen hundreds and hundreds in my time. It was marvelously memorable. Then, you seem to have departed from America more or less for good until two summers ago and that one Carnegie Hall appearance which, I sadly missed being far away in Maine. I've often wondered why, though I know you've done lots of variety in Britain and I've been there often before, during and after the war, I never seem to have been where you were appearing. Anyway, if I may . . . I'll come by with a friend backstage tonight for a few moments to tell you in person what indelible memories I've retained of you in *Blackbirds* . . . too long ago.

It will be grand to see you on stage again once more this evening.

Yours most sincerely,

H. D. Rothschild

1931/32 RKO
CONCERT TOUR ITINERARY

1931

Feb.
21–27 RKO Palace Theater, New York
28 Keith's Theater, Cincinnati, Ohio

Mar.
1–6 Keith's Theater, Cincinnati, Ohio
7–13 Palace Theater, Chicago, Illinois
14–21 Palace Theater, Cleveland, Ohio

Apr.
1–3 Fordham Theater, New York
4–10 RKO Palace Theater, New York
11–14 86th St. Theater, New York
15–17 Coliseum Theater, New York
18–21 81st Theater, New York
22–24 Kenmore Theater, New York

May
16–19 Chester Theater, Bronx, New York
20–22 Madison Theater, New York
23–29 Shea's Hippodrome, Buffalo, New York
30–31 Shea's Hippodrome, Toronto, Ontario, Canada

June
1–5 Shea's Hippodrome, Toronto, Ontario, Canada
6–18 Various Canadian cities
20–23 Jefferson Theater, 14th St., New York
27–30 Hippodrome Theater, New York

July
1–3 Hippodrome Theater, New York

4–10 Keith's Theater, Boston, Massachusetts
11–17 RKO Palace Theater, New York

Aug.
8–14 Earle Theater, Philadelphia, Pennsylvania
29–31 Lafayette Theater, Harlem.

Sept.
1–4 Lafayette Theater, Harlem.
7 Departs New York for British tour . . . arrives U.K. 14 September
21–27 London Palladium
28–30 London Palladium also doubles at Café de Paris

Oct.
1–3 London Palladium also doubles at Café de Paris
7 Departs Britain . . . arrives back in New York on 16 October
18–23 RKO Theater, Trenton, New Jersey
24–27 Schn'c't'dy, Keith's Theater, New York
28–30 Proctor's Albany Theater, New York
31 Keith's Troy Theater, New York

Nov.
1–3 Keith's Troy Theater, New York
4–10 Franklin Theater, New York
11 Armistice Night, Veterans' Benefit Ball, Renaissance Casino, New York
11–13 Royal Theater, New York
14–17 RKO Palace Theater, New York
18–20 Keith's Theater, Union City, New York
21–27 Albee Theater, Brooklyn, New York
28–30 Kenmore Theater, New York

Dec.
1 Kenmore Theater, New York
2–4 Keith's Theater, Yonkers, New York
5–8 Keith's Theater, Madison, New York
9–11 Keith's Theater, Chester, New York
12–18 Keith's Theater, Syracuse, New York
19–25 Keith's Theater, Rochester, New York
26–31 105th St. Theater, New York

1932

Jan.
1 105th St. Theater, New York
2–8 RKO Palace Theater, Columbus, Ohio
9–15 RKO Theater, Dayton, Ohio
16–22 RKO Rivoli Theater, Toledo, Ohio
23–29 RKO Riverside Theater, Milwaukee, Wisconsin
30–31 RKO Theater, Minneapolis, Minnesota

Feb.
1–5 RKO Theater, Minneapolis, Minnesota
6–12 RKO Theater, St. Paul, Minnesota

13–15 RKO Theater, St. Paul, Minnesota
19–25 RKO Theater, Spokane, Washington
26–28 RKO Theater, Spokane, Washington

Mar.
1–4
5–11 RKO Theater, Seattle, Washington
12–18 RKO Theater, Tacoma, Washington
19–25 RKO Theater, Portland, Oregon

Apr.
1–7 RKO Golden Gate Theater, San Francisco, California
9–15 RKO Orpheum Theater, Oakland, California
16–22 RKO Theater, Los Angeles, California
23–29 RKO Theater, Los Angeles, California
30 RKO Theater, Salt Lake City, Utah

May
1–6 RKO Theater, Salt Lake City, Utah
7–13 RKO Theater, Denver, Colorado
14–20 RKO Keith's Theater, Omaha, Nebraska
21–23 RKO Orpheum Theater, Sioux City, Iowa
25–27 RKO Paramount Theater, Des Moines, Iowa
28–30 RKO Orpheum Theater, Davenport, Iowa

June
18–24 Hippodrome Theater, Buffalo, New York

July
3–9 Lafayette Theater, Harlem, New York

* Please note this is not a comprehensive listing of all the tour dates as certain newspapers
containing relevant information to complete the itinerary could not be located.

CAREER DATES 1921–38

In chronological order:

1921
May 23   *Shuffle Along* premieres at Broadway's 63rd St. Theater.

1923
Aug. 23   *Runnin' Wild* opens at the Howard Theater, Washington, D.C.

Sept. 6   *Runnin' Wild*, Selwyn Theater, Boston, Massachusetts.

Oct. 29   *Runnin' Wild* premieres at Broadway's Colonial Theater.

1924
May   *Runnin' Wild* road tour opens in Philadelphia, Pennsylvania.

Fall   Adelaide appears in a five-month residency at the Everglades Club in Times Square, N.Y.

1925
Spring   Adelaide appears in revue at the Club Alabam, Manhattan, N.Y.

May 25   *Chocolate Kiddies* premieres in Germany at Berlin's Admirals Palast Theater.

1926
Mar. 8   *Lincoln Frolics* premieres at Harlem's Lincoln Theater.
Mar. 14   *Lincoln Frolics*, Broadway Theater, Washington, D.C.

Apr. 5   *Tan Town Topics* premieres at Harlem's Lafayette Theater.

May 17   *Bill Robinson Revue* premieres at Harlem's Alhambra Theater.

June 28   *My Magnolia* tryout at Atlantic City, New Jersey.

July 5   *Shake Rattle and Roll*, Harlem's Lafayette Theater.
July 12   *My Magnolia* premieres at Broadway's Mansfield Theater.

Oct. 18   *Desires of 1927* premieres at the Orpheum Theater, Newark, New Jersey.
Oct. 25   *Desires of 1927*, Harlem's Lafayette Theater. The show then goes on tour.

Nov. 14   *Desires of 1927*, Howard Theater, Washington, D.C.

Dec. 11   *Desires of 1927*, Globe Theater, Cleveland, Ohio.
Dec. 25   *Desires of 1927*, Grand Theater, Chicago, Illinois.

1927
Jan. 10   *Desires of 1927*, Palace Theater, Memphis, Tennessee.
Jan. 17   *Desires of 1927*, Lyric Theater, New Orleans, Louisiana.
Jan. 24   *Desires of 1927*, Frolic Theater, Birmingham, Alabama.
Jan. 31   *Desires of 1927*, Atlanta, Georgia.

Feb. 14   *Desires of 1927*, Lincoln Theater, Louisville, Kentucky.
Feb. 21   *Desires of 1927*, Roosevelt Theater, Cincinnati, Ohio.
Feb. 28   *Desires of 1927*, Grand Theater, Chicago, Illinois.

Mar. 4   Adelaide appears at Chicago's Café de Paris after Ethel Waters storms out of her
           engagement at the restaurant.
Mar. 7   *Desires of 1927*, Koppin Theater, Detroit, Michigan.
Mar. 21   *Desires of 1927*, Pythian Theater, Columbus, Ohio.

Apr. 12   Adelaide stars at Chicago's Café de Paris in *Parisian Follies*.
Apr. 18   Adelaide stars in revue at the Swiss Gardens in Cincinnati, Ohio.

May 23   Adelaide stars at Chicago's Sunset Café in *Sunset Revue* for an eight-week
           engagement.

July 15   Adelaide stars at Chicago's Sunset Café in *Sunset Glories* for a further eight weeks.

Oct. 10   *Messin' Around* revue opens at Lew Leslie's Plantation Café.
Oct. 26   Adelaide records "Creole Love Call" and "The Blues I Love to Sing" with Duke
           Ellington and his Orchestra.

Nov. 3   Adelaide records "Chicago Stomp Down" with Duke Ellington and his Orchestra.
Nov. 14   *Dance Mania* premieres at Harlem's Lafayette Theater.
Nov. 21   *Dance Mania*, Gibson's Standard Theater, Philadelphia, for a two-week run.
           The show should have continued on to Baltimore and Washington, D.C., but was
           canceled at the last moment. Adelaide returned to New York on 3 December.

Dec.   Adelaide appears nightly throughout December at Harlem's Cotton Club with Duke
           Ellington and his Orchestra.
Dec. 3   Adelaide appears at all three Florence Mills' Memorial Benefit Shows held at
           Harlem's Lafayette, Alhambra and Lincoln Theaters.

1928
Jan. 4   Adelaide opens in revue at the Ambassadeur's Club on 57th Street, New York.

Feb. 13   *Blackbird Revue* commences at the Ambassadeur's Club.

Apr.   Last week in April *Blackbirds of 1928* pre-Broadway tryout at Nixon's Apollo Theater in Atlantic City.

May 9   *Blackbirds of 1928* premieres at 42nd Street's Liberty Theater.
May 19   "Creole Love Call" still in the American sales-charts at number 19.

June 21   Adelaide records "I Must Have That Man" and "Baby" from *Blackbirds*, accompanied by George Rickson on piano.

Aug. 13–14 Adelaide records "I Must Have That Man" and "Baby" accompanied by Lew Leslie's Blackbirds Orchestra which is released on Brunswick Records.

Oct. 8   *Blackbirds of 1928* moves to 42nd Street's Eltinge Theater.

Dec. 24   Cast of *Blackbirds* record a Christmas radio greeting to the world.

1929
Jan. 22   Monster Benefit at Lafayette Theater with cast of *Blackbirds*, *Show Boat*, etc.

Feb. 27   Philadelphia Midnight Benefit at the Gibson Theater with the cast of *Blackbirds*.

Mar. 24   Midnight Benefit at the Lafayette Theater with the cast of *Blackbirds*, *Show Boat*, *Porgy* and Noble Sissle. Cuban boxer Kid Chocolate also makes an appearance.

Apr. 14   Midnight Benefit at the Al Jolson Theater given by Mayor James J. Walker for Harlem's Children Fund starring Al Jolson, Eddie Cantor, Bojangles, Adelaide Hall, the Hall Johnson Choir, the Sidewell Sisters, Jules Bledsoe, the New York Philharmonic Orchestra and stars from the Metropolitan Opera.

May 9   *Blackbirds of 1928* celebrates one year on Broadway.

June 7   *Blackbirds of 1928* opens with a grand gala at the Moulin Rouge in Paris, France.

Aug. 31   *Blackbirds of 1928* closes at the Moulin Rouge. Adelaide departs from Le Havre on 11 September and arrives in New York on 17 September.

Sept. 30   *Blackbirds of 1928* commences American road tour at the Shubert Theater, Newark, New Jersey.

Oct. 14   *Blackbirds of 1928*, Pittsburgh, Pennsylvania.
Oct. 28   *Blackbirds of 1928*, Cleveland, Ohio.

Nov. 4   *Blackbirds of 1928*, Wilson Theater, Detroit, Michigan.
Nov. 26   *Blackbirds of 1928*, Adelphi Theater, Chicago, Illinois.

1930
Jan. 27   Adelaide commences her first short RKO tour at the Central Theater, Jersey City, New Jersey. (For full itinerary see Chapter 12.)

May 17   *Lucky Sambo* revue at Harlem's Lafayette Theater for two-week engagement.
May 31   *Lucky Sambo* goes on tour and opens at the Howard Theater in Washington, D.C.

Aug. 9–15 Adelaide headlines Broadway's RKO Palace Theater with Bill Robinson.

Aug. 13   *Brown Buddies* rehearsals.
Aug. 29   Adelaide headlines RKO's *Theater of the Air* radio salute to Amos 'n' Andy live from Harlem.

Sept. 12 *Brown Buddies* dress rehearsal.
Sept. 15 *Brown Buddies* tryout at Nixon's Theater, Atlantic City, New Jersey.
Sept. 22 *Brown Buddies* plays in Baltimore, N. Maryland.
Sept. 29 *Brown Buddies* plays at Nixon's Theater, Pittsburgh, Pennsylvania.

Oct. 7   *Brown Buddies* premieres at Broadway's Liberty Theater.

Nov. 23   Adelaide stars in Harlem's Unemployment Benefit at the Lafayette Theater. The program also includes Ethel Waters, Bill Robinson and The Berry Brothers.
Nov. 30   Adelaide stars in the NAACP Benefit at Broadway's Waldorf Theater. The program also includes Duke Ellington, Ethel Waters and Bill Robinson.

Dec. 7   Adelaide stars in *Harlemia* Benefit for City Hospital Radio Fund at Broadway's Majestic Theater. The program also includes Bill Robinson, Duke Ellington, Fletcher Henderson, Aida Brown and Cab Calloway.
Dec. 14   Adelaide stars in a Ziegfeld Benefit at Broadway's Alhambra Theater. The program also includes Bill Robinson, Fred and Adele Astaire and Al Jolson.

1931
Jan. 10   *Brown Buddies* closes on Broadway.

Feb. 21   Adelaide appears at Broadway's RKO Palace Theater with Noble Sissle.
Feb. 28   Adelaide commences her second RKO concert tour which lasts over 18 months. (For full tour itinerary see 1931/32 RKO Concert Tour Itinerary.)

1932
July 3   Adelaide breezes back into New York to headline at Harlem's Lafayette Theater. She introduces the city to Art Tatum who accompanies her on stage.

Aug. 5   Adelaide records "I'll Never Be the Same" with Art Tatum and Francis J. Carter on piano.
Aug. 10   Adelaide records "You Gave Me Everything But Love" with Art Tatum and Francis J. Carter on piano.

Oct. 28   Adelaide stars with Ethel Waters in Lew Leslie's revue *Dixie to Broadway* which opens on Broadway at the Paramount Theater in Times Square. Adelaide remains with the show for six weeks.

Nov. 11   *Dixie to Broadway* plays at Brooklyn's Paramount Theater.

Dec. 21   Adelaide records "I Must Have That Man" and "Baby" with Ellington. On the record her name precedes his and reads, "Adelaide Hall with Duke Ellington and his Famous Orchestra." It was the first time Ellington had allowed a female artist's name to precede his.

1933
Jan. 7   Adelaide records "I Must Have That Man" with the Duke Ellington Orchestra for N.Y. Records.
Jan. 14   Adelaide appears in concert at Harlem's Opera House for one week.

May 20   Adelaide performs in concert at Harlem's Lafayette Theater for one week.

June 17   Adelaide tops the bill at Broadway's RKO Palace Theater for one week.

Sept. 4   Adelaide tops the bill at the special Labour Day *New Rochelle Ball* in New York.

Oct. 11   Adelaide headlines *Cotton Club Revue* tour that opens in Washington, D.C.

Nov. 25   Adelaide stars in the *Cotton Club Revue* at Harlem's Lafayette Theater for one week.

Dec. 4   Adelaide records "Drop Me Off in Harlem" with the Mills Blues Band for N.Y. Records.

Dec. 8   Adelaide stars in the *Cotton Club Revue*, which appears for one week in Rochester, N.Y. and then moves on for weekly engagements in Cleveland, Detroit, Cincinnati and Chicago in accordance with the RKO circuit.

1934
Feb. 16   Adelaide headlines in the *Chocolate Soldiers* revue at Harlem's Apollo Theater.

Mar. 11   Adelaide stars at Harlem's Cotton Club in *Cotton Club Parade*, which runs for eight months.

June 30   Adelaide tops the bill at Harlem's Opera House for one week prior to her evening shows at the Cotton Club.

1935
June 30–July 6 RKO summer concert tour that commences at the Odeon Theater in St Louis, Missouri.

July 6   Adelaide performs a benefit concert at Harlem's Apollo Theater with Al Jolson, Bill Robinson and Ethel Waters.

July 12–18 RKO concert tour at the State Theater in Chicago, Illinois.

Aug. 31   Film premiere of Vitaphone's movie short *All Colored Vaudeville Show* starring Adelaide and the Nicholas Brothers. Adelaide sings "To Have You, To Hold You."

Sept. 19   Adelaide opens for a limited season at Chicago's Grand Terrace Café. The revue ends on 31 October.

Nov. 6   Adelaide arrives back in New York to prepare for her European tour.

Dec. 6   Alhambra Theater, Paris, two shows daily.
Dec. 12   Sings live on Paris Radio Cité.
Dec. 21   Performs at the *Night of Stars* benefit at Les Ambassadeurs—a charity that aids the Paris poor.
Dec. 23   Adelaide proceeds to London for special Christmas and New Year's Eve concerts.

1936
Jan.   Adelaide returns to Paris to record "Truckin' " accompanied by Joe Turner on piano and "East of the Sun and West of the Moon" with the J. Ellsworth Orchestra.

Feb. 22   Adelaide resumes her European tour in Switzerland with the Albert Gaubiers Ballet Company and opens at Basel's Consul Theater for a two-week run.

Mar. 8   The tour proceeds to Zurich for a two-week engagement then performs at various Swiss cities until the end of March.

Apr.   Adelaide travels to the South of France for a two-week engagement in Monte Carlo.
Apr. 23   She returns to Paris to perform on Willie Lewis' popular radio show.

May 5   Adelaide records "I'm Shooting High" in Paris with the Willie Lewis Orchestra.

June   Adelaide is featured in a 90-minute radio special live on Paris Cité radio show accompanied by the Willie Lewis Orchestra.

July   Adelaide and the Willie Lewis Orchestra perform in cabaret at Knokke Casino in Belgium.

Aug.   Adelaide travels to Germany and performs in Berlin during the Olympic Games.
Aug. 23   Adelaide returns to Paris to prepare for her trip to Holland.
Aug. 25   Adelaide performs at the Bal Taharin in The Hague for a four-week residency.

Oct. 19   Adelaide arrives in San Remo to commence her Italian tour. She opens at San Remo's smart Casino Municipale for a limited residency then continues on a short tour across Italy until November.

Dec.   Adelaide returns to Paris to a surprise welcome back party thrown by Maurice Chevalier.

1937
Jan. 1   Adelaide and Bert open their first nightclub in Paris on the Champs-Élysées. She receives an offer from New York's Cotton Club to star in their spring revue which she declines.
Jan. 30   Adelaide appears in cabaret at the Ventouris supper club in Paris for a short engagement.

Mar.   Adelaide headlines a lavish show at Cannes Club O'Rio in the South of France for a six-week residency.

Apr.   Adelaide returns to Holland for a three-week engagement at the Scheveningen Casino.

May 7   Adelaide returns to Paris for a two-week engagement at the Bœuf sur le Toit.
May 22   Bert invests money in a new Parisian nightclub, The Cotton Club, situated in Montmartre.

Oct.   Adelaide's short tour of Scandinavia commences.

Nov. 7   Adelaide appears in concert with Kai Ewans Orkester at the Det Ny Teater in Klokken for one week.
Nov. 14   The tour moves to Copenhagen's National Scala Theater for one week.
Nov. 21   The tour plays Stockholm's National Scala Theater for one week.

Dec.   At the beginning of December Adelaide returns to Paris to prepare for the opening of her own nightclub—the Big Apple.
Dec. 9   The Big Apple opens for business.

Dec. 16   Adelaide returns to Sweden and resumes her Scandinavian tour for a further week's engagement at Stockholm's National Scala Theater after her previous dates sold out.

1938
Jan. 15   New floorshow opens at the Big Apple.

Feb.   Regular live radio broadcasts are transmitted direct from the Big Apple every Saturday night featuring Adelaide and the Quintette du Hot Club de France.

Mar.   Adelaide appears at the Shan Hab Club.
Apr.   Adelaide holds her own private dance classes, teaching students the latest dance crazes such as The Canned Apple and Truckin'.
British producer Charles B. Cochran invites Adelaide to co-star in his adaptation of Edgar Wallace's *The Sun Never Sets* to be staged at London's Theatre Royal Drury Lane.
Apr. 12   The Berry Brothers hold their "Farewell to Paris" party at the Big Apple.

May   Adelaide commences rigorous rehearsals at London's Theatre Royal, Drury Lane.

June 9   Premiere of *The Sun Never Sets* at London's Theatre Royal, Drury Lane.

July 9   *The Sun Never Sets* closes.
Towards the end of summer the show regroups and commences a twenty-week British tour.

Aug. 21   Adelaide records "I Can't Give You Anything But Love, Baby" and "That Old Feeling" with Fats Waller at London's Abbey Road Studios.

Dec. 10   The Big Apple nightclub in Paris closes, exactly one year and one day after it opened.

RECORDINGS 1921–38

New York, 26 October 1927
Adelaide Hall featured (vcl) with Duke Ellington and his Orchestra:
Duke Ellington, Bubber Miley, Louis Metcalf, Joe Nanton, Rudy Jackson, Otto Hardwick,
Harry Carney, Fred Guy, Welman Braud, Sonny Greer.

VI 39370–1	Creole Love Call	Victor
VI 39370–2	Creole Love Call	Victor
VI 39371–1	The Blues I Love To Sing	Victor
VI 39371–2	The Blues I Love To Sing	Victor

New York, 3 November 1927
Adelaide Hall featured (vcl) with Duke Ellington and his Orchestra:
Duke Ellington, Jabbo Smith, Louis Metcalf, Joe Nanton, Rudy Jackson, Otto Hardwick, Harry
Carney, Fred Guy, Welman Braud, Sonny Greer.

OK W81777–A	Chicago Stomp Down	Okeh
OK W81777–B	Chicago Stomp Down	Okeh
OK W81777–C	Chicago Stomp Down	Okeh

New York, 21 June 1928
Adelaide Hall (vcl): acc by George Rickson (piano)

Baby	Victor Rec. Co. (test)
I Must Have That Man	Victor Rec. Co. (test)

New York, 14 August 1928
Adelaide Hall (vcl) with Lew Leslie's Blackbird Orchestra:
Pike Davis, Demas Dean (tp), Herb Flemming (tb), Carmello Jejo, Alberto Socarras (cl, as, fl),
Ramon Usera (ts, vin), George Rickson (piano, arr), Benny James (bj), Henry "Bass" Edwards
(tu), Jesse Baltimore (d).

E–28059	I Must Have That Man	Brunswick 4031
E–28060	Baby	Brunswick 4031

London, October 1931
Adelaide Hall (vcl): acc by Joe Turner (stand-in Bennie Paine), Francis J. Carter (piano)

R–217	Doin' What I Please	Orp102
R–218	Rhapsody In Love	Brunswick 01217
R–221	Minnie The Moocher	Brunswick 01217
R–222	To Have And To Hold	Orp102
R–225	Too Darn Fickle	Orp108
R–229	I Got Rhythm	Orp109
R–230	Baby Mine	Orp109
R–232	I'm Red Hot From Harlem	Orp108

New York, 5 August 1932
Adelaide Hall (vcl): acc by Charlie Teagarden or Mannie Klein (tp), Jimmy Dorsey (cl, as), Larry Gomar (vib), Art Tatum, Francis J. Carter (piano), Dick McDonough (g)

12148–A	Strange As It Seems	Brunswick 6376, Eng 1348
12148–B	Strange As It Seems	Meritt 24
12149–A	I'll Never Be The Same	Brunswick 6362 , Eng 1348
12149–B	I'll Never Be The Same	Meritt 24

New York, 10 August 1932
Adelaide Hall (vcl): acc by Art Tatum, Francis J. Carter (piano) Larry Gomar (vib–1)

12166–A	You Gave Me Everything But Love (1)	Brunswick 6376, Eng 01442
12166–B	You Gave Me Everything But Love (1)	Meritt 24
12167–A	This Time It's Love	Brunswick 6362, Eng 01442
12167–B	This Time It's Love	Meritt 24

New York, 21 December 1932
Adelaide Hall (vcl) with Duke Ellington and his Famous Orchestra:
Duke Ellington (piano), Arthur Wetsol, Cootie Wiliams (tp), Freddie Jenkins, Joe Nanton, Lawrence Brown, Juan Tizol (tb), Barney Bigard (cl, ts), Johnny Hodges (as, sop–1), Otto Hardwick (as), Harry Carney (bar, cl, as), Fred Guy (g), Wellman Braud (b), Sonny Greer (d).

B12773–A	I Must Have That Man	Blu-Disc T1001
B12773–B	I Must Have That Man	Blu-Disc T1001
B12774–A	Baby	Col OL6770
B12773–B	Baby	Blu-Disc T1001

New York, 7 January 1933
Adelaide Hall (vcl) with Duke Ellington and his Famous Orchestra:
Duke Ellington (piano), Arthur Wetsol, Cootie Wiliams (tp), Freddie Jenkins, Joe Nanton, Lawrence Brown, Juan Tizol (tb), Barney Bigard (cl, ts), Johnny Hodges (as, sop–1), Otto Hardwick (as), Harry Carney (bar, cl, as), Fred Guy (g), Wellman Braud (b), Sonny Greer (d).

B12773–C	I Must Have That Man	Brunswick
B12773–D	I Must Have That Man	Col
B12774–C	Baby	Brunswick
B12773–D	Baby	Blu-Disc

New York, 4 December 1933
Adelaide Hall (vcl) with the Mills Blue Rhythm Band

BS 78827-1-2	Drop Me Off In Harlem	Victor (Rej)
BS 78828-1-2	Reaching For The Cotton Moon	Victor (Rej)

Paris, France, 20 January 1936
Adelaide Hall (vcl): acc by Joe Turner (piano)

P–77616	I'm In The Mood For Love	Ultraphone AP1574
P–77613	Truckin'	Ultraphone AP1574

Paris, France, 20 January 1936
Adelaide Hall (vcl) with John Ellsworth and his Orchestra:
Alex Renard (tp), Guy Paquınet (tb), Christian Wagner (cl, as), Max Blanc (as), Alix Combelle (ts), Joe Turner (piano), Stephane Grappelly (vin), Roger Chaput (g), Eugene D'Hellemmes (b), Maurice Chaillou (d), Jacques Methehen "pseudonym for John Ellsworth" (dir.).

P–77616	East Of The Sun And West Of The Moon	Ultraphone AP1575
P–77618	Solitude	Ultraphone AP1575

Paris, France, 5 May 1936
Adelaide Hall (vcl) with Willie Lewis and his Orchestra

CPT 2649–1	I'm Shooting High	Pathe PA-914
CPT 2652–1	Say You're Mine	Pathe PA-914

Paris, France, 15 May 1936
Adelaide Hall (vcl) with Willie Lewis and his Orchestra

CPT 1	After You've Gone	Pathe PA
CPT 1	Swing Guitars	Pathe PA

Berlin, Germany, Summer 1936
Adelaide Hall (vcl) with piano accompaniment
German theater promotional record of excerpts from the *Black and White* revue:
(A) Truckin', (B) Solitude, (C) I Can't Give You Anything But Love, Baby, (D) I Must Have That Man, (E) Diga Diga Do, (F) Truckin'.

Paris, France, 15 October 1936
Adelaide Hall (vcl) with Willie Lewis and his Orchestra.
Bill Coleman joins the Band.

CPT 1	I'm Shooting High	Pathe PA

Copenhagen, Denmark, November 1937
Adelaide Hall (vcl) with the Kai Ewans Orchestra:
Olof Carlson, Axel Skouby (tp), Peter Rasmussen (tb), Kai Ewans (cl, as, ldr), Kai Moller, Aage Voss (cl, as), Ewald Anderson (cl, ts), Amdi Riis (piano), Willy Sorenson (b), Erik Kragh (d).

C-596	There's A Lull In My Life	Tono K6001
C-597	Stormy Weather	Tono K6002

C-598   Where Or When   Tono K6002
C-599   Medley: "Dinah, Margie, After
                        You've Gone, I Ain't Got Nobody   Tono K6001

London, Britain, 28 August 1938
Adelaide Hall (vcl): acc by Fats Waller (org, vcl comments)

OEA6391-1   That Old Feeling   HMV B8849
OEA6392-2   I Can't Give You Anything But Love   HMV B8849

ALL COLORED VAUDEVILLE SHOW
6 September 1935. The Vitaphone Corp. LP5761.
USA 1935–1 Reel
Director Roy Mack   Arch—Distributor
Adelaide Hall, The Nicholas Brothers, The Five Rocketeers and Eunice Wilson. A musical short based on a variety show that includes various songs and routines from the featured artists. Adelaide performs "To Have You, To Hold You."

DIXIELAND JAMBOREE
31 August 1935. The Vitaphone Corp. LP5744.
USA 1935–1 Reel
Director Roy Mack   Arch—Distributor
Adelaide Hall, Cab Calloway and his Orchestra, The Nicholas Brothers, The Five Racketeers and Eunice Wilson. A musical short based on a variety show that includes various songs and routines from the featured artists. Adelaide performs "To Have You, To Hold You." *Dixieland Jamboree* is an extended repackaged version of the *All Colored Vaudeville Show* and was released on 24 April 1946.

NOTES

PART I. SING TO THE MOON AND THE STARS WILL SHINE 1901–27

Chapter 1. Taxi for Miss Hall

1. "Cabaret Comes to Carnegie," *New York Times*, 14 Oct. 1988.

Chapter 2. Sing to the Moon

1. Adelaide consistently claimed in interviews that her father taught music at the Pratt Institute in Brooklyn. A claim that, after searching the archives at the Institute's library, cannot be verified. Arthur Hall is not listed as a member of the full-time faculty in any of the annual catalogs published between 1887 through to 1916. Working as a local music teacher, one would have expected to find a record of his name in the Institute's files.

   The family's Brooklyn apartment was certainly in the same vicinity as the High School. The Institute's seven tall distinguished-looking brick and terracotta buildings ran the entire length of Ryerson Street and could be seen clearly from Steuben Street where the Hall family lived. Although the listings are comprehensive they fail to mention pianists or tutors who worked part time during evening classes. Such classes included "music instruction" and "physical training." Both of these classes were offered in the Department of Kindergartens and would have required a pianist to accompany the lessons. As only records of full-time staff were kept on file, without further evidence it must be assumed that Arthur was only employed at the Pratt Institute on a part-time basis, if at all.

   It was common practice for aspiring black artists in the Twenties to embroider their backgrounds during interviews. It helped make their credentials sound a bit more interesting to the public. It was far easier to couture a life story, to fit the image they wished to portray, than to tell the truth, which, more often than not, was probably quite uneventful. Ironically with age, when memories genuinely begin to fade, those that have tampered with their backgrounds usually become victims of their own discrepancies. This was certainly true in Adelaide's case. In later years, the further education she purportedly received became a reality, as did her father's full-time teaching post at the Pratt Institute.

2. "St. Paul, Letter to the Galatians," Chapter 6, Verse 7: "Be not deceived, God is not morbid: for whatsoever a man soweth, that shall he also reap."

3. Dr. Gertrude Curtis married Cecil Mack, who wrote the lyrics to the "Charleston." He also wrote material for the comic duo Williams and Walker. When Mack died, Gertrude

married Ulysses S. Thompson—Florence Mills' ex-husband.
4. Maude Mills, *Storyville* 31, page 9, Nov. 1970.
5. Ada Overton Walker, *Storyville* 31, page 8, Nov. 1970.
6. Lew Leslie's first meeting with Adelaide, *Storyville* 31, page 9, Nov. 1970.

Chapter 3. Shuffle Along Nicely
1. *Jim Jam Jems* opened at Broadway's Cort Theater on 4 Oct. 1920 and ran for 105 performances.
2. See page 142 in Ethel Waters' autobiography *His Eye Is on the Sparrow*.
3. The steps of the "Shuffle" dance consist of brushing the ball of the sole forwards followed by a heel brush backwards. The step can be executed in various directions.
4. *Billboard*, page 45, 11 June 1921.
5. For Adelaide's account of meeting Josephine's mother backstage at St. Louis, see *The Power of Pride*, page 25, by Carole Marks and Diana Edkins.
6. For the full tour itinerary see *Reminiscing with Sissle and Blake*, page 148, by Robert Kimball and William Bolcom.

Chapter 4. I've Been Waiting for Someone like You
1. As I could find no birth certificate for Bert, the birth date, 4 July 1894, has been taken from his British passport no. 126624, issued on 10 May 1946. Two other documents conflict slightly with this date: his marriage certificate no. 17084—1895 and his immigration identification card no. 400490—1896.
2. A flat-footed stepping style that works the foot by striking, rubbing or sliding the entire sole close to the ground with shuffling steps. The body movements are mostly from the hips down.
3. See page 142 in Ethel Waters' autobiography *His Eye Is on the Sparrow*.
4. During Adelaide's employment in *Runnin' Wild* Bert returned to the merchant navy and made several transatlantic trips from New York to Antwerp and Rotterdam.

Chapter 5. Runnin' Wild and Free
1. The dance used propulsive swing rhythms to move the arms and legs. One step consisted of crossing over and swinging one arm in front of the opposite knee and then repeating the movement in the opposite direction.
2. *New York Times*, page 17, 30 Oct. 1923.
3. *Variety*, page 18, 30 Aug. and page 20, 1 Nov. 1923.
4. Account in *Black and White in Colour*, edited by Jim Pines.
5. See *Valentino: A Dream of Desire* by David Bret and *The Real Valentino* by S. George Ullman.
6. "Charleston accidental discovery," letter from Elida Webb, *Variety*, 9 Dec. and response 16 Dec. 1925.

Chapter 6. The Chocolate Kiddies Come to Town
1. Extract from an unpublished poem, "Black Black Black," by Malcolm Crowthers, © Malcolm Crowthers 2001.
2. *New York Amsterdam News*, 6 May 1925.
3. See *Bricktop*, page 79, by Ada Bricktop Duconge and James Haskins.
4. See *Reminiscing with Sissle and Blake,* page 190, by Robert Kimball and William Bolcom.
5. "Lyons captures Berlin with *Chocolate Kiddies*," *New York Amsterdam News*, 3 June 1925.
6. "*Chocolate Kiddies* in Berlin," *Variety*, page 40, 17 June 1925.
7. Four instrumental tracks from *Chocolate Kiddies*: "By the Waters Of Minnetonka," "Shanghai Shuffle," "O Katharina" and "Alabamy Bound" were also recorded in Berlin by Sam Wooding's Orchestra at a later date.
8. *New York Amsterdam News*, 19 Aug. 1925.

9. See *Jazz Cleopatra*, page 78, by Phyllis Rose.
10. "Lottie Gee in Vienna . . . ," *New York Amsterdam News*, 23 Dec. 1925. "Lottie Gee tours Britain . . . ," *New York Amsterdam News*, page 5, 24 Mar. 1926. "Lottie Gee returns . . . ," *New York Amsterdam News*, page 5, 5 May 1926.
11. *Storyville*, 60, 131 and 132.
12. From January 1926 through to the middle of March, the *Chocolate Kiddies* revue visited Spain, France and Switzerland before returning to Berlin. From there it traveled to Italy and then on to the Soviet Union. In Moscow the show performed from 16 March until 5 May, then played for two weeks in Leningrad from 8 May. The troupe finally sailed to South America before returning to New York where they disbanded.
13. "Manhattan Madness," *Chicago Defender*, 28 Jan. 1928.
14. See pp. 173–5 in Ethel Waters' autobiography, *His Eye Is on the Sparrow*.
15. *Revue Nègre* played at the Théâtre des Champs-Élysées in Paris, where it ran for three months. The show only occupied the second half of the bill.

Chapter 7. No Place more so than in Harlem

1. Many theories exist regarding when and how New York was christened the Big Apple. Most historians agree the term evolved during the jazz era in the 1920s and came out of Harlem's Renaisssance. As happens with any new culture, a new language is created to express its ideals and aspirations. From Adelaide's account, it appears that regular customers to the Big Apple bar gradually began to connect the name with the geographical area where it was situated. When white New Yorkers from downtown visited Harlem they picked up on the name and over a period of time began to refer to the area in general as the Big Apple. When put into context, this story seems highly probable.

   See also, Alberta Hunter's biography *A Celebration in Blues*, page 115. Adelaide claims ownership of the Big Apple name to the book's author, Frank C. Tayler.

   Unfortunately, Adelaide couldn't accurately recall on which of the four corners of 135th Street and Seventh Avenue the Big Apple bar was originally located.
2. "New revue goes over big," *Chicago Defender*, 13 Mar. 1926.
3. *New York Amsterdam News*, page 5, 31 Mar. 1926.
4. Philadelphia *Tribune*, (date unknown) May 1926.
5. *New York Amsterdam News*, page 12, 7 July 1926.
6. *New York Herald Tribune*, 13 July 1926; *New York Times*, 13 July 1926; *Variety*, page 41, 14 July 1926; *New York Amsterdam News*, page 11, 14 July and page 11, 21 July 1926.
7. Tallulah Bankhead quote, source unknown.
8. "Harlem theaters packed," *New York Amsterdam News*, page 13, 7 July 1926.
9. *Variety*, page 41, 14 July 1926.
10. Rudolph Valentino died on 23 August 1926.
11. *Chicago Defender*: 25 Dec. 1926; 1 Jan. 1927; 8 Jan. 1927; 19 Feb. 1927; 5 Mar. 1927.
12. "A Coming Star." Section in "The Spotlight," *Baltimore Afro-American*, 30 Oct. 1926.

Chapter 8. You Ain't Heard Nothin' Yet!

1. *Chicago Defender*, 23 April 1927.
2. *Chicago Defender*, 16 April 1927.
3. "Café de Paris bomb," *Chicago Defender*, 2 July 1927.
4. "Café de Paris in Chicago reopens," *Chicago Defender*, 19 Oct. 1927.
5. *Chicago Defender*: 21 May 1927; 28 May 1927; 2 July 1927.
6. *Chicago Defender*, 23 July 1927.
7. During this period Armstrong and his band were doubling at the Vendôme Theater and the Sunset Café. On occasions he also worked at the Dreamland Café. In various articles in the *Chicago Defender* between April–September Armstrong is mentioned as still working at the Sunset Café. See *Chicago Defender*, 17 Sep. 1927.
8. Over the years Adelaide became confused over exactly which revues she appeared in with

Duke Ellington. In different interviews she claimed the concert/revue where the "Creole Love Call" incident happened took place in various locations, including Toronto, Cleveland, during an RKO tour, Upstate New York, etc. It seems more probable that the event took place in New York in either the revue *Messin' Around* or *JazzMania*. Ellington's band performed at Harlem's Lafayette Theater in *JazzMania* for two weeks from 10 until 23 October and doubled at the Plantation Café in the revue *Messin' Around*. "Creole Love Call" was recorded three days later on 26 October. See also *Storyville*, page 53, issue 80, Dec. 1978/Jan. 1979.

9. On 26 October, Adelaide recorded vocals of "Creole Love Call" and "The Blues I Love to Sing" with Duke Ellington and his Orchestra at Victor Studios. Adelaide returned to Victor Studios on 3 November to record "Chicago Stomp Down" with Duke Ellington and his Orchestra.

10. See *The Twenties*, notebooks and diaries of Edmund Wilson, page 294.

11. The word Creole has two interpretations attached to it. The first, and most widely accepted, is linked to any descendant of a European or black settler from the islands of the West Indies. The second translation, and less known, heralds from the Southwestern State of Louisiana where the term Creole is used when referring to any poor or common person, no matter what shade or color their skin might be, who speaks and uses the local French *patois* as their native tongue. Creole relates to the actual dialect that is spoken solely in a particular district, which can often be totally indecipherable to an outsider's ear.

12. *New York Amsterdam News*, 2 and 9 Nov. and *Chicago Defender*, 5 and 12 Nov. 1927.

13. "Dance mania," the *Age*, 12 and 18 Nov. 1927.

14. *New York Amsterdam News*, page 8, 9 Nov. 1927; *New York Amsterdam News*, page 8, 16 Nov. 1927; *Philadelphia Enquirer*, page 23, 22 Nov. and page 9, 29 Nov. 1927.

15. "Reminiscing in Tempo: Guitarist Freddy Guy's Ellington memories," by John McDonough, *Down Beat*, page 16, 17 April 1969. See also *Ellington: The Early Years* by Mark Tucker.

16. On 3 December Florence Mills' benefit shows took place at Harlem's Lafayette, Alhambra and Lincoln Theaters. The shows commenced at midnight and raised over $4,000. The night became a celebration of black talent and was much talked about for weeks after. Artists who appeared at all three theaters included Duke Ellington and his Orchestra, Fred and Adele Astaire, Al Jolson and Adelaide Hall with her Twelve Dance Mania Maidens.

17. See *Nightclub Nights* by Susan Waggoner, pages 66 and 67, for a copy of *Rhythmania*'s program.

PART II. FOUR AND TWENTY BLACKBIRDS BAKED IN A PIE 1928–29

Chapter 9. Blackbirds

1. "Manhattan madness," Leslie presents a successor to the late Florence Mills, *Chicago Defender*, 28 Jan. 1928.

2. "Adelaide Hall to London," *New York Amsterdam News*, page 13, 21 Dec. 1927.

3. *Variety*, 4 April 1928.

4. *Variety*, page 55, 18 Jan. 1928.

5. *Variety*, page 52, 21 Mar. 1928.

6. *Chicago Defender*, 7 April 1928.

7. See page 82 in *Jazz Away From Home*, by Chris Goddard.

8. *New York Amsterdam News*, 4 April 1928.

9. "Song hit of *Blackbirds* makes history," *Chicago Defender*, page 11, 21 Dec. 1929.

10. *New York Amsterdam News*, page 8, 19 Nov. 1930; *Chicago Defender*, page 7, 14 Feb. 1931.

11. *Blackbirds of 1928*, advertisement (without Bojangles) and caricature of Adelaide, *New York Sunday Times*, 6 May 1928.

12. *Variety*, front page, 9 May 1928.

13. Review by Burns Mantle, *Daily News*, 10 May 1928; review by Thomas Van Dyke,

Morning Telegraph, 10 May 1928; review by Julius Cohen, *Journal of Commerce,* (date unknown) May 1928; review by Leonard Hill, the *Telegram,* 10 May 1928; *New York Times,* page 31, 10 May 1928; review by William Weer, *Brooklyn Eagle,* (date unknown) May 1928; *N.Y. Evening World,* 12 May 1928; *Variety,* page 48, 16 May 1928; *New York Amsterdam News,* 16 May 1928.

14. *World,* 10 May 1928: "The Liberty Theater was given over last evening to a Negro revue called *Blackbirds of 1928.* It might be described as a kind of Harlem Follies and it would be better, I think, if it had some good songs or some good comedians, or to be extravagant in one's demands, both.

   "They tell me that the greater part of it was recently most successful as the midnight entertainment at a cabaret in the frenetic fifties. I can easily understand that it would seem more interesting after a few drinks. *Blackbirds of 1928* is just a third-rate Broadway musical show, tinted brown. The very first solo begins when an intense soprano bursts out, in part, as follows: 'Why did I go away from Dixie, heart of the South, my Mammy used to call me Dixie, part of the South.'

   "Indeed the whole show teems with the Congo memories and plantation melodies of Tin Pan Alley. But if you stray into the Liberty at all, do not leave until that moment which comes about a quarter before 11 o'clock. Then a sleek, pleased young man about Harlem named Bill Robinson walks nattily on. After bowing right and left in response to the hurrahs of a seemingly enormous following, proceeds to justify and increase them by dancing as an expert and tickling as delightful a tap dance as you may ever hope to see or hear. There is no sound in all the noisy, flagrant evening which approaches in gaiety and infectiousness the neat confiding whisper of his gifted shoon to that delighted stage."

15. *Billboard,* page 13, 19 May 1928.
16. Unknown newspaper, 10 May 1928.
17. *Chicago Defender,* 12 May 1928.
18. *Chicago Defender,* 25 Feb. 1928.
19. *New York Amsterdam News,* page 10, 30 May 1928.
20. "*Blackbirds of 1928,* one of the best of its kind," *New York Amsterdam News,* page 6, 23 May 1928.
21. *Daily News,* 24 Sept. 1928. See also Broadway's weekly box-office takings in *Variety.*
22. *Variety,* 3 and 10 Oct. 1928.
23. "Second company for Boston," *New York Amsterdam News,* 24 and 31 Oct. 1928.
24. "*Blackbirds* carrying on," "Only my faith . . . ," *New York Amsterdam News,* 3 Oct. 1928.
25. *Billboard,* 1 and 8 Dec. 1928.
26. See page 186, *Black Pearls,* by Daphne Duval Harrison.
27. *New York Amsterdam News,* page 10, 30 May 1928.
28. "Stars glad of each other's success," *Chicago Defender,* 16 Feb. 1929. Lew Leslie defends the Negro performer and *Blackbirds'* success, *New York Amsterdam News,* page 8, 20 Feb. 1929.
29. *Variety,* page 53, 6 June 1928.
30. "Lazy Moon," *World,* 31 May 1928.
31. *New York Amsterdam News,* 8 Aug. 1928.
32. "The dance that dazed Mother," *Baltimore Afro-American,* 10 Nov. 1928.
33. "Was 'Diga Diga Do' too hot?" *New York Amsterdam News,* 8 Aug. 1928. See also *Chicago Defender,* 18 Aug. 1928.
34. *Chicago Defender,* page 5, 11 Aug. 1928.
35. "Race riot," *New York Amsterdam News,* front page, 19 Sept.; "Bojangles threatens to beat rowdies," *Chicago Defender,* 21 Sept. 1928; *Daily News,* 24 Sept.; "Bill Robinson's stand," *New York Amsterdam News,* 26 Sept. 1928.
36. See *Black Pearls,* page 61, by Daphne Duval Harrison.
37. *Chicago Defender,* 17 Nov. 1928. To capture a slice of the huge Latin American market Brunswick translated the song title on the record label into Spanish: "Ese Hombre Tiene

Que Ser Mio." Much to Adelaide's horror (she couldn't speak a word of Spanish) occasional requests would arrive from Latin members of the audience for her to sing it in their native tongue. Rather than disappoint her fans Lew Leslie arranged for Adelaide to learn the chorus in Spanish.

38. "That Wonderful Adelaide Hall," 1970 album sleeve note account by Bill Borden who saw *Blackbirds of 1928* on Broadway.
39. *Chicago Defender*, 1 Sept. 1928.
40. *Chicago Defender*, 8 Sept. 1928.
41. "Leslie would not quit," *Chicago Defender*, 13 Oct. 1928; "*Blackbirds* packing them in," *Variety*, 10 Oct. 1928; "The matter of song hits," *New York Sunday Times*, 21 Oct. 1928; "When the pie was opened," *New York Sunday Times*, 28 Oct. 1928.
42. "*Blackbirds* overtakes Mae West's show," *Variety*, 17 Oct. 1928.
43. "Dinner given to entire company," *New York Amsterdam News*, page 7, 10 Oct. 1928.
44. Advertising campaign for Wavine Beauty Treatments, *Chicago Defender*, 17 Nov. 1928; advertisement of Adelaide promoting Florence Mills Beauty Preparations, *New York Amsterdam News*, page 3, 13 June 1928 and *Chicago Defender*, 16 June 1928; Youth Eternal Facial Cream advertisement in *New York Amsterdam News*, 10 April and 8 May 1929.
45. *Billboard*, 18 Aug. 1928 and "Dance schools having busy season," *Billboard*, 31 Dec. 1928.
46. See page 178, *Goldwyn*, by A. Scott Berg. Paramount film test discussed with Adelaide during interview with author in November 1992.
47. See page 52, *Alberta Hunter*, by Frank C. Taylor.
48. Adelaide couldn't recall which drag ball she was invited to attend but an account of a similar affair held in Harlem can be found in Chapter 11 of Blair Niles' novel *Strange Brother*.
49. "*Blackbirds* playing to capacity," *Billboard*, 8 Dec. 1928.
50. "Second place," *Chicago Defender*, 29 Dec. 1928.
51. *Chicago Defender*, 5 Jan. 1929.
52. *Chicago Defender*, 5 Jan. 1929.
53. *Billboard*, 2 Mar. 1929.
54. "Johnny Hudgins' Bronx home scene of fatal shooting," *New York Amsterdam News*, front page, 13 Feb. 1929.
55. "*Blackbirds* for Benefit," *New York Amsterdam News*, page 10, 11 July and page 10, 18 July 1928. On 24 July, the cast of *Blackbirds* headed a Pullman Porters Brotherhood midnight charity gala at Harlem's Lafayette Theater. It was the first time such a show had been staged to aid a mass of struggling Negroes, who were poorly paid and worked long hours in terrible conditions. The event was organized to awaken public awareness of their plight and helped raise over $10,000 for the cause.
   Reviews of other benefits that the Blackbirds' cast performed at are:
      Big benefit show staged at the Lafayette, with stars from *Blackbirds*, *Show Boat* and *Hello Yourself*, *New York Amsterdam News*, 16 and 22 Jan. 1929;
      Lafayette Benefit, *New York Amsterdam News*, page 8, 30 Jan. 1929;
      Lafayette Benefit featuring the cast of *Blackbirds* and *Show Boat*, *New York Amsterdam News*, page 6, 13 Mar.; page 6, 20 Mar.; page 8, 27 Mar. 1929; Harlem Children's Benefit organized by Mayor James J. Walker, starring Al Jolson, Eddie Cantor, Bojangles and Adelaide Hall, etc., *New York Amsterdam News*, page 8, 27 Mar. and page 13, 10 April 1929.
56. *New York Amsterdam News*, 20 Feb. 1929; *Chicago Defender*, 23 Mar. 1929.
57. "*Blackbirds* haven't got weary yet," *New York Amsterdam News*, page 8, 27 Feb. 1929; "*Blackbirds* are an institution," *Chicago Defender*, 9 Mar. 1929.
58. "*Blackbirds* are one of the most profitable attractions on Broadway," *Billboard*, (date unknown) April 1929.
59. *New York Amsterdam News*, 24 April 1929; "*Blackbirds* for Paris," *New York Times*, 16 May 1929.

60. "Anniversary dinner," *New York Amsterdam News*, 8 and 15 May 1929.
61. "*Blackbirds* May party," *Chicago Defender*, 11 May 1929.
62. *Blackbirds of 1928* chalked up 518 performances on Broadway, thus gaining entry in the record books as the longest-running all-black revue in Broadway's theatrical history, a statistic the show still retains to this date. For further information see the text written by Miles Kruger on the 1968 Columbia album *Blackbirds of 1928* issued to commemorate the fortieth anniversary of the revue.

    Variety placed "I Can't Give You Anything But Love, Baby" eighth in their "Golden 100 Tin Pan Alley Songs" of the Twenties. See *The Jazz Age*, page 319, by Arnold Shaw.

    For additional articles referring to *Blackbirds of 1928* see:

    Billboard, page 88, 7 Sept. 1929; "Brief history of *Blackbirds*," *Chicago Defender*, 13 Oct. 1928 and page 12, (date unknown) Nov. 1928; *New York Amsterdam News*, page 6, 23 May 1928. Lew Leslie mentions in this article that he had to ask Dorothy Fields and Jimmy McHugh to compose the score because he could find no suitable material written by black composers. Leslie did, however, commission Eubie Blake to write songs for the show but they were never included. The article has a quarter-page photograph of Adelaide with her Blackbird Chorus Girls. Also see separate article in *Chiacgo Defender*, 7 April 1928.

Chapter 10. You're not the only Oyster in the Stew

1. See *Jazz Cleopatra*, page 141, by Phyllis Rose.
2. Before Bert sailed to France he applied for a visa permit so he could re-enter the States. The U.S. Department of Labor replied with a letter stating he was temporarily admitted to America as a seaman for the purpose of reshipping foreign freight and that no subsequent record could be found of him having been admitted for permanent residence. In view of the fact that permits are only issued to aliens who have been legally admitted to the United States for permanent residence, the Bureau of Immigration declined to issue such a document to him. Permit file 496229, 29 May 1929. Bert subsequently traveled to France without an American re-entry visa.

    The misunderstanding came about because the Bureau of Immigration had no record of Bert's marriage. He had originally been resident in the country illegally. As Bert was now the husband of a U.S. citizen, he lodged a relative petition, which was finally approved by the Department of Labor on 30 August 1929. A re-entry visa to the States was issued to him at the American Embassy in Paris, permit number 269, card 400490.
3. Photograph of Adelaide onboard the SS *Ile de France*, *New York Amsterdam News*, 29 May 1929.
4. "French kiss Adelaide Hall on her arrival," *Chicago Defender*, 15 June 1929.

Chapter 11. Direct from Broadway

1. Paul Colin's fascination with the *Blackbirds* sketch prompted him to amend it at a later date. The original picture had a lop-sided red windmill to depict the Moulin Rouge painted on the forefront of the picture. The later version omitted the windmill completely which, Colin thought, made the picture more pleasing to the eye.
2. "Leslie show a big sensation, management forced to close the doors to the Moulin Rouge to keep out the large insistent crowds seeking entrance without tickets," *New York Amsterdam News*, 12 June 1929.
3. "*Les Oiseaux Noirs* se sont envolés," premiere gala report by Louis Léon-Martin, *Paris Midi*, 9 June 1929.
4. *Blackbirds*' Moulin Rouge reviews:

    "Les Premières," by Jacques Patin, *Le Figaro*, page 5, 13 June 1929; review by Louis Léon-Martin, *Paris Midi* (date unknown) June 1929; review by Henri-Jaunet, (newspaper and date unknown) June 1929; "Chronique des Théâtres de Paris," *Blackbirds*' appraisal by Théophile Gautier, *Le Figaro*, 21 June 1929; *Le Journal*, (date and writer unknown) June

1929; "Music Hall," *L'Intransigeant*, report, (writer unknown) 2 June and review 14 June 1929; "Les Premières," by Roger Cousin, *Excelsior*, 13 June 1929; "Les Premières," by Jean Prudhomme, *Le Matin*, 13 June 1929.

5. "Une brillante Fête de Natation," report and photographs of the swimming gala at Tourelles by René Lehmann, (unknown newspaper) page 4, 26 June 1929; "Black and White," report and photographs of the swimming gala at Tourelles by Edouard Beaudu, (unknown newspaper) page 6, 30 June 1929; Louis Cole's report of Paris Beauty Contest, *New York Amsterdam News*, page 12, 31 July 1929.

6. "Leslie show a big sensation," *New York Amsterdam News*, 12 June 1929.
"Paris receives *Blackbirds* with open arms." Quote: "They are seen to especial advantage in a jungle fantasy where, transformed into gorgeous Birds of Paradise, they form a magnificent and inspiriting spectacle of which the culminating attraction is Adelaide Hall, probably the next idol of the Paris music hall public: she has shapeliness, vitality and a bewildering voice rather suggestive of a contralto grafted on an unearthly yodeling instrument." "Adelaide Hall, the new Josephine Baker, with more talent in 'Diga Diga Do'. . . ," *New York Amsterdam News*, page 12, 3 July 1929.
"J. A. Rogers tells of *Blackbirds* . . . ," *New York Amsterdam News*, 10 July 1929.

7. Article by J. A. Rogers, page 12, *New York Amsterdam News*, 31 July 1929. "Adelaide takes Paris by storm," full-page article and photograph taken in Paris, quote: "The gay Parisians have taken the charming Adelaide Hall of *Blackbirds* to their hearts. Adelaide also won a Bathing Beauty Contest recently and when you can do that in France it means that you have won real international fame."

8. *Billboard* page 40, 6 July 1929.

9. *Chicago Defender*, (date unknown) July 1929.

10. "Members of *Blackbirds*, which is having such a huge success at the Moulin Rouge," are invited to the opening of Henri de Rothschild's new lavish Théâtre Pigalle in Montmartre, *Tatler*, Priscilla in Paris, 3 July 1929.

11. *Variety*, 31 July 1929.

12. "Lew Leslie assembling talent for forthcoming show . . . ," *Variety*, 16 July 1929.

13. *Variety*, 13 Aug. 1929.

14. "Adelaide Hall star of the world-famous *Blackbirds*," *Chicago Defender*, 10 Aug. 1929.

15. Advertisement in the *Chicago Daily Tribune*, page 46, 26 Nov. 1929. Quote: "Mr. Leslie will personally direct the orchestra tonight."

16. "As good as the late Florence Mills," by Frederick Donaghey, *Chicago Daily Tribune*, 27 Nov. 1929. Quote: "The performer entitled to the black hype, in the belief of the management, is Adelaide Hall, and she is entitled to it. She is far-and-away the best of the Negro soubrettes, easily better than Ethel Waters and at least as good as the late Florence Mills was. The show on at the Adelphi (Chicago) is just as good without Bill Bojangles Robinson."
"Famous *Blackbirds* opens at the Adelphi," *Chicago Defender*, page 10, 23 Nov. 1929. (See also an interview with Adelaide on page 11 in the same newspaper: "Star of *Blackbirds* says: 'We just do our stuff.'") Quote: "'We have no inferiority complexes, nor do we have any superiority complexes. We just do our stuff!' Thus does Miss Adelaide Hall, star of Lew Leslie's *Blackbirds* show, which opens Tuesday night at the Adelphi, explain why the production has been such a signal success. 'Nothing succeeds like pep,' Miss Hall elaborated. 'Nothing can take the place of push and drive in any activity. We Race artists do not think in terms of our public, we are just ourselves at all times and we give to our play, for our work is just that—our undivided energy. We are happy and we show it.' Adelaide Hall is particularly representative of this new pep and vigor. Perhaps that's why she is the star of the show."
"Critic says *Blackbirds* is best of musical shows," *Chicago Defender*, page 11, 30 Nov. 1929. Quote: "Adelaide Hall, scintillating star of the show, gives a performance, which marks her as one of the greatest artists in the business. Miss Hall in the 'Diga Diga Do'

number, with the entire befeathered and wriggling chorus back of her, gave me a thrill that I shan't forget for a long time. It is a barbaric number with a jungle tune that makes your blood pound."

17. "*Blackbirds* to be annual revue, promises Lew Leslie," *Chicago Defender*, page 11, 30 Nov. 1929.
18. *Chicago Defender*, 7 Dec. 1929.
19. *Chicago Defender*, 7 Dec. 1929 and 7 June 1930.
20. *Chicago Defender*, page 11, 14 Dec. 1929.
21. After Adelaide's departure from *Blackbirds* Harriet Calloway took over as the new star of the show, *Chicago Defender*, page 11, 14 Dec. 1929.
22. *New York Amsterdam News*, 18 Dec. 1929.
23. "Greetings from Adelaide Hall," New Year message from Adelaide to the theatrical editor of the *New York Amsterdam News*, page 8, 1 Jan. 1930. Quote: "May I express my appreciation of the generosity of your splendid paper during the past years . . ."

PART III. AND THE MONEY CAME ROLLING IN 1930–35

Chapter 12. Where to Now?
1. "Adelaide Hall RKO contract," *Chicago Defender*, 1 Feb. 1930.
2. "Adelaide Hall at the Palace," *New York Times*, page 20, 10 Feb. 1930.
3. "Adelaide Hall at the Palace," *Billboard*, page 16, 15 Feb. 1930.
4. After her Broadway Palace appearance Adelaide headlined at Chicago's Palace Theater and was also asked to appear as a special guest at The Hippodrome Indoor Circus, *Chicago Defender*, 29 Mar. 1930, advertisement on page 5.
   "Adelaide Hall in Europe," *Chicago Defender*, 5 April and 17 May 1930. On 5 April, the *Chicago Defender* printed a short bulletin stating Adelaide was booked to open at the Empire Music Hall in Paris on 18 April, with an engagement at London's Palladium to follow. Her trip was canceled at the last minute.
5. "Rehearsal hours at RKO," *Variety*, 7 July 1931.
6. "*Blackbirds* for talking screen," *Chicago Defender*, 27 Dec. 1929.
7. "Jimmy McHugh and Dorothy Fields sign publishing deal," *Chicago Defender*, 21 Dec. 1929.
8. "Song hit of *Blackbirds* makes history," *Chicago Defender*, page 11, 21 Dec. 1929.
9. "Lew Leslie broke," *Variety*, 13 Aug. 1930.
10. *New York Amsterdam News*, 21 May 1930. *Lucky Sambo* report, *Chicago Defender*, 31 May 1930. Adelaide also appeared in *Lucky Sambo* at the Howard Theater in Washington, D.C., *Chicago Defender*, 7 June 1930.
11. *Chicago Defender*, 2 May 1930 and *Variety*, 30 July 1930.
12. "Business booming at the Palace Theater," *Variety*, 1 Oct. 1930.
13. *New York Times*, page 13, 11 Aug. 1930 and *Billboard*, page 16, 16 Aug. 1930.
14. *Chicago Defender*, 30 Aug. and 6 Sept. 1930.
15. "*Brown Buddies*' rehearsals and tryout tour," *New York Amsterdam News*, 17 Sept. 1930.
16. "*Brown Buddies* here next week," *New York Amsterdam News*, 1 Oct. 1930; *New York Age*, page 6, 4 Oct. 1930.
17. "Bojangles shot by mistake," *New York Times*, 6 Oct. 1930; "Bojangles shot," *New York Amsterdam News*, front page, 8 Oct. 1930; "Bojangles shot," front page, *New York Age*, 11 Oct. 1930.
18. *Daily Mirror*, 8 Oct. 1930; *New York Evening World*, 10 Oct. 1930; *New York Times*, 8 Oct. 1930; *New York Evening Post*, 8 Oct. 1930; *Variety*, page 62, 15 Oct. 1930; *Billboard*, 18 Oct. 1930.
19. *New York Amsterdam News*, 15 Oct. 1930.
20. Adelaide performed numerous numbers throughout the show's run including "Happy," "My Blue Melody," "Is You, or Is You Ain't," "Ziggity-Zag" and "Give Me a Man Like That."
21. "Darky Rhythm," *New York Amsterdam News*, 19 Nov. 1930; "Truckin' dance added to

Brown Buddies," *Chicago Defender*, 29 Nov. 1930.

22. "I Hate Myself for Falling in Love With You," *New York Amsterdam News*, 10 Dec. 1930.

23. "Bojangles' dance class," *New York Amsterdam News*, page 8, 10 Dec. 1930.

24. Interview with Adelaide conducted by author, 14 Oct. 1992. Article about Marty Forkins and Bojangles' temper, *New York Amsterdam News*, 19 Nov. 1930.

25. Benefit show at the Alhambra on 14 Dec., Florenz Ziegfeld to direct Bojangles, Adelaide Hall, Jack Benny, Ann Pennington, the Roxyettes dancers, Ted Healy and his Racketeers, Frances Williams and an array of RKO stars, *New York Amsterdam News*, 3 and 17 Dec. 1930.

   Variety Benefit at the Ambassador Theater on 21 Dec. given by the Harlem Morningside League under the auspices of Radio Station WEVD, with Fred and Adele Astaire, Adelaide Hall and Bojangles, Guy Lombardo and his Orchestra and many other well-known names, *New York Amsterdam News*, page 9, 17 Dec. 1930.

   "Adelaide Hall, Harlem's theatrical favorite . . . will help in the crowning of the new 'Miss *Tatler*' at the 'Coronation Party' this coming Monday evening at the Dunbar Palace," *Tatler*, 21 Nov. 1930.

   NAACP Benefit at the Waldorf Theater on 30 Nov. Cast included Bojangles, Adelaide and other *Brown Buddies* members, Duke Ellington and his Orchestra, Ethel Waters etc. Carl Van Vechten bought four first row orchestra seats, *New York Amsterdam News*, 19 Nov. and 3 Dec. 1930.

   Harlemia Benefit show at the Majestic Theater on 7 Dec. 1930 for New York's unemployed and the City Hospital Radio Fund. Cast included Adelaide Hall, Bojangles, Duke Ellington and his Orchestra, Fletcher Henderson and his Orchestra, Cab Calloway and Ada Brown. The theater was donated by the Shubert Brothers. *New York Amsterdam News*, 12 Dec. 1930.

26. Interview with Bert Hicks, *Sunday Pictorial*, 12 June 1949.

Chapter 13. RKO, Coast to Coast

1. *Chicago Defender*, page 9, 21 Feb. and page 8, 28 Feb. 1931. Adelaide was added to the show as a special guest on the second week of Sissle's engagement and shared the bill with Beatrice Lillie and Bob Hope.

   In January 1931, Adelaide commenced rehearsals with the comedian Johnny Hudgins for a proposed tour to South America. After disagreements with Hudgins she pulled out. *Chicago Defender*, page 9, 21 Feb. 1931.

2. *Chicago Defender*, page 8, 14 Mar. 1931. Alex Hill mentioned as one of Adelaide's piano accompanists, *Chicago Defender*, 31 Mar. 1931. Alex Hill opens a publishing house with Fats Waller and Bud Allen, *Chicago Defender*, page 7, 14 Feb. 1931.

3. 1931 RKO reviews:
   The Palace, N.Y., *New York Times*, page 24, 6 Apr. 1931. The bill includes Phil Baker, Adelaide Hall and Burns and Allen.
   The Palace, N.Y., *Variety*, page 45, advertisement page 53, 8 Apr. 1931. (On page 45, it mentions the solo number her two piano accompanists perform.)
   86th St. Theater, N.Y., *Variety*, page 51, 15 Apr. 1931.
   81st St. Theater, N.Y., *Variety*, page 43, 22 Apr. 1931. Quote: "Adelaide Hall presents herself with class showmanship in a series of special numbers, rhythmic and melodious, by Mack Gordon and Harry Revel. Joe Turner and Alex Hill, her accompanists at the two baby grands, displayed musicianship in one long solo, a medley of pop tunes."
   The Hippodrome, Buffalo, *Billboard*, (date unknown) June 1931.
   The Palace, N.Y., *Billboard*, (date unknown) July 1931. (Alex Hill and Joe Turner mentioned as piano accompanists.)
   The Palace, N.Y., *Variety*, pages 32 and 40, 14 July 1931. (On page 32, the review mentions the two piano accompanists take a solo number.)

The Palace, N.Y., the *New York Times*, page 13, 13 July 1931. Advertisement on page 2x, *New York Times*, 12 July 1931.

The Earle, Philadelphia, *Billboard*, (date unknown) Aug. 1931.

The Royal, N.Y., *New York Amsterdam News*, 11 Nov. 1931.

Madison and Chester, N.Y., *Variety*, page 31, 1 Dec. and page 32, 15 Dec. 1931. Quote: "Miss Hall, recently back from the other side, has several enticing gowns, class drops and carries two colored pianists. Later acquit themselves creditably at the grands during a change. Opening with a Harlem special, Miss Hall follows with two other numbers, encoring with 'I Must Have That Man.' Equipped with a voice that has plenty of appeal, the colored singer entertainer sells her routine ably."

4. *Evening Telegram*, Toronto, 29 May, 30 May and 2 June 1931.
5. *Toronto Star Weekly*, pages 5 and 12, 30 May 1931.
6. *Toronto Daily Star*, 3 June 1931.
7. Reviews of Adelaide's performance at the Palace, N.Y. *New York Times*, page 13, 13 July; *Variety*, pages 32 and 40, 14 July; *Billboard*, (date unknown) July 1931. Advertisement on page 2x, *New York Times*, 12 July 1931. Vic Oliver at the Palace, N.Y., *John Bull*, 6 Mar. 1954.
8. *Variety*, page 32, 14 July 1931.
9. *New York Amsterdam News*, page 10, 26 Aug. 1931. See also a previous report regarding Lew Leslie dropping Ethel Waters from *Blackbirds of 1930* because he refused to pay her a high salary, *Chicago Defender*, page 7, 14 Feb. 1931.
10. *New York Amsterdam News*, 2 Sept. 1931. See also page 203 in Ethel Waters' autobiography *His Eye Is on the Sparrow*.
11. *New York Amsterdam News*, 2 Sept. 1931.
12. London *Evening Standard*, page 13, 16 Sept. and *New York Amsterdam News*, page 10, 30 Sept. 1931.
13. *The Stage*, 23 and 30 Sept. 1931 and *Storyville*, issue 114.
14. London *Evening Standard*, page 9, 22 Sept. 1931.
15. During a conversation the author held with Adelaide on 4 Nov. 1992, she claimed that Bennie Payne had also traveled to Britain on the SS *Ile de France* but not in her employment. He came over for a break and also to discover what the music scene in Britain was like. He hoped to find work in London. (His name does not appear on the official SS *Ile de France* passenger list.) See also *Melody Maker* (Gramophone review section), December issue 1931. In the review for Adelaide's record "Rhapsody in Love" and "Minnie the Moocher" the writer states that she is accompanied by the master pianists Francis "Fats" Carter and Bennie Payne.
16. *Variety*, page 53, 29 Sept. 1931.
17. See Lena Horne's autobiography *Lena*, page 51.
18. *Variety*, page 53, 29 Sept. 1931.
19. *Variety*, page 2, 13 Oct. 1931. "Adelaide Hall returns," *New York Amsterdam News*, page 10, 21 Oct. 1931. Adelaide denies the rumors that she will be joining Lew Leslie's next edition of *Blackbirds*.
20. *Variety*, page 45, 8 Apr. 1931.
21. *Billboard*, page 18, 5 Dec. 1931.
    In his illuminating novel *Strange Brother*, Blair Niles immortalized Adelaide as the jazz diva of the era. Set in New York in 1927, when the song "Creole Love Call" was all the rage, one of the book's characters, a sultry songstress named Glory, could almost have been based upon Adelaide—if Adelaide hadn't already been mentioned in the text. The story takes the reader on a fascinating, if somewhat flighty, journey through the nocturnal habits of a city hell-bent on hedonism.
22. *Variety*, page 36, 5 Jan. 1932 and page 38, 12 Jan. 1932.
23. "Strange As It Seems," Art Tatum Collector's Items Album 011. The album cover holds two photographs of Adelaide shot at White's Photographic Studio in New York during her role

in *Blackbirds of 1928*. On one photo signed to Ella, that shows her wearing a ragamuffin outfit, Adelaide wrote, "My honest opinion of this sweet and lovely lady is that she is an absolute asset to our race." The other photo, addressed to Mr. and Mrs. Stewart, in which Adelaide can be seen strumming a ukulele, the inscription reads, "Here's to Mr. and Mrs. Stewart, or should I say Bill, a very wise and witty personality looking strutter, ha ha!" Both photos are signed, "sincerely Adelaide," and dated 21 January 1932.

24. Reviews, *San Francisco Chronicle*, 2 and 4 April, photograph, 10 April 1932.

25. "Adelaide Hall to head show," *New York Amsterdam News*, page 8, 29 June 1932. "Harlem still likes Adelaide," *New York Amsterdam News*, page 8, 6 July 1932.

26. "When Hawkins deputized for Choo [sic] Berry," by Spike Hughes, *Melody Maker*, (date unknown) Jan. 1942. Quote: "One night John Hammond, Choo and I (Spike Hughes) drove to a small two-by-four room in Harlem. The air reeked of reefers, and there was a small blue light burning. In the corner of the room was a piano. In an armchair sat Art Tatum.

  The object of our visit was for me (Spike Hughes) to hear Tatum play; but he was a shy customer, and it wasn't until Choo sat down and took his saxophone out of its purple velvet bag that Tatum could be persuaded to play.

  Once having got him to accompany Choo, Art Tatum was well set, and when Choo dropped out of the performance he continued to play without realizing that we were listening to him. It was after this evening that John Hammond and I (Spike Hughes) persuaded Brunswick to record Tatum in his own right as a pianist instead of just Adelaide Hall's accompanist."

  See also an Art Tatum article in *Melody Maker*, page 9, 15 Oct. 1955.

27. Adelaide on Tatum, interview conducted between Adelaide and author, 1 Aug. 1993.

  In 1932, the movie, *Dancers in the Dark*, premiered in New York. A romantic melodrama set in a dance hall, the film starred Jack Oakie, Miriam Hopkins and Lyda Roberti. Certain film journals attribute songs in the soundtrack as being recorded by Adelaide accompanied by Duke Ellington and his Orchestra. Unfortunately, I have not been able to ascertain which, if any, songs were used in the movie.

  Dancers in the Dark movie advertisement, *Variety*, 19 Jan. 1932.

Chapter 14. The Lark on Larchmont Hill

1. "Adelaide Hall, colored actress, arrives at her Larchmont residence," *Larchmont Times*, page 6, 25 Aug. 1932.

2. "An American citizen born brown," by George E. Banks, *Larchmont Standard Star*, 28 Sept. 1932. Quote: "The Mayor was stormed with protests, men and women who are normally white are red with anger, letters written to newspapers for and against her case. The controversy of Adelaide Hall continues. A storm of indignation is brewing. She does not gain anything by living in Larchmont being surrounded by white people."

3. *New York Amsterdam News*, front page, page 2 and various other pages, 24 Aug. 1932. See also *Sunday Post News*, 21 Aug. 1932.

4. Quote taken from the United States Constitution, 17 September 1787.

5. Interview regarding the Mayor of New York, conducted by telephone with Rosemary Davis by the author, London, 26 Oct. 2000.

6. *New York Amsterdam News*, page 8, 29 June 1932.

7. *New York Times*, 28 and 30 Oct., 6 Nov.; *New York Amsterdam News*, 26 Oct. and 9 Nov.; *New York Times*, 6 Nov. 1932. See also Ethel Waters' autobiography *His Eye is on The Sparrow*, page 203.

Chapter 15. Lenox Avenue Blues

1. *New York Amsterdam News*, 11 and 18 Jan. 1933.

2. *New York Amsterdam News*, 17 and 24 May 1933.

3. *Variety*, 20 June 1933. See also *New York Sun*, 14 June 1933.

Rochelle Ball Benefit, *New York Amsterdam News*, 30 Aug. 1933.

4. In the Harold Arlen biography *It's Only a Paper Moon*, (publisher unknown) page 76, Arlen claims he had to get permission from the Cotton Club management to perform "Stormy Weather" himself—even though he had written the song—when he performed it at the Radio City Music Hall on 19 May 1933.

5. *New York Amsterdam News*, 27 Sept., 11 Oct., 22 Nov., 29 Nov., and 6 Dec. 1933.

6. "Ex-lawyer held in jail," *New York Times*, page 5, 27 Sept. 1933. "Adelaide Hall causes arrest," *New York Herald Tribune*, 27 Sept. 1933. "Adelaide Hall has white man jailed," *New York Amsterdam News*, front page, 4 Oct. 1933. "Adelaide Hall files suit for title to Marcus home," *New York Herald Tribune*, 28 Oct. 1933. "Adelaide Hall asks for title . . . ," *New York Amsterdam News*, front page, 1 Nov. 1933.

7. *New York Amsterdam News*, 17 and 24 Jan., 14 and 21 Feb. 1934.

8. "The house that Jack built," *New York Amsterdam News*, 29 Feb. 1936.

9. *New York Amsterdam News*, page 8, 28 Feb. 1934.

10. *New York Amsterdam News*, 17 Mar. 1934.

11. Description of Adelaide's performance at the Cotton Club in Lena Horne's autobiography *Lena*, by Lena Horne and Richard Schickel, pages 50–1. Interview conducted with Adelaide about the time at Cotton Club by the author, London, 24 Jan. 1993.

12. *New York Amsterdam News*, 31 Mar. 1934.

13. *New York Amsterdam News*, 23 June 1934.

14. *New York Amsterdam News*, 7 July 1934.

15. "Gloom chaser," *Daily News*, 19 Aug. 1934. Quote: "Now and then the fame of one of the inhabitants of the city spreads beyond its confines. Smiling Adelaide Hall, Harlem nightclub singer, is one of those who have graduated to a wider field, Broadway knows her as the prima donna of *Blackbirds of 1928* and *Brown Buddies*. Aristocratic Westchester County knows her as the colored singer who rented a home in exclusive Larchmont and moved into it despite all the legal efforts of her swanky neighbors." A large photograph of Adelaide clad in a swimming costume posing on her own private beach at Larchmont is included in the report.

16. *Chicago Defender*, page 13, 19 Dec. 1936.

17. *New York Amsterdam News*, (date unknown) 1935.

18. *New York Amsterdam News*, page 6, 19 Oct. 1935.

19. Incident related to author during interview with Adelaide, Nov. 1992.

20. *Chicago Defender*, page 8, 14 Sept. 1935; *Chicago Defender*, 21 Sept. 1935; *New York Amsterdam News*, 12 Oct. 1935.

21. *Chicago Defender*, 12 Oct. 1935.
    See also Ray Nance Band in variety with Adelaide Hall and Art Tatum, *Chicago Defender*, 12 Oct. 1935.

22. *Chicago Defender*, page 10, 19 Oct. 1935.

23. *Chicago Defender*, page 8, 2 Nov. 1935; *New York Amsterdam News*, page 13, 9 Nov. 1935.

24. Mayor (Bojangles) bids *bon voyage* to Calloway, *New York Amsterdam News*, page 8, 28 Feb. 1934.

PART IV. SOMEONE'S SITTING ON MY CLOUD 1936–38

Chapter 16. Paris Match

1. London's *Daily Mail*, page 19, 4 Oct. 1978.

2. *Le Figaro*, page 5, 6 Dec. 1935.

3. "Adelaide Hall in Paris for big time hit," *Chicago Defender*, page 13, 7 Dec. 1935.

4. *Storyville*, issue 124, 1986.

5. "Joe Turner threatens to quit Adelaide tour," *Chicago Defender*, 3 Jan. 1936.

6. "Strange Tale," *Chicago Defender*, 29 Nov. 1930.

7. *Le Figaro*, 13 Dec. 1935.
8. "Benefit for Paris poor," *Chicago Defender*, 3 Jan. 1936.
9. *Chicago Defender*, 1 Feb. 1936.
10. *Chicago Defender*, 28 Feb. 1936.
11. *Chicago Defender*, page 15, 20 June 1936.
12. Press release issued by Mlle. Maude Rumford (Adelaide's secretary) regarding Adelaide's Swiss tour which had disbanded in Zurich, *Chicago Defender*, 6 Mar. 1936.
13 *Chicago Defender*, page 15, 20 June 1936.
14. "Back to Lew?" *Chicago Defender*, page 10, 9 May 1936.
15. Review in an undated and unidentified French newspaper, 1936.
16. *Chicago Defender*, 29 Aug. 1936.

Chapter 17. The Queen of Montmartre, Mr. Hall and the Dukes of Deception

1. George Gibson's recollections from correspondence received by the author from Mr. Gibson.
2. *Chicago Defender*, 19 Dec. 1936.
3. "Adelaide Hall opens nitery in gay Paree," *Chicago Defender*, 9 Jan. 1937.
4. During conversations with the author Adelaide recalled appearing at the Lido on the Champs-Élysées. She believed its owners offered Bert the lease on the club.
5. *Chicago Defender*, 9 Jan. 1937.
6. "Adelaide Hall closes her café in gay old Paree," *Chicago Defender*, page 11, 23 Jan. 1937.
7. *Chicago Defender*, page 11, 23 Jan. 1937.
    Chicago Defender photo-chart showing national black stage celebrities. A splendid large photo of Adelaide dominates the feature, *Chicago Defender*, page 13, 20 Feb. 1937.
8. *Chicago Defender*, 6 Mar. 1937.
9. Adelaide Hall at the Bœuf sur le Toit in Paris for a fifteen-day engagement, *Chicago Defender*, page 13, May, 1937.
10. *Chicago Defender*, 10 April 1937. Adelaide Hall picture and short commentary regarding her support for the return of more live vaudeville shows in America, *Chicago Defender*, page 7, 22 May 1937.
11. *Chicago Defender*, 22 May 1937.
12. "Jim Crow hits Paris' Cotton Club," *Chicago Defender*, 28 May 1937.
13. *Chicago Defender*, 4 Dec. 1937.
14. "Adelaide Hall's Big Apple Opens," *New York Amsterdam News*, 29 Jan. 1938.
15. *Chicago Defender*, page 11, 21 Aug. 1937.
16. "Canned Apple is it," article in unknown newspaper, Paris, 8 Dec. 1937. Quote: "The Canned Apple dance, comprising the best features of the American Big Apple and the French Can-Can, has its world premiere tomorrow night. It will be introduced by Adelaide Hall."
17. "Adelaide Hall encounters many hardships with her Big Apple," *Chicago Defender*, 5 Mar. 1938.
18. "Adelaide Hall tops in Paris," *Chicago Defender*, 26 Feb. 1938. "Ol' Lady Hall," *Country Life*, U.S. edition, 3 April 1986.
19. Berry Brothers' farewell party held at the Big Apple, *New York Amsterdam News*, 29 April 1938.
     Actress Neeka Shaw held a farewell party at the Big Apple before her departure to New York. On 30 April, a few days after the party Miss Shaw died of consumption. Article and a photograph of Adelaide, Neeka Shaw and guitarist Maceo Jefferson, *Chicago Defender*, 14 May 1938.
20. See page 88, *Django Reinhardt* biography by Charles Delaunay.
21. Newspaper interview conducted with Bert Hicks about his success as a nightclub proprietor. The article ran for three consecutive weeks. In it he mentions Fats Waller's visit to the Big Apple nightclub in Montmartre. *Sunday Pictorial*, 5, 12 and 19 June 1949.

Chapter 18. A Call from C. B.

1. In May 1938, there was still a one-hour time difference between France and Britain; both countries adopted daylight saving time (Françoise Combes, Observatoire de Paris).
2. *London Evening News*, 6 June 1938.
3. *London Evening News*, 9 June 1938.
4. *The Times*, 10 June 1938; the *Daily Mail*, 10 June 1938; *Daily Telegraph*, 10 June 1938; the *Observer*, 12 June 1938; the *Sunday Times*, 12 June 1938.
5. "£25,000 deal in theater tickets," *The Stage*, 13 June 1938.
6. "Long live Sanders," *Tatler*, 29 June 1938.
7. *Chicago Defender*, 1 July 1938.
8. Poster advertising Josephine Baker's appearance in variety at London's Palladium, week of 27 June 1938 (Peter Barrett Archive).
9. "I worked behind the scenes at Drury Lane," by choreographer Bertha Slosberg, which includes information about twenty-week British tour, *Outspan*, pages 43, 45, 95 and 97, 17 Feb. 1939.
10. A taped interview with Adelaide Hall at the BBC Sound Archives. She talks about Fats Waller's visit to Britain in 1938.
11. *Chicago Defender*, 30 Sept. 1938.
12. Quote from Adelaide Hall interview with author, 14 Dec. 1992.
13. Spencer Williams' article in *Storyville*, issue 123, Feb.–Mar. 1986.
14. "The BBC stays up late for Fats Waller," report by the "Detector" of the BBC broadcast from St. George's Hall, London, *Melody Maker*, (date unknown) Sept. 1938.
15. Personal letter dated 21 May 1943, from Ray Sonin to Adelaide—Sonin become editor of *Melody Maker* after the previous editor Percy Brookes had resigned at the start of the Second World War. The letter was sent to London's Westminster Hospital (where Adelaide was recovering from a serious operation) to wish her a speedy recovery. Sonin—who had been news editor at *Melody Maker* in 1938—states in the letter that they had never met but shared a mutual friend, George Elrick. From the content of the letter it also appears that Adelaide (or possibly Bert) had recently written to the magazine regarding "short-wave listening" on the radio.

Chapter 19. November 1938

1. Friday 4 November, Jersey, Channel Islands. Two minutes after taking off from St. Helier airport a Jersey Airline DeHavilland aircraft bound for Southampton crashed into a field. Fourteen passengers were killed.

The Big Apple

1. *Chicago Defender*, 31 Dec. 1938.
2. "Adelaide Hall may replace Bricktop," *Chicago Defender*, 10 Dec. 1938.
3. "Adelaide Hall death rumor . . . proves to be a hoax," *Chicago Defender*, 25 Nov. 1938.

BIBLIOGRAPHY

Bechet, Sidney. *Treat It Gentle*, London: Cassell, 1960.

Berg, A. Scott. *Goldwyn*, London: Hamish Hamilton, 1989.

Bernhardt, Clyde E. B. *I Remember*, Philadelphia: University of Philadelphia Press, 1986.

Bret, David. *Valentino: A Dream of Desire*, London: Robson Books, 1998.

Chisholm, Anne. *Nancy Cunard: A Biography*, New York: Knopf, 1979.

Collier, James Lincoln. *Duke Ellington*, New York: Oxford University Press, 1987.

Cunard, Nancy. *Negro: An Anthology*, Paris: Ballantyne Press, 1934.

Damase, Jaques. *Les Folies du music hall*, London: Spring Books, 1970.

Delaunay, Charles. *Django Reinhardt*, New York: Da Capo Press, 1982.

Derval, Paul. *The Folies-Bergère*, London: Methuen, 1955.

Duconge, Ada Bricktop and Haskins, James. *Bricktop*, New York: Atheneum, 1983.

Fitzgerald, Scott F. and Fitzgerald, Zelda. *Bits of Paradise*, London: Penguin Books, 1976.

Gilbert, Douglas. *American Vaudeville: Its Life and Times*, New York: Dover Publications, 1968.

Goddard, Chris. *Jazz Away from Home*, New York: Paddington Press Ltd, 1979.

Grime, Kitty. *Jazz Voices*, London: Quartet Books Ltd, 1983.

Haedrich, Marcel. *Coco Chanel: Her Life, Her Secrets*, London: Hale and Co, 1971.

Hammond, Bryan and O'Connor, Patrick. *Josephine Baker*, London: Jonathan Cape Books, 1988.

Haney, Lynn. *Naked at the Feast: A Biography of Josephine Baker*, New York: Dodd, Mead, 1981.

Harrison, Daphne Duval. *Black Pearls: Blues Queens of the 1920s*, New Brunswick: Rutgers University Press, 1990.

Haskins, Jim. *The Cotton Club*, New York: Random House, 1977.

Henderson, Mary C. *The New Amsterdam Theater: The Biography of a Broadway Theater*, New York: Hyperion, 1997.

Heymann, C. David. *Poor Little Rich Girl*, London: Hutchinson, 1983.

Higham, Charles. *Wallis: Secret Lives of the Duchess of Windsor*, London: Sidgwick and Jackson, 1988.

Hill, Constance Valis. *Brotherhood in Rhythm*, New York: Oxford University Press, 2000.

Horne, Lena and Schickel, Richard. *Lena*, New York: Signet Books, 1966.

Hughes, Langston. *The Big Sea: An Autobiography*, New York: Knopf, 1940.

Jablonski, Edward. *Harold Arlen: Happy with the Blues*, New York: Da Capo Press, 1961.

Johnson, James Weldon. *Black Manhattan*, New York: Da Capo Press, 1991.

Kimball, Robert and Bolcom, William. *Reminiscing with Sissle and Blake*, New York: The Viking Press, 1973.

Kirkeby, Ed. *Ain't Misbehavin: The Story of Fats Waller*, New York: Da Capo Press, 1975.

Kobler, John. *Capone: The Life and World of Al Capone*, New York: Da Capo Press, 1992.

Kukla, Barbara J. *Swing City: Newark Life 1925–50*, Philadelphia: Temple University Press, 1991.

Longstreet, Stephen. *Jazz: A Graphic Dictionary*, New York: Catbird Press, 1989.

Longstreet, Stephen. *The Real Jazz: Old and New*, Baton Rouge, Louisiana: Louisiana State University Press, 1956.

Machlin, Paul S. *Stride: The Music of Fats Waller*, Oxford: Macmillan Press, 1985.

Mackenzie, Norman A. *The Magic of Rudolph Valentino*, New York: The Research Publishing Company, 1974.

Marks, Carole and Edkins, Diana. *The Power of Pride*. New York: Crown Publishers, Inc., 1999.

Niles, Blair. *Strange Brother*, London: GMP Publishers Ltd, 1991.

Ogren, Kathy J. *The Jazz Revolution: Twenties America and the Meaning of Jazz*, New York: Oxford University Press, 1989.

Oliver, Paul (ed.) *Black Music in Britain: Essays on the Afro-Asian Contribution to Popular Music*, Milton Keynes/Philadelphia: Open University Press, 1990.

Pessis, Jacques and Crépineau, Jacques. *The Moulin Rouge*, New York: St Martin's Press, Stroud, Gloucs: Alan Sutton Publishing, 1990.

Pines, Jim (ed.) *Black and White in Colour: Black People in British Television Since 1936*, London: British Film Institute, 1992.

Pinfold, Mike. *Louis Armstrong*, Tunbridge Wells: Omnibus Press, 1987.

Rose, Phyllis. *Jazz Cleopatra*, London: Vintage, 1990.

Schoener, Allon. *Harlem on My Mind: Cultural Capital of Black America*, New York: Random House, 1968.

Schuller, Gunther. *Early Jazz: Its Roots and Musical Development*, New York: Oxford University Press, 1968.

Shaw, Arnold. *Black Popular Music in America*, New York: Schirmer Books, 1986.

Shaw, Arnold. *The Jazz Age: Popular Music in the 1920s*, New York: Oxford University Press, 1987.

Shulman, Irving. *Valentino*, London: Leslie Frewin Publishers, 1967.

Singer, Barry. *Black and Blue: The Life and Lyrics of Andy Razaf*, New York: Schirmer Books, 1992.

Smith, Geoffrey. *Stephane Grappelly*, London: Pavilion Books Ltd, 1987.

Tayler, Frank C. with Cook, Gerald. *Alberta Hunter: A Celebration in Blues*, New York: McGraw-Hill, 1987.

Tucker, Mark. *Ellington: The Early Years*, Oxford: Bayou Press, 1991.

Ullman, S. George. *The Real Valentino*, London: C. Arthur Pearson Ltd, 1927.

Waggoner, Susan. *Nightclub Nights*, New York: Rizzoli International Publications, 2001.

Waller, Maurice and Calabrese, Anthony. *Fats Waller*, New York: Schirmer Books, 1977.

Waters, Ethel and Samuels, Charles. *His Eye Is on the Sparrow*, New York: Bantam Books, 1952.

Weill, Alain and Nennert, Jack. *Paul Colin: Affichiste*, Paris: Denöel, 1989.

Wilson, Edmund (edited by Leon Edel) *The Twenties*, London: Macmillan London Ltd, 1975.

Winer, Deborah Grace. *On the Sunny Side of the Street*, New York: Schirmer Books, 1997.

Woll, Allen. *Black Musical Theatre: From Coontown to Dreamgirls*, New York: Da Capo Press, 1991.

INDEX